Governing the World?

'Global governance' has become a key concept in the contemporary study of international politics, yet what the term means and how it works remains in question.

This book takes an alternative approach to understanding the concept by exploring how global governance works in practice through a set of case studies on both classical issues of international relations such as security, labour and trade, and more contemporary concerns such as the environment, international development and governing the Internet. The book explores the processes, practice and politics of global governance by taking a broad look at issues of human rights governance and focusing on detailed aspects of a topic such as torture and rendition to help explain how governance does, or does not, work to students and researchers of international politics alike. Bringing together a diverse and international group of scholars, each chapter responds to a set of questions as to what is being governed, how and who by and offers issue-specific case studies and recommended reading to develop a full understanding of the issue explored and what it means for global governance.

Sophie Harman is Senior Lecturer in International Public Policy at Queen Mary, University of London.

David Williams is Senior Lecturer in the School of Politics and International Relations at Queen Mary, University of London.

Governing the World?
Cases in global governance

Edited by Sophie Harman and David Williams

LONDON AND NEW YORK

First published 2013
by Routledge
2 Park Square, Milton Park, Abingdon, Oxon OX14 4RN

Simultaneously published in the USA and Canada
by Routledge
711 Third Avenue, New York, NY 10017

Routledge is an imprint of the Taylor & Francis Group, an informa business

© 2013 selection and editorial matter Sophie Harman and David Williams, individual chapters, the contributors.

The right of Sophie Harman and David Williams to be identified as editors of this work has been asserted by them in accordance with the Copyright, Designs and Patent Act 1988.

All rights reserved. No part of this book may be reprinted or reproduced or utilised in any form or by any electronic, mechanical, or other means, now known or hereafter invented, including photocopying and recording, or in any information storage or retrieval system, without permission in writing from the publishers.

Trademark notice: Product or corporate names may be trademarks or registered trademarks, and are used only for identification and explanation without intent to infringe.

British Library Cataloguing in Publication Data
A catalogue record for this book is available from the British Library

Library of Congress Cataloging in Publication Data
Harman, Sophie.
Governing the world? : cases in global governance / Sophie Harman, David Williams.
pages cm
1. International organization. 2. International cooperation. 3. International relations--Philosophy. I. Title.
JZ1318.H374 2013
341.2--dc23
2012046776

ISBN: 978-0-415-69040-9 (hbk)
ISBN: 978-0-415-69041-6 (pbk)
ISBN: 978-0-203-50839-8 (ebk)

Typeset in Times New Roman
by GreenGate Publishing Services, Tonbridge, Kent

Printed and bound in the United States of America by Publishers Graphics, LLC on sustainably sourced paper.

Contents

List of boxes and case studies   vii
Notes on contributors   viii
List of abbreviations   xi

Introduction: governing the world?   1
SOPHIE HARMAN AND DAVID WILLIAMS

1 Security and global governance   11
JAMIE GASKARTH

2 Governing development: power, poverty and policy   28
DAVID HULME AND JAMES SCOTT

3 Global financial governance: taming financial innovation   46
ANASTASIA NESVETAILOVA AND CARLOS BELLI

4 Corruption and global governance   62
CHARLES CATER

5 Governing trade   79
MARK LANGAN

6 The global governance of labour   96
JUANITA ELIAS

7 Governing communications   114
THOMAS RICHARD DAVIES

8 Problems and prospects for health in the twenty-first century   128
ADAM KAMRADT-SCOTT

9 Governing climate change and the planetary environment 142
CARL DEATH

10 Governing human rights: rendition, secret detention and torture in the 'War on Terror' 160
RUTH BLAKELEY AND SAM RAPHAEL

11 Governing forced migration 180
PHIL ORCHARD

Conclusion: governing the world? 197
SOPHIE HARMAN AND DAVID WILLIAMS

Bibliography 206
Index 233

Boxes and case studies

Boxes

2.1	Selected UN Summits and Conferences, 1990–2000	30
2.2	The Millennium Development Goals	32
5.1	Aid for Trade and Kenyan cotton	89
6.1	The Core Labour Standards	101
6.2	Indonesian domestic workers in Malaysia: the Memorandum of Understanding (MoU) as a bilateral form of labour governance	111
9.1	The growth of modern environmentalism	144
10.1	Core Universal Human Rights	163
10.2	Major global instruments of human rights law (1945–)	165
10.3	The 'Enhanced Interrogation Techniques'	169
11.1	Helping the displaced in Bosnia, 1992–5	189
11.2	Interdiction at sea and Australia's refugee policy	192

Case studies

1.1	Human security	18
1.2	Governing the use of force	21
4.1	Extractive industries	71
8.1	Indonesia, H5N1 and virus sharing	132
8.2	The Global Alliance for Vaccines and Immunization	133

Contributors

Carlos Belli is a researcher working on issues of global finance and a Visiting Lecturer in IPE in the Department of International Politics at City University London.

Ruth Blakeley is a Senior Lecturer in International Relations at the University of Kent. She is the author of *State Terrorism and Neoliberalism: The North in the South* (Routledge, 2009). She is interested in state violence, state terrorism and the use of torture. She was awarded an ESRC grant, with Sam Raphael, for their research on the globalisation of rendition and secret detention. For more information, see: www.therenditionproject.org.uk

Charles Cater is a Research Associate at the International Development Research Centre (IDRC) in Ottawa, Canada. He holds a doctorate in International Relations from the University of Oxford.

Thomas Richard Davies (MA, MPhil, DPhil Oxon) is a Lecturer in International Politics at City University London, where he researches transnational politics and history. He is the author of *The Possibilities of Transnational Activism: The Campaign for Disarmament between the Two World Wars* (Martinus Nijhoff, 2007) and *NGOs: A New History of Transnational Civil Society* (Hurst, 2013).

Carl Death is a Lecturer in the Department of International Politics, Aberystwyth University. His work has focused on environment and development issues, particularly with regard to sub-Saharan Africa. He is the author of a monograph entitled *Governing Sustainable Development: Partnerships, Protests and Power at the World Summit* (Routledge, 2010).

Juanita Elias is an Australian Research Council Future Fellow at Griffith Asia Institute, Griffith University, Australia. Her research takes a feminist perspective on issues such as migration, labour standards, the political economy of Southeast Asia, global governance and human rights. Recent works appear in the journals *Economy and Society*, *Review of International Political Economy*, *Australian Journal of International Affairs* and *Pacific Review*.

Jamie Gaskarth is Associate Professor (Senior Lecturer) in International Relations at Plymouth University. He writes on foreign policy, ethics and international society and has publications in the *European Journal of International Relations*, *International Affairs*, *Foreign Policy Analysis* and *Review of International Studies*, among others. He is co-author (with Oliver Daddow) of *British Foreign Policy: The New Labour Years* (Palgrave, 2011) and single author of *British Foreign Policy* (Polity Press, 2013). He is also the convenor of the BISA British foreign policy working group.

Sophie Harman is a Senior Lecturer in International Public Policy at Queen Mary, University of London. Her research focuses on the political economy of governance with particular reference to the World Bank and health. She has published several books with Routledge, most recently *Global Health Governance* (2012) and *The World Bank and HIV/AIDS* (2010).

David Hulme is Professor of Development Studies and Head of the Institute for Development Policy and Management at the University of Manchester. He is Director of the Brooks World Poverty Institute and CEO of the Effective States and Inclusive Development Research Centre at Manchester. He has worked on rural development, poverty and poverty reduction, microfinance, the role of NGOs in development, environmental management, social protection and the political economy of global poverty for more than 30 years. His main focus has been on Bangladesh but he has worked extensively across South Asia, East Africa and the Pacific. His recent books include *The Millennium Development Goals and Beyond: Global Development after 2015* (Routledge, 2012), *Global Poverty* (Routledge, 2010), *Just Give Money to the Poor* (Kumarian Press, 2010), *What Works for the Poorest?* (Practical Action, 2010), *Poverty Dynamics* (Oxford University Press, 2009) and *Social Protection for the Poor and Poorest* (Palgrave, 2008).

Adam Kamradt-Scott is a Senior Lecturer in International Security Studies at the Centre for International Security Studies, University of Sydney.

Mark Langan is a Senior Lecturer in Politics and Applied Global Ethics at Leeds Metropolitan University. He has held positions as Lecturer in International Politics at the University of Stirling as well as Research Fellow at Brooks World Poverty Institute at the University of Manchester and the Scottish Council Foundation, an independent think-tank in Edinburgh. Mark's research interests primarily lie in the political economy of African development and critical analysis of EU external trade regimes.

Anastasia Nesvetailova is a Reader in International Political Economy at City University London. Among her publications are *Fragile Finance: Debt, Speculation and Crisis in the Age of Global Credit* (Palgrave, 2007) and *Financial Alchemy in Crisis: The Great Liquidity Illusion* (Pluto, 2010).

Phil Orchard is a Lecturer in International Relations and Peace and Conflict Studies at the University of Queensland. His primary research focuses on international efforts to protect civilians and forced migrants. He is currently completing a book titled *Refugees and the Construction of International Cooperation* and, with Alexander Betts, an edited volume on *Implementation in World Politics: How Norms Change Practice*. His work has been published in the *Review of International Studies*, *International Affairs* and the *Global Responsibility to Protect Journal*.

Sam Raphael is a Senior Lecturer in International Relations at Kingston University, London. His research focuses on the intersection between US foreign policy, human rights and counterterrorism. He was awarded an ESRC grant, with Ruth Blakeley, for their research on the globalisation of rendition and secret detention. He is co-author, with Doug Stokes, of *Global Energy Security and American Hegemony* (Johns Hopkins University Press, 2010).

James Scott is Hallsworth Research Fellow with the Brooks World Poverty Institute at the University of Manchester. He works on issues of trade, aid and emerging powers. His principal research area is international trade, in particular developing countries' participation in the General Agreement on Tariffs and Trade and World Trade Organisation, and is co-editor (with Rorden Wilkinson) of the recent book *Trade, Poverty, Development: Getting Beyond the WTO's Doha Deadlock* (Routledge, 2013).

David Williams is a Senior Lecturer in the School of Politics and International Relations at Queen Mary, University of London. He is the author of *The World Bank and Social Transformation in International Politics: Liberalism, Governance and Sovereignty* (Routledge, 2008) and *International Development and Global Politics: History, Theory and Practice* (Routledge, 2011).

Abbreviations

ABHS	Advisory Board on Human Security
AMC	Advanced Market Commitment
APWG	Anti-Phishing Working Group
AU	African Union
BIS	Bank for International Settlements
BPI	Bribe Payers Index
BRICS	Brazil, Russia, India, China, South Africa
BWI	Bretton Woods Institutions
CAP	Common Agricultural Policy
CCR	Central Commission for the Navigation of the Rhine
CDM	Clean Development Mechanism
CFCs	Chlorofluorocarbons
CIA	Central Intelligence Agency
CLS	Core Labour Standards
CNOOC	Chinese National Offshore Oil Company
CNPC	China National Petroleum Corporation
CoP	Conference of the Parties
CPI	Corruption Perceptions Index
CRAs	Credit-rating agencies
CSD	Commission for Sustainable Development
CSOs	Civil Society Organizations
CSRTs	Combatant Status Review Tribunals
CSS	Cascading Style Sheets
DAC	Development Assistance Committee
DDA	Doha Development Agenda
DDT	Dichlorodiphenyltrichloroethane
DRC	Democratic Republic of Congo
ECHR	European Convention on Human Rights
ECSC	European Coal and Steel Community
EIB	European Investment Bank
EIR	Extractive Industries Review
EITI	Extractive Industries Transparency Initiative
EPZs	Export processing zones

ETI	Ethical Trading Initiative
ETS	Emissions Trading Scheme
EU	European Union
FAO	Food and Agriculture Organisation
FATF	Financial Action Taskforce
FCA	Financial Conduct Authority
FCPA	Foreign Corrupt Practices Act
FCTC	Framework Convention on Tobacco Control
FDI	Foreign Direct Investment
FPC	Financial Policy Committee
FSA	Financial Services Authority
FSB	Financial Stability Bank
GATT	General Agreement on Tariffs and Trade
GAVI	Global Alliance for Vaccines and Immunisation
GCB	Global Corruption Barometer
GCC	Gulf Cooperation Council
GDP	Gross domestic product
GEF	Global Environmental Facility
GFATBM	Global Fund to Fight AIDS, Tuberculosis and Malaria
GHG	Global Health Governance
GHPs	Global Health Partnerships
GNI	Gross national income
GPEF	Global Programme to Eliminate Filariasis
HDI	Human Development Index
HTML	HyperText Markup Language
IAB	Internet Architecture Board
IAEA	International Atomic Energy Agency
IANA	Internet Assigned Numbers Authority
IATA	International Air Transport Association
IBRD	International Bank for Reconstruction and Development
ICANN	International Corporation for Assigned Names and Numbers
ICC	International Chamber of Commerce
ICCPR	International Covenant on Civil and Political Rights
ICESCR	International Covenant on Economic, Social and Cultural Rights
ICFTU	International Conference of Free Trade Unions
ICISS	International Commission on Intervention and State Sovereignty
ICRC	International Committee of the Red Cross
IDA	International Development Association
IDGs	International Development Goals
IDP	Internally displaced person
IETF	International Engineering Task Force
IFIs	International Financial Institutions
IGF	Internet Governance Forum
IHL	International Humanitarian Law
IHR	International Health Regulations

IHRL	International Human Rights Law
IIED	International Institute for Environment and Development
IISD	International Institute for Sustainable Development
ILO	International Labour Organisation
IMF	International Monetary Fund
IO	International Organisation
IOM	International Organization on Migration
IPCC	Intergovernmental Panel on Climate Change
IRTF	International Research Task Force
ITO	International Trade Organization
ITU	International Telecommunications Union
KBR	Kellogg Brown & Root
LNHCR	League of Nations High Commissioner for Refugees
MDGs	Millennium Development Goals
MEA	Multilateral Environmental Agreement
MMV	Medicines for Malaria Venture
MNC	Multinational Corporation
MOSOP	Movement for the Survival of the Ogoni People
MoU	Memorandum of Understanding
NATO	North Atlantic Treaty Organisation
NGO	Non-governmental Organisation
NOCs	National Oil Companies
OCHA	Office for the Coordination of Humanitarian Affairs
ODA	Official Development Assistance
OECD	Organisation for Economic Cooperation and Development
ONGC	Oil and Natural Gas Corporation
OSCE	Organisation for Security and Cooperation in Europe
OSI	Open Society Initiative
PACE	Parliamentary Assembly of the Council of Europe
PEPFAR	President's Emergency Plan for AIDS Relief
PHA	People's Health Assembly
PHC	Primary Health Care
PHM	People's Health Movement
PIPF	Pandemic Influenza Preparedness Framework
PPPs	Public–Private Partnerships
PRA	Prudential Regulatory Authority
PRS	Poverty Reduction Strategy
PRSP	Poverty Reduction Strategy Paper
PSC	Private security company
PWC	Post-Washington Consensus
PWYP	Publish What You Pay
REDD	Reducing Emissions from Degradation and Deforestation
RWI	Revenue Watch Institute
RSPB	Royal Society for the Protection of Birds
SAPs	Structural Adjustment Programmes

SCI	Sustainable Consumption Institute
SCO	Shanghai Cooperation Organisation
SEC	Security and Exchange Commission
SIDS	Small Island Developing States
STC	Safe Third Country
TI	Transparency International
TRIPs	Trade Related Intellectual Property Rights
UDHR	United Nations Declaration of Human Rights
UNAIDS	Joint United Nations Programme on HIV/AIDS
UNCAC	United Nations Convention Against Corruption
UNCTAD	United Nations Conference on Trade and Development
UNCTOC	United Nations Convention Against Transnational Organized Crime
UNDP	United Nations Development Programme
UNEP	United Nations Environment Programme
UNESCO	United Nations Educational, Scientific and Cultural Organisation
UNFCCC	United Nations Framework Convention on Climate Change
UNFPA	United Nations Population Fund
UNHCR	United Nations High Commission for Refugees
UNICEF	United Nations Children's Fund
UNIFEM	United Nations Development Fund for Women
UNMOVIC	United Nations Monitoring, Verification and Inspection Commission
UPU	Universal Postal Union
USAID	United States Agency for International Development
WGI	Worldwide Governance Indicators
WHA	World Health Assembly
WHO	World Health Organisation
WIPO	World Intellectual Property Organization
WSSD	World Summit on Sustainable Development
WTO	World Trade Organisation
WWF	World Wildlife Fund/World Wildlife Fund for Nature
W3C	World Wide Web Consortium

Introduction

Governing the world?

Sophie Harman and David Williams

Financial and economic crisis, the threats from disease pandemics, preventing climate change and protecting individuals from violence, amongst many other things, all seem to require some form of global co-operation: some attempt to manage, regulate and control these issues and processes that threaten states, economies, societies and individuals. In some ways this is not novel. The idea that global actors ought to find ways to deal with common challenges has been a long-standing argument within international relations, and there are some important historical examples where forms of institutionalised co-operation have been developed. But in the contemporary period there seems to be a growth in the number of these challenges as a result of both the increasing integration of the global economy and the growing significance of new kinds of actors on the world stage. The ongoing global financial crisis demonstrates this very clearly.

In recent years it has become commonplace to label efforts to manage these issues forms of 'global governance'. While the term has become very popular in the academic study of international politics and in international public policy circles, there are intense disputes about what it might mean, what is involved in it, whether it really works and, in the end, what we should make of it. Is global governance something to be embraced as the best solution to global problems in a complex global age, or something to be feared as it erodes state sovereignty, and privileges some actors and some values above others?

This book makes no pretence to have provided any simple answers to these questions. What it does do is bring together a series of essays that explore the different ways in which events, issues and processes are managed, regulated and controlled in contemporary international politics, in the belief that a collection of this kind provides some necessary material for reflecting on these larger questions. The rest of this introduction tries to provide some background and context for the case studies that follow. It looks at the rise of global governance as a term of both academic and international public policy debate, at what might be meant by the term and at some of the questions that arise when we start to think about its significance in contemporary international politics.

The rise of 'global governance'

Within the academic study of international politics 'global governance' has become something of a growth industry. There are now lots of research centres, academic programmes and courses dedicated to the topic (including some of our own courses from which the impetus for this book springs). This interest in global governance is also relatively new. A quick search of the British Library catalogue reveals that that the earliest book with the term in the title was published in 1993. From 1993 to 1997 only 33 more were recorded in the catalogue. In the period 1997–2001 that figure is 56; in 2001–5 it is 132; in 2005–9 it is 176; and 155 books are recorded from 2009 to the present (spring 2012). A search of the Library of Congress catalogues reveals a similar trend: seven books in 1990–3; 32 in 1993–7; 103 in 1997–2001; 245 in 2001–5; 532 in 2005–9; and 533 from 2009 to the present. That the term only really entered into academic discourse in the early 1990s is confirmed by other developments during this period: the publication in 1992 of the first significant academic book that explored the concept (James Rosenau and Ernst-Otto Czempiel's *Governance without Government*) and the founding in 1995 of the academic journal *Global Governance* (Rosenau and Czempiel 1992).

Concern about global governance is not limited to the academy, of course. It seems fair to say that the recent global financial and economic crisis has intensified interest among international policymakers in how global processes, events and flows are to be better managed and regulated. This is more than just rhetoric. There has been a growing consensus, at least among western states, that they really ought to design mechanisms for managing processes that affect their common interests – even if there is also a recognition that it is hard to do so. The 1995 Commission on Global Governance report, *Our Global Neighbourhood*, argued that changes in the global situation made it imperative to improve arrangements for the governance of international affairs (Commission on Global Governance 1995). These changes included economic globalisation, the proliferation of weapons of mass destruction, civil conflict, persistent poverty and environmental change. Most importantly it argued that growing interdependence meant that individual states were less and less able to deal with these challenges on their own – thus the need for forms of co-operative management and the linking of states and non-state actors together in regimes of governance. This basic sentiment is one that has been repeated by many other politicians and global policymakers. In 2011, for example, the President of the UN General Assembly said that

> the world today is getting more interdependent and more integrated. Problems cross borders without asking for passports and visas. Information spreads instantly all over the globe. It is no longer possible to ignore what is happening abroad. Global challenges require co-ordinated and concerted action of the international community.
>
> (Diess 2011)

This kind of sentiment has been nicely summed up by Mark Duffield as 'the will to govern': the desire on the part of western states and global policymakers to impose an order on international events and processes, especially those that are thought to create 'challenges' for western states (2002: 1051).

The problem of getting *states* to agree collectively to deal with global problems is a familiar one to students of international politics, but the creation of regimes of global governance is not limited to this. Issues such as climate change and global poverty have engendered considerable interest among campaigning groups, NGOs and individual citizens in promoting a better global response to these kinds of problems. And a key problem for designing mechanisms of global governance is about the need to generate the participation of individuals, communities, faiths, genders, families, businesses and a host of collective endeavours and identities in the governance of global problems. Similarly, global governance is not only about getting states to respond to challenges but changing the behaviour of individuals and communities whether in regard to their consumption patterns, sexual practice, eating habits or neighbourliness, in a way that addresses common global problems.

Translating commitment to global governance into practice has not been straightforward, and there is no simple causal line from an argument for the necessity for new regimes of governance to their implementation in practice. But it is also true that since the mid-1990s there has been a proliferation of new regimes of governance emerging in international politics and the further development of existing regimes. Examples of the former include the Kimberley Process for controlling the export and sale of 'blood diamonds', the Kyoto Protocol, and efforts to control the use of land mines. Examples of the latter include, most obviously, the establishment of the World Trade Organisation (WTO), but also the strengthening of the global anti-money laundering regime. All this has led to the contemporary situation in which the establishment of practices of governance is seen as the answer to a host of problems in international politics – from climate change to small arms and from infectious diseases to global financial turmoil.

What's in a name?

All this academic and practical interest in global governance, however, has not necessarily led to any great clarity about what, exactly, might be meant by the term (Dingwerth and Pattberg 2006). One reason for this is that both component parts of the term are disputed. 'Global' implies a geographic reach that many regimes of governance simply do not have (and some do not aspire to). However the term 'global' also implies something more than just geography. It at least suggests something about participation in the construction of regimes of governance – that many (all?) states have some kind of say, with the obvious counter that in many cases it is the dominant states who in fact wield significant power in the construction of regimes of governance. 'Global' might also refer to something about the benefits that flow from regimes of governance: one of the justifications for global governance has been that states have *common* interests in resolving global problems. Yet it is also clear that regimes of governance often benefit some states more than others, and some (trade for example) have been regularly criticised for producing benefits that accrue disproportionately to the more powerful states. If regimes of governance are not global in reach, nor the result of wide participation, nor beneficial to large numbers of states, then the term 'global' may be inappropriate at best and downright disingenuous at worst. This in turn has led to a distinctive sub-set of arguments about the legitimacy of arrangements for global governance and the extent to which they ought to be more equitable and/or accountable (Held 1995; Falk 2000).

The term 'governance' is perhaps even more problematic. Some of this has to do with the fact that the term is a rather archaic one. Some of it has to do with the fact that it is appended to other words – 'good', 'multi-level', 'European' and so on – from which some single or straightforward definition is hard to establish. And some of it has to do with distinguishing 'governance' from other things: government, regulation, management, order, law and so on. This has led Lawrence Finkelstein to argue that 'we say "governance" because we don't really know what is going on' (1995: 368). These difficulties have not stopped academics and policymakers from trying to define the term. The Commission on Global Governance defined 'governance' as:

> the sum of the many ways individuals and institutions, public and private, manage their common affairs. It is a continuing process through which conflicting or diverse interests may be accommodated and co-operative action taken. It includes formal institutions and regimes empowered to enforce compliance, as well as informal arrangements that people and institutions have either agreed to or perceive to be in their interest.
>
> (1995: 4)

James Rosenau argued that global governance should be conceived so as to:

> include systems of rule at all levels of human activity – from the family to the international organisation – in which the pursuit of goals through the exercise of control has transnational repercussions ... Governance ... encompasses the activities of governments, but it also includes the many other channels through which 'commands' flow in the form of goals framed, directives issued and polices pursued.
>
> (1995: 13–14)

Thomas Weiss has argued that 'many academics and international practitioners employ "governance" to connote a complex set of structures and processes, both public and private' (2000: 795).

Some common themes emerge from these definitions. Two seem particularly important. The first is that global governance involves an often-complex relationship between public authorities (states and formal international organisations) and private authorities and organisations (NGOs, transitional activist groups, standard setting bodies, and businesses). As Rosenau has argued,

> global governance refers to more than the formal institutions and organisations through which the management of international affairs is or is not sustained. The United Nations system and national governments are surely central to the conduct of global governance, but they are only part of the picture.
>
> (1995: 13)

Second, and following from this, the mechanisms through which governance is exercised are a complex set of legal and coercive practices and other more informal mechanisms such as voluntary agreements, codes of conduct and 'naming and shaming'. International law is obviously central to global governance as a normative tool, a form of disciplinary 'new constitutionalism', or a primitive legal system (Slaughter 1993; Gill 2005; Bull 1977). But even here it is the case that international law provides the basis upon which other mechanisms of governance work, by highlighting non-compliance and mobilising campaigning groups. In both of these ways practices of global governance are complex in the sense that they often involve a variety of actors and mechanisms. It is this kind of complexity that is usually thought be the distinguishing feature of contemporary regimes of global governance and which provides some way of distinguishing it from other related terms.

Global governance and history

Even if we can define what global governance means, this does not get us very far in answering the question of how we should understand its significance as an analytical concept or an empirical reality. In tackling these questions several new kinds of difficulties immediately present themselves. The first relates precisely to the novelty of the term. The relatively recent academic use of 'global governance' suggests that something importantly new is going on in international politics. And some scholars have even gone so far as to suggest that the emergence of global governance is transforming the character of international politics – generating a new form of global order (Slaughter 2004). The history of international politics, however, shows that the idea that global processes ought to be better managed is an old one, and for some scholars the collective need to form governance arrangements is nothing new. Viewed in this light, the period from the 1990s is simply an acceleration of something that had been happening since the nineteenth century with the growth of industrialisation, the spread of disease and the need to maintain peace in Europe.

The idea that significant efforts ought to be made to better manage international issues goes back at least to the Enlightenment arguments about the need to control war and establish free trade. Famously Kant argued in *Idea for a Universal History* that 'the problem of establishing a perfect civil constitution is subordinate to the problem of a law-governed external relationship with other states', and much of liberal international thought subsequently has been convinced that the security of liberalism domestically requires various forms of international reform (1970a: 46). In Kant's brief remarks about Barbary pirates for example, whose actions were 'contrary to the right of nature', there is some indication that distant places ought to be the object of reform (1970b: 106). It was not really until the nineteenth century that more systematic efforts were made to regulate and manage international issues. The ending of piracy on the Barbary Coast, the ending of the transatlantic slave trade, and through the middle of the nineteenth century, the spread of free-trade agreements, are some obvious examples. Through the first half of the twentieth century attempts to govern international processes and events accelerated with the creation most obviously of the League of Nations, but also organisations such as the International Labour Organisation (ILO) and the Bank for International Settlements (BIS). At the end of World War II, a host of new organisations were created with the explicit purpose of better managing international political and economic affairs – the International Monetary Fund (IMF), the International Bank for Reconstruction and Development (IBRD) (now the World Bank), the General Agreement on Tariffs and Trade (GATT) and the UN, for example.

All this suggests that at least some of what we might now call global governance has been going on for some time. The difficulty this poses for our contemporary understanding of the term global governance is that it is not clear how we should understand its novelty: Is there something significant about contemporary forms of global governance that distinguish them from these earlier efforts? Is it an intensification of patterns of global management or qualitatively different? It is clearly animated by the same kinds of concerns – the idea that states have a common interest in dealing with the challenges they face – and in some cases it involves many of the same kinds of features. The novelty of contemporary global governance is, as we noted earlier, usually thought to reside in the complexity that results from the variety of actors and mechanisms involved, but even here there are significant precedents – the ILO for example, or the BIS. It is not just that 'global governance' might not really be new; it is that there is a long history of describing and explaining this using terms other than global governance.

Global governance and international relations theory

This points towards another set of analytical difficulties: how we might understand and explain 'global governance' in theoretical terms. Given the centrality of theoretical disputes to the history and self-image of the discipline of International Relations it is unsurprising that a good deal of effort has gone into theoretically inspired debates about global governance. This kind of engagement seems essential if we are to try to understand in broad terms what global governance really is. Is it simply the exercise of power by dominant states? Does it represent a 'hegemonic project'? Is it really about sustaining and expanding the reach of the global capitalist economy? Should we understand it as promoted by states or by classes or historical blocs? Does it embody and promote certain kinds of ideas and ideologies or should we understand it simply in terms of states' interests? And do states really matter anymore?

One obvious way of addressing these kinds of questions has been to use established theories of international politics to examine global governance (for a collection of essays that does just this see Ba and Hoffman 2005). These kinds of engagement have produced some important insights, but anyone familiar with the traditions of international relations theory will recognise that some of the results of this have been rather predictable. Realists have tended to argue that the world has not changed all that much, that states and their power remain the central determinants of international politics, that what regimes of governance do exist are the product of state power (particularly that of the US), that powerful states simply ignore these regimes when it is not in their interests to follow them, and that claims about how global governance (or globalisation) have transformed international politics are grossly exaggerated (Waltz 1999; Sterling-Folker 2005). From this perspective it is not just that there is nothing really new that can be captured under the label of 'global governance', it is also that there is nothing very important about it either. Marxists want to claim that contemporary patterns of global governance can be understood through the lens of historical materialism, or accounted for by the concepts of world hegemony. Here there has been some recognition that there might be something 'new' about contemporary practices of global governance, but this is only the case because the character of the global capitalist economy, and the problems and social forms it generates, have changed. Feminists argue that the institutions, forces, structures and processes of global governance are inherently gendered. In this sense, the project of global governance is about the reproduction and assertion of gender norms that take heteronormativity, women's role in social reproduction, and institutionalised male dominance as a basis for which issues are addressed. We could go on.

Rationale for the book

We think it would be foolish to adjudicate on these kinds of debates. There are good reasons to think that there can be no adequate resolution to such debates, and in any case we think that the diversity of approaches to global governance is probably desirable in the sense that it generates thought-provoking and often revealing arguments. We also think it would be foolish to advocate a simple theoretical eclecticism whereby we take bits from each of these theories. The differences between these theoretical positions are often so profound that they simply cannot be combined together in any coherent way. It seems likely then that debates about the real meaning and significance of global governance will continue. However, while there may be limits to what we can with confidence say about the significance and meaning of global governance, we also think that engagement with the term ought to take place on the basis of a familiarity with at least some of the concrete instances of global management or regulation. In other words, we think that students of international politics need to have more than simply an understanding of the debates about the term, its theoretical implications and the ways in which it is understood by different schools of international relations theory.

Our concern with this is not simply 'factual' – although we do think that is important, and we certainly do not think that we (or any of our contributors) can simply 'describe' in any theoretically neutral way what is going on. But, in our view, students need to know something about what is concretely happening in attempts to regulate, manage and control issues and processes in international politics. Having a set of cases about which we have asked the same questions – *What is being governed and why? Who are the key actors involved? What kinds of problems and issues have emerged? And, how successful or not has it been?* – allows students to get a sense of the complexity of the issues, make connections across the cases, and see similarities and differences between them. These are surely essential first steps in any analysis of what global governance might be and how we should understand its significance. We might in the end want to say that there is nothing really new about global governance, or that what we call global governance can be fully grasped by one or other theory, but in order to draw these kinds of conclusions we do need to be aware of the complexity and diversity of what is going on in international politics, and this book tries to give some sense of that.

The selection of any set of cases involves making judgements. We have been guided by a number of considerations. The first is what areas of 'global governance' are ones we as teachers of international politics would like our students to have some familiarity with. Teaching global governance often begins with some discussion of theoretical or conceptual approaches to global governance, with students attempting to define the term often by conceptions of what it is not or what it might be. It is often not until students are able to apply these conceptual understandings to a range of case studies or projects in which global issues are governed that the picture of global governance becomes less murky. The second is to pick some cases that have an obvious contemporary relevance to reflect the changing politics, issues, institutions, language and individuals involved in the governance of international politics. The cases included here show the rapid change and contemporary nature of old issues such as the management and politics of health and trade as well as the relatively new concern of how to govern the Internet. The third is to explore case studies within these issues and offer new perspectives on governance by specialists in specific fields. In this sense our aim was not to draw together a collection of experts strictly working on global governance but to involve a range of authors working in a variety of fields to apply their knowledge of a specific area to questions of global governance. The goal was to see how ideas of global governance are either broadly absorbed or challenged across disciplines and to offer insights into how different issues require similar or divergent processes of governance.

Overview of cases

These issues of what global governance might mean, how it operates and its history are all illustrated and explored in the chapters that follow. Almost all the chapters illustrate the centrality of the UN system to contemporary practices of governance, even if as with the governance of communications and labour, some of the institutions involved predate the establishment of the UN. So, with security we see the continued centrality of the UN Security Council, with migration the centrality of the United Nations High Commission for Refugees (UNHCR), with the environment the key role played by the United Nations Environment Programme (UNEP) and UN conferences and summits, with poverty the contemporary centrality of the Millennium Development Goals (MDGs), and with human rights the key role played by UN agreements. In this sense the chapters confirm Rosenau's claim that the UN system is 'central to the conduct of global governance'. But, and very importantly, all the chapters also illustrate the complexity of contemporary practices of global governance, as they all include a variety of agents and a variety of mechanisms of governance. These range from the involvement of the World Bank, NGOs and research institutes in global environmental governance, to the complex interaction of different types of agents in the governance of the internet, to the role of private forms of financial governance. The mechanisms involved range from international treaties, UN declarations, and domestic legal regimes, to 'naming and shaming', standard setting and campaigning.

All the chapters also illustrate the continued centrality of states, especially powerful states, to the establishment and functioning (and undermining) of regimes of global governance. The cases of migration and health bring out the key role played by states in shifting the focus of governance, and the case of human rights brings out the vital role played by domestic legal systems in holding governments to account for their actions. Acknowledging the centrality of states to contemporary practices of governance does not, however, mean that the 'realist' view of global governance is correct. Even in the hardest of hard cases, security, states are enmeshed in relationships that limit their unilateral room for manoeuvre, and even in the case of the invasion of Iraq, the United States struggled with its relationship with the UN (rather than simply ignoring it), and in the aftermath of the invasion relied on a host of other actors (the World Bank, private security companies, businesses) to achieve its objectives. So even if states are important and powerful, regimes of governance shape what they can do. In some cases, notably global financial governance, states can find themselves struggling to adapt to the unforeseen consequences of mechanism of governance they themselves helped establish. And in all the cases, states have found themselves at least having to respond to pressures from other agents, whether NGOs, businesses or international organisations.

The chapters also take as a central theme change over time. They trace the way regimes of governance emerge, develop and sometimes transform. This raises the important question of why they change. The chapters suggest a number of possible further lines of enquiry here. One that comes out forcefully is the role of moments of crisis or dramatic change: the end of World War I, the end of World War II, the end of the Cold War, and perhaps, the current global financial and economic crisis. It might be the case that prevention is better than cure, but it is also clear that more often than not the development and transformation of regimes of governance takes place in response to perceived failures in existing mechanism and practices. Another issue thrown up by the centrality of change over time is that we should perhaps think of global governance as an evolving process, rather then simply as something we have more or less of. An important corollary of this is that there will never be an 'end' to this process of change – never a time when we can safely say that this or that issue is 'governed' globally; all there is is a never-ending process of complex, messy and faltering adaptation involving intense contestation and argumentation.

Finally, and very importantly, the cases all illustrate the distinctly mixed record that regimes of global governance have had. The most egregious case is, of course, the governance of global finance – the failure of which has had extraordinarily far-reaching consequences. But in a host of other areas, failures and inadequacies are clear. The regime of governance of internally displaced persons remains weak. Global agreement on climate change is hard to achieve. The governance of labour remains fractured, and of course, human rights violations and poverty continue to be central aspects of the lives of many millions of people. In this sense we should put all the recent academic discussion of global governance in context: it is an important part of international politics, and has important consequences, but it has certainly not transformed global politics, and at the moment it seems unlikely that we will get away from the distinctly 'second-best' arrangements that we currently see. On the other hand, there is no sign that attempts to govern global processes will stop. In that sense the chapters that follow should perhaps be seen as snapshots of where we are at the moment with attempts to govern, manage and regulate global processes, flows and issues.

1 Security and global governance

Jamie Gaskarth

Analysing the global governance of security is difficult because the concept of security is so pervasive in public discourse. A host of issues, from the use of military force, intelligence and policing, to climate change, disease and development, even to exam results and pension liabilities have had the tag of security applied to them. How can any one actor, or group of actors, be considered to govern security across such a range of global problems?

The United Nations Security Council is the highest international authority supervising military security, supported by a series of agencies that seek to regulate and ameliorate particular security threats. The International Atomic Energy Agency oversees nuclear inspections and monitors the proliferation of nuclear technology and weapons. The Department of Peacekeeping supervises conflict resolution. The UN Office of Disarmament Affairs seeks to curb the spread of weapons and aid disarmament. There are then various UN bodies and programmes that exist to confront threats that could be incorporated into security discussions, such as the World Health Organization (WHO), and UNAIDS, devised to combat disease. However, economic security problems are dealt with by the separate bodies of the World Bank, International Monetary Fund (IMF), and the G8 and G20 groups of richer states. The latter have also sought answers to development problems and environmental threats but agreements have often proved elusive. Meanwhile, regional alliances such as NATO have also begun to exercise a global reach.

In an anarchic world, without a higher sovereign than the governments of nation states, the governance of security is fragmented and often contingent on ad hoc coalitions and the distribution of power. Moreover the meaning of security seems to shift according to the context. In some environments, security is understood as an objective condition, measurable according to casualties, economic growth or infection rates. In others, it appears to be less tangible, a matter of psychological health or freedom from fear. Used in so many different ways, by such a range of actors, in an array of contexts, the concept threatens to become an empty metaphor or cipher; a cliché used to suggest that what is being talked about is so threatening that it demands the transfer of extraordinary powers to policymakers so that they can deal with it.

To make sense of such complexity, this chapter will begin by returning to first principles and enquiring as to what we mean when we talk about security. It then builds on this by examining debates over the type of threat that global governance needs to confront – and what governance means in such a diverse range of policy environments. The actors in world politics have engaged in ever wider efforts to manage and control problems through the lens of security. Yet, as I will attempt to show using two case studies, that of the governance efforts to turn human security into reality and the governance of the use of force in the UN Security Council, the result has been political tension and fragmentation.

What is security?

The term 'security' is problematic because it seems to exist on the fault-line between the physical world and its social interpretation. Do we describe something (usually labelled the referent object) as being secure because it is not physically threatened by another actor? Or is security an emotional state, the feeling of being secure (which may or may not have a physical basis)? For post-structuralists, this is an artificial distinction since it is the actor's interpretation that gives the physical world meaning and so makes sense of any discussion of security/insecurity. But, in the world of security an actor's perception can be proved false in the most brutal way possible, through violent subjugation or even extermination. The practice of security often takes the form of a dialectic between the physical world and the world of ideas. Sometimes the idea of an actor's strength can lead to military victory even if they have fewer material resources. At other times, overconfidence and a misreading of capabilities can lead to defeat. As a result, it is very difficult for an actor to measure how secure they are – either in material or psychological terms.

Tied up with this confusion are debates about what exactly is the referent object that is being secured (or rendered insecure). The focus of security can be scaled down to the level of individuals or scaled up to encompass wider political communities, such as the family, tribe or clan, nation, state, regional body, religious community or civilisation. If we are trying to assess the physical safety of these units of analysis, we might look at threats to individual life and health, or the well-being of the community at the aggregate level, or the physical space, the territory, they occupy. Much of the traditional security studies literature is concerned with the latter two and explores how states maintain the integrity of their borders and protect their communities from external threats of violence.

Alternatively, the referent object of security could be an idea, such as an identity to which an individual or group places particular importance. Stuart Croft describes the latter as 'ontological security', which he defines as 'having a consistent sense of self and having that sense affirmed by others' (2012: 42). Having some idea of who we are and how we belong to a community is a major factor in the psychological well-being of social animals like humans. However, this can also create insecurity in others – particularly when attachment to a particular identity is used to exclude or dominate. When identity is grounded in a specific physical situation – ownership of a given territory, say – and this is disputed, insecurity can be especially rife and lead to violence. Many of the most protracted conflicts around the globe, from Israel–Palestine to Kashmir, are prolonged by the way protagonists see their ontological security as inseparable from ownership of territory. Thus, those who would enact global governance need to find a way to adjudicate on such claims.

A further problem implied in the above discussion is whether security entails stability over time. Is a territory only viewed as secure if it maintains the same borders? Do we have to continually reinforce a particular identity and preserve it in stasis for our ontological security? In his novel on the Sicilian aristocracy of the nineteenth century, the Italian writer Giuseppe di Lampedusa famously had one character opine that 'everything must change so that everything can stay the same'. In other words, we are faced with a paradox: to provide security for something, we have to accept its insecurity and be prepared to change it to fit the circumstances.

The challenge for agents of governance is to weigh what level of insecurity is acceptable. This is no easy task. If we equate insecurity with susceptibility to (negative) change, then we must ask how much change can an entity endure before it becomes something different entirely? Is there a core or essence that we are trying to preserve, for which we will sacrifice other extraneous aspects? Buzan, Waever and de Wilde advocate restricting the security agenda to 'existential threats' (1998: 21). However, when they seek to elaborate what kinds of existential threats apply in different sectors, they acknowledge that in the economic sector 'these are difficult to pin down', in the societal, it is 'extremely difficult to establish hard boundaries that differentiate existential from lesser threats', in terms of identity, they concede 'it is always possible to paint challenges and changes as threats' and when it comes to the environment, they accept that it includes 'a huge mass of problems that are more difficult, although not impossible, to construct in existential terms' (1998: 22–23). As a result, the fundamental nature of a referent object, and what changes might constitute a threat to its existence, resists objective description. The only kind of objectivity possible is that which derives from wider social agreement.

Although this discussion might seem very abstract it has some important ramifications. Security is not an objective or absolute condition. It resists binary classifications that suggest we are either wholly secure or insecure. Instead, policymakers need to judge how best to provide a reasonable level of physical safety for individuals and/or groups as well as stability for their identity and values, given the circumstances. Security/insecurity is closely associated with change. For traditional security approaches, particularly those of a realist disposition, security was often conveyed as about building the capacity to resist negative change. This emphasis is derived from the realist desire to privilege order over demands for justice. However, Ken Booth, arguing from a critical perspective, has asserted a more positive interpretation of security as 'emancipation' (1991). According to Booth, people are most secure when they are free to realise their potential. Thus, security becomes the freedom *to* do things, as well as the freedom *from* having to worry about your physical or mental well-being. In effect, security in this view is the ability to bring about positive change as well as resist the negative. Although the concept of human security (to be discussed in Case study 1.1) seemed to promise a similar progressive agenda, in reality its interpretation has been wholly concerned with freedom *from* threats.

What should the agenda of global security governance be?

So far we have discussed security in terms of a referent object being subject to change. The catalysts of that change are described as security threats. The end of the Cold War provoked a major debate about what threats the discipline of security studies should focus upon. In a famous 1991 article, Stephen Walt declared that 'the main focus of security studies is easy to identify ... it is the phenomenon of war'; more specifically, he delineated the study of security as concerned with 'the threat, use, and control of military force' (1991: 212). This interpretation implied that security was about managing threats of physical violence. The primary actors in this framework were either states or groups aspiring to statehood. However, even as Walt wrote these lines, his characterisation of the discipline represented an aspiration more than a statement of fact. The field of security studies was already crowded with non-military threats perceived as affecting the quality of life of individuals across the globe, as well as their very existence – along with that of the states or political communities to which they belonged.

A number of different processes contributed to this diversification. In the first place, war itself was ceasing to be the most serious global threat to human life. As Miall et al. (2005: 28) note there is general agreement among conflict analysts that the number of interstate wars has declined. Although after the Cold War there was an increase in intrastate war – war within a state's boundaries – this trend had subsided by the mid-1990s. Furthermore, according to Lacina and Gleditsch (2005), the annual death toll from war fell by more than 90 per cent between 1946 and 2002. This is not to make light of the problem of war, especially since the proportion of the casualties of war who are civilians has risen from an estimated 5 per cent in the First World War to 90 per cent in more recent conflicts (Miall et al. 2005: 32). Nevertheless, a host of more evident or more potentially deadly threats have been identified that demand policymakers' attention.

For instance, threats from the natural world have been increasingly apparent in recent decades. These have had a more serious effect in many regions, either in terms of deaths or degrading the quality of life of ordinary people, than the threat of war. The 2004 Asian Tsunami caused upwards of 220,000 deaths (BBC 2005). The economic cost of such disasters is difficult to measure but the International Labour Organization estimated that one million jobs were lost due to the economic disruption in Indonesia and Sri Lanka (ILO 2005).

In addition, a series of potential threats have emerged as scientific knowledge about human activity and its impact on the natural world has grown. To assess the risks to human health from the environment, the World Meteorological Association and UN Environment Programme set up an Intergovernmental Panel on Climate Change (IPCC) in 1988. Its aim was to 'provide the governments of the world with a clear scientific view of what is happening to the world's climate' (IPCC 2012). The IPCC's reports highlight the damaging effect industrialisation and human activity are having on the atmosphere and have led to a series of efforts by international governance bodies, from the UN (via the Kyoto Protocol) to the G20 (in the controversial Copenhagen summit in 2009), to seek agreement on carbon emissions reductions. A recent report by the IPCC into extreme weather events was interpreted to mean that in the future 'heavier rainfall, fiercer storms and intensifying droughts would wipe billions off national economies and destroy lives' (Harvey 2011).

Another threat highlighted through scientific inquiry and entailing potentially catastrophic outcomes is that of disease. The spread of HIV/AIDS in the 1980s created alarm that diseases may one day have a major impact on the quality of life for many humans. After all, infectious disease was instrumental in the social breakdown of the Roman Empire in the sixth century (Rosen 2008) as well as medieval Europe's feudal system (Herlihy 1997). The threat from airborne strains of virus – more contagious than HIV/AIDS – are now discussed in existential terms and models of potential infection and death rates have provoked major government and governance responses to outbreaks such as those of H1N1 (Swine flu), H5N1 (Avian flu) and SARS.

The most recent example of a transnational non-military threat is that of the current financial crisis in Europe. Economics had only really featured in traditional security studies' analyses where it had a bearing on the funding of military equipment and operations. Yet, in a 2010 poll by the British think tank, Chatham House, the two highest security threats to the UK identified by elite opinion formers were 'that the world's financial system might collapse and that our energy supplies might be disrupted' (Chatham House 2010: 4). In whatever way the crisis unfolds, it will clearly affect the quality of life of millions of individuals across Europe and so is an important matter for security studies despite having only marginal military connotations.

These are just some examples of how security threats are seen as diversifying in contemporary world politics. To address this diversification, Barry Buzan sought to widen the subject of security to encompass five sectors of analysis: the military, the political, the economic, the societal and the environmental (Buzan 1991; Buzan *et al*. 1998: 7). This 'broadening' of the agenda provides greater scope to address non-military threats that still impinge on the health and safety of individuals and communities. However, it does create a problem in that labelling something as a security issue is usually associated with 'emergency' or 'extraordinary' measures that endow actors (usually governments) with greater power, often at the expense of civil and political rights. If 'ordinary' problems in economics, society and politics are brought under the security umbrella then the extraordinary might become ordinary and this loss of rights might become permanent. For this reason, Ole Waever has argued that some issues should be 'desecuritized' and restored to the 'normal bargaining processes of the political sphere' (Buzan *et al*. 1998: 4).

To summarise, there is a lack of clarity in the discipline about what security means, what should be secured (the referent object) and what threats to the referent object are the most important. Broadening the subject of security implies a wider range of actors than just states as well as a greater diversity of referent objects. This represents a clear challenge to attempts to promote global security governance. Those trying to coordinate resources are likely to face a plethora of issues that could be defined in security terms and a host of actors at various levels of political aggregation clamouring for involvement. The discussion will now turn to global governance and how this has been conceptualised in security terms before my exploration of two practical case studies: promoting human security and regulating the use of force.

Global governance and security

Global governance is generally understood to mean the exercise of authority at the global level, through 'steering' or 'control' mechanisms that are used to shape political behaviour (Jreisat 2004: 1003; Rosenau 2005: 49, 57). The term governance implies a wider range of actors than just national governments and theorists emphasise that it operates in a 'variegated environment characterized by a multiplicity of actors and levels' (Christou *et al.* 2010: 343). Governance arrangements go beyond the nation state and encompass private and supranational actors as well as formal and informal mechanisms of policy formulation (Commission on Global Governance 2005: 26; Rosenau 2005: 45). This more dynamic sense of policymaking operating at multiple levels and conducted by multiple actors seems to fit the broader and deeper understanding of security outlined above more accurately than the traditional state-based model.

According to Emil Kirchner, security governance systems function through processes of coordination, management and regulation (2007: 3). Coordination relates to who takes leadership of policymaking and implementation and oversees the process; management refers to 'monitoring, negotiations ... and resource allocation' (as cited in Christou *et al.* 2010: 344); while regulation is 'conceived as the policy result: its intended objective, its fostering motivation, its effective impact and the institutional setting created' (as cited in Christou *et al.* 2010: 344). A different array of actors may be more or less influential at each stage. The question of who gets to coordinate, manage or regulate security problems in global politics is a complex one since the architecture of global security governance has undergone considerable fragmentation in the post-Cold-War era. As the subject matter of security began to encompass other sectors beyond the military, so the number and type of organisations that could be considered security actors has also expanded.

In the military sector, alliances such as NATO, regional security organisations like the Organisation for Security and Cooperation in Europe (OSCE), Gulf Cooperation Council (GCC) and Shanghai Cooperation Organisation (SCO), as well as regional political organisations like the ASEAN regional forum, Arab League, African Union and European Union operate as 'pockets of coherence' (Rosenau 2005: 49) where security policy is discussed and implemented above the state but below the global level. Nevertheless, their actions can have global reach – as in NATO's intervention in Afghanistan in 2001 (Webber *et al.* 2004: 10). In the economic and environmental sectors, international political groupings such as the World Economic Forum, G8, G20 and G77 provide opportunities for governments, regional actors and NGOs to meet to forge common policies on global problems.

In the societal sector, religious communities can experience insecurity across the world and posit their own responses and the influence of diaspora communities has in some notable cases transcended national boundaries to influence the agenda of global security.

We have also seen a privatisation of security governance. Private security companies (PSCs) have been deployed to protect personnel and property in Iraq and Afghanistan, as well as in New Orleans following Hurricane Katrina. PSCs have also begun to be accepted as useful providers of logistical support, training and firepower for peacekeeping missions in places like Sierra Leone. Furthermore, there are growing signs of a global civil society emerging. NGOs such as the Red Cross, Human Rights Watch and Amnesty International provide an important service in monitoring and reporting on the conduct of war. Global protest movements, from the anti-globalisation movements in the late 1990s to the recent Occupy activities have highlighted the economic and societal insecurities that have resulted from neoliberal economic policy. The advent of new social media and digital technology mean that non-governmental actors can have an increasing influence on the agenda of global security debates, mobilising public opinion and compelling governments to respond.

Despite the diversity of actors contributing to global governance, theorists have tended to emphasise the abiding significance of states as the primary actors in global governance, as in Webber *et al.*'s (2004: 6) suggestion that 'States are still the agents through which the structures of governance are instituted and financed, and the agents through which the efforts of these structures are largely realized'. James Rosenau acknowledges that 'The United Nations system and national governments are surely central to the conduct of global governance' even as he asserts that 'they are only part of the full picture' (2005: 45). The relative importance of states will depend on the security sector being discussed – with some transnational security threats, such as environmental ones, proving resistant to efforts by states to coordinate a response. However, in the military realm, states are the dominant actors and remain the only ones capable of projecting power at a global – or regional – level.

Yet, for all the importance of states in shaping the pattern of global governance, even the most powerful often have little room for unilateral action or creative thinking. The international society of states is replete with norms and rules that guide state behaviour, offering thick descriptions of what constitutes acceptable conduct on the part of its members. Whitman (2003: 269) notes the 'establishment and maintenance of legal, diplomatic and economic systems and norms' which he identifies as the reason why 'even in the absence of a supranational authority, most states obey most international laws most of the time'. This is particularly the case when it comes to military security, which, despite appearing to be an arena of state autonomy, is arguably one of the most regulated spheres of activity in global politics. When states opt to use force they do so within a complex pattern of norms and rules that structure their understanding and behaviour (Christou *et al.* 2010: 346; Webber *et al.* 2004: 4, 8).

The difficulty for contemporary security policymakers is that there is considerable disagreement over what these rules should be and how they should be applied. The widening of the security agenda has opened up the field of security provision to encompass new potential threats but this has unsettled established mechanisms of global governance. In the first case study, I explore these trends by analysing the potentially radical concept of human security and note how it has been incorporated into the policy rhetoric and bureaucratic machinery of the UN. Although seemingly transformative in its attitude to security, the concept has been integrated into development planning with little dissent from states. By contrast, the decision to use force to confront potential threats to order or actual threats to international justice – discussed in my second case study – have proved far more controversial. What this perhaps implies is that states are less concerned when security is applied to other fields such as development than when fields such as law, justice and human rights are applied to security.

Case study 1.1 Human security

Our first case study is concerned with how global governance mechanisms have tried to implement the new concept of human security. The term itself was promoted in the UN Human Development Report of 1994, which argued that:

> The concept of security has for too long been interpreted narrowly: as security of territory from external aggression, or as protection of national interests in foreign policy or as global security from the threat of a nuclear holocaust. It has been related more to nation-states than to people.
> (UN 1994: 22)

Instead, the report sought to orientate the referent object of security towards individuals and what makes them insecure in their everyday lives. Security was defined as 'first, safety from such chronic threats as hunger, disease and repression. And second, it means protection from sudden and hurtful disruptions in the patterns of daily life' (UN 1994: 23). Or, as it states later in the report: freedom from fear and freedom from want (UN 1994: 24). It then goes on to relate the idea of security to seven main categories of threat, namely: economic security; food security; health security; environmental security; personal security; community security; and political security (UN 1994: 24–25). Importantly, the report argues that human security in these areas 'cannot be brought about through force, with armies standing against armies. It can happen only if we agree that development must involve all people' (UN 1994: 24).

From this brief description we can see that the report is very much in accord with those arguing for a broadening and deepening of the security agenda – albeit with slightly different category headings to those of Buzan. The reference to 'sudden and hurtful disruptions' is a reminder that security, as noted above, is often concerned with resisting or ameliorating the effects of negative change.

Confronting these security threats is argued as about promoting equal opportunities for development rather than the traditional panacea of military force.

The UN Human Development Report of 2010 argues that the human security agenda represented a 'radical shift in thinking on peace and conflict prevention' (UN 2010: 17). Moving the focus from states to individuals knocks the former off their pedestal as the referent object of security and 'opens up the state for critical scrutiny' (Thomas 2001: 164). However, it does not go as far as Booth in moving security away from 'freedom from' questions to 'freedom to' (Booth 1991) and as such is arguably not as progressive an agenda as Booth offered. Recent discussion on the concept has tended to emphasise the mutual dependence between state security and human security, with a UNESCO questionnaire noting the view that: 'Human security and state ("traditional" or "national") security are no longer seen as being in tension: the HSQ responses affirm that a capable and well-functioning state is fundamentally important to the attainment of human security' (UNESCO 2008: 117).

The UN Human Development Report of 2010 is careful to draw a distinction between human development and human security, asserting that the first relates to: 'expanding people's freedoms and the second to ensuring against threats to those freedoms' (UN 2010: 17). In this reading, human security policy is essentially negative and designed to prevent threats to development from being activated. Nevertheless, the two are seen as fundamentally connected, with the UN Secretary General, Kofi Annan, arguing that: 'we will not enjoy security without development, development without security, and neither without respect for human rights' (UN 2005: 6).

The question arises as to how far this concept actually impacted on the global governance of security. An immediate effect could be seen in the range of international forums that sprung up to debate and analyse how the concept could be applied. Building on their successful campaign to promote a treaty against landmines, the Norwegian and Canadian governments, along with eleven other members including South Africa as an observer, developed a Human Security Network in 1998, which holds an annual meeting of foreign ministers and NGOs to consult on how human security might be furthered (Howard-Hassmann 2012: 99). Austria, a founding member, describes the network's activities on its embassy website as 'urging states to accede to the Anti-Personnel Mine Convention and the International Criminal Court' as well as focusing on issues such as: 'the control of small arms and light weapons, the promotion of women, peace and security, the protection of children in armed conflicts, questions of humanitarian international law, and dialogue between civilizations' (Austrian Foreign Ministry 2012). The network's membership is largely made up of smaller nations and for this reason it has been asserted that it 'does not appear to have had any significant impact on how the international community address the responsibility to protect people' (Howard-Hassmann 2012: 99).

A separate initiative spearheaded by Japan has arguably had a great effect, as a result of its integration into United Nations operations. In 1999, Japan established a UN Trust Fund for Human Security, at first under the Office of the UN Controller and since May 2004 maintained by the Human Security Unit (HSU) that operates out of the United Nations Office for the Coordination of Humanitarian Affairs (OCHA). The Unit proudly boasts on its website that since 1999 it has committed over $350 million to projects in over 70 countries (OCHA 2012). In 2000, the UN Secretary General affirmed in a number of speeches the importance of freedom from want and freedom from fear as 'building blocks of human, and therefore national, security' (Commission on Human Security 2003: 4). Following Annan's support for this approach at the UN Millennium Summit, Japan was again instrumental in establishing an independent commission on human security that submitted a report in 2003 to the Secretary General entitled *Human Security Now*. This recommended an Advisory Board on Human Security (ABHS) be set up to mainstream the concept across the range of UN operations (Commission on Human Security 2003: 142). The 2005 World Summit Outcome statement was seen as a particular success for the Advisory Board, the Trust Fund and the Human Security Unit in that UN member states agreed in paragraph 143 that: 'all individuals, in particular vulnerable people, are entitled to freedom from fear and freedom from want, with an equal opportunity to enjoy all their rights and fully develop their human potential' (UN 2005). The implication of this statement was that the principles of human security were accepted by all the states of the UN.

As a consequence of the efforts of these bodies, a series of UN reports have made reference to human security and highlighted its relevance to development in subsequent years (e.g. UN 2005, 2006, 2010). The governments of Canada and Japan have been noted as playing particularly important roles as 'norm entrepreneurs', advancing the concept of human security. Some have drawn a distinction between the Canadian emphasis on the military aspects of security and Japan's focus on the developmental ones (Howard-Hassmann 2012: 92). But what original divisions may have existed have largely been dissolved by the establishment of the 'Friends of Human Security' initiative in October 2006, co-chaired by Japan and Mexico. In 2010, the Japanese Ambassador to the UN noted that: 'More than 140 Member States have participated in the seven meetings held to date' (Takasu 2010). These meetings have entailed discussions on both the conflict and development branches of human security.

Importantly, the human security agenda has been taken up by NGOs and civil society activists, and many of the intergovernmental forums noted above include strong representation from the third sector. The HSU of the UN notes that their campaign draws 'input from a number of governments, non-governmental organizations and civil society groups as well as scholars and other prominent individuals' (UN 2006: 2).

The activities of 'international agencies, NGOs and the private sector' are seen as operating alongside states in promoting human security and acting to 'shield people from menaces' (CHS 2003: 10). It is also viewed as important for these groups to be co-opted to the aims of human security, as the Commission on Human Security puts it: 'Implementing a human security approach in post-conflict transition requires significant changes in the way donors, multilateral agencies, nongovernmental organizations and national authorities pursue their goals' (CHS 2003: 70). Just as traditional state security forces have to appreciate the importance of development to conflict resolution, so donors and NGOs working in development would need to take on board the physical security needs of vulnerable peoples across the globe.

Although the concept of human security has clearly received a bureaucratic impetus within the structures of the UN, it is still a controversial term. Some human rights advocates see it as subverting the already existing and more institutionally defined human rights regime (Howard-Hassmann 2012). Even its supporters concede that the idea of human security can appear too complex, involving too many actors and sectors, to be of practical use (Krause 2004: 43). Perhaps human security's most important legacy is in strengthening the delegitimisation of state appeals to national security to justify human rights abuses. In its 2001 report *The Responsibility to Protect*, the International Commission on Intervention and State Sovereignty (ICISS) noted that: 'The emerging concept of human security has created additional demands and expectations in relation to the way states treat their own people' (ICISS 2001: 7). Indeed, the authors explicitly use the human security concept to highlight how individuals can be put at risk from security forces within a state and criticise the military focus of much security discourses at the expense of guarding them against 'the omnipresent enemies of good health and other real threats to human security on a daily basis' (ICISS 2001: 15). In short, what talking about human security does is shift the governance of security away from the formerly dominant discourse of sovereignty and national security and towards the mutual obligations of international society and the security of the individual. It is a move that is also apparent in our second case study.

Case study 1.2 Governing the use of force

The key mechanism for the global governance of military security is the United Nations, especially its Security Council. The Security Council is made up of five permanent members: the United States, Russia, China, the UK and France – the victorious powers in the Second World War – and ten other member states elected by the General Assembly for two-year, non-consecutive terms. Controversy has surrounded the permanent status of the UK and

France and the non-inclusion of major powers such as Japan, Brazil and India in this select group. Yet, the permanent member states arguably remain the most militarily capable in world politics, evinced by the fact that they were the five highest spenders on military equipment in 2011. Permanent member status endows these countries with an exalted position in global affairs. As the former UK Representative to the Security Council David Hannay, recalls, the UN is: 'a kind of caste system ... In New York, the five permanent members of the Security Council are like Brahmins' (Hannay 1999).

Nevertheless, the public nature of Security Council debates means that all its members, even those with permanent membership, have to defend their position in a forum that attracts media and NGO comment and criticism. The UN Secretary General plays an important part in raising awareness of security threats and calling for a response by the Security Council. The UN more broadly, with its 'complex system of numerous associate agencies ... that amount to a vast bureaucracy' (Rosenau 2005: 60) also has an independent effect on the terrain of security discourse through the reports, press releases and actions of its various offices on security matters. As such, although it remains an intergovernmental body, the UN Security Council is influenced by debates across the spectrum of global and national civil societies.

For much of its history, the main purpose of the Security Council has been to promote the governance of interstate conflict. Under the auspices of the UN system, three justifications for warfighting are afforded to states, these are: self-defence, to maintain or restore international peace and security, and to prevent genocide. The first is regulated under Article 51 of the UN Charter, which stipulates that: 'Nothing in the present Charter shall impair the inherent right of an individual or collective self-defence if an armed attack occurs against a Member of the United Nations' (UN 2012). Although this does enshrine the right of states to act unilaterally (or with allies) where they face an imminent threat, measures are supposed to be 'immediately reported to the Security Council' with the implication that it is the latter body that is the ultimate arbiter of the justification for military action.

The second justification goes even further in establishing the Security Council as the main focus of the global governance of the use of force. Under Article 24(1) of the UN Charter, the Council is given the 'primary responsibility for the maintenance of international peace and security' by UN members who, in Article 25, agree to accept and carry out its decisions. This includes the right to 'take such action by air, sea, or land forces as may be necessary to maintain or restore international peace and security' afforded the Council under Article 42 of the Charter (UN 2012).

The third justification is acting to prevent or punish genocide, action which all signatories of the 1948 genocide convention have committed themselves to undertake. The convention defines genocide as 'acts committed with intent to destroy, in whole or in part, a national, ethnic, racial or religious group'

(Article 1). Although in an extreme situation, states could justify taking unilateral action to prevent genocide under the convention (provided there was sufficient grounds for believing it was imminent), in Article 8 the convention stipulates that contracting parties should 'call upon the competent organs of the United Nations to take such action under the Charter of the United Nations as they consider appropriate for the prevention and suppression of acts of genocide' – implying that it is for the Security Council to judge what constitutes a genocide and what action should be taken.

In short, the UN Security Council is, under international law, the primary conduit for the global governance of military security and the key reference point in any justification for the use of force. However, the council has faced major challenges in recent decades threatening to fracture it from within, as well as marginalise it in favour of alternative security forums.

The thorniest of these challenges relates to the problem of sovereignty. The states system is predicated on the norms of sovereignty and non-intervention. State sovereignty is often defined as about who successfully 'lays claim to the monopoly of legitimate physical violence within a particular territory' (Weber 2004: 33). National governments within states ultimately derive their authority from their right to use force in their territory and exercise state power to oversee their laws and customs – something recognised internally by their own people and externally by the international community. To provide for differences in how people live across the world, the norm of non-intervention suggests that where internal problems do not impinge upon other states, they should be left for communities within the state to resolve.

However, while acting as a theoretical underpinning of everyday state practice, these norms have long been in tension with the maintenance of the system as a whole. If disorder and violence is allowed to grow within a state it may threaten the stability of the wider region. Furthermore, the international community's failure to act to prevent atrocities within a state can lead to accusations of complicity. The question arises: when should the demands of international order or justice trump sovereignty? This can be a complex question, even in apparently straightforward cases such as the Iraqi invasion of Kuwait in 1990. Initially, this situation involved Iraq launching an unprovoked attack on its neighbour without any of the three justifications for military action outlined above. As such, it represented a clear threat to the prevailing international order. If states were allowed to annex weaker members at will then the stability of state borders would be threatened and with it the security of the state system itself. This is one reason why Iraq's actions brought such extensive condemnation from other states.

A coalition of states intervened to liberate Kuwait in 1991, authorised by UN Security Council Resolution 678, which allowed members to 'use all necessary means' to restore international peace and security in the area – thus evoking Chapter VII, especially Article 42 of the UN Charter (UN 1991).

Under the ceasefire agreement, enshrined in UNSC Res 687, Iraq consented to give up all its chemical and biological weapons and stocks, with international supervision, and agreed not to 'use, develop, construct or acquire' such weapons in the future (UN 1991). It also reaffirmed its obligations under the treaty on the Non-Proliferation of Nuclear Weapons. The reference to international supervision in the agreement was crucial. In accepting the right of the international community to manage the disarmament of their nuclear, biological and chemical programmes, Iraq was also implicitly accepting that their sovereignty was conditional on compliance with the ceasefire agreement. But, for seven years after the end of the conflict Iraq continued to pursue chemical and biological weapons programmes and for a period of twelve years Iraq obstructed international monitors, expelling them from the country in 1998 and failing to provide full cooperation in 2002–3 when they were re-admitted.

The dilemma the international community faced was how far Iraq's non-compliance represented a threat to international security. The British Prime Minister, Tony Blair, argued that: 'if the will of the UN is breached then the will should be enforced' (Blair 2003a). For him, Iraq's failure to comply with seventeen UN Security Council resolutions threatened to undermine the authority of the Council and with it the global governance of international order (Blair 2003b). Thus, the internal activities of Saddam Hussein's regime were perceived to have global implications. Yet, other states, notably France, Germany and Russia, felt that Iraq had been contained by sanctions and did not see the urgent need for military action. Jacques Chirac, the French President asked the rhetorical question in February 2003: 'does Iraq – controlled and inspected as it is – pose a clear and present danger to the region? I don't believe so' (Graff and Crumley 2003).

The Iraq case highlighted a number of other problems in the global governance of the use of force. The UN Charter locates the responsibility for adjudicating on military action with the Security Council, but what happens when the Council cannot agree? The conception of permanent members as being like 'Brahmins' implies a hierarchical model of security governance. These five states have particular privileges: either they can threaten to veto action (and thereby deprive it of wider international legitimacy); or they may go ahead on an equivocal legal basis, under the assumption that they are entitled to decide unilaterally how international law is interpreted and when it is enforced. Either way, the fiction of the equal rights of all states under the charter is exposed.

However, in the contemporary era, a host of actors are able to have an impact on global debates about security governance. Non-state agencies such as the United Nations Monitoring, Verification, and Inspection Commission (UNMOVIC) and the International Atomic Energy Agency (IAEA) provided evidence to the Security Council and offered an alternative source of information on the threat Iraq represented. Think tanks and NGOs presented arguments for and against the use of force and global protest movements were launched to express public disapproval with military action. Thus, states, and their national government representatives, were not the only arbiters of the decision to intervene. As a consequence, when the US and its allies decided to act without a further resolution explicitly authorising the use of force, they faced a high political cost in terms of their international legitimacy and authority.

Underlying these debates are conflicting views on who should coordinate, manage and regulate global security. The idea of certain privileged states having superior rights to others goes against the pluralist ethos that is supposed to inspire the United Nations. The growing discourse of human security noted above undermines the norm that statespeople are free to act with impunity where their national security interests are concerned. Yet, only a few states have the capacity to use force to compel other actors to comply with international rules. In this way, there is a continual tension between the wide array of actors who would contribute to debates on military security and the fact that only states, and few of those, can actually act to uphold global security governance.

The Iraq debate goes to the core of many of the conceptual problems with security discussed earlier in this chapter. Security is not an objective condition. The extent to which Saddam Hussein's regime was viewed as constituting a threat to global security depended on the interpretive efforts of global governance mechanisms such as the UN agencies, the Security Council and powerful states. Members of the Security Council disagreed over how far regular obstruction of monitoring efforts threatened the entire credibility of global security governance under UN auspices. For some, minor changes to the inspection regime would effectively mean its destruction as an enforcement mechanism. For others, it would simply reflect the restoration of sovereignty to Iraq that the passage of time from the first Gulf War seemed to merit. For those who decided to use force, they were faced with a dilemma: in intervening to restore the peace and security of the international system, were they undermining its fundamental norms, namely sovereignty and non-intervention?

Although interpreted at the time as a major blow to the importance of the UN Security Council, the invasion of Iraq in 2003 arguably reaffirmed its primacy as the locus of authority and legitimacy in the global governance of the use of force. The political fallout from this decision, and the consequences for the legitimacy of the occupation of Iraq, have meant that policymakers have subsequently been careful to achieve Security Council approval before using force. For instance, in the case of Libya in 2011, intervention was carried out under the authority of UNSC Res 1973 which explicitly allowed members to use 'all necessary measures' to protect civilians.

Yet, while the Council's status as the ultimate arbiter of the use of force may have been reaffirmed, the fact that certain (permanent) members can veto action continues to be controversial. In February 2012, the council voted on a resolution calling for President Assad of Syria to step down as part of an Arab League peace plan. The Assad government's brutal suppression of an uprising had led to allegations of widespread human rights abuses and nearly 6,000 deaths (UN 2012b). Thirteen security council members voted in favour of the motion but China and Russia both vetoed it. China defended its decision by arguing that Syria's 'sovereignty, independence and territorial integrity must be respected' and also added that 'The purposes and principles of the United Nations Charter must be respected' (UN 2012b).

The repeated use of the veto by China and Russia over Syria has led Amnesty International to criticise the UN Security Council as 'tired, out of step and increasingly unfit for purpose' (Amnesty International 2012). Thus, even though the processes of the Security Council have been respected over Syria, its authority and legitimacy have faced renewed questioning. The international community has so far not undertaken military action but instead pursued diplomacy, deployed an observer mission and sent the former UN Secretary General Kofi Annan to broker a ceasefire. In the meantime the death toll stands at 16,000. Evaluating global security in the aftermath of the invasion of Iraq in 2003, a UN Report argued that: 'The maintenance of world peace and security depends importantly on there being a common global understanding, and acceptance, of when the application of force is both legal and legitimate' (UN 2004: 62). Although the three criteria for the use of force noted above are universally accepted, there is no consensus on when they are applicable.

Conclusion

In this chapter I have attempted to highlight the conceptual problems in defining security and show how the widening agenda of security studies opens up the governance of global security to a greater range of actors in world politics. Yet, these developments are in tension with the continuing primacy of states as the most prominent security actors. The potentially radical idea of human security has been domesticated by intergovernmental forums and focused around freedom from threats rather than the furtherance of progressive, emancipatory ideals. In the process, the state has been reaffirmed as vital to individual security, even with the caveat that state sovereignty must be conditional on respect for human rights.

On the use of force, we still see powerful states deciding how international law should be interpreted and circumventing the will of the UN Security Council, either by blocking action or pursuing it outside the legal framework of the UN Charter. Yet, the growing power and number of alternative actors in security, from NGOs and international agencies to civil society groups means that the authority and legitimacy of such behaviour is under greater stress. At present, the sense of a global governance of security still holds. But, if this is to continue, there will either have to be more agreement on what the ultimate referent object of global security is (state sovereignty or individual rights); or, the architecture of security governance is likely to fragment further into regional or ideological groupings. In the process, the governance of security will lose much of its global character.

Recommended reading

Christou, G., Croft, S., Ceccorulli, M. and Lucarelli, S. (2010). 'European Union security governance: putting the "security" back in', *European Security*, 19(3): 341–359.

Commission on Human Security (2003). *Human Security Now*, New York: CHS.

Kirchner, E.J. (2007). 'Regional and global security: changing threats and institutional responses' in E. Kirchner and J. Sperling (eds), *Global Security Governance*. London: Routledge, pp. 3–22.

Krahmann, E. (2003). 'Conceptualizing security governance', *Cooperation and Conflict*, 38(1): 5–26.

Ralph, J. (2011). 'A difficult relationship: Britain's "Doctrine of International Community" and America's "War on Terror"' in O. Daddow and J. Gaskarth (eds), *British Foreign Policy: The New Labour Years*. Basingstoke: Palgrave Macmillan, pp. 123–138.

Recommended websites

Human Security Gateway: http://www.humansecuritygateway.com/aboutUs.php
International Relations and Security Network: http://www.isn.ethz.ch/
Council on Foreign Relations: http://www.cfr.org/thinktank/iigg/
United Nations Human Security Unit: http://www.unocha.org/humansecurity/

2 Governing development
Power, poverty and policy

David Hulme and James Scott

Introduction

The global governance of poverty has a long, but not particularly illustrious, history. It can be traced most directly to the first United Nations (UN) 'Development Decade' launched in 1961, but also stretches beyond this to include the 1919 creation of the International Labour Organization (ILO) that sought to ameliorate the 'injustice, hardship and privation to large numbers of people' that prevalent labour conditions caused. Indeed, poverty governance may be said to begin with one of the first international standard-setting conventions, namely the First International Sanitary Conference of 1851, which aimed to create standardized quarantine measures to help prevent the spread of infectious diseases such as cholera, plague and yellow fever. However, the apogee of international efforts to tackle poverty is found in the UN Millennium Development Goals (MDGs), derived from the UN Millennium Summit in 2000, and it is these that frame present-day efforts to improve the plight of the poor.

The MDGs set out a list of targets to be achieved by 2015 that would blunt or remove the worst aspects of extreme poverty, covering income, health, education, gender equality and environmental sustainability. They are targets to be achieved by developing countries but include (weak) stipulations for how developed countries should assist in the fight against poverty. Perhaps surprisingly, the origins of the MDGs lie to a greater extent in rich rather than poor countries, and their character may be said to reflect rich country concerns as much or more than those of poor countries.

This chapter examines the process of the MDGs' creation, before situating their content within the broad parameters of development theory. It then examines efforts made to implement the Goals, using this to explore the debates that rage around aid from rich to poor countries and the role of trade in development. The conclusion draws some lessons from the preceding analysis concerning the highly contested and complex character of global poverty governance, and the often-contradictory impulses of the main players involved.

Origins of the MDGs

As noted in the introduction to this book the concept of global governance stretches back at least to the Enlightenment. The global governance of poverty can be traced to the creation of some of the earliest international institutions, but it is in the post-Second World War period that development and poverty reduction begin to be treated more directly and this has intensified over time. In 1948 the UN Declaration on Human Rights was signed, granting all citizens the 'right to a standard of living adequate for the health and well-being of himself and of his family' (Article 25). Shortly before at the 1944 Bretton Woods conference the International Bank for Reconstruction and Development (now more generally known as the World Bank) had been created, tasked with providing long term, concessional lending to Europe and the developing world to finance their infrastructure needs. A further step was taken in the 1960s driven by US President John F. Kennedy, who was alarmed by the growing influence of the Soviet Union in the global South. Kennedy played a central role in the creation of the World Food Programme in 1961 and went on to call for the 1960s to be declared the 'Decade of Development'. This project was strongly linked to Kenneth Rostow's 'modernization' approach to development – the idea that the countries of the global South could relatively easily follow the experience of the Western states in developing a modern, industrial economy given sufficient investment and reform. Indeed, Rostow worked closely on the idea of the Decade of Development (Toye and Toye 2005: 141). For Rostow, a 'big push' on aid would see developing countries propelled over the hurdles they faced onto the path of rapid modernization.

The optimism sparked by the UN Decade of Development saw a rash of target-setting; however, enthusiasm to set targets outstripped the commitment to action and results often fell far short of the rhetoric. In 1970 the Second UN Development Decade was inaugurated by the General Assembly, again pushing for aid to drive sustained economic growth, though recognizing that developing countries themselves bore primary responsibility for their development. As before, results were less than hoped for and by the 1980s the process of summitry and goal-setting had stalled, amid a wider crisis in development thinking. The modernization approach had been found wanting, with developing countries no closer to catching up with the rich countries and mired in unserviceable mountains of debt. Meanwhile, more critical development theory stemming from the political left was similarly under a sustained critique, being found unable to account for the rise of the newly industrialized countries of East Asia and facing the collapse of the socialist alternative (Schuurman 1993: 2–16). The theory of development found itself entering an 'impasse' (Booth 1985).

In the 1990s the UN process of summitry re-emerged, most notably with the Children's Summit of 1990, which partly managed to break the pattern of 'strong rhetoric but no action' (Emmerij *et al.* 2001: 112) seen in previous processes. The success of the Children's Summit reignited the practice of setting targets for ameliorating problems related to poverty, and summits were launched over the next ten years covering a range of areas including food, gender, population, habitation and the environment. These underpinned the subsequent creation of the MDGs at the UN Millennium Summit.

However, UN summits were only one element of the process and a number of other institutions played significant roles, most notably the Organization for

Economic Cooperation and Development (OECD) – the club of rich nations (see Hulme 2009 and 2010 for a more detailed history). While the 1990s saw the creation of many targets across a range of development challenges, aid agencies in the donor countries were facing cut-backs following the end of the Cold War. The OECD's Development Assistance Committee (DAC), which oversees the aid given by donor nations, felt that something needed to be done to protect aid budgets from being squeezed any further.

To this end, in 1996 DAC set up a group to review the future of development aid and the role DAC would play therein. This group drew up a list of goals contained in the declarations that had been agreed at the various UN summits over the 1990s (see Box 2.1) and attempted to make these form a coherent set. Following the inevitable political wrangling between DAC members over the prominence given to various elements the final report was published, titled *Shaping the 21st Century* (DAC 1996). This was 20 pages long but could be easily summarized by the list of its 'International Development Goals' (IDGs) that had been agreed by all DAC members.

Box 2.1 Selected UN Summits and Conferences, 1990–2000

2000 Millennium Summit: 'The role of the United Nations in the 21st century' (New York)
1996 World Food Summit (Rome)
      Second UN Conference on Human Settlements (HABITAT II) (Istanbul)
1995 Fourth World Conference on Women (Beijing)
      World Summit for Social Development (Copenhagen)
1994 International Conference on Population and Development (Cairo)
1993 World Conference in Human Rights (Vienna)
1992 United Nations Conference on Environment and Development (Rio)
      International Conference on Food and Nutrition (Rome)
1990 World Summit for Children (New York)
      World Conference on Education for All (Jomtien, Thailand)
      UNCTAD Conference on Least Developed Countries (Paris)

Meanwhile, the UN faced its own problems. The abject failure of the Security Council to respond to the Rwandan genocide of 1994, the aborted UN-backed intervention in Somalia in 1993–5 and the widely perceived failure of the fiftieth Anniversary Summit in 1997 had dented the organization's credibility. Secretary-General Kofi Annan felt that it was imperative to make the 2000 General Assembly Summit a success and worked hard to seize the opportunity offered by the new millennium to galvanize agreement among members on an ambitious topic. Furthermore, he recognized that it was imperative that the summit declaration achieved unanimous approval.

To help facilitate the necessary consensus Kofi Annan published a report in the lead-up to the Assembly for comment from interested groups, drawing from

the declarations made at previous UN conferences and summits. This report was titled *We the Peoples: The Role of the United Nations in the 21st Century* (Annan 2000). Though ostensibly based on the same material as *Shaping the 21st Century*, this report differed in a number of areas. The Beijing Women's Conference goals on gender equality, women's empowerment and reproductive health were already weakened in *Shaping the 21st Century*, but were almost absent from *We the Peoples* to cater to the sensitivities of strongly conservative religious states (see Hulme 2009). *We the Peoples* also gave greater prominence to spreading the benefits of technology, the environment, the particular problems faced by Africa and the setting of goals for rich countries to provide assistance to poor countries in their efforts to achieve the poverty targets.

The publication of *We the Peoples* by the UN and the IDGs by the DAC was partly a means of drawing NGOs into the process. NGOs responded generally in line with the degree to which their particular issue area was included. Most welcomed the broader approach of both documents, expanding the area of concern away from merely extreme income poverty to include a range of social development issues. Many women's groups were angry at the watering down of the gender goal that had taken place and lobbied for its restoration.

Following the process of additions, deletions and compromises that accompany all UN statements, *We the Peoples* formed the basis of the UN Millennium Declaration which received unanimous approval on 8 September 2000. The Declaration contained all that was necessary for drawing up an authoritative set of goals for poverty reduction that had the support of all 189 member states – a moment of unprecedented global unity around the issue of poverty. However, a problem remained. There were now two sets of competing goals – those set out by the UN and those set out by the DAC. To continue with the two operating side by side looked messy and would provide fuel to the anti-aid lobby, which would argue that even the world's development agencies were unable to agree on a single set of objectives. The alternative was to merge the two, but this posed problems for both agencies. Kofi Annan could not be seen to be changing the Millennium Declaration when it had been endorsed unanimously, while the DAC, keen to raise ODA spending among donor countries, felt that its IDGs were simpler, monitorable and achievable – key considerations for aid agencies – and had been endorsed by the World Bank, IMF and UN in June 2000.

The issue was resolved at a meeting held in March 2001. It was agreed that the two would be merged, and that there would be a division of labour between the Bretton Woods Institutions (BWIs, i.e. World Bank and IMF) and the UN. The BWIs would oversee implementation of the MDGs at the national level, primarily through the existing Poverty Reduction Strategies (PRSs), while the UN would drive the MDG process. PRSs would integrate the MDGs to ensure that countries were making progress towards their achievement. With this compromise, Kofi Annan was able to complete the required report on how to fulfil the commitments set out in the Millennium Declaration, which became the *Road Map Towards the Implementation of the United Nations Millennium Declaration* (UN 2001). At the end of the document were the eight MDGs along with a set of indicators to measure progress (see Box 2.2).

Box 2.2 The Millennium Development Goals

Goal 1: Eradicate extreme poverty and hunger
Target 1.A: Halve the proportion of people whose income is less than one dollar a day
Target 1.B: Achieve full and productive employment and decent work for all, including women and young people
Target 1.C: Halve the proportion of people who suffer from hunger

Goal 2: Achieve universal primary education
Target 2.A: Ensure that children everywhere, boys and girls alike, are able to complete primary schooling

Goal 3: Promote gender equality and empower women
Target 3.A: Eliminate gender disparities in all levels of education

Goal 4: Reduce child mortality
Target 4.A: Reduce by two-thirds the under-five mortality rate

Goal 5: Improve maternal health
Target 5.A: Reduce by three-quarters the maternal mortality ratio
Target 5.B: Achieve universal access to reproductive health

Goal 6: Combat HIV/AIDS, malaria and other diseases
Target 6.A: Have halted and begun to reverse the spread of HIV/AIDS
Target 6.B: Achieve, by 2010, universal access to treatment for HIV/AIDS for all those who need it
Target 6.C: Have halted and begun to reverse the incidence of malaria and other major diseases

Goal 7: Ensure environmental sustainability
Target 7.A: Integrate the principles of sustainable development into country policies and programmes and reverse the loss of environmental resources
Target 7.B: Reduce biodiversity loss
Target 7.C: Halve the proportion of people without sustainable access to safe drinking water and basic sanitation
Target 7.D: By 2020, to have achieved a significant improvement in the lives of at least 100 million slum dwellers

Goal 8: Develop a global partnership for development
Target 8.A: Develop further an open, rule-based, predictable, non-discriminatory trading and financial system
Target 8.B: Address the special needs of the least developed countries, including through tariff and quota free access for the least developed countries' exports; debt relief for heavily indebted poor countries; and more generous ODA for countries committed to poverty reduction
Target 8.C: Address the special needs of landlocked developing countries and small island developing states
Target 8.D: Deal comprehensively with the debt problems of developing countries
Target 8.E: In cooperation with pharmaceutical companies, provide access to affordable essential drugs in developing countries
Target 8.F: In cooperation with the private sector, make available the benefits of new technologies, especially information and communications

Source: UN, *Report of the Secretary-General on the Indicators for Monitoring the Millennium Development Goals*, New York: UN, 2008. Unless otherwise stated all targets are to be achieved by 2015.

Though the Millennium Declaration represented a moment of profound global convergence around the issue of poverty, at the same time the MDGs were not greeted with wholesale enthusiasm. The IDGs were viewed with suspicion by many developing countries as being the product of the OECD – a club of rich nations from which the developing world was excluded – and this suspicion was transferred across to the MDGs when the two were merged. Both the MDGs and IDGs were weak with regard to what the rich countries were expected to contribute, and implementation was to be through the distrusted BWIs – institutions that have had a decidedly problematic history with regard to development (to which we return below). As such the IDGs, and by extension the MDGs, were viewed partly as the rich countries telling the poor countries what to do, without any binding commitment to provide the resources needed to do it.

Several lessons may be drawn about the nature of poverty governance from the process of creating the MDGs. First, the global governance of poverty is institutionally 'messy' with numerous overlapping institutions involved, all needing to please different constituencies and facing different pressures. The MDGs were a UN project that was deeply entwined with the OECD and which had to include the two principal de facto global development institutions, the World Bank and the IMF, despite their highly dubious record with regard to many of the areas included in the MDGs. Second, the developing countries often play a secondary role in global poverty governance despite being its 'subjects'. There is a disconnect between the rich countries, which provide some of the development finance needed to tackle poverty (especially in aid-dependent countries), and the poor countries, which are expected to implement poverty-reduction programmes into which they had partial or little input. The developing countries broadly saw the MDGs as just another donor-led development project, and were generally more concerned about nationally defined development plans (rather than internationally imposed ones) and maintaining good relations with the BWIs, the gatekeepers of access to international finance.

These issues are better understood when placed within the context of the competing paradigms of development, to which we now turn.

The content of the MDGs and paradigms of global development

One of the reasons for the complex and overlapping institutional architecture in which the global governance of poverty takes place is the different paradigms, resting on different broad theoretical approaches, that underlie different understandings of development. One way of understanding this was developed by Jean-Philippe Thérien, who identifies two competing interpretations of international poverty: the 'Bretton Woods paradigm' and the 'UN paradigm' (Thérien 1999). Each encapsulates a different interpretation of what development constitutes and how it should be achieved. The Bretton Woods paradigm is closely linked with the practices and discourse of the Bretton Woods institutions and the World Trade Organization (WTO), and is closely linked to their shared neo-liberal agenda. It views globalization as contributing greatly to poverty reduction, and places the primary explanation of continued poverty as being the economic policies of poor countries themselves. Overcoming poverty is achieved by increasing economic growth through freeing the private sector, though there is a role for state programmes targeted at the poorest. Poverty in this analysis 'far from being the product of an asymmetrical structure invariably biased against the South, is more the result of a temporary misadaptation of markets' (Thérien 1999: 732). Markets can be got right by following the standard prescriptions of the Washington Consensus – liberalization, privatization, fiscal discipline and labour market flexibility. Since the general trend over recent decades has been in the direction of Washington Consensus policies, not least (though not exclusively) due to the imposition of these policies by the BWIs themselves, adherents of the Bretton Woods paradigm are generally optimistic with regard to the overall direction of global poverty reduction (for example Dollar and Kraay 2002; see also Deaton *et al.* 2006 for a critique of the Bank's selective use of research in support of its ideological position).

The UN paradigm is less optimistic about the direction of poverty, and less convinced that the way of achieving poverty reduction is through handing greater power to markets (Thérien 1999: 732–7). The UN system involves too many institutions for this to be a fully formed, coherent approach across all UN agencies. Rather, it is designed as an analytical construction drawing from the various analyses of poverty advocated by a range of UN agencies, particularly the United Nations Development Programme, International Labour Organization, UNICEF, and the Economic and Social Council. The UN paradigm is concerned with rising global inequality, which it attributes to the processes of globalization and the economic structures that keep poor countries (and poor people) poor. Drawing from Amartya Sen's Capability Approach it views poverty in a multidimensional way, highlighting social, political and ethical aspects in addition to the income poverty focused on by the Bretton Woods paradigm. Poverty in this view certainly includes having a low income, but it also includes lacking such things as education, health services, political representation and social respect. Through this, 'the UN paradigm seeks to take into account all the complexity of the social environment in which poverty exists' (Thérien 1999: 735). The recent trends towards liberalization and globalization are recognized as generating enormous wealth, but also seen as generating inequality and human insecurity as government capacity to pursue policies aimed at social cohesion and redistribution is reduced by transferring power to the market.

The MDGs can be seen to be a compromise between these two paradigms. The MDGs reflect a basic-needs, multi-dimensional approach to poverty characteristic of the UN paradigm, encompassing the need to improve education, health, gender equality, access to contraception, conditions in urban slums and so on. Meanwhile, the Bretton Woods paradigm is visible in the prominence given to extreme income poverty, which forms the first MDG and the most prominent target – that of halving the proportion of people living in dollar-a-day poverty by 2015. In addition, the approach of the MDGs – that of nested, quantifiable and time-bound targets – is lifted directly from business school textbooks on results-based management (see Hulme 2007).

Perhaps as a result of this compromise between two different analyses of the nature and causes of poverty, the MDGs say a great deal about what should be achieved but next to nothing about how to go about achieving it (see Wilkinson and Hulme 2012; Hulme 2010). For instance, target one (of tackling dollar-a-day poverty) says nothing about how growth might be increased and whether the impediments to growth are to be found in the policies of poor countries themselves (in line with the Bretton Woods paradigm) or global structural factors, such as structures of trade that restrict developing countries' exports (in line with the UN paradigm). Areas that previously have been considered to be central to development, such as the need for poor countries to industrialize and the importance of building economic infrastructure, are entirely absent. This partly reflects the 'development impasse' mentioned above, in that the neo-liberal, BWI paradigm that emerged in the 1980s downplayed such issues, leaving the allocation of resources to the market. But perhaps to a greater extent it reflects the UN's need for a consensus. While everyone can agree that extreme poverty, children unable to go to school and so on are bad, there is no consensus around the best way to tackle these problems. As the two paradigms of development outlined above demonstrate, there are conflicting approaches to questions concerning the correct role of the state within development, the importance of inequality and the importance of social structures in generating poverty. The MDGs bypassed such conflicts by being silent about how they were to be realized.

The formulation of the MDGs with regard to women and gender has also drawn criticism. Women feature prominently in the MDGs, explicitly in Goal 3 (promote gender equality and empower women) and Goal 5 (improve maternal health) but implicitly in others such as Goal 6 (combat HIV/AIDS etc.) which cannot be achieved without addressing women's unequal access to sexual and reproductive rights and lack of empowerment. While the MDGs are usually seen as positive with regard to women's rights, being seen as a means of addressing gender equality more broadly (e.g. Unterhalter 2005) and symbolizing the success of the feminist movement over previous decades (Subrahmanian 2004), problems remain. Naila Kabeer (2005), for instance, demonstrates that since improvements in each of the specific indicators used in MDG3 to assess progress on gender equality – education, employment and political representation – are linked to improvements in women's well-being, efforts must be made to improve the ability of women to overcome and to challenge the social and cultural impediments to their equal participation in society and in decisions that affect them. Significant, more contentious areas, were excluded from the MDGs such as gender-based violence and women's reproductive and sexual rights, though the latter was reintroduced having initially been cut to appease conservative religious groups (see Hulme 2009). Furthermore, the MDGs reinforced stereotyped roles for women, treating them as 'fundamental to the development process, but only within a narrow gendered frame that sees their role as the production and protection of children and carers within the community' (Harman 2012a).

As noted above, almost nothing was included in the MDGs as to how they were to be implemented. What little there was in this regard can be found in Goal Eight – Develop a Global Partnership for Development. This contained the targets for rich countries and specified what they should do. Unlike the targets for developing countries, no concrete deadline was given for those in Goal 8 and for only one was a quantifiable measure of progress set. The following section examines the progress made in achieving the MDGs, focusing particularly on aid.

Efforts to achieve the MDGs

The UN reports on progress towards achieving the MDGs in its annual *Millennium Development Goals Report*, and more detail can be found at http://mdgs.un.org. Progress has, inevitably, been mixed. Dollar-a-day poverty has declined significantly from its 1990 level of almost half the world's population and is projected to fall to below 15 per cent by 2015, exceeding the requirements of the MDGs. Though it was inconceivable that universal primary school enrolment would be achieved by 2015 given the starting point (Clemens *et al.* 2007), considerable progress has been made including among some of the poorest countries. Child mortality has fallen from 12.4 million in 1990 to 8.1 million in 2009. Deaths from malaria have dropped sharply in a number of countries, particularly in Africa, while new HIV infections and AIDS deaths are declining steadily (UN 2011: 4).

While this is all to be applauded, the links between the MDGs and poverty reduction are not direct and may be limited. The drastic fall in income poverty is almost entirely the result of high growth in China and India, which has had nothing to do with the MDGs. Other areas of improvement may well have more to do with relatively robust growth rates across much of the developing world, the emergence of sub-Saharan Africa from the two 'lost decades' of development of the 1980s and 1990s, and high commodity prices improving the incomes of those countries exporting raw materials, which tend to be the poorest. Though it is impossible to disentangle the various causes and effects, this should not detract from the real improvements in life prospects for hundreds of millions that have occurred over the past 20 years. It must also be noted that the way in which the MDGs are framed, as progress towards global targets rather than improvements on past performance, makes Africa appear to be 'failing' when it is improving its poverty reduction achievements (Easterly 2009: 26–35).

Other areas of deprivation remain stubbornly persistent. Opportunities for employment have not improved, particularly for women. The number of people living in slum conditions has increased dramatically. Progress on maternal mortality is a long way off track, especially in sub-Saharan Africa, and there is little improvement on unmet contraceptive needs. Though falling, HIV/AIDS prevalence rates in Africa continue to be so high as to threaten progress on a range of other MDGs. Where progress is being made, often it is not reaching the poorest and socially disadvantaged groups (women, the disabled, minorities, etc.) (UN 2011).

Though NGOs were highly involved in the formulation of the MDGs after 2000 they became somewhat marginalized. The specific role for NGOs in implementing the MDGs was left largely unaddressed by the UN's implementation plans. In addition, Western donors have been moving towards channelling aid towards direct budget support in developing countries, further undermining the role played by NGOs in development (Brinkerhoff *et al.* 2007: 2). Many NGOs continued to use the concept of the MDGs where appropriate in fundraising but played relatively little part in direct implementation. At the same time the role of the private sector as contractors and as partners (in public private partnerships, or PPPs) has risen. Most prominent was the rise of GAVI (formerly known as the Global Alliance for Vaccines and Immunisation). The UN has made increasing use of such PPPs. Some of these are driven by the UN itself, essentially outsourcing the implementation of a particular programme to the private sector but remaining organizationally rooted in the UN and funded by governments. Others have been driven instead by individuals of a 'global elite', the most prominent of whom is Bill Gates, which is organizationally outside the formal organizations of global governance (see Bull 2010). As Benedicte Bull argues, though there have been clear successes in a number of areas, such elite initiatives threaten to sideline the multilateral organizations of global governance and thereby undermine their authority. From an analytical point of view, the emergence of this elite and the role it plays in driving measures to tackle poverty highlight the importance of non-state actors in the global governance of poverty.

Though NGOs and PPPs have played a role in the implementation of the MDGs, the bulk of the money that has gone to their achievement comes from aid budgets. In the following section we look at this in more detail.

Official development assistance

One consequence of the basic-needs basis of the MDGs was the fact that they concentrated almost entirely on the social elements of development to the exclusion of economic infrastructure. Indeed, as the implications of the MDGs and the efforts toward their achievement filtered through to donor aid programmes, aid spending both by governments and the World Bank has shifted towards the social sectors. This has benefits of course – more schools and hospitals are built, etc. – but to the extent that this has come at the expense of improving economic infrastructure it may come at the cost of undermining the future basis for growth, and therefore for financing future schools and hospitals without relying on aid.

The effectiveness of aid, and its impact on developing countries, have become critical topics of recent debate, particularly following the publication of two highly influential books critiquing the whole aid project: William Easterly's (2006) *White Man's Burden: Why the West's Efforts to Aid the Rest Have Done So Much Ill and So Little Good,* and Dambisa Moyo's (2009) *Dead Aid: Why Aid is Not Working and How There is a Better Way for Africa*. Both critique the aid industry as failing to achieve its objectives and even perpetuating poverty through fuelling corruption and undermining incentives among the elite to build successful businesses. On the other side of the debate aid also has its strong proponents, such as Jeffrey Sachs, who argues fervently that the MDGs can be achieved so long as enough money is made available by donors (Sachs 2005).

Between these extreme pro- and anti-aid positions lies the middle ground occupied by the majority of practitioners, experts and academics. Possibly the most detailed and balanced recent review of aid and its impact on the recipient countries is Roger Riddell's (2007) *Does Foreign Aid Really Work?* This provides a comprehensive examination of what is best practice in delivering aid and how the benefits of aid programmes might be promoted. These good practices include untying aid (that is, avoiding attaching conditions to aid money that stipulate for example that it has to be spent on goods and services provided by companies based in the donor country), using aid to put cash directly into the hands of the poor, making aid flows more predictable, coordinating aid across donors more effectively and reducing policy conditionality.

Whether one considers aid to be a positive thing or not, it is a fact that the world's poorer countries have consistently demanded more aid from rich countries, and the rich countries in turn have consistently promised to deliver more. This stretches back to the pledge made in 1970 at the UN General Assembly that the world's rich countries would commit 0.7 per cent of gross national income (GNI) to aid, subsequently re-affirmed with monotonous regularity, most recently at the 2002 International Conference on Financing for Development in Monterrey, Mexico. Some countries have managed to achieve or even exceed this target (2010 figures) – Norway (1.1 per cent), the Netherlands (0.81 per cent), Luxembourg (1.05 per cent), Sweden (0.97 per cent) and Denmark (0.91 per cent). Others are less generous – including the US (0.21 per cent), New Zealand (0.26 per cent), Japan (0.2 per cent), Greece (0.17 per cent) and Italy (0.15 per cent). The average across all DAC countries has been rising since the creation of the MDGs (see Figure 2.1), but this has only recovered the lost funds following the steep post-Cold War decline. The current level of 0.31 per cent is similar to the level in 1970 when the 0.7 per cent pledge was first made. But it must be noted that the composition of aid has begun to change. Over the last decade China, and to a smaller extent India and Brazil, have become major donors but their contributions are not included in OECD statistics.

Despite this poor history, it would perhaps be wrong to dismiss the pledges made more recently on financing the MDGs. It may be argued that aid agencies have followed a particular evolutionary path (Lancaster 2007; Lumsdaine 1993). Though rhetorically they are always claimed to be targeted at achieving development, in reality countries initially create aid agencies as a means of increasing their international influence and those agencies are closely tied to the government's international political and economic aims. As a consequence, the aid distributed is usually tied (it must be spent on goods and services supplied by the donor countries' companies) and concentrated among countries that have a strategic political or commercial importance for the donor. However, over time this grounding of aid budgets in self-interest begins to be eroded and replaced by a 'moral vision', often through the campaigning of civil society, though this has taken place at different speeds in different donor countries.

This process was helped by the end of the Cold War and the removal of that 'need' to use aid to prop up regimes on the 'right' side of that conflict. Over recent years efforts have been made to realign aid budgets towards development goals. In 2005 the DAC countries signed the Paris Declaration on Aid Effectiveness, which sought to use the lessons of past aid programmes to increase the extent to which aid spending met development goals (OECD 2005). In 2001 the DAC countries agreed to move towards untying aid to least developed countries (OECD 2001). Though this is only a 'recommendation' and therefore not binding, it helps to create pressure on donors to move towards untying their aid. Implementation is inevitably uneven, but some countries have gone beyond the demands of the 2001 agreement, and overall untied bilateral aid rose from 46 per cent when the agreement was signed to around 82 per cent in 2008 (Clay et al. 2009).

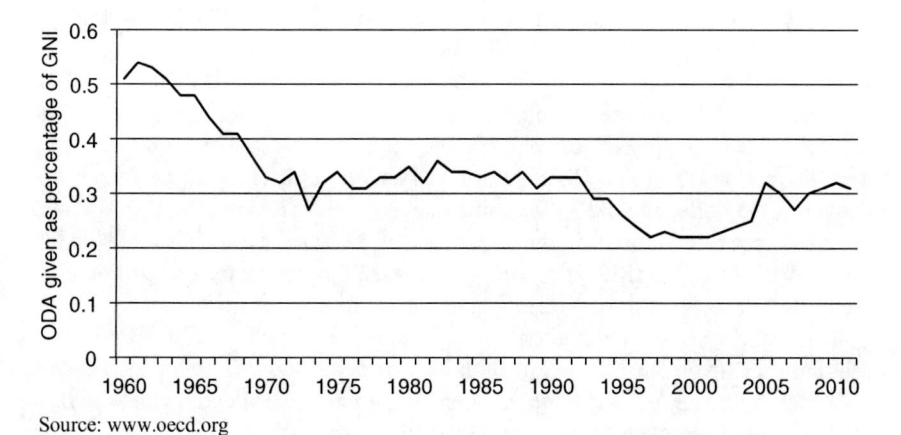

Source: www.oecd.org

Figure 2.1 Total ODA from DAC countries, 1960–2011, percentage of GNI

All EU countries and New Zealand have officially agreed a timetable to meet the 0.7 per cent target. Though some of the growth in ODA over recent years has been in the form of debt relief – the removal from the books of debt that was not going to be repaid anyway, particularly to Iraq (the 2005 peak in Figure 2.1 above), and which does not represent any new flows of real money – the underlying trend upwards since 2000 is genuine. That said, ODA fell slightly in 2011 as donors faced the fiscal squeeze from the ongoing economic crisis. In the UK the Conservative Party, traditionally somewhat hostile to ODA, pledged before the 2009 election to maintain progress towards the 0.7 per cent target and has protected the budget of the Department for International Development from the cuts. Within the EU at least, the idea that rich countries have a moral obligation to provide development assistance to tackle global poverty appears to be an emergent norm promulgated as an integral element of what it means to be part of the European project (Fukuda-Parr and Hulme 2011).

The World Bank, IMF and poverty reduction strategies

The MDGs were not simply about increasing aid levels and could not be achieved through aid alone. Other policies and other institutions were involved, most notably the World Bank, IMF and WTO – three of the most powerful international organizations. Their input into achieving the MDGs has not, however, been as positive as it might have been. As noted above, in the compromise agreed by the UN and OECD, the World Bank and IMF retained their oversight role of developing countries' economic policies and the measures they were taking to achieve the MDGs. This was done through the existing Poverty Reduction Strategy Paper process. To understand the significance of this requires a brief examination of the Bank and Fund's impact on developing countries.

The World Bank (originally the International Bank for Reconstruction and Development) was created in 1944 at the Bretton Woods Conference with a remit to provide long-term credit to countries for reconstruction following the Second World War and for infrastructure projects. The Bretton Woods Conference also saw the creation of the IMF. The IMF had two purposes. First, to provide short-term finance to help countries in balance of payments difficulties – that is, countries that find themselves unable to pay their international bills. Second, it was tasked with overseeing the post-war currency regime in which all currencies were tied to the US dollar which in turn was tied to gold. This currency regime – known as the dollar standard – was abandoned in 1971, leaving the IMF without one of its core roles. However, the emergence of the 'third world debt crisis' in the early 1980s thrust the IMF, alongside the World Bank, into a new role of managing the debt problems most developing countries found themselves in.

This process was undertaken through the use of 'Structural Adjustment Programmes' (SAPs), in which developing countries had to implement reforms drawn up by the Bank and Fund in order to gain access to loans with which to pay off other debts. SAPs were designed to increase the ability of developing countries to service their debts. They were based in the emerging neoliberal ideology being championed by Ronald Reagan and Margaret Thatcher that placed an emphasis on freeing markets and reducing the size of government (closely tied to the Washington Consensus and underpinning the Bretton Woods paradigm examined above). SAPs aimed at increasing economic efficiency, reducing government spending, increasing export earnings and cutting imports. Though they reversed some of the excessive trade and other restrictions that had arisen over the years in many countries and brought about greater macro-economic stability, these policies often came at an enormous social cost as education and health services withered through lack of funds and government policies aimed at protecting the poor (such as subsidizing basic foodstuffs) were abandoned. Africa suffered more than most, as trade liberalization squeezed the incomes of the rural poor by opening countries up to highly subsidized agricultural goods from the US and EU, and inefficient and/or industries were destroyed by cheaper imports.

Following criticism of the social impact of SAPs and growing recognition within the Bank and Fund that countries resented the imposition of these conditions and did all they could to resist implementing them, a new approach was adopted. In 1999, the Bank and Fund introduced Poverty Reduction Strategy Papers (now shortened to PRSs). It was claimed that this would increase country ownership of economic reforms, include greater attention to the social impact of reforms and engage with civil society over the policy reform. Developing countries are required to draw up a PRS before they are able to access funds from either of the BWIs, and virtually all OECD aid agencies require a PRS to be in place before they will consider a country for aid. PRSs, therefore, act as the 'ticket' to access BWI and OECD development finance.

As noted above, the MDGs were linked to the PRS process as the means of securing implementation. This, however, has been problematic. Institutions tend to show a large degree of resistance to change, and it remains an open question as to the extent to which PRSs have changed from the SAP process (for a range of discussion on this, see Pender 2001; Stewart and Wang 2003; Craig and Porter 2006). To many commentators, the country ownership of PRSs has been limited. Many countries lack the capacity to produce their own PRS, not least because the Bank and Fund spent 20 years requiring borrowing countries to dismantle national planning institutions. For the poorest countries their first PRSs were often produced by foreign consultants. Over recent years some countries have built greater planning capacity and are now able to drive their PRS process to a greater extent, or bypass it altogether by shifting to national five-year plans, but this is by no means universal. Even when domestically drafted, ultimately the Bank and Fund act as final arbiters and countries know that they must produce a PRS that chimes with the pro-market and anti-state ideology of these institutions if it is to be approved.

Leaving the governance of MDG implementation at the national level to the BWIs distanced developing countries from both the MDGs and PRSs and it tied the MDGs to the institutions that continue to subscribe to the Bretton Woods paradigm of development, albeit moderated somewhat from the days of the Washington Consensus. In particular the IMF had little time for the social aims contained in the MDGs, seeing them as little more than a distraction from the real task of continuing with fiscal restraint, liberalization and privatization. This has hampered the extent to which developing countries were willing to engage with the MDGs and has eventually led to a number of countries abandoning the PRS process and introducing five-year national plans.

The WTO

In important regards the rich countries also have failed to take the MDGs altogether seriously. One example is found in the WTO. Just one year after the Millennium Summit, the WTO launched a round of trade negotiations in Doha, Qatar, known as the Doha Development Agenda (DDA) or Doha Round. This, it was claimed, would 'place [developing countries'] needs and interests at the heart of the Work Programme' (WTO 2001) and redress the imbalance of previous trade rounds, and it has been linked with MDG Goal 8. The decision to make the Doha Round a 'development' round appears to have marked the pinnacle of MDG influence on trade negotiations, and it has been downhill ever since. Now more than a decade old, the DDA has hit an impasse. Promises of reforming the global trade system to benefit the world's poorest countries and open opportunities through trade for the poorest people have proved to be vacuous. Space does not allow for a detailed examination of the DDA (for such a discussion see Scott and Wilkinson 2011; Wilkinson and Scott 2012), but two examples will illustrate the failure of the rich countries to respond to the needs of the poor. First, the US and EU have refused to agree to any proposal that would require them to reduce their agricultural subsidies, while simultaneously demanding of the developing countries (particularly the emerging powers of Brazil, India and China) that they provide significant new market-opening in manufactured goods and services. Some poor countries are extremely badly affected by these subsidies. For example, cotton subsidies paid by the rich countries (particularly the US) amounting to $6 billion annually have been shown to depress world prices, robbing the cotton producers of West and Central Africa of export income and pushing farmers below the poverty line (Lee 2012). Despite this, the US has resisted efforts to tackle the issue and refused any agreement that reduced its cotton subsidies.

A second example of the lack of will shown by the rich countries can be found in the negotiations with the DDA for a deal by which the least developed countries would receive duty-free quota-free market access for all their exports. In a rather cynical way, illustrative of much of the approach of the rich countries to the governance of poverty, in 2005 the US offered duty-free quota-free access on 97 per cent of tariff lines. Though this sounds good, it must be remembered that least developed countries tend to export only a very narrow range of items. As such, the exclusion of 3 per cent of tariff lines meant that the vast majority of their exports could be excluded. The least developed countries were effectively being offered free market access for any product, except for those that they actually produce (Oxfam 2005; Stiglitz and Charlton 2006). As the DDA negotiations have stalled, pressure has grown for a duty-free quota-free deal to be put in place as an 'early harvest', but the US has refused.

As we have seen, the reforms of the global governance of poverty promised around the Millennium Summit have made little progress. The implementation of the MDGs has been rather patchy. Aid has increased and has been redirected towards social sectors but remains a long way from the agreed target of 0.7 per cent of GNI, though more countries are moving towards the target. Implementation of the MDGs within developing countries themselves is handled by the World Bank and IMF, though how 'deep' their commitment runs is questionable, particularly with regard to the IMF. Elsewhere, there has been little change in the architecture of global poverty governance. The WTO's DDA has reached an impasse and the member states refused to shift their policy in a more development-friendly direction. The promises made at Kyoto about mitigating climate change so that it does not disproportionately impact on poor countries and poor people have been dishonoured.

Conclusion

Global governance across all areas is contested, complex and often contradictory, as illustrated by the MDGs and wider governance of poverty. This was a project that was partly pushed by the UN Secretariat, but was also deeply entwined with political machinations in the club of rich nations, the OECD, and its efforts to justify aid budgets. But it was the developing countries themselves that were required to achieve the MDGs and the donor countries both resisted (successfully) any inclusion of quantified and time-bound targets for themselves relating to their expected contributions in such areas as aid, trade and tackling climate change, and have been decidedly reticent about changing their own policies to assist the achievement of the MDGs. Many developing countries have been sceptical of the MDGs and see them as somewhat imposed on them by the developed countries.

The method of overseeing MDG implementation through PRSs and the previous history of Bank and Fund SAPs generate questions over the role of sovereignty within the global system. Though sovereignty is supposedly a cornerstone of the international system, the governance of poverty highlights how it is in some regards honoured more in the breach than in the observance (for a wider discussion of this, see Krasner 2001). Developing countries have only limited control over their own economic direction, being both highly constrained by exogenous forces and (for some at least) to a significant degree controlled by the BWIs. Conditionality imposed as part of SAPs can be seen as a direct derogation from the principle of sovereignty. While the PRS process supposedly involved greater 'country ownership', questions remain over the extent to which this has been achieved. If changes are occurring then these arise more from the recent arrival of China on the aid scene, with its 'no strings attached' development finance, rather than changes in OECD countries or international institutions.

Indeed, China's aid to Africa can be usefully contrasted with that of the traditional donors and potentially opens up opportunities for Africa to escape the straightjacket of reliance on the West. While the MDGs have driven a shift in aid spending from OECD countries towards social sectors – merely the latest in a long line of shifting aid fads and fashions – China's aid focuses consistently on building infrastructure (Brautigam 2009: 11). As its economic growth has taken off China has been compelled to increase linkages with other countries to secure access to the raw materials it needs. Part of this outward turn has seen a massive and rapid expansion of its building of roads, ports and other economic infrastructure across Africa. This is partly philanthropy, but is also closely linked with China's own economic needs. Western states have criticized China's aid as being unscrupulous, ignoring social and environmental standards and being tied to the use of Chinese companies for building the infrastructure. Much of this criticism is of dubious accuracy and some of it is rather hypocritical. African governments have generally welcomed the new source of development and investment finance that China's expansion has brought and are keen to see it continue. However, as UNCTAD (2010) argues, if the rise of such South–South cooperation is to deliver benefits to Africa, African states must have an active policy of ensuring that such assistance fits with and promotes their national development plan.

For rich countries, the global governance of poverty highlights the ways in which states should not be seen as unitary actors but as complex entities pursuing multiple, sometimes contradictory, activities simultaneously. Concerns expressed about global poverty are, without doubt, genuine, but are compromised by the domestic political battle taking place within each country and by geopolitical interests of the state. The US, to take one example, is not blind to the effects of its cotton subsidies on an estimated 10 million poor farmers in Africa and is aware of the contradiction between its free-market rhetoric and the continued use of subsidies, but these considerations are trumped by the interests of a powerful set of 25,000 cotton businesses. Likewise, aid agencies are staffed by people genuinely concerned with poverty, but they operate in a highly political environment and aid spending is compromised by the need to respond to domestic groups hostile to 'wasting' money on feckless and corrupt countries, or pushing for aid to be used for the purposes of furthering state commercial and strategic interests.

Just as each country has many forces shaping policy, the international landscape has many global institutions involved in poverty governance. These subscribe to differing understandings of the nature of development and the means to overcome poverty, and have their own constituencies to satisfy. Disagreement is particularly strong over the appropriate role of markets, the effect of globalization on poverty and inequality and the importance of domestic policy versus international structural constraints for understanding the causes of poverty. The rich countries, and especially the United States, mostly incline towards what has been called the Bretton Woods paradigm, and consequently the most powerful international organizations involved in governing poverty also take this position. Other institutions, especially the UN with its 193 country membership, advocate alternative outlooks but they are more peripheral, underfunded and have limited real influence.

It is easy to be cynical about international efforts to tackle poverty, but there are signs of hope. There is evidence that the levels of human deprivation witnessed in what is an affluent world are slowly being recognized as morally unacceptable and demanding both attention and policy changes. Progress towards delivering more, and crucially better, aid is being made, and the rising powers of China, India and others are opening up new trading opportunities, demanding reforms to global institutions and providing new sources of development finance and models of development. The MDGs represent a moment of global solidarity around the problem of poverty and though progress has been patchy, it is nonetheless real. The MDGs will not be fully achieved but progress towards them has accelerated in most parts of the world, including Africa. As the world moves beyond the MDGs when they expire in 2015 the challenge is not to produce a 'better' set of global goals but how to build a new global movement around poverty, in which citizens of developing countries themselves play a greater role in setting and achieving their own goals.

Recommended reading

Birdsall, N., Rodrik, D. and Subramanian, A. (2005). 'How to Help Poor Countries', *Foreign Affairs*, 84(4): 136–52.

Easterly, W. (2006). *The White Man's Burden: Why the West's Efforts to Aid the Rest Have Done So Much Ill and So Little Good*, Oxford: Oxford University Press.

Hulme, D. (2010). *Global Poverty: How Global Governance is Failing the Poor*, London: Routledge.

IDS Bulletin Special Issue (2010). 'The MDGs and Beyond', 41(1). A collection of articles on aspects of the MDGs and what will replace them.

Lancaster, C. (2007). *Foreign Aid: Diplomacy, Development, Domestic politics*, London and Chicago: University of Chicago Press.

Recommended websites

http://www.worldbank.org/
http://www.oecd.org/development/
http://www.southcentre.org/
http://www.un.org/millenniumgoals/

3 Global financial governance
Taming financial innovation

Anastasia Nesvetailova and Carlos Belli

Introduction: the paradox of financial regulation

One of the many paradoxes of the global financial system is that while capital flows are commonly considered to be one of the most footloose elements of the global economy, and while the financial industry is believed to be largely unregulated, finance is in fact one of the most heavily regulated segments of economic activity. At the global level, the financial sector is governed by international financial institutions such as the International Monetary Fund (IMF), the World Bank, the Bank for International Settlements (BIS) and the Financial Stability Board (FSB). At the national level, central banks, financial services authorities, ministries of finance, Treasury departments and other bodies carry out the tasks of financial regulation and supervision of individual institutions. Within the financial markets, it is private structures of market authority, such as credit-rating agencies (CRAs) or even market standards (such as accounting standards or valuation rules) that are supposed to guide and discipline the behaviour of market participants. Finally, at the level of the individual financial institutions, various departments are mandated to carry out the tasks of supervision and control of specific functions and operations, as well as the overall state of the bank or a financial company. In fact, the architecture of global financial governance is so sophisticated that in 1996, Ethan Kapstein observed that:

> [o]ver the past 20 years the leading economic powers have created a regulatory structure that has permitted the financial markets to continue toward globalization without the threat of systemic collapse. The elimination of financial contagion has required painstaking efforts by dedicated public servants who have had to navigate between domestic political pressures and concerns about the well-being of the international system.
>
> (Kapstein 1996: 2)

Within ten years of the date the above lines were published, the world economy was confronted with the biggest financial meltdown since the Great Depression of the 1930s. In August 2007, problems of several financial institutions linked to the losses on the so-called subprime mortgages (those offered to clients with no or inferior credit history) in the USA spurred an international liquidity crisis.

Within days the perceived phenomenon of 'global excess liquidity' turned into a problem of a global liquidity crunch. In the course of that year, as the real-estate markets continued to stagnate or fall, the crisis entered into its second phase – the international banking crisis, heralded by the collapse of several large institutions, including Lehman Brothers. Without decisive action by the public authorities to stop the tumbling markets, international credit flows simply would have ceased to function. The governments in the USA and the UK did intervene, announcing massive bailout packages of financial aid to the markets and specially designated programmes aimed to relieve the banks of bad debts they had incurred during the boom years of 2000–07. Yet despite aggressive government stimulus measures, coordinated internationally, by late 2008 the financial crisis had become a global recession.

The size of the bailout schemes, totalling around $9 trillion, illustrated that contrary to the vision suggested by Kapstein, the ostensibly sophisticated network of financial regulation had not eliminated risk out of the economic system. Notwithstanding the developed web of regulatory structures governing finance at national and international levels, the crisis showed that the globalization of financial markets over the past 30 years has advanced at the cost of an exponential increase in the threat of systemic collapse. Indeed, at the time of writing (spring 2012), the global credit crunch has entered into its third stage – the crisis of European sovereign debt. Despite some isolated rallies in the financial markets, many analysts believe that the risk of a 'double-dip' recession and possibly a depression (especially in the case of the UK and Europe) remains high.

While in its most immediate form the financial meltdown of 2007–12 has become associated with the crisis of the securitization industry in finance, its long-term roots lie in the tendency of financial institutions to exploit unregulated financial spaces. Accordingly, the major lessons of the credit crunch can only be understood when placed in the historical context of the long-running tension between regulation and innovation.

The aim of this chapter is not to analyze a particular financial crisis or its regulatory response. These questions have been a subject of a large and growing body of scholarship on financial fragility and the global financial crisis (e.g., Brunnermeier 2009; Crotty 2009; Schwartz 2009). Our aim here is to explore the foundations of the contemporary system of financial governance, and analyse the relationship between the perennial financial instability of the economy and the regulatory responses to financial innovation, in a historical setting. We focus, in particular, on the important nexus between technological and financial innovation on the one side, and regulatory environment on the other.

The global financial crisis as a crisis of governance

One of the major theoretical perspectives on the origins of the global financial crisis of 2007–09 can be identified under the heading of 'behavioural' explanations for the crisis. Rehearsed mainly in the framework of formal economics, these analyses emphasize the skewed structure of incentives in the financial industry that produced a sub-optimal outcome: namely, an inefficient price mechanism for allocating risk in the financial system. Outside the boundaries of economic orthodoxy, behavioural accounts emphasize the dominant role of the human factor, and more precisely, human failure, in precipitating and escalating the global crisis.

Stressing the role of incompetence, greed and fraud, behavioural accounts of the crisis reveal the incompetence of senior management at individual financial institutions; unaccountable traders and salesmen who knowingly sold risky products to their customers; the financial space exploited by individual crooks of various calibres; the warnings about the risk of the coming malaise that were repeatedly dismissed or silenced; and finally, the untrained, unskilled and not sufficiently savvy regulators, statesmen and even academics who did not discern or were not sufficiently clued in to the actual developments in the financial industry (Nesvetailova 2010). In other words, a major perspective on the origins of the global financial crisis suggests that in essence the meltdown was not about finance or banking as such; rather, it was a crisis of a complex mechanism and principles of governance (Toporowski 2009; Rajan 2010). It was bad practices of regulation and control at individual financial institutions that had led their managers to underestimate and often misrepresent the risks they were taking upon and trading in. It was the search for profit and the conflict of interest that led the institutions of private market discipline – the credit-rating agencies – to rate obscure complex and inferior debt products as AAA securities; it was the focus on consumer price inflation and a firm commitment to the optimizing force of liberalized markets that had led many central bankers and financial regulators to rely on the self-discipline of the free market, rather than aim for a systemic overview of the build-up of risks in international banking. It was the idea that financial and banking crises tend to happen in emerging markets and developing economies, and not in the economies of advanced capitalism, that led institutions like the IMF and the FSB to completely overlook the signs of the coming financial crisis.

In November 2009, when Queen Elizabeth II paid a visit to the London School of Economics and asked an audience of reputable economists why no one had foreseen the global financial crisis, the sophisticated answer given to Her Majesty's simple question was that, somehow, they had missed systemic risk. That answer is indicative for at least two reasons: first, it was actually true. Indeed, despite the growing sophistication of financial models and economic techniques, mainstream economic and financial theory offers very little by way of understanding the behaviour of *an economy as a system* (Nesvetailova 2013). Second, the answer given to the Queen also illustrated the basic fact that the constellation of structures, agents, networks, nodes of data and sets of relationships that constitute the contemporary financial system, is extremely complex. From a functional point of view, this complexity means that any regulatory effort to keep pace with the progress of financial innovation driven by the private agents' search for profit, is likely to encounter enormous practical, ideological and even cultural difficulties. The opaqueness and sophistication of most of today's financial products and techniques make it virtually impossible for those outside the trading desks or financial platforms to decipher the nature and function of many financial products. Moreover, the banking sector lobbyists and financial industry representatives have been putting enormous pressure against any effort by governments or international organizations to introduce new codes and rules of financial regulation (Seabrooke 2006).

At the same time, the complexity that is inherent in a financial system that thrives on financial innovation is also a powerful agent by itself. Gillian Tett, citing the French philosopher Pierre Bourdieu in her own account of the 2007–09 financial crisis, reminds the reader that in a range of tools employed by elites to exercise control over society, the so-called areas of social silence are no less important than, say, ownership of the means of production or financial resources. What matters in a given socio-political context, in other words, is not defined simply by the control over financial, intellectual or physical capital of a society, but also by the way a society talks about itself and understands its behaviour. In influences over this cognitive map, Tett argues, 'what matters is not merely what is publicly discussed, but also what is *not* mentioned in public' (2009: xiii, italics in the original). Tett then continues her own story about a credit derivative – the actual instrument that brought down the world financial system in 2007–09 – explaining that an important area of social silence, both inside and outside the banking world, developed about credit derivatives during the boom years of 2000–07. Such silence was partly a reflection of the opacity necessarily built into the process and products of financial innovation, but such silence was also accepted, publicly and politically, because of the presence of so-called silos – 'self-contained realms of activity and knowledge that only the experts in that silo can truly understand' (Tett 2009: xiv).

It is through these knowledge silos, as well as through the political opportunities offered to the governments on both sides of the Atlantic who were able and willing to capitalize on the economic boom driven by finance, that the financial sector has successfully arrogated for itself a position of overwhelming predominance, influence and control over the so-called real economy. This process is often understood as *financialization*. Although many definitions of the concept of financialization exist, in a few words, the financialization of capitalism has encompassed a variety of processes by which the financial market spread and embedded its influence into every aspect of modern life (Langley 2008; Montgomerie 2009). As the ongoing turmoil illustrates, the cost of this process is the heightened vulnerability of economy and society to the growing variety and complexity of financial risks and ultimately, systemic breakdowns.

The financial stability of the Bretton Woods

The foundations of the contemporary system of financial governance can be traced back to the Depression of the 1930s, and the chains of policy reactions to it. The banking crisis of the early 1930s and the succeeding economic meltdown around the world exposed the structural weaknesses of the financial system and induced policymakers to rethink the global structure of financial architecture. The financial and economic chaos during the 1930s, aggravated by the experience of two catastrophic wars in less than 30 years, encouraged political leaders to reconsider their approach towards international economic cooperation. In the wake of the Second World War, most world leaders agreed on a number of principles notably: the need to avoid the mercantilist logic and economic nationalism that ruled over the 1930s. A major contribution came from the British economist John Maynard Keynes who formulated this idea in his seminal publication *The Economic Consequences of the Peace* (1919). Keynes, as designated lead negotiator for the British Treasury, was a key player in the design of the new international economic order established at the United Nations Monetary and Financial Conference in 1944, commonly known as the Bretton Woods agreements.

Despite Keynes' prestige and influential ideas, however, he could not overcome the prevailing authority of the United States in the negotiations. The United States had an overwhelming position after the war: it owned 70 per cent of the gold reserves in the world; it had a sound economic system, thus replacing the UK as the biggest world creditor; and last but not least, over the years the US had built an unrivalled military, industrial and financial capacity.

Although American and British delegations to the Bretton Woods conference had alternative visions of how to organize the new structure, they ultimately agreed on an unprecedented system of multilateral international institutions, including two highly influential institutional bodies: the IMF and the International Bank for Reconstruction and Development (IBRD, now known as the World Bank). The third institution aimed to establish and enforce the rules of international trade, was also proposed: the International Trade Organization (ITO). Ultimately, the refusal of the US Congress to ratify the ITO charter brought to an end this third project. In its place the more informal General Agreement on Tariffs and Trade (GATT, renamed as the World Trade Organization in 1995) served as the multilateral body to discuss trade affairs.

One of the most divisive issues at the Bretton Woods gathering concerned the international mobility of capital. In order to guarantee the autonomy of national economic policies, all countries were allowed to impose capital controls. This measure was not meant to block all cross-border capital movements, rather it was seen as a tool of national policy to control speculative flows or tax evasive domestic capital. It was also meant to allow greater independence to each country in adjusting its national rates of interest (Keynes 1980: 149). In this way, control over currency exchange rates and national interest rates was managed directly by the Treasuries of member governments rather that by the agents of private finance. As Miles Kahler (2002: 50) put it, 'the rules under this regime of relatively fixed parities were constructed by governments, for governments.'

It was not long, however, before the world of finance would find new ways to circumvent the obstacles imposed on their continual search for profits, managing to regain increasing influence over the world's financial architecture. Key innovations in the international financial markets during the late 1950s led to further transformations in the structure of the UK and US banking model, thereby eroding the effect of official regulatory measures, and augmenting the part of the financial system that would be *de facto* privately governed.

The rise of the Euromarket and the erosion of regulation

> It is natural enough that London banks – and merchant banks in particular – with their expertise and international connections […] have sought to participate actively in this [Euromarket] business. It is par excellence an example of the kind of business which London ought to be able to do both well and profitably. That is why we at the Bank, have never seen any reason to place any obstacles in the way of London taking its full and increasing share […] There are of course risks involved […] we have not however thought that the existence of risks provided any reasons for our seeking to restrict the development of this market. We have rather felt that we ought to be able to rely on the judgement of London banks to conduct their operations in accordance with sound banking principles and we have been entitled to assume that, in exercising their banking judgement they would not overlook the experience of 30 years ago. To drive the business from London would be wrong […] and the reputation of London as a monetary centre would suffer in the process.
>
> Letter from the Deputy Governor, Sir Humphrey Mynors, to Sir Charles Hambro, Director of the Bank of England and Chairman of Hambros Bank
> (written in early 1963)

In the late 1950s, a new type of a financial market emerged in the City of London. A peculiar regulatory niche offered by the City allowed international private finance to effectively escape from the restrictions imposed by the Bretton Woods system and national domestic regulations. The innovations brought by the Euromarket reconfigured the international financial system, ultimately leading to the ultra-liberal and unregulated financial order that characterizes the world of finance today.

The origins of the Euromarket can be traced in the early stages of the Cold War, when the Soviet and Chinese communist governments, fearing the confiscation of their deposits held in New York, decided to transfer their dollars to European banks, mostly based in London. Around the same time, an increasing amount of US dollars was passing through the same space, under the implementation of the Marshall Plan and military assistance budgets, thus flanking the growing US external payment deficit. The Bretton Woods arrangements, by designating the dollar as the dominant currency of the new international monetary system, further encouraged companies and states worldwide to hold dollar cash reserves.

In this environment, the City of London assumed a key role as an international financial hub. The Euromarket was able to grow dramatically in a short period of time, re-establishing the City as the most important financial centre in the world. In effect, by the early 1970s, it accounted for almost 80 per cent of the Euromarket (Burn 1999). This was made possible because while the domestic market in the UK was regulated, the international market was not. As Gary Burn observed:

> the Defence Regulation of 1939 (reaffirmed by the 1947 Exchange Control Act), designed to protect Britain's currency reserves by controlling the movement of capital out of the sterling area [...] effectively compartmentalized the British banking system into a highly regulated domestic market and a totally unregulated international market, thereby giving a *de facto* offshore condition to all banking activity segregated into the latter.
>
> (Burn 1999: 226)

Thus, distinguishing residents from non-residents, the UK political and financial authorities considered that transactions undertaken by non-residents on behalf of a lender or borrower who themselves were not located in the UK, were not, for regulatory purposes, to be officially viewed as having taken place in the UK, even though they effectively did happen in London. In other words, financial transactions in the UK between non-resident actors carried out in foreign currency were not under UK regulations. But since transactions did effectively take place in London, they were not regulated by any other regulatory authority, thus creating a financial 'black hole' in the international system, the London Euromarket offshore. A growing number of financial institutions began to run, effectively, two accounting books: one for domestic operations and the other for international transactions (Palan *et al.* 2010: 161).

Meanwhile, US constraints on capital flows, an outcome of the Glass Steagall Act and the Bretton Woods legacy, encouraged American multinationals, who were increasingly expanding their operations worldwide, to use the 'expatriate dollars' of the Euromarket, circumventing the restrictive domestic legislation in the USA. Immediately, US banks followed their corporate clients, opening new branches in the unregulated environment of the City and transferring all their international transactions beyond the control of any national monetary authority. The new configuration of the international financial market was thus characterized by an asymmetry between the highly regulated national domestic environments and the totally unregulated Euromarket, which was operating de facto as an offshore paradise. Foreign banks (mostly American) and multinational corporations simply moved where the least regulatory restriction was placed and where more favourable tax treatment was offered.

The UK chief financial authority, the Bank of England (which was nationalized in 1946), was not willing to regulate the Euromarket because of its role in catalysing a large inflow of US dollars that benefited the UK economy and re-established the City of London's position as the world's premier financial centre. The Bank of England was therefore acting as an interface between the state and the market: the 'government's arm in the City, and the City's representative in the government' (McRae and Cairncross 1973: 193, cited in Burn

1999: 241). Thus for the British government, pressured by the instability of the sterling (in particular after the Suez crisis in 1956), the Euromarket represented a discounted option to finance its balance of payments deficits, allowing local authorities, for instance, to borrow foreign currency from the Euromarket on a medium- and long-term basis (at very competitive rates) in order to finance its repayments of shorter term debt or to make investments, thus protecting the UK sterling reserves. Gradually, the offshore Euromarket replaced the international institutions of Bretton Woods in the role of financing budgets and balance of payments deficits.

For private finance, the Euromarket created freedom to carry out countless financial transactions without any institutional control or established rules, thus allowing for much higher returns than the restrictive domestic markets. On the other hand, it also led to increased volatility and higher financial instability. In fact, while the Euromarket, effectively avoiding national regulations, evolved from the pursuit of higher profits by the private financial sector, its further development served to erode domestic regulations by providing all market operators with more lucrative alternatives. The result was further deregulation of financial markets and the liberalization of capital movements during the 1970s and early 1980s, which formally declared the death of the Bretton Woods legacy.

The international arrangement of 1944 was meant to bring stability to the currency exchange markets, but was also designed as a way to prevent competitive currency devaluations, associated with the floating exchange rates. To further guarantee the autonomy of national economic policies, all countries were given the right to impose capital controls. Although the goal was to control speculative flows and 'harmful' movements of capital, the result was perverse: the development of the Euromarket after the 1950s which gradually corroded national domestic controls.

The two international financial institutions established at Bretton Woods, the IMF and the World Bank, were seen as a common ground to promote monetary and financial collaboration. Specifically, they were intended to provide liquidity as international lenders, a role previously held by the private markets (Helleiner 2008). The IMF was designed to provide short-term loans to member states with temporary cash-flow problems, while the World Bank was given the task of providing long-term loans for reconstruction and development to countries affected by the war. Thus by replacing private markets in the provision of liquidity, these institutions were thought to reinforce national autonomy of the member states and make them more independent from market restraints. In practice, the UK and other governments often found it more convenient to borrow in the private Euromarket rather than require provisional liquidity from the IMF. By 1970, the volume of private capital in the form of deposits available to borrow in the Euromarket was considerably higher than all the gold and dollar reserves held by the IMF and the governments who financially supported it (Strange 1976: 176).

The discussion at Bretton Woods did not focus solely on the creation of new public international institutions. In July 1944, a resolution was proposed for the liquidation of the BIS, the 'bank of the bankers' created in 1930 under the Hague agreements. Harry Dexter White, who negotiated on behalf of the US at Bretton Woods, supported the abolition of the BIS because he feared that it might interfere with the newly created financial institutions. In fact, to many of its opponents, the 'BIS and its central bank members represented the policy preferences of private finance' thus challenging 'the dominant role of governments in the direction of monetary affairs' (Kahler 2002: 47). Norway, jointly with the United States and other national delegations, accused the BIS of collaborating with Nazi Germany during the Second World War, suggesting that it be liquidated as soon as possible. Although prominent Nazi officials had been members of its executive board and although the resolution had been approved at the Bretton Woods conference in 1944, the BIS was not dismantled. Instead, it has increasingly gained relevance, in particular since the Bretton Woods order collapsed in the early 1970s, and especially through the Basel committee on banking regulation.

Since the end of the Second World War it has become a convention for individuals holding key positions in national or international politics to be offered a place in a private bank or other financial institution; and vice versa. During the 1960s, when the Euromarket expanded, the Bank of England, a (recent) public institution, was still dominated by governors and directors recycled from the private banking community. In a similar fashion, several executives of the World Bank were recruited directly from Wall Street, and the same applies for many financial or economic related chairs within national governmental ministries. As a result, the private financial sector has acquired an organic power to influence, directly and indirectly, national and international policy decisions (Strange 1986).

This close relationship makes global financial governance, and more specifically, public control over the financial system, an extremely complex and difficult task. It is not surprising that many exponents of privately regulated finance, while holding political power, had strongly advocated the reduction of government controls and less regulation. They argued that if the market was free to allocate financial resources, it will always be more efficient and thus more profitable than a heavily regulated market. The tension between the expansion of a privately governed market sphere and the regulatory role of the state in the context of a US-led agenda for financial governance has always been at the heart of the analyses in the discipline of international political economy (Cohen 2007; Helleiner 1994; Palan 2009; Phillips and Weaver 2010). While the advance of financialization and the emergence of new forms of financial institutions, products and practices has revealed the limitations of IPE approaches to financial governance, the issue of the balance between the gains from privately regulated markets, and the social costs of financial and economic crises, remains essential for understanding the evolution and challenges of global financial governance (Wigan 2009, 2010; Montgomerie 2008).

Neoliberalism and private financial governance, or the golden age of financial innovation

Less than 30 years after its creation, the financial system envisaged by the architectures of Bretton Woods was overthrown. Compared with an arrangement in which governments were supposed to control transnational capital mobility, where international institutions were created to provide short- and long-term liquidity, and where fixed exchange rates were designed to guarantee systemic stability, the post-1970 financial system turned out to be very different. The erosion of government controls throughout the 1960s initiated a massive cross-border expansion of capital, accelerated after 1971 by progressive trade liberalization and deregulation of financial markets. The international allocation of financial resources was mainly undertaken by the private market, thus obscuring the lending role of the IMF and World Bank. Finally, the system of floating exchange rates was formalized in 1973, encouraging further circulation of currencies across national political frontiers. This in turn accelerated the process of 'deterritorialization', which describes the increasing disconnection between the domain of currency usage and the geographic borders of issuing states (Cohen 1998).

This process was strongly influenced (and justified) by a new economic paradigm which promptly turned into the dominant ideology among the most influential circles of economic power. Neoliberalism, the ideology that has preponderantly inspired the evolution of the financial system over the past 30 years, is essentially supported by a set of claims originated from standard neoclassical theory of economics: if markets were to be allowed to operate without any restrictions, they would optimally 'serve all economic needs, efficiently utilize all economic resources and automatically generate employment for all persons' (McKenzie 2011: 202). Supported by the scientific and quantitative turn in economic and political theories, advocates of the neoliberal doctrine launched an attack on the regulatory framework that started to be established with the New Deal in the United States and then consolidated in Western Europe after the Second World War.

Defending the natural capacity of financial markets to self-correct, the new doctrine advocated a minimal role of the state, fewer rules and less overall control. In the context of the international recession during the 1970s, neoliberal visions found a favourable audience among policymakers. The overburdened (Keynesian) state, it was argued, by running continuous deficits to finance the domestic economy and boost internal consumption, was increasing inflationary pressures. Additionally, wage bargaining and trade unions were pushing wages up while rendering the labour market too rigid, cutting down productivity and profits and feeding even more inflationary pressures. Keynesian principles of monetary and fiscal stimuli were seen as inflationary, while increased government expenditures to maintain demand, good infrastructure and unemployment measures were seen as wasteful and damaging for national balance of payments and exchange rates (Cerny 2008).

In the wake of the high inflationary pressures of the 1970s, aggravated by the two oil crises of 1973 and 1979, the driving force behind macroeconomic thinking has been to keep inflation low and stable. Policymakers, particularly in the US and UK, became less concerned with control of domestic economy and more inclined to provide favourable 'business-friendly' policies to boost growth. In addition, states sought to liberalize the restrictive capital controls imposed under the New Deal and in the early post-war years. The British government, as we have seen, greatly contributed to this process by tolerating the growth of the unregulated Euromarket since the late 1950s. In these circumstances, the United States, keen to attract private financial capital into its national borders, abolished national capital controls in 1974. Soon the British government followed the same path, eliminating domestic capital controls in 1979 (Helleiner 2008). Caught up in this competitive deregulatory pressure, and in order to avoid the migration of domestic capital and financial business outside of borders, other advanced industrial countries adopted the same policies, leading to a spiral of market and financial deregulation throughout the 1980s and the 1990s.

These shifts produced two major effects: not only did they make public regulation and governance extremely difficult, but they have also led, over the past two decades, to some perverse interactions between finance, risk and the so-called 'real economy'. In light of this, although neoliberalism in the global financial architecture is often associated with the removal of state from the regulatory space of the market and liberalization of the economy, it is more appropriate to understand the rise of neoliberal governance as, essentially, the rise of private mechanisms and institutions of economic regulation and governance (Seabrooke 2006; Sinclair 2008).

The historical process of financialization, intended as the ability to locate, price and then shift risk from one's books, has been the heart of the new important segment of the financial sector, the securitization industry. Securitization is a process through which an issuer creates a financial instrument by combining different types of financial assets and then marketing different tiers of the repackaged instruments to investors. Mortgage-based securities are a typical example of securitization. By combining mortgages into one large pool, the issuer divides the large pool into smaller pieces based on each individual mortgage's inherent risk of default and then sells those smaller pieces to investors. The key to financial institutions' ability to shift risky products to other parts of the financial system, in turn, lay in their newly found apparent control over risk and ability to create 'liquidity'. The very essence of financial innovation and securitization more narrowly was to transform inherently illiquid assets (and more specifically, very low quality debts) into liquid securities. For a while, the alchemy seemed to have worked wonderfully: banks reaped more and more profits because they were able to remove credit risk from their books; customers and clients, equipped with the purchasing power of debt, felt better off; credit-rating agencies were happy to charge high fees for their stamps of approval and politicians were content as they gained on the political benefits of the economic boom. The continually expanding frontier of liquid assets only reinforced the idea that financial innovation created liquidity, and therefore wealth. At first cut therefore, the subsequent burst of the bubble was simply the unravelling of a grandiose illusion of wealth and liquidity (Nesvetailova 2010).

Thus, the advances in 'scientific' finance, the expansion of exotic credit products and crucially, the belief that sophisticated techniques of parcelling debts, creating new products, arranging structured deals and opening up new markets was prone to create additional and plentiful liquidity, had hidden, for a while, the 'dark shadow' of the evolution of the global financial markets. In effect, the proliferation of obscure techniques of valuing risk and even more obscure financial securities had driven the financial system into a structurally illiquid, and crisis-prone, state. At the level of the financial system, securitization had produced an incredibly complex and opaque hierarchy of credit instruments, whose liquidity was assumed but in fact never guaranteed.

The second impact of financial innovation was more long term. Financial innovations were introduced for a reason: they helped financial institutions to gain profits by further circumventing existing barriers on profit-making. These barriers, as we have seen, tended to arise out of the introduction of official regulations and rules. Although since the 1970s, deregulation and liberalization of financial markets were the major priorities for most national governments, the continuous outbreak of international financial crises persuaded the 'international community' to improve (or attempt to) the global system of financial governance. During the 1980s, the Latin American debt crisis, which caught up large western banks (mainly European and North American), led to a new regulatory response. The Basel Committee on Banking Supervision, formed in 1974 under the auspices of the BIS and representing central bankers around the world, introduced a set of minimum capital requirements for banks in 1988. The agreement established that banks should have 8 per cent in core ('tier one') capital against its total risk-weighted assets. The essence of the Basel accord of banking regulation was to establish the concept of risk-weighted capital and risk-based capital requirements for banks. The introduction of the concept of risk-weighted capital, however, gave banking institutions both *the motive* and *the means* to start searching for ways to redistribute the official amount of risk held on their books. According to Victoria Chick, for instance, the experience of the Basel accord – a first major attempt at international banking regulation – illustrated well the law of unintended consequences. Regulations intended to strengthen the balance sheets of banks by weighting assets on the basis of their riskiness (thus rewarding the holding of safe assets), actually drove risky assets off the balance sheet. As a result of the introduction of the Basel rules, securitization was undertaken not just as a small part of bank operations when banks needed liquidity, but on a scale such as to change the whole manner in which banks operated (Chick 2008). Once more, financial institutions have found new ways to conduct business, avoid international and domestic regulations, and gain higher profits.

Therefore, the structural conflict between the legislatively defined regulatory space and the real operating realm of financial institutions has been increasingly apparent over the past few decades. Since 1975, after the oil crises of the early 1970s, the leaders of the six richest nations in the world (US, UK, Japan, West Germany, France and Italy) have held periodic annual meetings to discuss global issues and possibly, to coordinate eventual solutions. Soon this group, known as the G6, became the G7 with the inclusion of Canada, and latterly the G8, when Russia joined the meetings in 1997. At the same time, the G7 also became the platform where the finance ministers (Russia excluded) attempted to coordinate financial policies and discuss global problems. After the financial crises in East Asia, Latin America and Russia in 1997–9, G7 finance ministers decided to expand the membership of the forum, inviting another twelve countries plus the European Union to join in, thus becoming the G20 (Wade and Vestergaard 2011).

Simultaneously, a plethora of new private and public bodies emerged to control and oversee the financial system. In 1974, the already mentioned Basel Committee on Banking Supervision (BCBS) was established by the G10. The 1980s saw the founding of more specific bodies, like the International Organization of Securities Commissions (IOSCO). In 1985, the International Swaps and Derivatives Association (ISDA) was established. It is a private organization of more than 800 over-the-counter derivatives dealers – banks and securities firms that are so-called 'repeat players' in the privately negotiated industry of financial derivatives, or the market for derivatives that are not traded on organised platforms (Riles 2011: 30). The 1990s saw the birth of the International Association of Insurance Supervisors (IAIS) and attempts to coordinate the various bodies more efficiently at the Joint Forum, an international group who gathered together supervisors from the three fundamental sectors of the financial world: banking, securities and insurance.

Therefore, the international financial system is shaped and governed by an enormous variety of public and private actors and multilevel structures. In addition to national governments, there exist supra-national organizations such as the European Commission, older international organizations such as the IMF, the World Bank or the OECD, national and supranational monetary authorities, national regulators responsible for banks and other financial intermediaries. supranational meetings of regulators with specific regulatory tasks such as CEBS (Committee of European Banking Supervisors), CESR (Committee of European Securities Regulators) or CEIOPS (Committee of European Insurance and Occupational Pensions Supervisors), but also many other private bodies and influential lobby groups, such as the IIF (Institute of International Finance, a global association whose membership includes most of the world's largest commercial and investment banks, as well as many insurance companies and investment management firms). This list could continue further.

Yet the global credit crunch revealed that all the post-Bretton Woods systems of privatized financial regulation have failed. The international banking accord, Basel 2, while not implemented fully, proved to be pro-cyclical and is believed not only to have failed in maintaining the stability of the financial system, but actually to have aggravated the crisis. The credit-rating agencies – profit-seeking companies whose role as privatized institutions of regulation was promoted by the Reagan administration to ensure market stability – failed most scandalously (Sinclair 2008). Many of the central bankers, notionally independent from the political agenda of governments, have failed to spot cracks in the system and recognize the growing build-up of risks. Lacking a holistic vision and a systemic approach to economic policy-making, traditional monetary authorities appeared impotent in preventing the crisis. The IMF in turn, about the only institution with a global overview of the financial system, not only failed to anticipate and diagnose the crisis correctly and in time, but was painting a rosy picture of global economic prospects only months before the crisis erupted in August 2007 (IEO 2011).

The extraordinary sophistication and opaqueness of the financial system that thrives on the notion of risk and is driven by financial innovation is challenging not only because of its sheer scale. The complexity of the contemporary financial system makes it hard even to get a meaningful understanding of *what is* financial governance today. Kern *et al.* (2006: 15) identified three main characteristics that define systems of global financial governance: '*effectiveness* in devising efficient regulatory standards and rules; *accountability* in the decision-making structure and chain of command; and *legitimacy*, meaning that those subject to international regulatory standards have participated in some meaningful way in their development'.

In this framework, the current structure of financial governance does not conform to any of the three criteria outlined by the authors. First, the crisis and its aftermath illustrated that the system of governance is ineffective, primarily because of the ease with which financial institutions are able to circumvent obstructive regulations in their pursuit of profits. Second, the institutions of financial governance are rarely accountable for its failures: even in the midst of the current crisis many financial institutions were bailed out by the state, while their managers resigned with unreasonably lofty bonuses. Moreover, it was the decision of the credit-rating agencies – the institutions discredited most in the midst of the credit crunch – to downgrade the rating of some European countries in 2011–12, that pushed many sovereign borrowers in the Eurozone to the brink of a debt trap. Finally, the existing structure of financial governance may well be considered illegitimate if we reflect not only on the enormous disparity of power to influence the international regulatory standards between powerful corporate interests and many developing countries, but also on the seemingly unmitigated capacity of financial markets to demarcate and restrict the public sphere. The harsh and ideologically driven austerity programmes launched by many European countries, including the UK, will impose high costs on societies and economies in most of the affected countries for decades to come. The sector that would suffer least from the reduction of public spending and tax increases is the financial industry and the City of London.

Conclusion

The global financial crisis of 2007–09 has led to one of the most far-reaching revisions of the principles, norms and institutions of international financial governance since the Depression of the 1930s. New financial bodies have been established on both sides of the Atlantic and new laws aimed to better protect societies from financial crises have been passed in several countries. In the USA, a Consumer Financial Protection Bureau was set up to tackle 'abusive' mis-selling of mortgages, credit cards and other loan products. In the EU, a series of legal changes proposed by the European Commission will enhance the consumer protection (for bank account holders and retail investors) maintained by the existing directives on Deposits Guarantee Schemes and Investor Compensation Schemes. In the UK, the Financial Services Authority (FSA) will be split into two new bodies, a Financial Conduct Authority (FCA) and a Prudential Regulatory Authority (PRA). In parallel, a new Financial Policy Committee (FPC) will be set up within the Bank of England which, in turn, will assume much greater role in the overall supervision and control of the financial system. In addition, a new international banking accord (Basel 3) is under way, and individual financiers in the UK and USA had to withstand a politically administered curb on their bonus pay.

Can the new set of regulatory bodies and norms suffice in preventing a contagious financial crisis in the future? The continuing debt crisis in the Eurozone makes any answers to this question far too premature, yet the analysis presented above suggests that most likely, not. The fundamental reason for this is that the regulations initiated in light of the credit crunch of 2007–09, as indeed, earlier attempts at global financial regulation, tend to target some of the repercussions and specific practices of the financial sector rather than the structural logic and the institutional environment facilitating financial innovation. In this sense, the global credit crunch has produced a rather paradoxical outcome. On the one hand, the crisis has launched the most radical reform of the world financial regulation since the 1930s. New measures targeting banks' derivatives trade, new restrictions imposed on the credit-rating agencies and new controls on the hedge fund industry would have been inconceivable had the crisis of 2007–09 not exposed the failure of the privately regulated financial system. On the other hand, the cumulative change in the world economy driven by private finance throughout the twentieth century and specifically in the wake of the 1970s financial revolution, is simply too gigantic to be reversed by a new set of policies and rules, however refined. The challenge to achieve a more robust system of financial governance at the global level lies not only in a new refined set of policies and regulatory measures to be applied to the increasingly complex web of financial markets. Fundamentally, it requires a different paradigm of thinking about the function of finance in political economy and specifically, addressing the politically sensitive question of *which parts of financial activity today are socially useful.*

Recommended reading

Bello, W. *et al.* (eds) (2000). *Global Finance: New Thinking on Regulating Speculative Capital Markets*, London and New York: Zed Books.

Blackburn, R. (2006). 'Finance and the Fourth Dimension', *New Left Review*, 39, May–June.

Eichengreen, B. (1998). *Globalizing Capital*, Princeton, NJ: Princeton University Press.

Gamble, A. (2009). *The Spectre at the Feast: Capitalist Crisis and the Politics of Recession*, London: Palgrave.

Germain, R. (1997). *The International Organization of Credit: States and Global Finance in the World Economy*, Cambridge: Cambridge University Press.

Krugman, P. (2008). *The Return of Depression Economics and the Crisis of 2008*, London: Allen Lane.

Strange, S. (1997). *Mad Money*, Manchester: Manchester University Press.

Recommended websites

http://www.ft.com/intl/indepth/global-financial-crisis
http://www.worldbank.org/financialcrisis/
http://www.levy.org

4 Corruption and global governance

Charles Cater

In December 2010, Tunisian street vendor Mohamed Bouazizi's self-immolation served as a catalyst for civil uprisings eventually leading to regime changes in Tunisia, Egypt and Libya known as the Arab Spring; in April 2011, veteran social activist Anna Hazare initiated more than six months of hunger strikes and mass demonstrations which stunned the political establishment in India; in September 2011, protestors took over part of Manhattan's financial district as Occupy Wall Street, which then prompted similar direct action in many other cities; and in January 2012, thousands of Nigerians took to the streets and instigated a labour strike paralyzing the country. What have all these people been protesting? To a certain extent, the answer is simple: *corruption*. Corruption can take various forms, whether kleptocratic political elites such as in Tunisia, institutionalized bribery within the civil service such as in India, a conspicuous lack of accountability for corporate fraud such as in the US, or the chronic looting of a nation's natural resource rents such as in Nigeria. Meanwhile, anti-corruption legal frameworks have reached unprecedented levels of scope and jurisdiction with the contemporary adoption of international conventions, national laws with extra-territorial reach, and numerous 'soft law' multi-stakeholder initiatives; yet corruption appears to remain as intractable as it has ever been.

This chapter assesses the globalization of anti-corruption mechanisms, including in relation to the extractive industries. The analysis proceeds as follows: first, an overview of corruption in terms of how we define and understand it, corruption's economic and socio-political costs, and the historical context for how corruption became a concern for global governance; second, a summary of anti-corruption mechanisms such as international law, national laws with extraterritorial reach, and non-binding soft law; and third, a case study of the extractive industries including UN commodity sanctions and policies of international financial institutions, national laws regulating oil and mining, and multi-stakeholder initiatives. A few different dimensions of analysis resurface throughout the chapter: relations between governments and intergovernmental organizations, relations between governments of developed and industrialized countries ('the North'/'the West') and governments of developing countries ('the South'), relations between governments and corporations, and relations between governments and civil society. Anti-corruption mechanisms seem more likely to work if they are mandatory rather than voluntary, not perceived as externally imposed, implemented by governments that are both able and willing to enforce the rule of law (including with respect to the private sector), and meaningfully backed by civil society within the country. Despite a contemporary trend toward the globalization of anti-corruption law, perhaps the more critical (and more effective) work to be done is located within states rather than between them.

Corruption

Defining corruption

Corruption may be difficult to define but most people intuitively know it when they see it. A good starting point for a working definition of corruption is the following concise formulation by Transparency International: the abuse of entrusted power for private gain. Notably, the use of the word 'entrusted' implies an emphasis on the public sector rather than the private sector, which is compatible with Western conceptions of corruption and thus the principal focus of anti-corruption mechanisms as well. The United Nations Convention Against Corruption (UNCAC), the only global law specifically dedicated to corruption, does not actually define the term per se. Rather, articles 15–25 of UNCAC outline a series of offences which are each determined to be corrupt: bribery of (and the solicitation of bribes by) national public officials, bribery of (and the solicitation of bribes by) foreign public officials and officials of public international organizations, embezzlement and diversion of property by a public official, trading in influence, abuse of functions, illicit enrichment, bribery within the private sector, embezzlement of property in the private sector, laundering proceeds of crime, the retention or concealment of corruptly attained property, and obstruction of justice (UN 2004a: Articles 15–25). Despite the absence of a specific definition of corruption within UNCAC, such a comprehensive list of acts to be criminalized could indicate an international consensus regarding what constitutes corruption and what should be done about it. However, a closer examination reveals that many articles merely *suggest* that states enact implementing legislation (e.g. regarding bribery and embezzlement in the private sector), while 'most provisions of the Convention make some reference to working within the principles of a State's domestic law, which allows significant room for different interpretations of the Convention's requirements in any given country' (U4 Anti-Corruption Resource Centre 2010). This was not an accidental by-product of negotiation among UN member states, but instead reflects national differences regarding conceptions of corruption.

The contemporary emergence of a global anti-corruption regime has also prompted a proliferation of academic scholarship critiquing mainstream discourse. Criticisms regarding the modern anti-corruption campaign – or what one author has collectively termed the 'anti-anti-corruption' position – include the following issues: the definition of corruption, the measurement of corruption, dominant liberal–rationalist premises of the concept, the legitimacy deficit of anti-corruption programmes, and insufficient contextualization to accommodate national and regional variation (Gephart 2009; Bukovanksy 2006). For example, Transparency International's Corruption Perception Index (CPI) and the World Bank Institute's Worldwide Governance Indicators (WGI) have been criticized for their over-reliance on the opinions of experts and businessmen rather than data collected from a larger sample size of average citizens, thus reinforcing preexisting Western conceptions of corruption – particularly regarding the assumed disparities between developed and developing countries. One study has compared the results of household surveys of more than 35,000 people in eight African countries and the opinions of 350 'experts' on the issue of corruption: the experts considerably overestimated the frequency of corruption, mistakenly ranked the countries in terms of their relative levels of corruption, wrongly assumed a high level of tolerance for corruption among the general population, and underestimated the degree to which the public cared about good governance (Razafindrakoto and Roubaud 2006). Beyond issues of defining and measuring corruption, critics have also argued that developing countries have been inadequately consulted in the design of anti-corruption mechanisms by institutions such as the World Bank and the International Monetary Fund (IMF), that the role of Western corporations in paying bribes and laundering money is under-represented within mainstream analyses, and that a zero-tolerance approach to corruption ultimately serves to delegitimize governments and societies in the South.

The costs of corruption

There is a general consensus (although not without dissenting views) that corruption has a high economic cost for governments, corporations and society. According to the former director of the World Bank Institute's programme on global governance, Daniel Kaufmann, the total annual bribery of public officials by individuals and the private sector can be estimated at $1 trillion. However, this includes neither the incidence of fraud within the private sector (which the available evidence suggests is substantial in both developing and industrialized countries) nor the embezzlement of public funds at all levels, including by leaders such as Suharto in Indonesia (estimated at $15–35 billion), Marcos in the Philippines, Mobutu in Zaire, and Abacha in Nigeria (estimated at $5 billion each). Furthermore, Kaufmann also cites statistics regarding an associated development cost of corruption: a 2–4 per cent reduction in annual income growth rates for countries, about a 3 per cent reduction in annual growth rates for businesses, and an estimated 20 per cent 'tax' on foreign direct investment. Likewise, corruption is positively correlated with increases in income inequality and also functions as an indirect form of regressive taxation because it has a disproportionate impact on poor households and small businesses (World Bank nd). Corruption – and in many cases even just the perception of corruption – also deters foreign aid. Thus, some developing countries may fall into a 'corruption trap' of ineligibility for precisely the assistance they may need most for institutional reforms. On the other hand, high growth rates in countries such as

India and China do raise interesting questions about the correlation between corruption and poor economic performance, prompting the claim that in weak institutional environments corruption may actually 'grease the wheels' of capitalism (Méon and Weill 2008).

The social and political impacts of corruption are perhaps best understood within the context of confidence in public institutions and governmental legitimacy. According to a recent study based on household survey data from the Gallup World Poll, confidence in public institutions is fundamentally undermined by corruption, which then leads to lower levels of political participation in democratic processes, an increased tendency to 'vote with one's feet' through emigration, and a higher tolerance for using violent means to achieve political ends (Clausen et al. 2011). For example, although the causes of the Arab Spring in Tunisia, Egypt and Libya were undoubtedly complex, a loss of governmental legitimacy caused by public perceptions of corruption amongst the elite was an integral part of the equation (Partridge 2011). Furthermore, as cases such as intrastate conflict in Sierra Leone, Angola and the Democratic Republic of Congo (DRC) demonstrate, war economies can also facilitate incentive structures that financially reward political and military elites for corruption, thus leading to conflict perpetuation rather than conflict resolution. Corruption also poses challenges for post-conflict peacebuilding as there are difficult trade-offs involved in maintaining stability and reforming institutions, not least at the risk of armed opposition by those who had previously benefitted from the status quo (Rose-Ackerman 2008). Furthermore, tackling corruption through liberal peacebuilding – democratization and market liberalization – may also entail substantial risks and can under certain circumstances even exacerbate corruption (Le Billon 2008). Overall, while the political and social costs of corruption affect all countries, they are particularly adverse for developing countries.

Perhaps more than any other state, the DRC illustrates the high costs of corruption – such as economic decline, poor governance, and large-scale violence – especially among developing countries dependent on natural resources. During the protracted authoritarian rule of Mobuto Sese Seko (1965–97), corruption became the norm. Following the renaming of the country as Zaire in 1971, Mobutu implemented a policy of 'Zairianization' in 1973. Ostensibly, the goal was to increase the so-called 'authenticity' of the economy through the nationalization of foreign owned companies; in practice, it meant the wholesale theft of businesses and their redistribution to political and military elites loyal to Mobutu. The country's economy never recovered. Kleptocracy had a particularly cruel, self-perpetuating logic in Zaire: the arbitrary exercise of power and appropriation of public goods at the highest level amplified and exacerbated insecurity for each lower level of society (e.g. generals stole from their own troops, the troops stole from civilian populations). The transnational dimensions of corruption were also evident as Western banks, mining companies and governments were complicit in Mobutu's embezzlement. By the mid-1990s, Mobutu had amassed a personal fortune estimated at $5 billion, but Zaire was on the verge of state collapse. The overthrow of Mobutu by Laurent Kabila in 1996 precipitated a series of natural resource-related conflicts which have caused as many as five million deaths and created more than two million refugees and internally displaced persons. In a country with abundant natural resource wealth in the form of cobalt, copper, diamonds, gold, coltan, tin, tungsten and other mineral deposits, per capita income remains less than $300 and the quality of life is the world's worst as measured by the United Nations Human Development Index (HDI). Admittedly, the DRC is an extreme case, but the costs of failing to address corruption, particularly when associated with the extractive industries, are evident.

Historical context

The origins of contemporary anti-corruption law can be traced to political reforms in the aftermath of the Watergate scandal in the United States. The ensuing investigation discovered a pattern of illegal campaign contributions to the Nixon Administration from American corporations using money that had been laundered in foreign countries. The Senate Subcommittee on Multinational Corporations, chaired by Senator Frank Church, subsequently also uncovered widespread bribery overseas by American firms. President Ford appointed a 'Task Force on Questionable Corporate Payments Abroad', whose recommendations formed the basis for the Foreign Corrupt Practices Act (FCPA) enacted by Congress in 1977. The FCPA mandated corporate accounting procedures to facilitate government oversight and criminalized bribery of foreign officials. Eventually, political reforms that had been the catalyst for the FCPA transformed into economic drivers for the international extension of anti-corruption law as American corporations were at a competitive disadvantage to their European counterparts (who in some cases even legally benefitted from tax deductions for bribes they paid abroad). With strong backing from the US business lobby, an amendment to the FCPA in 1988 directed the President to initiate negotiations for multilateral anti-bribery legislation with the Organization for Economic Cooperation and Development (OECD), which eventually led to the adoption of the Convention on Combating Bribery of Foreign Public Officials in International Business Transactions in 1997 (Darrough 2009). The initial target of anti-corruption law in the US – American corporations – had become a critical constituency for its internationalization.

With the end of the Cold War, there was increased interest by UN member governments in emerging security threats – including money laundering connected with organized crime and terrorism – and a belated realization that kleptocratic leaders were actually an impediment to development. The intergovernmental Financial Action Task Force (FATF) was formed in 1989 at the G7 summit in Paris in order to address mounting concerns regarding money laundering. The FATF released an initial forty recommendations to combat money laundering in 1990, and then issued nine special recommendations on links between money laundering and terrorist financing following the attacks of 11 September 2001 (Financial Action Task Force 2004, 2008). During the interim, the World Bank 'ended decades of studied silence' on the issue of corruption with President James

Wolfensohn's pivotal 'Corruption is cancer' address at the organization's 1996 annual meeting, thus signalling an intent to reform operations and lending practices (Heineman and Heimann 2006). Meanwhile, 18 months of negotiations at the UN eventually led to the adoption of the United Nations Convention Against Transnational Organized Crime (UNCTOC) in December 2000, the organization's first legally binding instrument to address corruption. Realizing the need to also target other forms of corruption beyond organized crime, the General Assembly immediately established an Ad Hoc Committee to negotiate the text for an international anti-corruption treaty, which was then adopted as the United Nations Convention Against Corruption (UNCAC) in October 2003. Finally, the global anti-corruption agenda has also been promoted by the advocacy of influential non-governmental organizations, particularly Transparency International, which was founded in 1993 and now has more than 90 national chapters.

Anti-corruption law

This section summarizes anti-corruption law in three parts: intergovernmental organizations and international law, states and national law with extraterritorial jurisdiction, and soft law including multi-stakeholder initiatives. These consist of the OECD Convention on Combating Bribery of Foreign Public Officials in International Business Transactions, the United Nations Convention Against Corruption, the US Foreign Corrupt Practices Act, the UK Bribery Act 2010, the OECD Guidelines for Multinational Enterprises, and the United Nations Global Compact. There are also five main regional anti-corruption laws which fall outside the scope of this chapter: Inter-American Convention Against Corruption (adopted March 1996, entered into force June 1997); Council of Europe Civil Law Convention on Corruption (adopted November 1999, entered into force November 2003); Council of Europe Criminal Law Convention on Corruption (adopted November 1998, entered into force July 2002); The European Union Convention on the Fight against Corruption Involving Officials (adopted May 1997, entered into force September 2005); and the African Union Convention on Preventing and Combating Corruption (adopted July 2003, entered into force August 2006).

Intergovernmental organisations and international law

The OECD adopted the Convention on Combating Bribery of Foreign Public Officials in International Business Transactions, the first international anti-corruption treaty, on 21 November 1997. The convention entered into force on 15 February 1999. There are currently 38 state parties (all 34 OECD members, plus non-members Argentina, Brazil, Bulgaria and South Africa). Although the OECD Convention is not fully global in terms of jurisdiction, OECD members do account for a majority of global gross domestic product (GDP), international trade and foreign direct investment (FDI). The OECD Convention criminalizes the bribery of foreign public officials for the purpose of advantage in international business.

In other words, it takes a 'supply side' approach to anti-corruption. Interestingly, state parties are not required to enact legislation regarding the bribery of their own officials. The OECD Convention also does not apply in cases where the bribery is entirely domestic, when the recipient is other than a public official, or where the intent is other than gaining advantage in business. Furthermore, the various forms of corruption other than bribery are not covered. While the OECD Convention is not self-executing (i.e. it is dependent on domestic law), state implementation and enforcement is monitored by the OECD Working Group on Bribery through a peer-review system and public reporting process. Nonetheless, despite conditions conducive to implementation – widespread ratification, narrow scope and thorough monitoring mechanisms – enforcement has been lacking. According to Transparency International, there has been active enforcement in less than a fifth of countries, moderate enforcement in less than a quarter of countries, and little or no enforcement in more than half of countries (Transparency International 2011).

The UN General Assembly adopted the UNCAC, the most global and comprehensive anti-corruption treaty to date, on 31 October 2003. It entered into force on 14 December 2005; there are currently 158 state parties to UNCAC, plus the European Union. UNCAC incorporates a broad range of mechanisms, including preventive measures (Chapter II), criminalization and law enforcement (Chapter III), international cooperation (Chapter IV), asset recovery (Chapter V), and technical assistance and information exchange (Chapter VI). The preventive measures are dependent upon substantial state institutional capacity for implementation: reform of the civil service, transparent public finances, oversight of the private sector, an independent judiciary, and regulation of the financial sector to prevent money laundering. Chapter III obligates state parties to enact legislation criminalizing the following: offering/giving bribes to national public officials, offering/giving bribes to foreign public officials and officials of public international organizations, soliciting/accepting of bribes by a national public official, embezzlement by public officials, laundering proceeds of crime, and obstruction of justice. For several other offences, UNCAC suggests that states should consider enacting legislation: soliciting/accepting bribes by foreign public officials and officials of public international organizations, trading in influence, abuse of function, illicit enrichment by public officials, bribery and embezzlement in the private sector, and the concealment of illicit assets. Perhaps the most significant aspects are the asset recovery provisions outlined within Chapter V, which obligate states to adapt their civil and criminal laws to enable the tracking, freezing, forfeiture, and return of assets acquired through corrupt means. During negotiations over UNCAC, asset recovery was a main selling point among developing countries and had strong backing from the US delegation as well (Webb 2005).

States and national law

First passed by the US Congress in 1977 and then amended in 1988 and 1998, the Foreign Corrupt Practices Act (FCPA) utilizes a two-pronged approach: an anti-bribery clause and record-keeping/accounting provisions. The FCPA prohibits payoffs to foreign public officials or foreign political parties in order to 'obtain or retain business' (US 1977: Sections 78dd-1 to 3). The anti-bribery clause applies to US 'persons' (i.e. individuals and businesses) and foreign issuers of securities that are listed on US exchanges. As amended in 1998, it also applies to foreign firms and individuals who make illicit payments within the US. The FCPA further requires corporations to keep accurate records of transactions and implement a system of internal accounting controls (US 1977: Section 78m). While the FCPA has been a landmark anti-corruption law with innovative extraterritorial jurisdiction, numerous drawbacks have diminished its impact in practice: first, there has been a conspicuous lack of enforcement by the executive branch; second, loopholes mean that private firms (i.e. non-issuers) are not covered by the accounting and record-keeping requirements, while foreign subsidiaries with less than 51 per cent ownership by the parent company are completely exempt from the FCPA; and facilitation payments (i.e. money paid for the performance of routine public services), which can be difficult to distinguish from bribes, are allowed by the FCPA (Weismann 2009). Interestingly, the FCPA case which has led to the largest fines to date (more than $1.7 billion to the US government, the German government and the World Bank) was brought against a foreign firm, Siemens AG, for bribery in Argentina (Darrough 2009). However, to the extent that the FCPA has influenced the behaviour of corporations, it may also have had the unintended consequence of not merely deterring corruption by American firms abroad but actually reducing FDI towards those countries perceived to be most corrupt – thus acting as a de facto sanction on developing countries (Spalding 2010).

Based in part on the FCPA and intended to satisfy the UK's requirements as a state party to the OECD Convention, the Bribery Act 2010 was passed on 8 April 2010. The UK Bribery Act criminalizes both active and passive bribery by corporations and individuals and establishes four principal offences: offering, promising or giving of an advantage; requesting, agreeing to receive or accepting an advantage; bribery of a foreign public official; and failure by a commercial organization to prevent bribery (UK 2010: Sections 1, 2, 4, 6 and 7). The fourth offence is unprecedented in international anti-corruption law; the burden of proof has effectively been shifted onto corporations to document that they have adequate institutional controls to preclude bribery by their staff or representatives. Thus, the UK Bribery Act is broader in scope than the FCPA and the OECD Convention; it also establishes more extensive jurisdiction. Not only does the law apply to both the domestic and foreign operations of UK-based corporations, but it also asserts extraterritorial jurisdiction over 'any other body corporate (wherever incorporated) which carries on a business, or part of a business, in any part of the United Kingdom' (UK 2010: Section 7 (5)(b)). In other words, as Transparency International UK recently concluded, 'A foreign company which carries on any part of its business in the UK could be prosecuted for failure to prevent bribery even where the bribery takes place wholly outside the UK and the benefit or advantage to the company is intended to accrue outside the UK' (Transparency International UK 2010: 9). Perhaps unsurprisingly, the UK Bribery Act has met resistance from the private sector. This delayed its entry into force until after notes of guidance from the Ministry of Justice were issued, which NGO advocates claim watered down the legislation by exempting corporations that are listed on UK stock markets but do not operate within the UK (Reuters 2011).

Corporations, NGOs and 'soft law'

There are two principal international initiatives addressing corruption that could be categorized as 'soft law' (i.e. non-binding and/or voluntary mechanisms): the *OECD Guidelines for Multinational Enterprises* and the United Nations Global Compact. The OECD Guidelines were first adopted in 1976 and have been revised five times, including most recently in 2011. A wide range of issues are covered, such as human rights, labour, the environment, consumer interests, technology, competition and taxation. Section VII concerns bribery, bribe solicitation and extortion:

> Enterprises should not directly or indirectly, offer, promise, give or demand a bribe or other undue advantage to obtain or retain business or other improper advantage. Enterprises should also resist the solicitation of bribes and extortion.
>
> (OECD 2011)

Unlike the OECD Convention, UNCAC, the US FCPA and the UK Anti-Bribery Law, the OECD Guidelines are non-binding for both states and corporations. Meanwhile, following the adoption of UNCAC in December 2003, the UN Global Compact added an anti-corruption principle in June 2004: 'Businesses should work against corruption in all its forms, including extortion and bribery' (UN 2004c: Principle 10). The Global Compact is a multi-stakeholder initiative incorporating NGOs, corporations and the UN. The first nine principles cover human rights, labour and environmental issues. Similar to the OECD Guidelines, participation in the Global Compact is voluntary and the ten principles – phrased as recommendations for corporations – are non-binding. Through the establishment and promotion of general standards for business conduct, the Global Compact seeks to further the international development of certain norms. However, in practice the track record has been mixed, with critics noting that the multi-stakeholder initiative can be exploited by corporations for public relations purposes. The UN's own internal review has acknowledged this risk (Arevalo and Fallon 2008).

Non-governmental organizations, particularly Transparency International, have also been significant in terms of shaping an evolving global anti-corruption regime. TI's annual Corruption Perceptions Index (CPI), first released in 1995, ranks international perceptions of corruption in nearly 200 countries; the Bribe Payers' Index (BPI), initiated in 1999, evaluates the supply side of corruption by source country and industry sector; and the Global Corruption Barometer (GCB), dating back to 2003, tracks trends in domestic public opinion regarding corruption. Although the CPI is not the only composite ranking of corruption available (alternatives include 'Control of Corruption', one of six Worldwide Governance

Indicators tracked by the World Bank) it has arguably been the most widely covered by media and most influential on public policymaking. Nonetheless, the CPI has been criticized for its narrow focus on the demand side of corruption within the public sector and its reliance on the opinions of Western executives and experts, which may then lead to regionally biased country rankings (Anderson and Heywood 2009). On the other hand, one could also argue that Transparency International (TI) has made some effort to address these limitations of the CPI through its subsequent introduction of the BPI (which focuses instead on the supply side of corruption) and the GCB (which is based on a large-N survey of people regarding the levels and types of corruption within their own countries). Overall, Transparency International's approach does not fit the typical profile of advocacy NGOs in one key respect: its infrequent use of 'name and shame' tactics, particularly with regard to the private sector. In fact, the global anti-corruption agenda of TI and the interests of international business have frequently been complementary. For example, the US chapter of TI has had strong backing from the private sector, which has also lobbied for extending FCPA provisions through global mechanisms (Rose-Ackerman 2011).

Case study 4.1 Extractive industries

This section assesses recent initiatives within a sector known for a high incidence of corruption, the extractive industries. The emergence of these anti-corruption mechanisms is indicative of both the limits of the global anti-corruption laws surveyed above and the need for a more targeted approach.

Intergovernmental organisations and international law

The World Bank and the IMF have undertaken several initiatives related to transparency and anti-corruption within the extractive industries. The World Bank published an exhaustive, multivolume *Extractive Industries Review* (EIR) in 2003, while the IMF also released a *Guide on Resource Revenue Transparency* in 2005. Both reports identified governance as a key challenge and advocated increased transparency in areas such as revenue flows, project documents and budget processes. The EIR also noted the fundamental importance of developing governmental capacity for natural resource management and industry regulation (World Bank 2003; IMF 2005). The IMF's staff monitoring programme in Angola offers some insight into corruption and the constraints for IFIs to impose reforms. According to the IMF, nearly 30 per cent of Angolan government expenditures from 1997 to 2002 – $8.3 billion of $27.9 billion – either went inexplicably missing or were spent on extra-budgetary items and then inadequately accounted for after the fact (IMF 2003 and 2002).

Meanwhile, President Jose Eduardo dos Santos publicly criticized the 'police action of the IMF' and stated that the Angolan government would not be pressured into disclosing oil sector data (Hodges 2004: 121). The World Bank Group's involvement in the Chad–Cameroon oil pipeline project also suggests there can be critical limits to reform. In 2002, the International Bank for Reconstruction and Development (IBRD) and the International Development Association (IDA) agreed to provide nearly $100 million in financing for the governments of Chad and Cameroon, but with conditions applying to the former: the establishment of a dedicated offshore escrow account, financial oversight by an independent panel, and a revenue management plan committed to poverty reduction. In 2008, the IBRD and IDA withdrew from the project due to repeated diversions of oil revenue from social programmes by the government of Chad (World Bank 2008).

In terms of international law focusing on natural resources, UN Security Council resolutions imposing commodity sanctions have been the most prominent. In most instances, the goal has been to reduce the amount of income that rebel groups can derive from natural resource exports. These cases include Afghanistan, Angola, Cambodia, Côte d'Ivoire, Democratic Republic of Congo, Liberia and Sierra Leone, while in Libya the intent was to compel cooperation with investigations and prosecutions related to the Lockerbie bombing. Certainly, war economies are highly conducive to corruption and present an intractable problem for UN peace operations. The Oil-for-Food programme in Iraq suggests there are risks associated with UN administration of natural resource finances. As allowed by UN Security Council Resolution 986 of April 1995, Iraq resumed the sale of oil on the international market in order to finance the purchase of humanitarian goods. The purpose of the Oil-for-Food programme was to alleviate the widespread suffering of civilian populations caused by the comprehensive sanctions regime imposed on Iraq after the first Gulf War, while at the same time limiting the Iraqi government's capacity to finance further military expenditures through oil exports. However, according to the final report of the Independent Inquiry Committee, chaired by former US Federal Reserve Chairman Paul Volcker, the Iraqi government of Saddam Hussein benefitted from more than $1.8 billion in illicit payments through the Oil-for-Food programme. There were at least $229 million in illegal surcharges paid by 139 companies buying oil and more than $1.55 billion in kickbacks by 2,253 companies selling humanitarian goods. An estimated $11 billion in oil exports were also smuggled by the Iraqi regime outside the UN administered programme (Independent Inquiry Committee 2005). With respect to UN management, Volcker concluded, '… the gatekeepers of the Programme, the Secretariat, the Security Council and UN contractors failed most grievously in their responsibilities to monitor the integrity of the Programme' (Independent Inquiry Committee 2005b).

States and national law

Transnational resource corporations are typically bound by the laws of the countries in which they operate, while the laws of the country in which they incorporate come into play less frequently. Assertions of extraterritorial jurisdiction – such as with the FCPA – are the exception rather than the norm (but nonetheless useful for analysis of emerging trends in global governance). Following a three-decade-long period of lax enforcement of the FCPA, there was a radical shift in the Security and Exchange Commission's (SEC) approach coinciding with the election of Barack Obama. The upsurge in enforcement undoubtedly caught American corporations by surprise, particularly companies within the extractive industries which had thus far enjoyed de facto immunity from prosecution under the previous administration. Halliburton, an oil services company, came under investigation for a bribery scheme from 1994 to 2004 related to the Bonny Island liquefied natural gas facility in Nigeria. Kellogg Brown & Root (KBR), a Halliburton subsidiary at the time, had offered $180 million in bribes to Nigerian officials in order to win $6 billion in contracts for the corporation and its joint venture partners. From February 2009 to April 2011, these corporations paid the SEC more than $1.5 billion in settlements to avoid criminal and civil prosecution: Halliburton ($579 million), Paris-based Technip SA ($338 million), Snamprogetti Netherlands BV and its former parent company Eni ($365 million) and Tokyo-based JGC Corp ($219 million). Meanwhile, the Nigerian government launched its own investigation, including charges against former US Vice President Dick Cheney in his capacity as CEO of Halliburton from 1995 to 2000. Halliburton settled this case for $35 million in December 2010 and the charges were dropped. Most recently, Albert 'Jack' Stanley, the former CEO of KBR, was also sentenced to two-and-a-half years in prison for his role in the bribery scheme (Calkins 2012). Despite the magnitude of the settlements with the SEC, it remains to be seen whether the Halliburton/KBR cases will have a significant deterrent effect on corruption within the extractive industries.

The US Dodd–Frank Wall Street and Consumer Protection Act of July 2010 is principally concerned with regulation of the financial industry in the aftermath of the global financial crisis; however, the last ten pages of the 848-page law also include unprecedented provisions regarding tracking conflict minerals from the DRC and reporting requirements for oil and mining corporations listed on US exchanges (US 2010: Sections 1502 and 1504). The underlying assumption of Section 1504 is that mandatory public disclosure of detailed financial data regarding what oil and mining corporations pay to the states where they operate will promote transparency and therefore mitigate corruption. The Dodd–Frank Act has faced significant opposition from corporations who have claimed that Section 1504 puts US-based corporations at a competitive disadvantage, that the reporting requirements will impose unreasonable compliance costs on firms, and that disclosure will violate contractual terms of confidentiality with host countries. Unsurprisingly, the private sector has been lobbying the SEC to weaken the forthcoming implementing rules of Dodd–Frank, but their objections are overstated (Kaufmann and Penciakova 2011). Dodd–Frank will apply to all US-listed firms, which includes most of the internationally operating oil and mining companies in the world, and similar draft legislation in the EU would expand the scope even further; preliminary SEC analysis shows that implementation will increase compliance costs for corporations by about 0.3 per cent; and studies indicate that disclosure is not incompatible with most existing contracts (Revenue Watch Institute 2011). Section 1504 of Dodd–Frank represents a major victory for advocacy organizations such as Global Witness and the Revenue Watch Institute that have been campaigning for transparency in the oil and mining sectors. However, the polarized public debate between advocacy NGOs and transnational corporations may have obscured an even more fundamental underlying question as to whether Dodd–Frank will actually work. At best, corporate disclosure of governmental resource revenue is a necessary but insufficient initial step toward combating corruption. For transparency to work, presumably data on state expenditures (which are outside the scope and mandate of Dodd–Frank) would be an equally fundamental part of the anti-corruption equation.

Corporations, NGOs and 'soft law'

Non-governmental organizations – particularly the US-based Open Society Institute (OSI) and the associated Revenue Watch Institute (RWI), UK-based Global Witness and the Publish What You Pay (PWYP) coalition – have been highly influential in advocating for anti-corruption measures within the extractive industries. PWYP includes more than 600 member organizations worldwide, many of which are based in resource-rich developing countries. In an effort to promote transparency, PWYP calls for full disclosure in three areas: payments by resource corporations to the countries where they operate, revenues earned by governments from the extractive industries, and licensing arrangements and contracts. The underlying assumption is that publicly available information regarding precisely how much governments earn from oil/gas and mining will then reduce corruption and more fiscal transparency will yield better political accountability. PWYP also recognizes the importance of civil society in resource-dependent countries as part of the potential equation for better accountability of governments. National coalitions have been formed by PWYP members in at least 30 countries for this purpose, but the extent to which these have been effective in practice is debatable. Perhaps most importantly thus far, the PWYP advocacy campaign was the principal catalyst for the Extractive Industries Transparency Initiative (EITI).

Overall, PWYP is more comprehensive than EITI in terms of disclosure regarding contracts and licensing arrangements. Perhaps unsurprisingly, EITI consequently has more backing from both corporations and governments than PWYP. Corporations typically consider the details of contracts to be proprietary information, the disclosure of which may put them at a competitive disadvantage in relation to other firms; while numerous governments for various reasons (protecting sovereignty, maintaining negotiating leverage or concealing corruption) have also resisted disclosing contractual information such as concession agreements and signature bonuses.

Initially launched by the UK in 2002, the Extractive Industries Transparency Initiative now includes 35 countries in various stages of implementation (11 countries are EITI 'compliant' and 24 countries are EITI 'candidates'). EITI utilizes a multi-stakeholder format which also includes participation by more than 50 of the world's largest oil and mining companies; the PWYP coalition and other civil society organizations; and the World Bank, the IMF, and regional development banks, which also supply financing and technical assistance to EITI. At first glance, the approach of EITI appears to be straightforward: companies disclose what they pay to governments, governments disclose what they receive from companies, and the two sets of data are independently verified, with oversight by a multi-stakeholder group. However, there are several weaknesses within EITI which detract from its potential as an anti-corruption mechanism. First, numerous countries and corporations remain outside the EITI framework, including national oil companies (NOCs) from countries such as Russia, China, India, Malaysia, Saudi Arabia and Angola, including include Gazprom, Rosneft, PetroChina, Chinese National Offshore Oil Corporation (CNOOC), China National Petroleum Corporation (CNPC), Sinopec, Oil and Natural Gas Corporation (ONGC), Petronas, Saudi Aramco and Sonangol. Notable exceptions include EITI participants Petrobras (Brazil), Pemex (Mexico), Statoil (Norway) and QatarPet (Qatar). Second, participation and compliance with EITI is voluntary rather than mandatory. Third, even within the limited parameters of disclosure regarding corporate payments and governmental income, there are critical gaps within the data collected by EITI. Fourth, it remains questionable whether civil society organization participation has functioned as an adequate oversight mechanism for corporations and governments. Lastly, EITI does not cover a broader range of financial information such as concession contracts and government expenditures, which are equally important as aggregate revenue data for promoting transparency and mitigating corruption. Arguably, it may be precisely some of these drawbacks for EITI – narrow scope, voluntary implementation and limited oversight – which are a principal source of its appeal for corporations and governments, even if this might reduce its effectiveness.

Conclusion

Contemporary globalization of anti-corruption law can at least partly be understood as a manifestation of the collective realization by states that emerging threats are increasingly transnational – such as corruption and its linkages with organized crime and terrorism – and thus also require an international response. Yet, there also remain substantial limits to how much and in what ways states are willing to cede sovereignty. UNCAC and the OECD Convention, the two principal international anti-corruption laws, are more like coordinating mechanisms among member states than a form of supranational legislation regulating corruption. Neither of these instruments is self-enacting as both require enabling legislation at the domestic level to take effect, and enforcement is dependent upon states. This also raises the question of capacity: international conventions impose substantial requirements on states which they may not actually be able to implement, thus potentially resulting in what has been termed 'obligation overload' for developing countries (Davis and Kingsbury 2010). As the IMF's advocacy for oil revenue transparency in Angola and the World Bank's financing of the Chad–Cameroon pipeline indicate, there are also significant limits to what extent institutional reforms can be externally imposed by international actors. At least from the perspective of critics of the IFIs, this is undoubtedly a good thing; but from the viewpoint of people actually coping with corruption, the maintenance of state sovereignty may be small consolation. On the other hand, the UN's Oil-for-Food Programme in Iraq also serves as a cautionary reminder that international administration of resources and finances entails its own risk of systemic corruption.

To some extent, the globalization of anti-corruption law can also be attributed to state and corporate motives to create a 'level playing field' for international business. This partly explains how the FCPA served as a catalyst for the OECD Convention, and then how the OECD Convention subsequently mobilized support for UNCAC. Of course, domestic politics also play an important role in determining how transnational corporations are regulated by the states in which they are incorporated. As the Watergate scandal shows, it was only once the integrity of the American political system had been compromised by illegal campaign contributions from corporations that Congress took an interest in the payment of bribes internationally. (A similar pattern can be observed more recently with the Elf affair, where the systematic bribery of African leaders by the former French state oil company was exposed only because some of the money had returned to France in the form of illegal campaign contributions.) However, for more than 30 years the FCPA was only minimally enforced and therefore did not have much of an impact in terms of reducing corruption. Anti-corruption legislation can only be effective to the extent that it is adequately enforced, which is often an issue of political will but can also be a question of the state's institutional capacity – particularly in developing countries. Lastly, the rapid economic development of countries such as China, India and Brazil has also had important implications for changing relations between transnational corporations and states; this is particularly true in the extractive industries where national oil and mining companies are now in global competition with Western firms. The well-founded stereotype of international corruption being a problem of bribes paid by transnational corporations from developed countries to public officials in developing countries probably now captures less of the full picture than it once did.

Much of the recent scholarly debate regarding corruption, particularly the critiques generated by those who have taken a position that could be termed 'anti-anti-corruption', has been framed in terms of conflict between industrialized countries of 'the North' and 'the West' and developing countries of 'the South'. These critics have probably overstated their case. There are valid points to be made regarding the CPI's reliance on the opinions of Western executives and experts, the index's exclusive focus on the demand side of corruption, and its reinforcement of stereotypes regarding global disparities in levels of corruption. Likewise, it is also true that much of the IFI's anti-corruption agenda has been imposed on developing countries without their consultation during its formulation. Nonetheless, cultural relativist claims (ironically, usually made by Western academics) regarding how developing country societies conceive of corruption fundamentally differently to developed country societies, can also be taken too far. While, certain forms of patronage and clientelism perceived as corrupt in one national context may instead have traditional legitimacy in another national context, but this does not therefore mean that people in developing countries do not consider the wholesale embezzlement of public assets by political elites to be corrupt. Furthermore, to the extent that there is variation in how corruption is conceived and regulated, UNCAC leaves considerable scope for adaptation to national legislation. Finally, the economic progress of emerging market countries (i.e. BRICS – Brazil, Russia, India, China and South Africa) in comparison with the economic stagnation of the United States, Europe and Japan is transforming power relations among states, which in turn affects their relative influence over international institutions. Critiques of 'the North' imposing anti-corruption mechanisms on 'the South' are increasingly at odds with this new reality.

Finally, the long-term keys to fighting corruption are probably at the domestic level in terms of the role of civil society and the degree of state capacity. Contemporary anti-corruption mechanisms have perhaps overestimated the power of civil society to ensure the accountability of states and corporations. For example, civil society oversight is intended to act as a check on both states and corporations within EITI, but this ignores the reality that the stakeholders have unequal amounts of political and economic power. Is it reasonable to assume that civil society can meaningfully deter state or corporate corruption despite the absence of an independent media, educated citizenry, and the rule of law in a developing country? By contrast, the problem in the US is not inadequate state capacity but that private sector campaign contributions have purchased undue political influence leading to a conspicuous lack of corporate accountability. As Jeffrey Sachs notes, 'Poor-country governments probably accept more bribes and commit more offences, but it is rich countries that host the global companies that carry out the *largest* offences' (Sachs 2011). Nonetheless, in democracies there is the potential for social movements and other forms of protest to exert sufficient pressure on governments for meaningful reform. This was notably more successful in India with the anti-corruption movement led by activist Anna Hazare than it was in the US with the Occupy Wall Street protests. Ultimately, there are no easy or quick-fix solutions to the endemic problem of corruption, but it is clear that any future successes will require the sustained and active engagement of citizens within both developed and developing countries. Meanwhile, it is perhaps unrealistic to assume that the international anti-corruption mechanisms analyzed in this chapter will yield significant progress on their own.

Recommended reading

Bracking, S. (ed.) (2007). *Corruption and Development: The Anti-corruption Campaigns*, Basingstoke: Palgrave Macmillan.

Fisman, R. and Miguel, E. (2010). *Economic Gangsters: Corruption, Violence and the Poverty of Nations*, Princeton: Princeton University Press.

Graycar, A. and Smith, R. (eds) (2011). *Handbook of Global Research and Practice in Corruption*, Northampton: Edwin Elgar.

Rose-Ackerman, S. (ed.) (2006). *International Handbook on the Economics of Corruption*, Northampton: Edwin Elgar.

Rotberg, R. (ed.) (2009). *Corruption, Global Security, and World Order*, Washington, DC: Brookings Institution Press.

Recommended websites

Corruption Currents: http://blogs.wsj.com/corruption-currents
Global Witness: http://www.globalwitness.org
I Paid a Bribe: http://www.ipaidabribe.com and http://www.ipaidabribe.or.ke
Revenue Watch Institute: http:// www.revenuewatch.org
U4 Anti-Corruption Resource Centre: http://www.u4.no

5 Governing trade

Mark Langan

Trade has long been a source of contention in the international system. Peaceful disputes over access to markets have escalated into situations of 'gunboat diplomacy' as occurred, for instance, at the outset of the opium wars between the British Empire and Imperial China in the nineteenth century (Greenberg 1969). In the twentieth century, however, global governance institutions were established in the hope of mediating trade arrangements between nations and of facilitating greater international economic exchange. The creation of the World Trade Organisation (WTO) in the 1990s embodied, in particular, hope that trade would bind the international community together in friendship. The global governance of trade – led by the WTO – would facilitate global economic integration and bring about mutual reliance among prosperous and peaceful trading partners (Wilkinson 2006).

Trade remains, however, a controversial issue in international affairs, particularly in terms of the global governance of trade between countries of the global North and global South (North–South trade). WTO negotiations that aim to complete further market-opening in developing countries under the Doha Development Round have provoked bitter accusations of neo-colonialism (cf. Wade 2003; Scott and Wilkinson 2011; Oxfam 2005; Jawara and Kwa 2004). Trade unionists, civil society organisations, as well as developing country officials, have raised concerns regarding what they term 'premature' trade liberalisation. They claim that fledgling industries in the global South will be strangled at birth by an influx of cheaper goods from the global North upon liberalisation (Chang 2003; Morrissey *et al.* 2007; George 2010; Nunn and Price 2004; Traidcraft 2005; Langan 2012). The Kenyan textiles industry, for example, lost 70,000 jobs in the early 1990s upon entry of cheap clothing from the European Union (Republic of Kenya 2001: 4). Critics also claim that agricultural production in the global South – so important for food security – may be adversely affected by the WTO's pursuit of freer North–South trade. The North's 'dumping' of excess agricultural produce upon the developing world has, in the past, led to loss of livelihoods for local producers due to falling agricultural prices and broader agricultural decline (Clover 2003).

Rather than support further trade liberalisation and market-opening in the global South, therefore, there are a wide range of global governance actors who oppose WTO free-trade agendas and who claim that developing countries must be allowed policy space to protect their industries and agricultural sectors from unfair competition. This, it is argued, is asking for no more than what countries of the global North enjoyed during their own time of economic and social development. The United Kingdom and the United States of America practised 'protectionist' trade policies in the not so distant past (and in fact, continue to do so), putting up barriers to foreign imports during periods of rapid industrialisation and agricultural modernisation (Chang 2003: 139; Goodison 2007: 280; Moss and Bannon 2004: 53).

This chapter will examine the global governance of trade as it relates to economic ties between countries of the global North and global South. It will first examine the theories that inform global governance actors' perspectives on free trade. This will assess, in particular, disagreements surrounding the WTO Doha Development Round. Second, the chapter will examine practical attempts by global governance actors to marry free trade agendas to poverty reduction objectives. In particular, it will consider 'top-down' global governance interventions in the form of WTO-led 'Aid for Trade' programmes. Third, the chapter will examine 'bottom-up' global governance initiatives. It will consider the role of civil society and private sector actors in promoting 'ethical trade' agendas allegedly conducive to poverty alleviation in developing countries. The conclusion will then recap broader lessons surrounding the global governance of trade.

The global governance of trade: theories and actors

Global governance actors – whether WTO officials, trade unionists, private sector investors, civil society groups or trade representatives from developing countries – are guided (knowingly or unknowingly) by theoretical perspectives that inform whether they view free trade as a vehicle for global development, or conversely, a vehicle for neo-colonial penetration. It is these theoretical debates that lie at the heart of recent controversies surrounding the global governance of trade and that continue to provoke fierce disagreement as to the policies that global governance actors ought to pursue. These theoretical positions, while wide-ranging and nuanced, can broadly be grouped into two main schools: a 'liberal' school that holds that global free trade is a necessary tool for economic and social progress, and a 'critical' school that voices concerns as to asymmetric (that is, unequal) economic ties between poorer and richer nations. Global governance actors (re)articulate both liberal and critical perspectives as they seek either to advance, or to stall, movement towards global free trade.

This first school – the liberal school of global trade – has historically held sway within the corridors of the WTO and its key member countries within the global North (Goldstein 1998: 143–4). John Ruggie (1982) provides a succinct account of the adoption of liberal economic precepts by global governance institutions in the aftermath of World War II. He maintains that a 'liberal internationalist orthodoxy' held sway in the United States, particularly among financial elites. This owed both to ongoing normative (ethical) beliefs in the productive potential of free trade, as well as a more 'realist' (interest-based) pursuit of open markets for US commercial and industrial gain. In opposition to liberal precepts, however, developing countries sought to protect emerging producers from premature liberalisation and (hence) from more advanced competitors in the industrialised world. Accordingly, a 'compromise' was struck in relation to what Ruggie terms 'embedded liberalism' as the US sought to accommodate international opinion. Negotiations for open global markets would be pursued through multilateral endeavours within liberal international economic institutions. Nevertheless, a degree of domestic economic interventionism would be allowed (even welcomed) within individual nation states. This compromise underpinned newly founded liberal global governance bodies such as the General Agreement on Trade and Tariffs (GATT). Embedded liberalism would eventually give way, however, to 'neoliberal' principles as richer nations – again led by the US – called for greater liberalisation, deregulation and privatisation in developing countries.

Established in the 1990s as a successor to the GATT, the WTO builds upon earlier advancements towards the liberalisation of global trade pursued by its predecessor in the aftermath of World War II. As a successor institution the WTO aims, however, 'to be the centre piece of a much consolidated and significantly widened regulatory framework'. It is 'designed not only to administer a series of legal agreements [as per the GATT] ... but to also provide a permanent forum in which further liberalisation could be pursued through periodic negotiations' (Wilkinson 2002: 129). In this context, the WTO includes strengthened procedures for trade dispute settlement, introducing strict timetables for case resolution while ensuring that rulings are automatically enforced (unless a broad consensus exists against a particular conclusion). This is in stark contrast to the GATT, where a losing party had been able to unilaterally object to the enforcement of a ruling (WTO 2012). This reform arguably benefits developing countries since they have much to gain from a 'rules-bound' global trade system in which richer nations are held accountable for infringement of free-trade principles. The WTO also oversees a broader range of trade issues than its GATT forebear. Notably, it incorporates legal text on intellectual property rights as well as access in agriculture, textiles and clothing and services. It further includes provisions in relation to 'non-tariff barriers' (that is, barriers to trade other than traditional import taxes, for instance in terms of hygiene requirements placed upon agricultural produce (Sally 2002). This wider remit reflects the 'success' of the GATT Uruguay Round (concluded in the 1990s) which culminated in the foundation of the WTO as a global governance institution.

The institutional robustness of the WTO, moreover, arguably brings greater 'coherence to global economic policymaking' by complementing the powers and functions of the World Bank and International Monetary Fund

(IMF) within an overarching global governance architecture (Wilkinson 2007: 172). This is again in contrast to the GATT which had 'limped along for nearly forty years with almost no "basic constitution"' (Jackson, cited in Srinivasan 1999: 1050). Interestingly, there had been hope of establishing an International Trade Organisation (ITO) in the 1940s as part of the Bretton Woods negotiations that led to the creation of the IMF and World Bank. Due to opposition within the US Congress, however, the ITO was never formally ratified – hence the emergence of the GATT as an ad hoc (and stop-gap) trade body. The creation of the WTO in the 1990s, in this context, sought to rectify a historical anomaly and to establish a bolder, stronger global trade institution. This would, in turn, lead to greater peace and prosperity amongst trading partners within ever freer global markets.

This optimistic vision of global free trade embodied within the GATT/WTO drew (and continues to draw) upon long-standing arguments advanced by classical liberal theorists – most famously, Adam Smith – that free trade provides a fair means of exchanging resources between countries, and hence of avoiding military confrontation (Oneal and Russett 1999). Classical liberal theories also maintain that free trade will lead to a more efficient and (hence) productive international economic order. Nations with a 'comparative advantage' in a particular product or service will capitalise on this economic strength through exports in global markets, while importing commodities or services when these are more efficiently produced elsewhere (Chenery 1961). This will result in 'win–win' outcomes and prosperity for all trade participants. In addition, classical liberal theories of free trade maintain that global economic exchange leads to mutual reliance between trading partners and (hence) to a better cultural understanding between peoples. In some cases, co-operation on trade might in fact encourage formal political and social co-operation, as witnessed in relation to the evolution of the European Union – given its humble origins as the European Coal and Steel Community (ECSC). Scholars known as liberal institutionalists advance here what is termed a 'functionalist' argument in favour of global free trade. Namely, that trade liberalisation gives rise to later, more intensive forms of political co-operation. The successful global governance of *free* trade will lead not only to increased economic exchange but also lay the grounds for a more stable international realm (Nye 1970: 796–9).

Central to recent debates surrounding the global governance of trade, meanwhile, many liberals in the period of 'embedded liberalism' in the mid-twentieth century argued that the state – and by extension, global governance institutions – ought to play an active part in maintaining the stability of international economic exchange (Ruggie 1982: 380). In the immediate post-war period, liberal economists such as John Maynard Keynes argued that governments should regenerate economic activity during periods of global depression. Governance institutions should stimulate job creation and economic growth by encouraging the investor confidence necessary for overcoming troughs in the global economy. At the international level, newly established post-war global governance institutions such as the World Bank and the IMF should similarly intervene to provide financing to stimulate growth, particularly in developing country contexts (ibid.).

Importantly, however, with the rise of free market 'fundamentalism' from the late 1970s onwards, prominent '*neo*-liberals', such as Milton Friedman, have argued for the wholesale retreat from any form of governance intervention that involves economic regulation or trade interventionism. David Harvey (2005: 2) explains that, for neo-liberals:

> State interventions in markets (once created) must be kept to a bare minimum because, according to the theory, the state cannot possibly possess enough information to second-guess market signals (prices) and because powerful interest groups will inevitably distort and bias state interventions (particularly in democracies) for their own benefit.

Neo-liberal theories were translated into practical action during the 'Washington Consensus' between the 1980s and mid-1990s. Global governance institutions, particularly the World Bank and IMF, enacted neo-liberal policy prescriptions, rolling back the frontiers of the state in the global South through the promotion of privatisation, deregulation and trade liberalisation (Mailafia 1997: 253). Structural adjustment programmes (SAPs) funded by these International Financial Institutions (IFIs) necessitated developing states' adherence to neo-liberal economic reform (particularly, trade liberalisation) in return for loans and overseas development assistance.

While more recent 'embedded liberals' such as Joseph Stiglitz (1998) have criticised neo-liberal policies in their articulation of a 'post' Washington Consensus, nevertheless, neo-liberal ideologies continue to influence the WTO in its approach to the global governance of trade. Notably, the WTO is currently pursuing freer North–South trade within its Doha Development Round. This round of WTO trade negotiations, launched in 2001, seeks to bring about developing countries' successful 'integration' into global free markets. Building on the 'success' of the GATT Uruguay Round, the Doha Round seeks to facilitate poverty reduction in the global South by stimulating more intense forms of North–South trade. Developing country liberalisation in terms of tariff barriers and other 'at-the-border' trade regulations will ostensibly allow greater levels of job-creating North–South trade. Specifically, it is claimed by WTO officials that the conclusion of the Doha Round will allow developing countries to benefit from 'comparative advantages'. That is, the conclusion of further free-trade arrangements will allow them to export surplus goods in greater quantities (for instance, agricultural products) while more easily importing commodities that are produced more efficiently in others parts of the global economy (for instance, high-tech manufactures). This will be a 'win–win' scenario for countries of the global North and the global South.

Significantly in terms of *neo-liberal* policies, however, the WTO Doha Round also aims to facilitate what has been termed 'deep' trade liberalisation in the global South (Young and Peterson 2006). This entails not only the traditional removal of tariffs (taxes) upon imported goods (as per classical liberalism), but also involves 'deeper' regulatory, 'behind-the-border' liberalisation within developing countries. This 'deep' liberalisation, for instance, in terms of national policies concerning foreign investment and government procurement, aims to enable corporations in the global North to more easily compete for lucrative contracts in the global South, particularly in emerging services sectors such as banking and construction. This, however, arguably disadvantages firms originating from developing countries themselves. It also arguably erodes the sovereignty of nation states in terms of their ability to regulate commercial activities within their own borders. Disagreement surrounding 'deep' liberalisation has in large part accounted for the failure to conclude the Doha Round, which is currently in deadlock (Scott and Wilkinson 2011). Meanwhile, neo-liberal policies continue to be pursued within the broader global governance architecture. Both the World Bank and IMF, for instance, have recently funded Poverty Reduction Strategy Papers (PRSPs) that compel recipient governments to implement further neo-liberal privatisation, deregulation and liberalisation (Cammack 2004; Craig and Porter 2003; Gore 2004). This, it is claimed (in accordance with neo-liberal theory) will establish the macro-economic environment conducive to the creation of jobs and to the alleviation of poverty.

In stark contrast to liberal, and neo-liberal, perspectives dominant within the WTO, critical theories of global trade articulate the dangers of 'premature' market-opening for countries of the global South. Ha-Joon Chang (2003: 139–146), in a seminal contribution, argues that unrestricted North–South free trade will 'kick away the ladder of development'. He states that developed countries such as the United Kingdom utilised protectionist policies during their own phase of development in order to successfully shield emerging producers from external competition. While industrialisation was taking place and agricultural modernisation proceeding, Northern states actively discouraged foreign imports through a mixture of high tariff barriers and stringent regulations. This facilitated domestic economic growth and the development of an advanced industrial base (ibid.).

In this historical context, Chang argues that the imposition of premature market-opening upon developing countries deprives them of the same opportunity to gradually grow competitive enterprises capable of attaining global market share. The pursuit of neo-liberal trade policies by the WTO, in particular, will 'kick away the ladder of development' by flooding poorer countries with cheap goods from the industrialised nations. Emerging industries and producers in the global South will thereby lose out to more advanced foreign competitors (ibid.). Developing countries will subsequently be left with little choice but to compete in international markets on the basis of their low-cost, dollar-a-day labour. This will encourage exploitative (and short-term) forms of foreign investment within 'enclaves' isolated from the wider domestic economy, for instance, within export processing zones (EPZs) servicing Northern retailers such as Walmart and Nike. In turn, governments of the global South will be deprived of the opportunity to build a competitive industrial base capable of generating lucrative tax revenues and more fairly remunerated jobs for poorer citizens.

Importantly, Chang's 'kicking-away-the-ladder' thesis builds upon long-standing critical perspectives concerning the merits (or otherwise) of global free trade. In the immediate period of decolonisation, African leaders including President Kwame Nkrumah of Ghana and President Sekou Touré of Guinea raised concerns regarding Northern actors' pursuit of neo-colonial trade agendas. While admitting that Europeans had abandoned formal colonialism, nevertheless they viewed inequitable trade arrangements and associated foreign corporate domination as a 'Trojan horse' for the imposition of neo-colonial control (Nkrumah 1965: 19). Premature free trade between African states and the global North would undermine the economic, and hence political, independence of former colonies. This would lead to the perpetuation of poverty in countries of the 'periphery', since less-developed states would remain as exporters of raw materials while remaining dependent on the importation of higher-value manufactures from developed nations. In short, developing countries would remain subordinate (both politically and economically) to the global North within colonial patterns of trade. This would deprive their peoples of the opportunity to attain better living conditions historically associated with mass industrialisation. Accordingly, Sekou Touré (1962: 149) argued that former African colonies must unite to resist skewed North–South free-trade arrangements:

> African nations are realising that in order to solve their urgent social problems they must speed up the transformation of their trade economy; and if this is to be done through industrialisation, it cannot be done within the limits of our national micro-economies [that is, it must be achieved through pan-African co-operation]. But unconditional integration into a multi-national market consisting of highly developed and underdeveloped nations negates the possibility of industrial development in advance; it could only be the association of the horse and the rider.

Neo-colonialism would only be halted through pan-African economic co-operation in opposition to premature North–South free trade arrangements.

Crucially, critical perspectives continue to influence a wide range of global governance actors – including developing country officials, trade unionists and Trade Justice campaigners – in opposition to what they deem as the WTO's pursuit of regressive trade liberalisation under the Doha Round. Indian activist Vijay Gawandia, the former president of the Maharashtra Cotton Growers Association, remarked of the stalled WTO Doha Round negotiations:

> the WTO is nothing but an instrument to implement neo-colonialisation ... the rich countries of the world again want to exploit poor countries of the world. This point is proved because America and Europe are not ready to

[expose] their markets to the efficient producers of developing and underdeveloped countries [while simultaneously calling for trade liberalisation in the global South].

(ABC News 2008)

This reflects serious concern from producers in the global South that, despite the rhetoric of free trade, countries of the global North maintain protectionist barriers to agricultural imports while subsidising their own farmers. The European Union, in particular, maintains its generous Common Agricultural Policy (CAP), dispensing subsidies to European farmers while failing to fully liberalise its agricultural markets to imports from developing countries (Traidcraft 2012; Oxfam 2004). Oxfam, meanwhile, in a report entitled *A Recipe for Disaster: Will the Doha Round Fail to Deliver for Development?* (re)articulates critical concerns that premature trade liberalisation will prevent developing countries from attaining genuine development, with strong echoes of Ha-Joon Chang (Oxfam 2006). In this fashion, both critical and liberal theories continue to strongly influence debates surrounding the global governance of trade – as well as to motivate global governance actors in either opposition to, or support of, North–South free-trade regimes.

Aid for Trade: 'top-down' global governance

Controversies surrounding the WTO Doha Round have, however, given rise to global governance initiatives that seek to more explicitly align free trade agendas to legitimising goals of poverty reduction. The WTO itself has taken the lead among donors to promote what have become known as Aid for Trade initiatives. This 'top-down' global governance agenda encompasses an array of potential aid interventions targeted at three main areas (Ismail 2008: 46–49). First, Aid for Trade involves the giving of aid monies to government ministries in the global South which are involved in trade negotiations. This is done (ostensibly) to improve their ability to defend their interests in multilateral, and bilateral, trade talks. Second, it involves aid assistance to what is termed the business 'enabling environment' – that is, to the infrastructure necessary for promoting and sustaining pro-poor free trade, for instance, better roads, ports and railways. Third, it includes direct aid to private sector businesses (in terms of marketing know-how, technological upgrades and so forth), as well as to private sector associations which exist to co-ordinate sector-wide activities (ibid.). The Director-General of the WTO, Pascal Lamy, proudly states that Aid for Trade will ensure that free market-opening under the Doha Round will be conducive to human well-being in developing countries (WTO 2011).

By disbursing Aid for Trade, richer members of the WTO in the global North thereby promote what they term as 'pro-poor' market-opening agendas. Developing countries will be made sufficiently competitive (via Aid for Trade) and successfully adjust to external market pressures upon liberalisation. In this vein, 'critical' concerns surrounding asymmetric North–South trade linkages are strategically downplayed. This is reflected in the historical context in which Aid for Trade became consolidated into the WTO's policy agenda. Notably, the emergence of Aid for Trade programmes coincided with the WTO Hong Kong Summit of 2005, which came soon after the embarrassing failure of WTO talks at Cancun in 2003. The promotion of Aid for Trade, in this context, provided a means by which the WTO and Northern states could seek to redress developing country concerns surrounding the imposition of premature trade liberalisation within the Doha Round (Langan and Scott; forthcoming).

Aid for Trade, accordingly, reinforces liberal perspectives of a global free trade system working to the benefit of all within the international community. As such it has become popularised among a wide number of donor institutions in the global North, particularly within the European Commission which has championed WTO-led Aid for Trade initiatives in its own public policy discourse. In particular, the European Commission's *Towards an Aid for Trade Strategy* echoes liberal theories on the benefits of trade liberalisation when coupled with transitional aid assistance (2007: 3). The Commission's adoption of Aid for Trade agendas, meanwhile, fits neatly with its own pursuit of bilateral trade agreements, particularly in its relations with the African, Caribbean and Pacific (ACP) countries. By mirroring the discourse of the WTO, the European Commission can portray attempts to achieve bilateral trade liberalisation (in tandem with multilateral liberalisation within the WTO) as a benevolent contribution to international development.

Promises of Aid for Trade, moreover, appear to have been coupled with necessary financial allocations. The European Union, for instance, promised that its Aid for Trade contribution would reach a total of €2 billion by 2010. Japan, in similar fashion, promised $10 billion over a three-year basis, while the United States of America pledged to annually distribute $2.7 billion (Langan and Scott forthcoming). Consequently, there are a number of 'success stories' that point to the potential of Aid for Trade to align free trade agendas to pro-poor economic growth in the global South. Itaye (2011), for instance, positively reports on UK-funded Aid for Trade assistance to a major transport corridor in East Africa. This has led to a reduction of vehicle waiting times by 66 per cent, as well as a saving of $600,000 for local trucking companies. Moreover, Itaye hails the Business Environment Strengthening Technical Assistance Project (BESTAP) in Malawi. Funded jointly by the European Union, the World Bank and the International Development Agency, BESTAP (worth $18.7 million) has resulted in a reduction in commercial dispute settlement times from an average of 200 days to 98 days over a two-year period. Such practical interventions to support the private sector in the global South are widely seen in donor circles as a means of aligning trade liberalisation agendas to poverty reduction objectives.

Crucially, however, there remain critical interpretations of Aid for Trade programmes that view these top-down global governance interventions as antithetical to genuine development. In particular, there are claims that Aid for

Trade is merely a sweetener for bad trade agendas (George 2010: 132). In the short term, Aid for Trade measures might assist businesses in particular sectors, but in the long term they help to 'lock in' developing countries to particular forms of asymmetric economic relations with more advanced nations in the industrialised world. Sheila Page (2006: 26), for instance, reflects that the giving of aid might compel developing country officials down the path of premature trade liberalisation. Jan Orbie (2007: 308) similarly points to the strategic purposes of Aid for Trade in complementing neo-liberal trade agendas, by mitigating criticisms levied by civil society groups and governments of the global South regarding the consequences of trade liberalisation. In this context, Orbie (2007: 297) memorably refers to Aid for Trade as a 'low-cost legitimacy enhancing device' for global governance actors who seek to pursue freer North–South trade.

Perhaps most disconcertingly, there are also concerns that Aid for Trade does more to assist foreign corporations to lever profits and resources from developing countries, than to alleviate poverty. In the case of EU Aid for Trade to Africa, for example, there are mounting concerns that this form of assistance is used to subsidise regressive forms of European investment. The European Investment Bank (EIB) has been particularly criticised for funding mining activities that lead to environmental destruction and to the exploitation of workers. Rather than promote equitable forms of North–South trade, the EIB has been accused by non-governmental organisations, such as CounterBalance (2010: 5), of rolling back human development. EIB investments in the Zambian copper mining industry, for instance, are seen to assist Glencore (a Swiss firm), but to result in developmentally questionable outcomes for workers in a privatised, largely foreign owned mining sector (2010: 10). While the EIB's investments of around €650 million in mining activities in Africa since 2000 are counted as part of EU Aid for Trade disbursements, nevertheless, such 'development' interventions do not necessarily align free trade structures to moral goals of poverty reduction – quite the contrary (2010: 5). For such reasons, donor Aid for Trade agendas are often viewed with considerable scepticism on the part of 'critical' actors such as trade unionists, Trade Justice activists and certain developing country governments as 'boomerang aid' – benefitting foreign companies rather than poorer citizens (Eurodad 2011).

Box 5.1 Aid for Trade and Kenyan cotton

Kenya's cotton sector illustrates the possible repercussions of 'premature' trade liberalisation. The sector enjoyed rapid growth in the immediate period after independence, with cotton-lint production growing from 20,000 bales in 1965–6 to around 70,000 bales in 1984–5 (Ikiara and Ndirangu 2002: 5). Upon the implementation of structural adjustment programmes (SAPs) in the 1980s, however, domestic manufacturers' demand for cotton plummeted as local textiles firms suffered upon an influx of cheap secondhand clothes from Europe. The cotton sector sufficiently recovered, however, to employ around 140,000 workers by the mid-2000s (Export Processing Zones Authority 2005: 2). Nevertheless, this figure represented a decline of around 60,000 livelihoods in relation to pre-liberalisation levels (Omolo 2006: 148). It appears appropriate that, in this context, Aid for Trade should be given in support of the Kenyan government's efforts to sustain a cotton-textiles value chain capable of generating impressive livelihood creation in poorer rural communities. Crucially, the Government of Kenya requested that the European Commission investigate the potential for its Aid for Trade assistance to support the country's cotton producers. This followed on from the European Commission's (2007: 6) promise to promote 'country-ownership' – by supporting recipients' own economic priorities (HTSPE 2003). When EU (non)interventions are assessed, however, it becomes clear that there remain considerable problems in translating donor language into tangible help for producers in the global South. One senior cotton sector stakeholder, when asked if Kenyan cotton production had received help from the Europe Commission, responded:

> Europe? Not particularly … they did a study that recommended we should stop growing cotton altogether – ridiculous! No assistance from the European Union – there has been assistance from the World Bank but in our view it has been structured wrongly … let me say that when we approached the EU … the lack of interest on their part was the only thing that was remarkable.
> (Personal communication 2007)

The senior stakeholder viewed EU Aid for Trade as mere rhetoric unsubstantiated by material assistance:

> we haven't seen anything from the EU to cotton – it's high talk surrounded by all the language … I frankly cannot understand. My encounter with that study left me with a very negative impression.
> (Personal communication 2007)

> The EU-sponsored report in question, Assessment of the International Competitiveness and Value Adding in the Kenyan Cotton Industry, published by a British consultancy firm, did conclude, as the stakeholder stated, that a fully fledged cotton textile value chain in Kenya was uncompetitive (HTSPE 2003). Citing electricity costs and other production factors, it recommended that attempts to rebuild a viable cotton-textiles chain were unfeasible. As a result, it concluded that cotton should be produced mainly for export and that garment manufacturing should be supported in export processing zones, where 'low pay' allows clothes-making to be internationally competitive. In rather bleak terms the report stated:
>
>> only lint production for export and garment manufacture under the AGOA Act [US African Growth and Opportunity Act] are promising in future, and that there is little promise of long-term high volume international sales of Kenyan-made fibres and cloth to the main consuming countries as well as of sales of garments outside the preference regulations of the AGOA Act.
>>
>> (HTSPE 2003: vi)
>
> The report also stated that cotton production would only be viable in particular regions of Kenya, with cotton in many areas said to be unprofitable in international markets. The senior cotton sector stakeholder, in this context, was angered that the EU-sponsored report had effectively condemned the cotton-textiles chain to stagnation – a stagnation that, from his perspective, had been brought about in the first instance through EU sponsorship of premature trade liberalisation in conjunction with the IMF and World Bank. Despite promises of country-ownership, Europeans had dismissed Kenya's request for assistance in rebuilding the cotton-textiles value chain. Interestingly, meanwhile, the report avoided historical analysis of the key role that cotton-textiles value chains have played in linking agricultural growth to mass industrialisation.

Ethical trade: 'bottom-up' global governance

It is important to note that there are also 'bottom-up' global governance initiatives led by non-governmental organisations (NGOs) and private sector actors that seek to more fully align North–South free trade structures to poverty reduction objectives. In particular, many businesses and civil society actors have supported 'ethical trade' programmes. These aim to promote life-enhancing employment in the global South by ensuring that private sector firms abide by certain ethical standards – for instance, relating to the payment of a minimum wage, agreement to respect 'social dialogue' with workers, and practical reform to ensure safer work conditions. Notably, the Ethical Trading Initiative (ETI), a UK umbrella association of retailers, trade unions and civil society campaigners, promotes ethical trade throughout global supply chains (also known as global value chains or GVCs) that deliver goods to the British high street. The ETI (2012) usefully defines what it means by the promotion of 'ethical trade':

> ethical trade means that retailers, brands and their suppliers take responsibility for improving the working conditions of the people who make the products they sell. Most of these workers are employed by supplier companies around the world, many of them based in poor countries where laws designed to protect workers' rights are inadequate or note enforced. Companies with a commitment to ethical trade adopt a code of labour practice that they expect all their suppliers to work towards. Such codes address issues like wages, hours of work, health and safety and the right to join free trade unions.
>
> (ibid.)

Ethical trade programmes, accordingly, align with liberal visions of global free trade as working to improve the lives of poorer peoples in the global South. While recognising that working practices have not always been suited to the needs of 'the poor', nevertheless, there is liberal optimism that global supply chains (made possible, and sustained, within North–South free-trade structures) can be reformed to serve the interests of developing countries.

Interestingly, there is some evidence that ethical trade programmes have successfully impacted upon poorer workers in the global South. The ETI Impact Assessment, for example, provides case study analysis of ethical trade interventions across an array of commodity sectors. It finds that improvements have been made across a number of indicators relating to child labour, health and safety, working hours and wages (Barrientos and Smith 2006: 14). In addition, there are broader indications that ethical trade initiatives have raised employer awareness of labour standards through the promotion of corporate codes of conduct. One garment factory owner in India, for example, commented that 'codes have brought in an understanding of the rights and basic standards that a worker should have. We never thought about it earlier and feel it is fair enough that minimum wages should be given to workers' (2006: 16). The Impact Assessment found, however, that across other indicators – namely freedom of employment, freedom of association, harassment, discrimination, and regular employment – that less progress had been made through ethical trade initiatives (2006: 14). The report's authors, meanwhile, in an academic paper on the subject explain that:

> ongoing tensions exist between corporate and civil society actors. While these tensions have driven positive change in outcome standards, in that corporates have responded to demands from civil society to adopt codes of labour practice, they have not done much to improve workers' access to process rights. Our analysis suggests this is partly because buyers and retailers prioritise commercial imperatives and take a technocratic approach to code compliance which does little to challenge embedded social relations or business practices that undermine labour standards in global production systems.
>
> (Barrientos and Smith 2007: 727)

This view regarding the limitations of codes, and the need to challenge 'embedded' workplace practices, is supported by Tallontire *et al.* (2005: 568) in their analysis of the implications of ethical trade for women workers in North–South free trade networks. Pragmatically – and within a liberal theoretical prism – Tallontire *et al.* recommend that participatory social auditing (PSA) be enacted to ensure that workers' perspectives can be heard through engagement and dialogue. Participatory methods, in this setting, are understood to enable a fuller understanding of the gender issues 'embedded in local employment practice and culture' (ibid.).

Crucially, however, there are a number of critical perspectives on ethical trade agendas that question the viability of such bottom-up global governance initiatives to meaningfully redress entrenched power inequalities within GVCs and North–South free trade regimes. Lone Riisgard (2007: 5) questions whether workers do in fact gain from ethical trade measures. She notes that it is:

> A tremendous task to challenge a governance structure [within global supply chains] that is driven by large powerful retailers employing strategies such as cost-cutting and just-in-time ordering – strategies that put additional pressures on suppliers and promote labour flexibilization [resulting in greater job insecurity and worsening conditions] and not labour organization.
>
> (ibid.)

In short, it is questionable whether ethical trade agendas can meaningfully challenge global capitalist relations and the ensuing demand to continually drive down production costs at the expense of workers. Equally significantly, Riisgard (2007: 9) points to trade union fears that ethical trade initiatives' emphasis on private codes of conduct leaves workers wholly dependent upon employers' good (or bad) intentions. Rather than rely upon voluntary compliance, many argue that it would be much preferable to seek formal legal regulation of workers' rights through government intervention. Meanwhile, Riisgaard also highlights the ambivalence of many trade unionists who feel that interventions from Northern NGOs on labour rights issues often do more to undermine workers' representation than to secure it (ibid.).

Additionally, there are 'critical' concerns that any improvement won through ethical trade initiatives is necessarily fleeting and short-term – owing to the instability of North–South value chains. Bair and Werner (2011: 989) convincingly argue that academic analysis of GVCs (and by extension, the rationale of the ethical trade movement itself) fails to understand that value chains necessarily entail processes of both inclusion and *exclusion*. Namely, that the competitive impulses of global free markets mean that value chains regularly shift from geographical location to geographical location. As production costs fluctuate – whether due to demands for higher wages or energy costs – production shifts from one area to another. Subsequently, gains for workers' rights are lost when production patterns shift to another country or region (ibid.).

From a critical standpoint, this bias within the GVC literature – and within ethical trade programmes inspired by GVC analysis – downplays the often deleterious consequences of North–South production networks (in free market conditions) for workers, the environment and host communities. This is arguably exacerbated by the utilisation of 'ethical trade' language to sanitise popular perceptions of corporate activities in the global South, and of North–South free trade regimes more broadly. The *Capturing the Gains* programme, for instance, unites researchers who seek to promote both economic and *social* upgrading in global production networks, with strong parallels to the rationales of the wider ethical trade movement. As part of its sector-based research in mobile telecommunications, for instance, the programme seeks to assess 'how ... industries can uphold decent work standards' and how 'civil society organisations [are] using "brand image" to promote social upgrading for workers' (Capturing the Gains 2012).

Notably, *Capturing the Gains* has received funding from the Sustainable Consumption Institute (SCI), alongside other funding sources. The Sustainable Consumption Institute was itself founded with generous financial support from Tesco, the supermarket retailer (Tesco 2011). In this context, it appears that the apparent underlying assumption of the *Capturing the Gains* programme, that GVCs *can* be reformed to uphold decent work standards, sits neatly with corporate agendas, such as that of Tesco Mobile, that seek to ameliorate concerns surrounding exploitative practices in order to prevent possible disruption to business activities. The language of achieving social upgrading, ethical trade, better livelihoods, and of 'capturing the gains' within North–South free-trade structures arguably gives rise to the impression that progressive reform *will* be successfully attained (eventually), and that workers lives *will* benefit from incorporation into GVCs (again, in due course). It arguably does little, however, to critically challenge overarching systemic inequalities within North–South free-trade regimes or to question whether foreign investment (often) based on low-cost labour is necessarily the best strategy for developing countries. Instead, it arguably forecloses attention to alternative economic policies premised upon developing countries' rejection of 'premature' trade liberalisation. Instead of helping developing countries to 'capture the gains' from North–South trade, therefore, such ethical trade discourse might, from a critical perspective, help to legitimise asymmetric (and fundamentally unstable) GVCs in which workers are compelled to capitulate the gains of production to predatory foreign investors.

Conclusion

This chapter has examined the global governance of trade, particularly as it relates to economic linkages between countries of the global North and countries of the global South. It has examined the theoretical perspectives that underpin global governance actors' approach to free trade agendas. It has demonstrated that liberal and critical theories continue to find resonance in the actions, and interventions, of global governance actors – whether in terms of WTO officials, developing country governments, civil society organisations or private sector bodies. Liberal perspectives, and their neo-liberal variant, continue to hold significant influence within the corridors of the WTO and its members within the global North. Actors such as WTO Director Pascal Lamy maintain that North–South free trade structures are an undoubted 'good' within international politics. Trade liberalisation will lead to economic growth, more jobs, and hence poverty reduction within developing countries.

Accordingly, global governance actors (from a liberal standpoint) must do all they can to promote, and to sustain, global free-trade structures. As noted, Aid for Trade initiatives in particular represent a 'top-down' governance strategy that seeks to build competitive enterprises in the global South. Trade liberalisation will thereby align to moral goals of poverty reduction since Aid for Trade will ensure that emerging producers in developing countries can fairly compete with rivals in the developed world. Meanwhile, in a 'bottom-up' endeavour, civil society actors and private sector representatives work together to promote ethical trade within global value chains. Through judicious interventions and the promotion of corporate codes of conduct, North–South free-trade structures can be made to work for poorer individuals, providing them with life-affirming employment free from harassment or exploitation.

Crucially, however, those from a critical standpoint oppose further global governance interventions that seek to impose 'premature' trade liberalisation upon developing countries. Following the logic of analysts such as Chang (2003), many Trade Justice campaigners and academics argue that the imposition of free-trade regimes will kick away the ladder of development from countries in the global South. Rather than secure economic growth and job creation, premature liberalisation will instead destabilise emerging industries and condemn developing countries to a cycle of dependency – importing high value manufactures while exporting lower value commodities, either agricultural produce or goods made by dollar-a-day labour for foreign investors. Developing countries will not attain meaningful, long-term poverty reduction unless they resist free-trade regimes and pursue alternative, more interventionist industrial policies.

In this context, critical perspectives are highly sceptical of both 'top-down' and 'bottom-up' interventions that seek to marry trade liberalisation policies to moralising goals of poverty alleviation. Rather than create conditions for genuine development, many view Aid for Trade initiatives as sweeteners for bad trade deals. Moreover, Aid for Trade programmes are, contrary to their development discourse, often seen to subsidise regressive forms of foreign investment in developing countries. In similar fashion, critical analysts are often sceptical of the efficacy of 'bottom-up' ethical trade interventions. While ethical trade initiatives hold out the (false?) promise of 'capturing the gains' of global trade for poorer workers, there are fears that these endeavours may popularly sanitise and legitimise exploitative GVCs in which workers are compelled to capitulate the gains of production to predatory foreign investors. Given this contrast between liberal and critical perspectives, it is necessary to remain reflexive as to the benefits of free trade structures for 'the poor'. Current stalemate within the WTO Doha Round indicates that there is potential to slow down movement towards ever freer North–South trade structures as global governance actors, not least developing country officials, begin to imagine alternative strategies to more effectively combine trade policies to development objectives.

Recommended reading

Chang, H. (2003). *Kicking Away the Ladder*, London: Anthem Press.
Njinkeu, D. and Cameron, H. (eds) (2008). *Aid for Trade and Development*, New York: Cambridge University Press.
Scott, J. and Wilkinson, R. (2011). 'The Poverty of the Doha Round and the Least Developed Countries', *Third World Quarterly* 32(4): 611–27.
Tallontire, A., Dolan, C., Smith, S. and Barrientos, S. (2005). 'Reaching the Marginalised? Gender Value Chains and Ethical Trade in African Horticulture', *Development in Practice*, 15(3–4): 559–71.
Touré, S. (1962). 'Africa's Future and the World', *Foreign Affairs*, 41: 141–51.

Recommended websites

Directorate General for Trade of the European Commission: http://ec.europa.eu/trade/
Ethical Trading Initiative: http://www.ethicaltrade.org/
Oxfam: http://www.oxfam.org.uk/
Traidcraft: http://www.traidcraft.co.uk/
World Trade Organisation: http://www.wto.org/

6 The global governance of labour

Juanita Elias

Profound and continuing changes in our global economic and political system present persistent challenges for the way in which the problems and issues facing workers around the world are addressed in global policy circles. This chapter focuses on the global governance of labour by examining some of the global policy initiatives that have ostensibly been designed to improve the position of workers and their families around the world. These globally focused initiatives involve policy-making, standard setting, activism and labour organizing. Limiting the discussion of the global governance of labour in this manner is important from the outset because, given the centrality of labour to the capitalist economic system, the term 'the global governance of labour' could also be used to discuss the very workings of the contemporary global economic system. The 'governance' of labour could, for example, be understood in terms of the way in which the organization and control of labour is central to the pursuit of profit in the capitalist system. Nonetheless, the discussion presented here does seek to situate labour issues within the context of the current transformation of the global political economy – namely the increased flexibilization, informalization and feminization of work that has accompanied the industrial decline experienced in Northern states and the uneven experience of industrial growth in the developing world.

Recent years have witnessed the increased transnationalization of production as firms have sought to expand their operations in order to take advantage of lower labour costs. The organization of industrial production is now transnational in scope, leading to perceptions that workers in, for example, the US steel or garment industry are in competition with workers based in, say, China or India. In addition, the globalization of production in this manner is associated with the rise of new technologies that make it possible for production lines to be increasingly fragmented and globally dispersed. Thus faster shipping times and improvements in information communication technologies make just-in-time production processes associated with fragmented production and increased dependence on informal and casualized work possible. Proponents of a 'race to the bottom' argument suggest that these changes are undermining nationally bounded forms of labour regulation (such as national minimum wages or trade union rights) as increasingly 'footloose' firms seek to discover ever cheaper sources of labour.

The rise of informal and casualized forms of work is of great significance to discussions of the global governance of labour because these, often highly feminized, groups of workers are consistently marginalized within existing approaches. Other important developments include the growth of enormous global conglomerates through merger and acquisition activities and the rise of global financial markets that increase the structural power of capital at the expense of labour and trade unions that tend to be organized at a local (usually national) level (Bieler and Lindberg 2011a: 7).

The use of the term global governance is very useful when discussing labour issues given the numerous actors and initiatives that are involved in this issue area. These include formal intergovernmental institutions, states, trade unions (organized on both national and international bases), and other non-governmental actors such as corporations, employer organizations and activist groups. A particular focus of this chapter is on the role of the International Labour Organization (ILO) in the global governance of labour – but in doing so, it points to the significant role that states and non-state actors such as unions or activists play within this governance regime. The chapter provides a brief history of the ILO, and then turns to look at how the ILO sought to reposition itself in the post-Cold-War era via its adoption of the 'Core Labour Standards' – a development that for some is seen as significantly strengthening the ILO's contemporary role in the global governance of labour. For others, however, recent developments at the ILO are viewed as merely serving to shore up the ongoing privatization of labour governance through corporate-led initiatives such as the United Nations Global Compact and corporate codes of conduct. Of considerable importance to the discussion is a concern with what these new and emerging practices of labour governance mean for workers around the world. In doing so, it is useful to employ 'gender lenses' – looking at the extent to which existing approaches to labour governance are able to protect the interests and needs of some of the most marginalized, low paid and disorganized groups of workers in the world – female factory workers, domestic workers and home-based workers. Although this chapter adopts a somewhat cynical take on the ability of current practices of labour governance to meet the needs of marginalized groups of workers, it ends on a note of optimism with a discussion of the opportunities and possibilities for labour activism within the current governance regime.

The International Labour Organization

The International Labour Organization (ILO) has played an important role in the global governance of labour issues since its inception in 1919. Recognizing the way in which labour issues need to be understood as a global issue, the preamble of the ILO constitution states that 'the failure of any nation to adopt humane conditions of labour is an obstacle in the way of other nations which desire to improve the conditions in their own countries' (ILO 1919). The ILO matters to those of us with an interest in global governance issues because its establishment represented 'the projection of worker needs into the realm of international relations' (Hughes and Haworth 2011: 7). There exists considerable critical debate over the role of the ILO but no discussion of the global governance of labour can ignore the significant role that this organization has played in shaping the way in which global labour issues are understood and responded to (see for example Standing 2008; Alston and Heenan 2004; Alston 2004; Prügl 2002; Cooney 1999; Vosko 2002).

The ILO is a unique international organization – it was established as part of the League of Nations system following the end of the First World War, yet managed to survive the collapse of the League. In part, its longevity can be explained by its organizational structure based on tripartism, meaning that it includes representatives from governments, trade unions and employer organizations. This structure afforded the ILO a level of autonomy from the League, enabling the ILO to pursue its own agenda. Thus as the League collapsed in the face of the Great Depression, rising militarism and national isolationism, the year 1934 actually saw the USSR and the USA join the organization. This is not to suggest, however, that the aims and objectives of the ILO were at odds with the broader vision of the League of Nations. For example, the organization's first director, Albert Thomas, was committed to the view that the pursuit of peace needed to involve a commitment to social justice. In the context of the aftermath of the First World War, such a concern was not only aligned to broad commitments to peace, but also reflected specific efforts to curb the spread of communism following the 1917 Bolshevik revolution. In the post-war period, Hughes and Haworth (2011) argue that the ILO managed to continue to play an important role in the global governance of labour. This involved successive director generals seeking to find a direction for the organization in the face of both the power politics of the Cold War and the rise of neoliberal orthodoxies from the early 1980s onwards, in which many states in the developing world were forced to adopt 'Washington Consensus' policies that were considerably at odds with the ILO's commitment to a social justice (see Hughes and Haworth 2011: 5–19). Other commentators, however, are more critical suggesting that in the post-War period, the ILO continually acted to perpetuate the hegemony of American Capitalism (Cox 1977; Whitworth 1994).

The ILO directs a system of international labour standards contained in over 190 conventions. Once a convention is adopted by the ILO, states are expected to ratify them into domestic law. Standing (2008) suggests that a key assumption underpinning this system was a recognition that states would be able to pick and choose those conventions that best suited their economic and welfare systems – a recognition of the diversity of national capitalist systems that also meant that once states did ratify what are, effectively, rather loosely worded conventions, there was considerable flexibility in the application of standards within domestic contexts. Inevitably then, even when governments ratify a convention, implementation is a deeply contested process. International labour standards are set through ILO enactments and recommendations that are designed to be 'aspirational' in that they establish standards to which states ought to adhere. The ILO's role in enforcing labour standards, however, is limited since the organization lacks the right to impose sanctions upon states that fail to comply. The enforcement of the ILO's resolutions and conventions is dependent on their ratification and enforcement by individual states, and the ILO relies largely on forms of 'shaming' states into responding positively to their ILO obligations (Mackelm 2002: 615; Weisband 2000: 665). One problem is that international labour standards compete with other norms and ideas within local contexts (for example, a state may well have signed up to conventions requiring equal pay for equal work, but may struggle to implement such practices in the face of entrenched gender discriminatory practices). Thus, ensuring that ILO conventions result in progressive outcomes for the targeted groups of workers often requires the work of dedicated activists intent on ensuring that international standards are translated appropriately into local settings.

The trade-labour standards debate and the rise of the Core Labour Standards

Attempts at creating a binding approach to labour standards regulation were seen during the establishment of the World Trade Organisation (WTO) when calls for a 'social clause' were raised. Arguments in favour of the social clause put forward the view that the ILO was too weak in the sense that it could not prevent violations of its conventions. This stands in contrast to the WTO who possesses, in its trade disputes mechanism, one of the few international adjudicative mechanisms able to impose (economic) sanctions on those states found to be in breach of WTO rules. Supporters thus argued that a social clause would enable the enforcement of internationally agreed labour standards as well as forcing the WTO itself to be a more socially responsible institution and thereby mitigate against the worst impacts of free trade on the lives of ordinary people (what has been termed a 'social floor' in trade agreements). Critics, however, have suggested that demands for a social clause are flawed because, given the fact that the WTO is a state-centric organization, only governments are able to make complaints (rather than say, NGOs or trade unions). Since the rights of workers are not generally a core priority for governments around the world, it is likely that workers' rights would simply become a bargaining tool in foreign policy and trade issues. Indeed, the objections of many states in the developing world to a social clause at the WTO were based on the assertion that the clause represented more a form of trade protectionism than a genuine commitment to worker rights. In light of these claims of trade protectionism, demands for a social clause had all but disappeared from the agenda of the WTO by the time of the fourth ministerial meeting in Doha in 2001.

Nonetheless, the ILO was keen to build a role for itself in a post-Cold War world in which (as the WTO labour-standards debate showed) labour issues were slipping off the agenda (Lee 1997). Furthermore, as the ongoing globalization of production continued apace into the 1990s, it appeared that the rights of workers were being consistently subordinated to corporate interests in the face of governments' commitments to free market ideologies that stressed the need to roll back worker rights in order to maintain international competitiveness. Murphy (2010) suggests that despite the failure of the social clause debate at the WTO, a renewed concern with labour standards at the international level contributed to a reinvigorated ILO. These activities led to the formation of important transnational pro-worker networks involving states, trade unions (in particular the International Confederation of Free Trade Unions – ICFTU) and NGOs. Hence '[d]espite not achieving their goals at the WTO, the ICFTU and pro-labour states did contribute towards developments on the issue in other international arenas' effectively keeping the debate about compliance with international labour standards 'alive' (Murphy 2010: 91). One outcome has been that a concern with labour standards has been incorporated into bilateral trade arrangements made by the EU and the US. Given the stalling of trade negotiations at the WTO and the current burgeoning of bilateral trade agreements, the inclusion of a social clause in bilateral trade agreements could be viewed as an important site for the governance of global labour issues. However, it has been pointed out that these social clauses rarely (if ever) result in sanctions being imposed against non-compliant states and there has been considerable resistance on the part of increasingly economically important Southern states such as India to the inclusion of these clauses (Orbie and Babarinde 2008).

In the aftermath of the failure of the social clause debate, the ILO itself sought to recapture the issue of labour standards by launching the Core Labour Standards (CLS). The ILO adopted the Declaration of Fundamental Principles and Rights at Work in 1998, which confirmed four issue areas as the CLS: freedom of association and the effective recognition of collective bargaining; elimination of all forms of forced and compulsory labour; effective abolition of child labour; and elimination of discrimination in respect of employment and occupation (see Box 6.1). The CLS were presented as 'fundamental' standards that ought to be applied to all workers around the world regardless of whether or not their state had ratified the associated ILO conventions. In this sense, many commentators at the time stated that the CLS could be viewed effectively as more 'universal' in character, more akin to human rights, than mere technical conventions that states could choose whether or not to ratify (Petersmann 2004; Valticos 1998). The ILO's successful promotion of the CLS has meant that these standards have come to be seen as central components of business-led initiatives in the area of labour standards such as corporate codes of conduct and the United Nation's Global Compact initiative (which sought to promote the voluntary adoption of the CLS alongside other human rights and environmental standards within the corporate sector).

> **Box 6.1 The Core Labour Standards**
>
> The 1998 Declaration of Fundamental Principles and Rights at Work states that:
>
> > all Members, even if they have not ratified the Conventions in question, have an obligation arising from the very fact of membership in the Organization to respect, to promote and to realize, in good faith and in accordance with the Constitution, the principles concerning the fundamental rights which are the subject of those Conventions, namely:
> >
> > (a) freedom of association and the effective recognition of the right to collective bargaining;
> > (b) the elimination of all forms of forced or compulsory labour;
> > (c) the effective abolition of child labour; and
> > (d) the elimination of discrimination in respect of employment and occupation.
>
> These four Core Labour Standards are associated with the following ILO conventions:
>
> (a) Freedom of Association and Protection of the Right to Organize Convention (No. 87)
> (b) Right to Organize and Collective Bargaining Convention (No. 98)
> (c) Forced Labour Convention (No. 105)
> (d) Abolition of Forced Labour Convention (No. 105)
> (e) Minimum Age Convention (No. 138)
> (f) Worst Forms of Child Labour Convention (No. 182)
> (g) Equal Remuneration Convention (No. 100)
> (h) Discrimination (Employment and Occupation) Convention (No. 111)
>
> See ILO (1998)

It is important, however, to recognize that whilst the CLS are linked to certain ILO conventions, they are not viewed as being necessarily linked to ILO enforcement mechanisms. Notably, the CLS were introduced at the behest of a US administration who were keen to see a labour standards regime in place that did not require states to ratify conventions into domestic law (after all, the US had an exceptionally poor record on this); '[the] bottom line is ... that the choice of standards to be included in the CLS was not based upon the consistent application of any coherent compelling economic, philosophical or legal criteria, but rather reflects a pragmatic political selection of what would be acceptable at the time to the United States' (Alston 2004: 485). Setting apart the CLS from other ILO conventions is thus viewed as setting them apart from the key mechanism through which labour standards are implemented – ratification into domestic law. The danger of this, Alston argues, is that:

> The Declaration has laid the groundwork for a decentralised system of labour standards implementation which significantly reduces the emphasis on governmental responsibilities and encourages a diverse range of actors, from transnational corporations to consumers, to take the lead in defining, promoting and even enforcing core labour standards.
>
> (Alston 2004: 460)

Although the development of the CLS is generally regarded in policy circles as a good thing that has raised the profile of the ILO, it is clear that not all commentators share this view. Concerns have been raised, for example, over the selection of some standards as 'core' and others as non-core. For example, nowhere in the CLS is a commitment made to the right to earn a fair wage (Alben 2001). The disappearance of the issue of fair wages is hardly surprising given the way in which dominant neoliberal development paradigms tend to emphasise a model of economic development based upon the attraction of FDI on the basis of labour costs. The ILO has attempted to counter criticisms that its Core Labour Standards fail to address everyday issues facing workers around the world (such as low pay or poor working conditions) through the parallel development of its 'Decent Work' agenda which emphasises the need for governments around the world to work to provide employment characterized by fair incomes, workplace security, social protection and opportunities for advancement (in addition to these commitments to trade union freedoms and non-discrimination already covered by the CLS). In 2008, the ILO reaffirmed this commitment with the Declaration on Social Justice for a Fair Globalization (ILO 2008). As Vosko (2002) suggests, the Decent Work agenda represented an attempt by the ILO to reconcile competing interests between corporate interests backed by industrialized states and actors representing more marginalized states, trade unions, NGOs and women's movements. The outcome is an agenda that is broadly compatible with the interest of capital but is also one in which potential challenges to the hegemony can emerge (see for example the discussion of indigenous, domestic and home worker rights in the final section of this chapter).

It has been suggested that the longevity of the ILO stems from its ability to continually 'reposition itself as global circumstances change' (Hughes and Haworth 2011: 48). The CLS are one example of this strategic respositioning – an attempt by the organization to maintain and enhance its role and relevance after the end of the Cold War. Another aspect of this institutional survivalism has been the ILO's ever-increasing engagement with International Financial Institutions (IFIs) such as the World Bank and the International Monetary Fund. The ILO's Decent Work agenda had much in common with the emphasis on poverty reduction that emerged within the IFIs from the late 1990s onwards (a policy shift often referred to as the Post Washington Consensus (PWC)).

Under the PWC the IFIs sought to move away from top-down neoliberal reform projects and, instead, sought to emphasize the importance of poverty reduction to development and to extend country ownership of development programmes through the Poverty Reduction Strategy Paper (PRSP) approach. Within this context the ILO sought to integrate its Decent Work agenda into the PRSP process – emphasizing the need to strengthen the role of 'tripartite partners' (ministries of labour, employers and worker organizations) in the drafting, implementation and monitoring of the PRSP process amongst other issues (see Hughes and Haworth 2011: 43). It is notable therefore that much of the World Bank's commentary on labour issues is framed in terms of commitments to the ILO's Decent Work and CLS agenda. But for critics of the organization, such activities merely represent the way in which the aims and activities of the ILO have been fundamentally undermined, in that the organization has been weakened by the need to deliver an approach to labour issues that fits a broadly neoliberal policy agenda.

Women, work and the Core Labour Standards

Having raised some general concerns about the CLS approach, the discussion now turns to look specifically at what the CLS means for marginalized groups of women workers around the world. The development of the labour standards debate has not adequately addressed the needs of women workers located in forms of employment such as export-sector factory work, domestic work, home-based work and in other forms of informal and casualized work. Many of the problems that women face in the workforce are a result of the way in which women tend to be regarded as a key source of low-waged employment in many of the most globalized (and most low-wage dependent) industries (Elson and Pearson 1981). Women are often viewed as a passive, flexible workforce that will accept low wages without demanding labour and human rights. Thus they tend to be recruited into the lowest paying jobs within industries, and tend to be over-represented in part-time, temporary and informal sector employment (Standing 1999). The prevalence of female employment is notable in particularly labour-intensive export industries such as garment production, electronics and horticulture. And, furthermore, the feminization of these sectors has been directly related to a process of degradation of the jobs that women move into. A 2005 United Nations Development Fund for Women (UNIFEM) report claimed that in the South, the informal sector (which includes home-based work and temporary and contract labourers) is a larger source of employment for women than the formal sector, and that women are more likely than men to be found in the informal forms of employment (Chen 2005). Women employed in sectors that fall outside of conventional understandings of 'labour force participation' are often among the most vulnerable groups of workers in the world – beyond the purview of trade unions, protective legislation and voluntary codes of conduct.

Given these factors, it could be argued that women workers in particular have most to gain from improvements in labour standards (Brasted 2004). Mechanisms for protecting labour standards are often targeted at protecting the rights of workers in low-waged industries with poor working conditions, the kinds of jobs found in low value-added industries at the bottom end of global supply chains located in the developing world. However, feminist authors have suggested that the promotion of the CLS advances a view of worker rights that often leave the specific problems and concerns of women workers on the sidelines of the labour standards debate. Shaw and Hale (2002: 109), for example, comment that whilst the 'human rights approach' (meaning the CLS) 'has much to recommend it – not least if it contributes to a revitalised ILO with a stronger international role', such an approach may not benefit women workers all that much, since particularly gendered issues such as low wages and workplace harassment are not generally considered to be core issues.

Ultimately, the CLS fall foul of what the human rights scholars Kaufman and Lindquist (1995) label 'gender-neutral treaty language'. There is no recognition of the specific problems that women workers face and many of these CLS may have the effect of benefiting male workers more. For example, the CLS have been interpreted as standards that are most applicable to (predominantly male) workers in formal employment – thus predominantly female, informal sector workers are overlooked, effectively marginalizing the female-dominated domestic, home-workers and many informal sector workers within the labour standards debate. As Standing (2008: 357) notes, the ILO was very much founded on assumptions concerning a 'standard' employment relationship – full-time workers in trade unions (see also Whitworth 1994: 134–140). This is a situation considerably at odds with the employment conditions under which most informal sector workers find themselves.

An interesting issue through which to evaluate the CLS concerns the rights of female migrant workers. A feminization of migration has occurred over the past few decades characterized by women increasingly seeking to move from one country to another in order to seek work and the rise of deeply feminized forms of employment within which migrant women predominate. One such example of this is the growth in the market for migrant worker employment as domestic workers within households. Huge numbers of women from labour-sending countries located in the less developed states of the world seek out employment in wealthier countries, including both rich Western nations and middle-income states such as Malaysia, Mexico or Thailand in which there is an expanding middle class but little in the way of state welfare support for things like childcare. Migrant women working as 'maids' within their employers homes are a particularly vulnerable group and face numerous forms of exploitation. The ILO has long been a key source of international human rights law in relation to the rights of migrant workers, however, until very recently, there has been a failure to address issues facing female migrants (Cholewinski 2006) (although in the final section of this chapter I examine the newly established ILO Domestic Worker Convention). Concerns can also be raised about the extent to which the ILO's approach to migrant worker rights has been framed in relation to the CLS. Whilst many of the CLS do have the potential to offer protection to vulnerable groups of women such as migrant domestic workers, the extent to which they are able to accommodate protection for those groups of workers whose work falls outside of conventional definitions of 'labour' (such as caring for household members) is questionable. For example, although the CLS prioritize the protection of trade union rights, trade unions often fail to meet the needs of marginalized groups of female migrant workers whose needs are concealed behind 'layers of invisibility' that construct them as neither 'proper' workers nor citizens (Amoore 2006: 21). Indeed, to take an example from the Southeast Asian region, it has been noted that more informal forms of labour organizing (such as that undertaken by NGOs) has often been far more successful in meeting the needs of marginalized groups of female workers (much as migrant domestic workers) compared to traditional trade unions (Ford 2005).

This is not to suggest that the ILO has not played an important role in seeking to address the problems facing migrant domestic workers. Again, using examples from Southeast Asia, we can point to ILO programmes and initiatives for domestic workers. In Malaysia, for example, the ILO worked with the national trade union body, the Malaysian Trade Union Congress, in attempts to establish as domestic worker association. The Jakarta ILO office in Indonesia operates a programme aimed, through both advocacy work and technical assistance, at addressing problems faced by migrant domestic workers in the region (in particular, focusing on Indonesian domestic workers employed in the receiving countries of Malaysia, Hong Kong and Singapore). The project does, however, reflect the way in which the work of the ILO has come to be increasingly framed around the CLS – specifically, the problems facing migrant domestic workers are presented in terms of the issues of trafficking and forced labour rather than in terms of socio-economic equality or wages. Such an approach is illustrative of the effective downgrading of an economic and social rights agenda at the ILO in the context of the CLS (Standing 2008: 368). For more on the issue of migrant domestic work in Southeast Asia see Box 6.2 at the end of this chapter.

Labour standards and the privatization of global governance

The CLS approach has in certain respects undermined some of the solid foundations that the ILO had developed in the enforcement and monitoring of labour standards and has consequently legitimated the role of the corporation as a key regulatory agent in enforcing labour standards throughout their supply-chains. The main mechanism thorough which this voluntarist approach to labour standards is directed is the corporate code of conduct. Codes typically consist of a statement of minimum labour conditions focusing on issues such as working conditions, environmental impacts and health and safety standards, assurances that the firm will comply with local laws and guarantees that the firm will uphold anti-discriminatory employment practices. Some codes also contain commitments to putting pressure on/compelling contractors or suppliers in respect of certain ethical standards. Many writers support codes because they view them as filling a regulatory vacuum, in that they act to enforce labour standards in states where the regulatory and enforcement mechanisms for upholding labour standards are lacking (Frenkel and Scott 2002). It has been suggested that labour codes of conduct within multinational firms place firms in a 'role model' position vis-à-vis local firms and thereby act to drive up labour standards across countries in the developing world (UNCTAD 1994: 201). In this sense, multinational corporations (MNCs) are regarded as socially responsible progressive actors that are willing to take on greater commitments in ensuring the well-being of their employees. Much of this literature presents the 'business case' for CSR with labour standards portrayed as being basically compatible with the operations of corporations – and even helping them to deliver higher profits.

Unsurprisingly, the voluntaristic codes of conduct approach has been thoroughly criticised. Concerns have been raised, for example, about the ethics of allowing firms to become essentially self-regulating on this issue. The suggestion is made that codes come to be regarded as a substitute for binding regulatory responses when they really should be viewed as complementary to them (Jenkins *et al.* 2002: 1). An OECD study from 1999 analysed the content of company codes of conduct; the findings seem to bear out the claim that codes are designed in a manner that best suits corporate interests. For example, few codes address the issue of freedom of association or are accompanied by meaningful systems of implementation (OECD 1999). Most notably they found that only 18 per cent of the codes studied contained a reference to international standards such as ILO conventions (OECD 1999: 5). It has also been suggested, in another survey of codes, that where international standards are referred to, the company has interpreted its original meaning or intention differently (Uriminsky 2001: 19). But it is worth noting that recent research from the clothing industry suggests that societal and activist pressure has had a significant impact not just on the uptake of codes, but in pressuring firms to opt for more rigorous codes and/or labour certification schemes (Fransen and Burgoon 2012). Nonetheless, Taylor (2011) notes that codes of conduct are taken up unevenly – with companies that are part of high-profile multinational supply chains tending to be more rigorous in the enforcement of standards, whilst other firms either falsify compliance with standards or ignore them completely. Codes thus act to perpetuate, rather than undermine, the unevenness in labour standards found across the industrial sector.

The problems with codes of conduct are further exposed in a variety of feminist studies. Pearson and Seyfang's study of women and codes of conduct found that women face a number of problems that stem from this secondary position within the labour market (Pearson and Seyfang 2002). These include: low wages and wage inequality, a lack of protection and respect for pregnant workers, inadequate occupational health, safety and social security rights (especially for part-time workers), absence of freedom of association, the right to collective bargaining and human rights, enforced overtime and over-long working days and the intensity of work. Furthermore, they also raise issues relating to women homeworkers (usually self-employed workers employed at home and taking in work such as garment or small product assembly). Because homeworkers tend to work in conditions that are far worse than those found in factories, the imposition of codes that impose minimum working conditions on workers may have a negative impact on the ability of some of the poorest groups of women in the world to find waged employment (Brill 2002: 118). Academics and practitioners working in the area of women and codes of conduct have also pointed to a number of practical problems – most notably, that women are often not aware that the codes even exist. They also point to 'tick-box' approaches to code monitoring and verification, whereby independent monitoring organizations (such as accountancy and consultancy firms) generally fail to talk to the women workers themselves, relying on information provided by company managers to ensure that codes are being enforced. Such a situation is indicative of the top-down nature of the implementation of codes that fails to take into account the reality of women's employment whereby 'there has been no place for women workers or their interests to be represented in the process' (Pearson and Seyfang 2002: 51).

Despite the fact that a high proportion of codes contain a commitment to anti-discrimination, this does very little to enhance the role and position of women in the workforce. In certain respects this reflects the weak enforcement mechanisms that accompany codes of conduct, thus although provisions to ensure discrimination does not take place are written into the codes, this has little impact in reality. But more importantly, it highlights the way in which global labour markets contain structures of gender inequality, and how firms have both perpetuated and drawn upon these gendered inequalities in order to secure a supply of low-cost female labour (Elias 2004). For example, the exclusion of homeworkers from most codes is indicative of the way in which codes are an inadequate tool for dealing with the gendered structures of inequality that characterize multinational systems of production (Brill 2002). Carr *et al.* (2000) also point to the exclusion of homeworkers from corporate codes of conduct – highlighting how the structural power of multinational firms enables them to construct labour conditions based upon fragmented production lines and supply chains. As a result, an increasing number of women in the export sector are employed as home-based workers, placing them beyond the reach of most codes of conduct and transferring many risks and costs from the subcontractor onto the worker. In Barrientos *et al.*'s work on women's employment in South African horticulture, another problem is highlighted. They found that codes often failed to cover large groups of women workers because women workers were generally employed on temporary contracts and not included in the provisions of the code. Thus the authors criticise the way in which codes of conduct are designed around norms relating to employment that are biased towards the male experience of full-time, permanent employment (Barrientos *et al.* 1999: 22).

Possibilities and opportunities for labour activism, resistance and change

As noted above, national trade union bodies are represented within the tripartite structure of the ILO. But labour unions play a role in the global governance of labour in other ways too. One example would be the role of international trade union federations such as the ICFTU which later became the International Trade Union Congress (ITUC) in 2006 when it merged with the World Confederation of Labour. Croucher and Cotton (2009) highlight the significance of the emergence of the ITUC as the largest union umbrella movement in the world suggesting that '[t]he international [union] movement is now closer to being worthy of the global description than ever before' (p. 36). International unions (which include both the ITUC and global union federations such as the International Transport Workers Federation or the International Federation of Building and Wood Workers) matter, argue Croucher and Cotton, because, given the globalization of production, they offer one of the only ways to bring about coordinated action by workers and introduce workers' voices into multinational corporations. The history of international trade union organisations is overviewed in the work of Myconos (2005), who charts the way in which these international federations have consistently struggled in reconciling the often deeply nationalist sympathies of national trade unions with a broader commitment to labour internationalism and solidarity. Myconos, while optimistic about the potential for labour internationalism, points to the real challenges that these movements confront in a global economy in which workers located in different states of the world are conventionally conceptualised as in competition with one another. Hyman (2011) argues that internationalist forms of trade unionism are of declining importance, with international trade union bodies becoming the distant and technocratic realm of the 'professional labour diplomat' (p. 27). It is a concern that is partially addressed by Croucher and Cotton's point that international trade unions ought to play an 'educative' role – seeking to maintain the relevance and legitimacy of unions as the voice of labour rather than focusing exclusively on issues such as collective bargaining, an issue that privileges the experiences of formal sector workers over those employed in more informal, flexibilized (and indeed, feminized) forms of work (Croucher and Cotton 2009).

Many scholars remain committed to the view that transnational forms of solidarity in the labour movement remain one of the few avenues open to labour in an era of neoliberal globalization. One issue therefore is to think about what new forms labour internationalism might take – for example, we could point to the rise of social movement unionism as trade unions seek to embrace social issues that fall outside of traditional understandings of trade union roles and necessitate international organizing and the formation of networks across and beyond the labour movement (see for example the studies presented in Bieler and Lindberg 2011b). Furthermore, might these newer forms of unionism provide forms of labour solidarity that are more accommodating to female workers employed in non-traditional occupations? Examples of this include the networks of alliances between activist groups and unions on issues such as domestic and migrant worker rights (see below), or new forms of internationally linked trade unions engaged in mobilising sex workers which, given the informality of working arrangements in this sector, operate more like advocacy networks (see Gall 2006).

Although scholars such as Waterman (2001) see more potential for labour activism in forms of social movement unionism than through engagement with organisations such as the ILO or international trade union federations, it is notable that the work of the ILO remains very important in terms of how activists and unionists approach the struggle for the rights of marginalized and oppressed groups of workers. Campaigns for new ILO conventions, for example, often stem from a coming together of networks of activist groups at the transnational level in order to campaign for the rights of the groups that they represent. One of the earliest examples of such a struggle concerns the rights of indigenous peoples. Interestingly, ILO was at the forefront of the development of instruments to protect the rights of indigenous workers. This work grew out of a concern that indigenous or 'native' populations were frequently amongst the most exploited and discriminated against groups of workers. In the early 1920s it undertook studies on the situation of indigenous populations, establishing the Committee of Experts on Native Labour in 1926 – work that fed into Convention 29 on Forced Labour (1930), the Recruiting of Indigenous Workers Convention (number 50) of 1936 and, later, the Indigenous and Tribal Peoples Convention (number 107) of 1957. And yet, although the ILO has this long history of involvement in issues pertaining to indigenous peoples, the adoption of ILO Convention 169 (the Tribal Peoples Convention) in 1989 was a direct response to the rise of an organized and politically significant indigenous peoples movement. Activism by and on behalf of indigenous peoples started to take a specifically transnational form in the second half of the twentieth century. The 1989 convention is the only international legal instrument to refer to indigenous rights. It is framed around ideas that indigenous populations have a right to preserve and protect their cultural traditions and practices and that they should have a say in development projects that affect them. Thus it has been designed to overturn the 'assimilationist' assumptions that were made in the 1957 Indigenous and Tribal Peoples Convention whereby indigenous peoples would simply become extinct as they were absorbed into dominant (and, by assumption, more 'modern' and less 'backward') cultures.

We can observe similar activist coalitions utilizing campaigns for new ILO conventions in the areas of home work (see Prügl 1999 on the campaign for a home workers convention) and domestic worker employment. These are, as was noted above, deeply feminized areas of work. The Domestic Worker Convention (number 189) was adopted at the 100th conference of the ILO in June 2011. Described by Prügl (2011) as 'a significant victory for an international coalition of domestic worker organizations who have lobbied for ILO action' (p. 428), the convention covers issues such as freedom of association for domestic workers, national minimum wage arrangements, standard hours of work, overtime compensation, decent working conditions and a safe working environment, social security and maternity protection. Activism around the rights of domestic workers has grown significantly since the 1990s, in part reflecting the expansion in paid domestic work, much of which is performed by migrant workforces in highly exploitative working conditions, in both the developed and developing world. It is recognized by both activists and academics that the ILO convention is a set of minimum standards for the protection of domestic workers and that many states will be unwilling to ratify it. Nonetheless, considerable hopes are placed on the ability of activists both to push for the ratification of the convention within states and to utilize the convention to push for further reforms once ratified. It is anticipated that such activities will serve to consolidate pro-domestic worker activism and raise awareness of the issues faced by domestic worker in society more generally (Hobden 2011). It is notable, for example, that the ITUC currently has in place a high-profile campaign to encourage states to ratify the Domestic Worker convention. Although this chapter has raised concerns about the ILO's approach to labour governance (especially in relation to the CLS), it is important to point out that the work of the ILO does embody commitments to worker rights and dignity – something that, as the discussion in Box 6.2 at the end of this chapter indicates, is frequently missing in state-centric approaches to governing the 'market' for migrant domestic work. Furthermore, as one activist pointed out, the very act of being involved in the discussions and debates over the convention can play a role in reshaping understandings of what constitutes 'work' within both the ILO and the economy more generally:

> I think that this is very much a historic time for domestic workers all over the globe, and it is long overdue that attention is given to domestic workers. I feel proud as a domestic worker, and I also believe in our union, that we, as workers and as the most oppressed workforce in all countries, have the opportunity to sit with the big bosses and the technical people of the ILO so that we can be declared a 'workforce'.
> (Hester Stephens, cited in Schwenken and Pabon 2011: 445–6)

The activities of the ILO in the global governance of labour, in certain respects, are broadly supportive of a view of globalization in which corporate interests and the interests of the most powerful states predominate (as the discussion of the CLS presented in this chapter indicates). Nonetheless, the ILO also acts as one of the few global forums for advocacy by and on behalf of some of the most marginalized groups of workers in the world. In this regard, I would stress in particular the ILO's work in the area of Decent Work and the possibilities for the emergence of new conventions such as the domestic worker convention under this decent work agenda. The portrayal of the global governance of labour provided in this chapter is certainly partial in its scope (for example, I have not considered those global labour regimes that pertain to forced and trafficked labour). But, by focusing on the issues facing female factory workers, home workers and domestic workers and the extent to which the international labour regime is or isn't able to meet the needs of these groups, the chapter reveals the thoroughly gendered and complex power relations that are at work in the governance of global labour issues.

Box 6.2 Indonesian domestic workers in Malaysia: the Memorandum of Understanding (MoU) as a bilateral form of labour governance

In the Southeast Asian state of Malaysia, the ready availability of low-cost female workers from neighbouring Indonesia combined with the increased presence of women in the workplace has led to a situation in which domestic workers are ubiquitous in middle-class households. And yet, the Malaysian state's non-recognition of domestic workers as 'workers' within both state legislation and public discourse underscores how domestic work remains an 'unconscious' or invisible component of the economic system. Migrant domestic workers in Malaysia constitute a key group of vulnerable and unprotected workers invisibly providing the 'flexible' low-wage work so central to the Malaysian state's pursuit of economic competitiveness and the growth of a prosperous middle-class society. A dominant construction of domestic workers as 'members of the family' has engendered an attitude that it is impossible to legislate for things like hours of work or enforce labour law within the domestic setting. The problems facing migrant domestic workers in Malaysia have been well documented (Chin 1998; Elias 2008; Human Rights Watch 2004). Domestic workers are employed directly by households, with their work permit tied to their employer and their freedom of movement curtailed by practices of employers holding onto their passport and repressive state action against undocumented migrants (including runaway domestic workers). They are subject to high levels of control and surveillance by employers, are not granted rest days and frequently experience difficulties such as the non- and under-payment of wages or are expected to perform additional household labour for friends/neighbours or to work in their employers' businesses (see Chin 1998).

Many Indonesian migrants employed in Malaysia are what we would term 'undocumented' workers (the term illegal migrant is purposefully avoided here because of the way in which this term is used to criminalize migrant workers). However, the market for migrant domestic work in Malaysia represents an example of a formalized system of return-migration whereby workers (usually women) are granted employment for a fixed period of time in Malaysia and are not permitted to bring family members with them. Such systems of return migration ensure that migrant workforces remain marginalized, controlled and locked into extremely low paid forms of work. The migration of domestic workers to Malaysia generally constitutes a 'regularized' form of migration organized through state-sanctioned brokerage agencies with workers taking up live-in positions in households. Systems of return migration are governed under the terms of a bilateral agreement made between host and sender countries known as a Memorandum of Understanding (MoU).

MoUs have been subjected to severe criticism from labour activists who regard them as instruments designed to protect the interests of (capitalist) states rather than the rights of workers. Thus MoUs tend to focus on which brokerage agencies are to be involved in the transportation of workers from one state to another, how wages and conditions are to be set and who should bear the costs of transporting and training workers. The example of MoUs provided here thus provides an example of an alternative, more state-centric, and indeed less worker-centred form of global labour governance to the more multilateral approach embodied by the ILO that was the main focus of this chapter.

Recent negotiations between Malaysia and Indonesia over a new MoU led to a major diplomatic dispute between these two states. In 2009, responding to domestic outrage over the treatment of Indonesian migrant domestic workers, the Indonesian government placed an embargo on its citizens taking up employment as domestic workers in Malaysia (a similar embargo was subsequently imposed on Saudi Arabia following the execution of an Indonesian domestic worker in 2011). In May 2011 the MoU was finally agreed and signed by the respective labour ministers in both states, although as yet few workers have actually arrived in Malaysia under the revised MoU. The revised MoU sought to ensure that workers could hold onto their passports, were entitled to a day off per week, and placed limitations on the extent to which employers could deduct recruitment fees from their employees pay. The problem is that MoUs are not actually binding on either state party. The 2011 MoU between Indonesia and Malaysia failed to specify a minimum wage, allowed employers to pay an unspecified amount of overtime in lieu of a day off and failed to specify exactly what kind of accommodation and rest was considered adequate for domestic workers. These shortcomings reflect the fact that the Indonesian government's bargaining position is rather weak, with certain provinces of Indonesia highly dependent on the remittances that workers send home. Although many within the Indonesian government and parliament have pressed the case for Indonesia taking a much stronger role in protecting the rights of its citizens overseas, and has even declared a policy of ending labour migration into low wage sectors by 2017, these sentiments and policies are significantly constrained by economic realities.

Activist groups in Indonesia have sought to pressure the government to ratify the ILO Domestic Worker convention – an approach that embodies a more multilateral approach to the rights of domestic workers than the MoU bilateral agreements. For example, the ILO convention makes very clear stipulations regarding how workers are paid, their right to be paid in line with national minimum wage policies (where such policies exist) and their entitlements to a day off per week.

Whilst this pressure on the Indonesian government may well produce positive results, it is unlikely that Malaysia would seek to ratify this convention considering the country's high dependence on low wage migrant domestic work and its poor human rights record. MoUs are often the only sets of regulatory arrangements that are in place for governing the employment and migration of domestic workers – these workers often do not have access to domestic labour legislation in host states because they are not recognized as workers and multilateral frameworks to protect their rights are very much in their infancy or have garnered insufficient support from states around the world. For example, alongside the ILO Convention on Domestic Work exists the UN Convention on the Rights of Migrant Workers and their Families, overseen by the UN Committee on Migrant Workers, which was signed in 1990 and entered into force in 2003 when the threshold of 20 ratifying states had been reached. It currently has around 40 signatory states most of which are net migration sender countries.

Recommended reading

Bieler, A. and Lindberg, I. (eds) (2011). *Global Restructuring, Labour and the Challenges for Transnational Solidarity*, Abingdon: Routledge.

Hughes, S. and Haworth, N. (2010). *The International Labour Organization: Coming in from the Cold*, Abingdon: Routledge.

Pearson, R. and Seyfang, G. (2002). '"I'll Tell You What I Want...": Women Workers and Codes of Conduct', in R. Jenkins, R. Pearson and G. Seyfang (eds), *Corporate Responsibility and Labour Rights: Codes of Conduct in the Global Economy*, London: Earthscan, pp. 43–60.

Standing, G. (2008). 'The ILO: An Agency for Globalisation?' *Development and Change*, 39(3): 355–84.

Recommended websites

International Labour Organization: http://ww.ilo.org
Core Labour Standards: http://www.ilo.org/global/standards/lang--en/index.htm
International Trade Union Confederation: http://www.ituc-csi.org

7 Governing communications

Thomas Richard Davies

Cross-border communications and global governance are mutually dependent: neither one would be possible without the other. For this reason, communications have been central to global governance since its earliest origins. As this chapter will show, the global governance of communications is unusual not only in terms of its extensive history, but also in terms of the range of issues and the variety of actors involved. Non-governmental actors, in particular, are especially central to the global governance of communications. After introducing the broad range of issues, actors and mechanisms involved in the global governance of communications, this chapter will explore the problems that arise using the case study of the Internet, which has transformed both transnational communications and global governance in the past two decades.

What is being governed and why?

'Communications' may be understood to encompass a vast range of methods by which people connect with one another. Their historical development includes such landmarks as the Phoenician alphabet, Sumerian cuneiform writing, Egyptian ships, Greek libraries and homing pigeons, Roman roads, and the invention of postal services, paper and moveable type in China, amongst many other innovations long predating the modern era. It is in the period since the French and industrial revolutions, however, that the global governance of communications has developed its contemporary characteristics.

Cross-border communications have become considerably more diverse on account of the multiple technological innovations of the past two centuries. The world's oldest intergovernmental organization – the Central Commission for the Navigation of the Rhine (CCR) – was established in 1815 to facilitate communication by river transportation, and since that point arrangements have been made for the international governance of transportation by sea, railway, road and air, growing as technological innovations have facilitated an expanding number of means of transportation. Since the invention of the electrical telegraph in the 1830s, electronic communications – expanding in scope from electrical telegraphy to the telephone, radio, television, satellite communication, and most recently the Internet – have necessitated increasingly complex structures of international governance.

The origins of the global governance of communications in its contemporary form can be traced at least to the French revolution. It was in this context that the first optical telegraph was developed, and that standard units of measurement such as the meter and kilogram were adopted. The notion that means of communication required cross-border co-operation was implicit in a French Executive Council Decree dating to 16 November 1792, which stated: 'The flow of rivers is a common asset, not given to transfer or sale, of all states whose waters feed them' (Cioc 2002: 40). Twelve years later, an international organization for centralizing tolls on the Rhine was established by the French Empire. Following the defeat of Napoleon, amongst the earliest agreements of the Vienna peace settlement of 1815 were the 'regulations concerning the free navigation of rivers', by which was set up the CCR as 'an authority with the power to serve as a means of communication between the river-bordering states, in respect of everything concerning navigation' (CCR 1815).

Between the establishment of the Rhine Commission and the expansion of its mandate in 1868, technological developments such as the electrical telegraph and the steamship facilitated a growing sense of global consciousness. As early as 1827, Swiss economist Jean Charles Léonard de Sismondi argued that:

> Since all communications have become so easy among men; since the dangers, distances, and difficulties of travel have almost disappeared; since trade is speedily connecting all climates, all industries and all the world's products; since the written thought circulates with ever greater speed, since books spread to all parts of the world, and since all in return send us their journals, our interest focuses on the entire human race ... for each generation the horizon of man has been extended, comprising successively his province, his country, his neighbours, Europe, and today the world.
>
> (Sismondi 1827: 17)

Eighteen years later the Welsh pioneer socialist Robert Owen argued that:

> The world itself is in the highway to be governed by the principle of union, through federation, annexation, joint stock companies, or corporations; by uniting interests and powers which, wisely combined, can effect much more conjointly than can be accomplished by isolated individual efforts.
>
> (Owen 1845: 1)

A key role in the development of such cross-border co-operation was to be played by the numerous new international NGOs that were established in the mid-nineteenth century (Davies 2013: chapter 1). Several of these – such as the Universal Office of Navigation and Commerce and the International Association for Obtaining a Uniform Decimal System of Measures, Weights and Coins – were to pioneer international organization for the promotion of international communications.

The multiplication of intergovernmental organizations for this purpose followed from 1865 onwards. Some, such as the International Commission of the Cape Spartel Light set up that year, extended the precedent set by the Rhine Commission in respect of fluvial navigation to the sea. Others were set up to facilitate international electronic telecommunication following the invention of the electrical telegraph. The intergovernmental organization that is now the principal United Nations specialized agency concerned with information and communications technology – the International Telecommunication Union (ITU) – was established in 1865 as the International Telegraph Union. The previous system of numerous bilateral agreements for the interconnection of national telegraph systems had become unmanageable, so an international organization to standardize such links was perceived as necessary (ITU 2010). Even though postal communication systems were of much earlier origin than the electrical telegraph, it was only following the precedent set by the ITU that a Universal Postal Union (UPU, also now a UN specialized agency) along similar lines was set up in 1874.

As the range of forms of communication expanded, so too did the number of international organizations set up to facilitate them, including the Central Office for International Carriage by Rail in 1893, the International Radiotelegraph Union in 1906, the World Road Association in 1909, and the International Civil Aviation Organization in 1944. The facilitation of communication was also central to the creation of international agreements and organizations for the standardization of units of measurement, such as the 1875 Metre Convention which set up the International Bureau of Weights and Measures; the 1881 International Conference of Electricians which agreed upon the ampere, ohm and volt; the 1884 International Meridian Conference which established the Greenwich Meridian as the Prime Meridian; and the creation in 1906 of the International Electrotechnical Commission for electronic standards, and in 1926 of the International Federation of National Standardizing Associations (succeeded in 1947 by the International Organization for Standardization) for standards in other areas.

From the mid-nineteenth until the early twentieth century, there also developed a significant movement for the global agreement on the most fundamental means of communication: language. Schemes for international auxiliary languages proliferated from the 1860s onwards, with two of the most popular being Volapük (invented in 1879 by German priest Johann Martin Schleyer) and Esperanto (invented in 1887 by Lejzer Ludwik Zamenhof). Both attracted large international followings before the First World War, but declined in popularity following the conflict (Eco 1995). Over the course of the twentieth century, English became the de facto lingua franca, although Esperanto and Volapük among other constructed languages remain spoken among a small minority today. Of more enduring significance was the movement which developed at the same time for the global governance of copyright. The International Literary and Artistic Association set up in 1878 by eminent literary figures including Victor Hugo was dedicated to promotion of an international convention protecting copyright around the world of literary and artistic works, and succeeded in persuading governments to agree to such a convention in Bern in 1886. The World Intellectual Property Organization (WIPO), a United Nations specialized agency set up in 1970, is the successor to the international organization for the protection of copyright established by this convention.

It is evident from the foregoing discussion that the variety of aspects of international communications is considerable, and that international co-operation for their facilitation has an extensive history. As the means of communication diversified, existing bodies often provided the framework for their management. Following the development of the telephone, for instance, an International Telephone Consultative Committee was established under the auspices of the ITU; following the development of satellite communication, the ITU took on responsibility for allocation of radio frequencies for this purpose; and more recently the ITU has been important in facilitating the infrastructure of Internet communication (ITU 2010; Lyall 2011).

The development of the Internet has brought with it some of the most complex arrangements of any issue area of global governance, with the ITU being just one actor among many involved, as the next section will highlight. The complexity of governance arrangements reflects the ambiguity of what constitutes the Internet: as one of the key NGOs involved in the global governance of the Internet, the Internet Society, has argued 'defining the Internet isn't easy. Because unlike any other technology, the Internet can be whatever we make it' (ISOC 2012). Lawrence Solum defines the Internet as 'a global network of networks, with communication between networks enabled by a communications Protocol Suite, currently TCP/IP' (Solum 2009: 48). The Internet does not consist merely of the World Wide Web, but also e-mail, file sharing, instant messaging, social networking, virtual private networking, and many other activities facilitated by the Internet Protocol Suite, including criminal activities associated with the 'dark Internet'. While the Internet may be far more complex than any older means of communication, the core rationales for the mechanisms of global governance of this as of other means of communication may still be divided into two core aspects: (i) to set standards that make communications possible; and (ii) to ensure that the benefits of communications are maximized and the harm produced minimized. As was noted in the Tunis Agenda for the Information Society of 2005, Internet governance 'includes more than Internet naming and addressing' and involves 'many cross-cutting international public policy issues' such as facilitating access to and 'equitable distribution of resources', combating cybercrime and spam, and ensuring that the governance processes are democratic and legitimate (WSIS 2005).

Who are the key actors involved?

The range of actors involved in the global governance of communications extends far beyond the specialized agencies of the United Nations system which constitute the primary focus in many other issue areas. Nevertheless, the United Nations system remains important, especially with respect to older forms of communication. Many of the principal United Nations organs concerned with communications predate the United Nations and were only later placed within the United Nations framework, such as the UPU in 1948 and the ITU in 1949. The UPU is a traditional intergovernmental organization, its membership consisting of states and its activities limited in scope to the facilitation of the sending of mail between the jurisdictions of the postal services of its member countries

(UPU 2010). The ITU, on the other hand, has a much broader membership and mandate. It describes itself as 'an organization based on public–private partnership since its inception, [with] a membership of 193 countries and over 700 private-sector entities and academic institutions' (ITU 2011a). The ITU's constitution lists no less than eighteen objectives for the organization, varying from the technical such as 'allocation of bands of the radio-frequency spectrum' and 'the worldwide standardization of telecommunications', to social objectives such as 'to promote the extension of the benefits of the new telecommunication technologies to all the world's inhabitants' and 'facilitating peaceful relations' (ITU 2011b: 3–6). It has therefore not only provided the standards that prevent radio interference and enable satellite and international telephone communications, but also has development programmes aimed at bridging the 'digital divide', and facilitates discussion forums such as the World Summit on the Information Society (ITU 2012; Lyall 2011).

Further intergovernmental organizations concerned with communications within the UN system include the International Civil Aviation Organization, the International Maritime Organization, the World Intellectual Property Organization and the World Tourism Organization. Several intergovernmental organizations concerned with communications remain outside the UN system, including the oldest – the Rhine Navigation Commission – and the Intergovernmental Organization for International Carriage by Rail, the International Bureau of Weights and Measures, and the World Road Association.

States influence the global governance of communications not only through participation in intergovernmental organizations. Some states have also done so through the setting of standards that other states have adopted. In the nineteenth century, for instance, the rules of the British Board of Trade concerning navigation at sea and its code of signals were adopted around the world. More recently, the system by which domain names and IP addresses are allocated globally was developed by agencies of the United States government. In 1998, this function was transferred by the US government to an international 'non-profit public benefit corporation' it set up for the purpose: the Internet Corporation for Assigned Names and Numbers (ICANN), which to the present day is responsible for overseeing the allocation of domain names and IP addresses worldwide (NTIA 1998). This organization has an exceptionally complex multi-stakeholder structure, aiming to represent not only governments (in a Government Advisory Committee), but also individual Internet users (the 'At Large Community'), alongside bodies such as the Generic Names Supporting Organization which includes both commercial and non-commercial constituencies (ICANN 2011).

ICANN is just one among many actors involved in the numerous different aspects of Internet governance, many of which are non-governmental. Amongst the most important is the Internet Society, which oversees technical standards-setting bodies including the Internet Architecture Board (IAB), the Internet Engineering Task Force (IETF) and the Internet Research Task Force (IRTF), whose memberships consist of volunteer specialists concerned with today's Internet protocols and the longer-term development of Internet standards respectively. While the

IETF is responsible for the Internet Protocol Suite, another organization, the World Wide Web Consortium (W3C), develops the standards for the World Wide Web, such as HyperText Markup Language (HTML) and Cascading Style Sheets (CSS). Like ICANN, W3C is a multi-stakeholder organization: it comprises 372 for-profit, governmental and non-profit organizations, ranging from Apple and CERN to Yahoo! and Zhejiang University (W3C 2012). While the fact that many aspects of the Internet have their roots in US government agencies is well-known, Peter Willetts has argued that 'NGOs were pioneers in creating the Internet', on account of their role in developing Internet service provision to the general public, a function subsequently dominated by profit-making corporations such as AOL (Willetts 2011: 111).

Analyses of Internet governance should not be limited to discussion of technical bodies such as ICANN, IETF and W3C whose standards make the Internet possible. As was noted in the previous section, Internet governance involves far more than this. A vitally important feature to note is that much of the Internet represents a comparatively ungoverned space, exploited by hackers and criminal organizations involved in activities such as piracy, pornography and fraud. On the other hand, the Internet has also been used by activists to challenge authoritarian regimes such as in the Arab uprisings of 2011, and the Internet can be a vitally important tool in facilitating international development. The vast range of issue-areas addressed by the Dynamic Coalitions of the Internet Governance Forum is indicative of the huge variety of international public policy issues associated with the development of the Internet. Currently, these include climate change, accessibility and disability, child online safety, gender, freedom of expression and freedom of the media, linguistic diversity, Internet rights and principles, open standards, core Internet values, youth, global localization, social media and legal issues, and public access in libraries; and in the past also included were issues such as rural access, privacy and spam (IGF 2012a).

It is on account of this vast range of public policy issues linked to the development of the Internet that the Internet Governance Forum (IGF) was founded in 2006 on the recommendation of the World Summit on the Information Society convened by the United Nations. Like ICANN and W3C, IGF is a multi-stakeholder organization, its meetings arranged by an Advisory Group comprising members from governmental, non-governmental, commercial, academic and technical sectors (IGF 2012b). A significant contrast, however, as Markus Kummer has noted, is that IGF 'has no decision-making authority', and aims to exercise influence by 'preparing the ground for negotiations and decision making in other institutions ...while the IGF has no power of redistribution, it has the power of recognition – the power to identify key issues' (Kummer 2011, vii). The Tunis Agenda of the World Summit on the Information Society by which IGF was established contains the most commonly accepted definition of Internet governance: 'the development and application by governments, the private sector and civil society, in their respective roles, of shared principles, norms, rules, decision-making procedures, and programmes that shape the evolution and use of the Internet' (WSIS 2005).

The transformative social, economic and political impacts of the Internet have ensured that many international bodies concerned with public policy issues have made special arrangements to deal with the impact of the Internet. The public policy issue of cybercrime, for instance, has been dealt with by the establishment by the Group of Eight of a Subgroup on High-tech Crime in 1997 and four years later by the Council of Europe in the form of a Cybercrime Convention. In the non-governmental sphere, public policy issues associated with the development of the Internet have resulted in the creation of multiple grassroots initiatives to handle them, such as WiredSafety, which claims to be 'the largest and oldest online safety, education and help group in the world' which began 'in 1995 as a group of volunteers rating websites' (WiredSafety 2012). Corporate actors also collaborate to contribute towards global governance of public policy issues associated with the development of the Internet, such as in the Anti-Phishing Working Group (APWG) – whose sponsors include Hitachi, Facebook and Cisco –which describes itself as a 'global pan-industrial and law enforcement association focused on eliminating the fraud, crime and identity theft that result from phishing, pharming, malware and email spoofing of all types' (APWG 2012).

What are the key mechanisms of governance?

The different mechanisms of global governance of communications vary according to the different actors involved and the novelty of the form of communication. This section will explore the mechanisms of the global governance of communications under three headings. The first is *traditional inter-state governance*, through intergovernmental agreements enforced by an intergovernmental organization: this framework is most commonly associated with the older forms of communication. The second is *multi-stakeholder governance*, involving multiple actors, both governmental and non-governmental, associated with some older forms of communication such as radio, as well as more recent forms such as the Internet. The third, building from Paul Wapner's identification of 'politics beyond the state' in global environmental governance (Wapner 1995), is *global non-state governance* by which non-state actors including non-governmental organizations, activist networks and transnational corporations handle the governance of communications and associated public policy issues independently of governments.

(i) Traditional inter-state governance

The oldest model of governance of communications may be illustrated with the examples of two of the three oldest intergovernmental organizations: the Commission for the Navigation of the Rhine (CCR) and the Universal Postal Union (UPU). In both cases states agreed at an intergovernmental congress upon an international convention, and an intergovernmental organization was established to oversee its implementation. With respect to CCR, the original provisions of the Final Act of the Congress of Vienna for freedom of navigation of the Rhine were refined by the Conventions of Mainz and Mannheim in 1831 and 1868 respectively, while the UPU (initially the 'General' Postal Union) was established to oversee the provisions of the 1878 Treaty of Bern by which member countries established a single postal territory (UPU 2010: ix). In both cases, these organizations' mandates, although expanded over time, have remained comparatively narrowly delimited. The territorial nature of the communications with which these organizations are concerned – river navigation and national postal services – lend themselves to exclusive control by sovereign territorial states.

The same cannot be said for Internet communications. Nevertheless, traditional inter-state governance remains relevant here too, especially with respect to those aspects most associated with the properties of the state, such as combating cybercrime. The first international convention on cybercrime was that of the Council of Europe, and deals with public policy issues traditionally governed by states which have been affected by the development of information and communications technology, such as child pornography, copyright and fraud, as well as network security violations (Kierkegaard 2008: 469). It has been credited with being 'an important tool in the global fight against those who seek to disrupt computer networks, misuse private or sensitive information, or commit traditional crimes utilizing Internet-enabled technologies', but has also been criticized for being 'fundamentally imbalanced' by giving 'law enforcement agencies powers of computer search and seizure and government surveillance, but no correspondingly procedural safeguards to protect privacy and limit government use of such powers' (Kierkegaard 2008: 474).

(ii) Multi-stakeholder governance

In the post-Cold War era, the multi-stakeholder governance model is superseding the traditional inter-state model. Governments can be important in the multi-stakeholder model, but there is a spectrum of approaches varying according to the centrality of the state's role. At one end of the spectrum are frameworks which place the state as the principal actor, dealing with those aspects of communications that require co-ordination of territorial infrastructure. The ITU is the prime example of this state-centric form of multi-stakeholder governance. It consists primarily of member states with one vote each in the principal decision-making organs such as the Plenipotentiary Conference. Non-state actors, on the other hand, are limited in their participation to specialist activities such as world radiocommunications conferences, the radio regulations board and the world telecommunication standardization assemblies (ITU 2011b).

At the opposite end of the spectrum are many of the multi-stakeholder initiatives responsible for global governance of the least territorial aspects of the Internet, such as the mark-up languages of the World Wide Web handled by W3C. Governmental participation in W3C is restricted to member organizations under their control, such as the Australian Bureau of Statistics and the National Aeronautics and Space Administration – organizations which are greatly outnumbered by private sector members, both profit-making and non-profit. W3C decision-making is centred around a bottom-up process by which members introduce proposals which need to secure consensus among the membership before publication as official 'W3C Recommendations' (W3C 2005). These recommendations – as their name suggests – lack enforcement provisions, but although it has been noted that Microsoft's 'dominant position [in the web browser market] has allowed it to accept or reject new specifications without having to consider the competition' (Alvestrand and Lie 2009: 145), the standards set by W3C with respect to languages such as HTML and CSS have often secured much wider implementation than many intergovernmental agreements considered to have the status of 'international law'.

(iii) Global non-state governance

Given the indirect nature of the role of governments in some multi-stakeholder bodies such as W3C, the activities of such organizations may be considered to constitute one aspect among the many dimensions of non-state governance of communications. The function of the IETF is not dissimilar from that of W3C, except that its standards relate to another aspect of the Internet (the Internet Protocol Suite), but its decision-making process is even more informal: as Alvestrand and Lie (2009: 138) have noted, it has 'no formal membership, no voting rules, and no explicit representation from companies, governments or organizations'. IETF's mission statement makes it explicit that 'any interested person can participate in the work' of the IETF, and that its standards are set 'based on the combined engineering judgement of our participants and our real-world experience in implementing and deploying our specifications' (IETF 2004). As with W3C, IETF standards are enforced 'not by formal requirements or policing', but instead 'by social networks and by the marketplace' (Alvestrand and Lie 2009: 138).

Beyond IETF standards setting, non-state governance of communications can be seen in the very different work of organizations such as WiredSafety and the Anti-Phishing Working Group. Like IETF, WiredSafety consists of volunteers. These volunteers, divided into groups such as CyberMoms, Teenangels, WiredCops and WiredKids, 'regularly "patrol" the Internet for child pornography, child molesters, and cyber stalkers', as well as 'helping cybercrime victims, … providing information about privacy and security online', training 'police officers on investigative techniques' and rating websites for child-friendliness (Kshetri 2010: 20). The APWG has a different composition to WiredSafety – consisting predominantly of corporate institutions – but a similar method of operation: monitoring and reporting, in this case of phishing websites, as well as information provision on phishing.

It should be noted that global non-state governance of communications is not exclusive to the Internet. In the field of air transportation, for instance, one of the most influential standards setters is the International Air Transport Association (IATA), which accepts only airlines as formal members (IATA 2012). IATA's three-letter airport codes are much better-known than the four-letter codes of the intergovernmental ICAO, and as Karsten Ronit and Volker Schneider (2000: 19) have noted, it 'has continually updated the IATA Dangerous Goods Regulation and established stricter standards than its intergovernmental parallel organization', the ICAO.

Discussions of non-state governance would be incomplete without consideration of the role of Internet activism. The Internet has greatly expanded the repertoire of activist methods. In many cases, rather than politics *beyond* the state, Internet activism has involved politics *against* the state. By far the most notable example of this in recent years has been the use in the Arab uprisings of 2011 of social media networks to facilitate mobilizations against the *ancien régimes*. Different social media perform different functions in such protest movements: YouTube, for instance, has been critical in information dissemination to mobilize people to *take part* in protests; while Twitter has been critical *during* protests, enabling activists to share information on their own and their opponents' movements. Among the transformative aspects of Internet communication for activists in the 2011 uprisings was the greater *speed* and *geographical reach* of communication that was facilitated in comparison with earlier forms of communication. Another transformative aspect of Internet communication for activists has been the *volume* of data that can be communicated: the 'secret US embassy cables' released by WikiLeaks, for instance, are said to comprise no less than 261 million words (WikiLeaks 2011).

With respect to politics beyond the state, the Internet has expanded the repertoire of activist methods for targeting non-state as well as state opponents. Many of these include 'hacktivist' methods, such as 'web site defacements, web site redirects, denial-of-service attacks, information theft, site parodies, virtual sit-ins, [and] virtual sabotage' (Samuel 2004: 6). Less aggressive methods have been arguably more effective in bringing about change: as early as 1990 consumer activists effectively used online message boards to mobilize 30,000 people to request that they be removed from Lotus Development Corporation's planned database, *MarketPlace: Households*, which resulted in the corporation never launching the product (Gurak and Logie 2003: 26–8). It should be noted that the use of the Internet by some activists may have counterproductive impacts on other activists: the release of US embassy cables by WikiLeaks, for instance, may have led to the identification of several human rights workers in authoritarian regimes (Beckett and Ball 2012: 160).

What are the problems and issues that arise?

Given their diversity, different aspects of the global governance of communications have attracted varying critiques. This section will explore a selection of those that have been raised in relation to global governance of the Internet, divided into two broad categories: (i) power relations, especially the preponderance of the United States government in aspects of Internet governance and the ability of authoritarian regimes to control Internet communications; and (ii) efficacy, especially with respect to wider public policy issues influenced by the development of the Internet such as cybercrime.

(i) Power relations

Despite the multi-stakeholder and non-governmental nature of many of the key institutions involved in Internet governance, one of the most common concerns to be raised is the extent to which the United States government is perceived to maintain a hegemonic position in aspects of Internet governance, even after having apparently transferred many of its previous functions to organizations such as ICANN, which has come under particular scrutiny. Mueller *et al.* (2007: 239) have argued that 'in the ICANN regime, the United States ... government privatized and internationalized key policymaking functions but retained considerable authority for itself, acting as contractor to ICANN and also asserting "policy authority" over the domain name system's root'. Mueller (2010: 62–3) has indicated three instruments of US oversight of ICANN: the first instrument is control over the contract between ICANN and the Internet Assigned Numbers Authority (IANA): 'Without this contract, ICANN would have little, if any, hierarchical authority over the co-ordination of the Internet's identifier systems'; the second is the Joint Project Agreement, which provides 'a list of policy-making tasks that ICANN is supposed to perform ... [which] clearly reflected the interests of the U.S. government'; and the third is the contract with VeriSign which 'requires Verisign to implement all the technical coordination decisions made via the ICANN process and to follow U.S. instructions regarding the root zone file'.

This privileged position of the United States, as well as concern with respect to the privileged role of non-state actors over governmental actors in many of the instruments of Internet governance, has led to calls from other states for new arrangements. In 2011, for instance, Vladimir Putin is reported to have been interested in the possibility of 'establishing international control over the Internet using the monitoring and supervisory capabilities of the International Telecommunication Union'. Given opposition of the United States to such proposals, and the position of the ITU that 'whatever one single country does not accept will not pass', such proposals have limited prospects in the immediate future (BBC 2012).

Calls for greater intergovernmental supervision of the Internet may reflect not only concern about the preponderance of the US government, but may be one strategy by which authoritarian regimes are seeking to limit the functioning of communications technology that has the potential to be used to challenge them. The failure of the Mubarak regime in Egypt to inhibit protest activity in 2011 by temporarily shutting down Internet communications might appear to support the assertion that the Internet is beyond national control, it having been claimed that the Egyptian government had to restore such communications due to the dependence of Egyptian business upon them (Bruen 2012: 99). However, Bill Clinton's remark in 1998 (quoted in Goldsmith and Wu 2006: 90) that efforts on the part of the Chinese government 'to crack down on the Internet' are 'like trying to nail Jell-O to the wall' has looked far from substantiated in the light of subsequent experience. Jack Goldsmith and Tim Wu (2006: 89, 101) have noted the success of the Chinese government in 'trying to create an Internet that is free enough to support and maintain the world's fastest growing economy, and yet closed enough to tamp down political threats to its monopoly on power', not only through effective barriers to foreign sites, but more significantly through the development within China of 'its own sphere of influence over network norms'. Goldsmith and Wu (2006: 89) conclude that 'the China example shows ... [that] a government's failure to crack down on certain types of Internet communication ultimately reflects a failure of interest or will, not a failure of power'.

(ii) Efficacy

The issue of the efficacy of global governance of the Internet should be separated into the technical aspects such as the Internet Protocol Suite, and the wider public policy aspects, such as cybercrime. The technical aspects of Internet governance include the domain name system overseen by ICANN, the web languages handled by W3C, and the Internet Protocol Suite managed by IETF. Despite being divided amongst numerous organizations with highly unusual decision-making processes, many of the technical aspects of Internet governance are managed remarkably smoothly. As Alvestrand and Lie (2009: 138) remark of the IETF, even though it has neither formal membership nor formal voting rules this 'is a standardization body that works': it 'has worked to build the Internet we have today' and 'there is a good chance it will continue working'.

The same cannot be said for many of the organizations that aim to handle the numerous broader public policy issues which the Internet has influenced. The IGF, in particular, has been criticized for being 'an ineffectual "talking shop" unable to influence significantly the hard issues and choices at stake' (Dutton and Palfrey 2007: 3). In 2010, when considering renewal of the IGF's mandate, the Secretary-General of the United Nations noted that stakeholders believed that 'the IGF, despite its role in promoting dialogue and understanding ... had not provided concrete advice to intergovernmental bodies and other entities involved in Internet governance', and 'that the contribution of the IGF to public policy-making is difficult to assess and appears to be weak' (UN 2010a: 5, 9; Malcolm 2012: 162–3). Responsibility for the IGF's ineffectuality has been attributed to 'early decisions made by its Secretariat and Multistakeholder Advisory Group', which constituted the Forum as 'an atomistic annual conference, without an agenda of specific issues to address, suitable processes for addressing them, or institutional structures to support such an exercise'; efforts to reform the IGF have been inhibited by the opposition of 'those same stakeholders who had originally spoken against the IGF's formation at WSIS (rich countries such as the USA, technical community groups such as ISOC and business groups such as the ICC [International Chamber of Commerce]), and often also by its incumbent Secretariat' (Malcolm 2012: 162).

Many of the wider public policy issues influenced by the development of the Internet are inadequately regulated at the global level. With respect to the issue of cybercrime, for instance, Knake (2010: 17–18) has noted that the Council of Europe's Cybercrime Convention 'has not led to an appreciable reduction in cyber crime', its mechanisms 'are bilateral and prosecutorial, providing no conduits to coordinate law enforcement activity across borders or for network security professionals to coordinate technical solutions when attacks occur', many members 'include some of the worst cyber criminal havens', and 'many countries, most notably Japan, have been unwilling to ratify the Treaty simply because it was constituted under the Council of Europe'. Knake argues that 'a similar organization should be established to do for cyber crime what FATF [the Financial Action Task Force] has done for money laundering'. It has been claimed that 'the drafting of the Convention demonstrated how difficult it can be to gain consensus on cybercrime': provisions relating to hate-speech, for instance, failed to make it into the Convention on account of concerns in respect of free expression among several states including the USA (Brenner 2007: 716). Although it is argued that 'there is no obvious explanation' for the limitations of the Cybercrime Convention, it is claimed that it 'attests to the futility of trying to adapt traditional, nationally based law enforcement to non-territorially based crime' (Brenner 2007: 717).

Conclusion

Communications were crucial in the early development of global governance, and developments in communications such as the Internet are playing a transformative role in the present day. This chapter has discussed a selection of the great diversity of governance frameworks that have evolved with respect to global communications, including pioneering multi-stakeholder and non-state governance processes. However, this chapter has also shown that the limitations of these frameworks are in some cases also considerable, especially with respect to the wider public policy issues that have accompanied the 'information revolution' of the contemporary era.

The limitations of existing arrangements for the governance of communications cannot be ascribed simply to the obstinacy of governments alone. In the case of the Internet Governance Forum, non-governmental and corporate actors share responsibility with governments for the failure to develop the Forum's capacity to influence public policy. In respect of many of the broader public policy issues associated with the development of the Internet such as cybercrime, the lack of progress in international cooperation to handle such issues stems in large part from their multifaceted nature, blending aspects traditionally associated with governmental responsibility such as security, with aspects transcending the boundaries of states' traditional roles. This chapter has discussed some of the varied multi-stakeholder approaches which have developed to date: in order adequately to address the broad range of public policy issues associated with the development of the Internet, it will be necessary to promote further innovation in multi-stakeholder forms of global governance, which should aim adequately to blend the state's capacity to assert authority within territorial limits, and transnational actors' capacity to do so beyond these limits.

The topic of global communications puts into sharp relief some of the key characteristics of global governance more generally, such as the existence of issues that states cannot handle alone and the vital role played by actors other than states. It also shows that even in one of the most transnational of issue areas, power relations among states remain important and must not be neglected. At the core of this issue area, as in the case of many others, is the problem of reconciling the considerable residual capabilities of an actor that emerged when power could be drawn in large part through control over territory, with the requirements of the present day, where territorial boundaries are more often than not an obstacle to the meeting of human needs.

Recommended reading

Bygrave, L. and Bing, J. (eds) (2009). *Internet Governance: Infrastructure and Institutions*, Oxford: Oxford University Press.
Lyall, F. (2011). *International Communications: The International Telecommunication Union and the Universal Postal Union*, Farnham: Ashgate.
Mathiason, J. (2008). *Internet Governance: The New Frontier of Global Institutions*, Abingdon: Routledge.
Mueller, M. (2010). *Networks and States: The Global Politics of Internet Governance*, Cambridge, MA: MIT Press.
Zacher, M. with Sutton, B. (1996). *Governing Global Networks: International Regimes for Transportation and Communications*, Cambridge: Cambridge University Press.

Recommended websites

Anti-Phishing Working Group: http://www.antiphishing.org/
International Telecommunication Union: http://www.itu.int/
Internet Corporation for Assigned Names and Numbers: http://www.icann.org/
Internet Governance Forum: http://www.intgovforum.org/
Internet Society: http://www.Internetsociety.org/
WiredSafety: https://www.wiredsafety.org/
World Wide Web Consortium: http://www.w3.org/

8 Problems and prospects for health in the twenty-first century

Adam Kamradt-Scott

Introduction

Since the turn of the twenty-first century, health has enjoyed wide acceptance as a legitimate foreign policy issue, but this has not always been the case. For many years the notion that health issues should hold comparable status to economic and trade issues, or military and security issues, was derided. While the emergence of HIV/AIDS in the 1980s began to shift opinions, in more recent years several adverse events such as the 2003 SARS outbreak, H5N1 'Bird Flu', and terrorist-related incidents such as the 1995 sarin gas attack on a Tokyo subway and the 2001 anthrax letters in the United States have reinforced the need for a different outlook (McInnes and Lee 2006). As a result, since 2000 the international community has launched a variety of new initiatives and programmes aimed at improving global health. New targets have been set, new agendas have been agreed, and new laws and regulations have been passed. New actors have also emerged to join an already complex and dense array of state and non-state entities; and new resources, worth billions of dollars, have been allocated to tackling (mostly) acute health issues such as infectious disease outbreaks. For a time, the future of global health looked bright indeed. However, in the wake of the 2008 global financial downturn that is challenging political structures and international relations, global health now sits, once again, at a crossroads.

This chapter sets out to examine some of the key challenges confronting global health governance in the twenty-first century by exploring three inter-related questions of 'who', 'how' and 'what' is being governed. Accordingly, the chapter is broadly divided into three parts. The first section explores the reconfiguration of power politics that has occurred within global public health following the rise of new actors such as the BRICS countries (Brazil, Russia, India, China and South Africa) and Global Health Partnerships (GHPs), thereby addressing the question of surveying 'who' is (re)shaping global health. The second section, which engages with the central question of 'how', examines the various processes, mechanisms and forums by which government and non-government based actors govern the global health commons and the extent to which they remain fit-for-purpose. The third section examines the 'what' in terms of existing global health agendas, what continues to be included and excluded, and how recent events such as the 2008 global financial crisis have begun to affect those priorities.

The phrase 'Global Health Governance' (GHG) remains highly debated, eliciting a diverse range of responses from those who seek to define it. This is principally because each of the terms within GHG are themselves contested. The term 'global', for instance, has been used interchangeably at times with terms such as 'transnational', 'transboundary' and 'transborder' (see Betsill and Bulkeley 2004), making conceptual clarity difficult. While confusion over the exact nature of the term continues, when used in the context of governance it is usually taken to mean 'beyond international', or in other words, involving more than only state-based actors (Aginam 2004). At the same time, the difficulty that has emerged with even this conceptualization has been that, as Finkelstein (1995: 368) has noted, '"Global governance" appears to be virtually anything.'

In 1946, delegates attending the conference that established the World Health Organization (WHO) controversially defined health to be 'a state of complete physical, mental and social well-being and not merely the absence of disease or infirmity' (WHO 2005). Although other definitions exist (Awofeso 2005), the WHO definition has enjoyed considerable support throughout the years. Even so, it has still been challenged on numerous fronts with detractors ranging from those that argue on the one hand that the definition is far too expansive and difficult to operationalize, while yet others insist that it remains too narrow or is 'oversimplified' (Larson 1996). Similar confusion has also emerged around the related phrases of 'international health' and 'global health' and what these terms refer to, but here Lee (2003: 191) has attempted to bring some precision by noting:

> Where a national government can assert relative control over crossborder flows that impact on the health of the population within its territorial boundaries, the term international health is more accurate. Where there is an erosion of that control by transborder flows that undermine, or even disregard territorial space, the term global health is more appropriate.

The third term, 'governance', has also suffered from much of the same ambiguity as 'global' and 'health'. What is generally agreed is that governance is not synonymous with *government* (Rosenau and Czempiel 1992; Rhodes 1996; Finkelstein 1995), although as noted in the Introduction to this book, commonly agreed definitions prove elusive. Having said this, conceptual clarity is not always essential for meaningful communication to still occur (Dingwerth and Pattberg 2006). It is in this regard that despite continuing divergences of opinion over the nature, scope and extent of GHG, as a field of research and practice GHG has continued to grow primarily because it is now widely accepted that individual governments – acting in isolation – no longer have the tools or means to adequately protect the health and well-being of their citizens in a highly interconnected, globalized world (Gostin and Mok 2009). As a result, multilateral activity specifically aimed at addressing health issues has expanded considerably, so much so that as Williams and Rushton (2011: 1) observe, 'we have seen both the generation of a whole new institutional architecture (a process which is still ongoing) and the foregrounding of health in international politics as never before.' The corresponding difficulty that accompanied the development of this new architecture, however, has been that the vast array of actors, resources and new rules have emerged in an ad hoc manner, and have often reflected political and economic interests as much as they have represented legitimate health needs (Lee 2010).

The reconfiguration of power within GHG

The field of global public health is no different from any other area of public policy with regard to the balance between individual states and the need for collective action through forms of international organization and global governance. The WHO, for example, arguably still remains the premier intergovernmental health organization despite several challenges to its authority over its more than 60-year history. Established in 1948 as the first specialized agency of the United Nations system, the WHO was charged to serve as the international community's directing and coordinating authority in health. In so doing, it subsumed the activities of a number of predecessor institutions such as the Health Organization of the League of Nations, and merged with other regional health bodies such as the Pan American Health Organization (which subsequently became the WHO regional office for the Americas). While other United Nations agencies such as the United Nations Population Fund (UNFPA) and the United Nations Development Programme (UNDP) have often contributed in significant ways to improving global health outcomes by procuring health supplies or advocating human rights-based approaches, their roles and influence have often been limited (see Harman 2012a for further discussion).

Until the early 1990s the WHO's directing authority in global health effectively remained unopposed. However, the emergence of several new actors – a number of which had not previously been traditionally associated with health – combined with perceived failings of the WHO to respond effectively to emerging health threats, significantly altered the global health governance architecture. For example, the World Bank's decision in 1993 to substantively expand its funding of health initiatives openly challenged the WHO's supremacy in international health – a position which, given the extent of Bank's deployable financial resources, it has largely maintained (McCoy *et al.* 2009). In this new role, the Bank was joined by other financial and/or trade actors such as the International Monetary Fund (IMF) and World Trade Organization (WTO) in initially promoting market-based solutions and privatization of health services, although in more recent years these institutions have been observed to amend many of their former policies to promote more inclusive, holistic sector-wide reforms (Harman 2012). In addition to this, other state-based forums such as the G8 and G20 have pursued a particularly active (and some would argue, more effective) health agenda, setting various goals around the control of infectious diseases, trade and intellectual property issues associated with pharmaceuticals, and access to affordable medicines. Given that these organizations are also comprised of the world's wealthiest states, the G8 in particular has been observed to make substantial contributions to – and even help create – global health partnership organizations (GHPs) like the Global Fund to Fight HIV/AIDS, Tuberculosis and Malaria (GFATBM or 'The Global Fund') (Kirton and Guebert 2009). At the same time, the creation of the United Nations Programme on HIV/AIDS (UNAIDS) in response to the WHO's perceived inaction in addressing the disease, combined with several controversies surrounding the WHO Director-General, Dr Hiroshi Nakajima, served to further undermine the organization's overall standing amongst member states. The appointment of Dr Gro Harlem Brundtland to the position of Director-General in 1998 on a platform of reform of the WHO assisted in reinvigorating the organization's reputation; but it was the 2003 SARS outbreak, and subsequent outbreaks of H5N1 avian influenza and the 2009 H1N1 influenza pandemic that have arguably reaffirmed the importance and relevance of having a robust and independent public health authority (Kamradt-Scott 2011).

Critics have often lamented the role and influence that powerful member states such as the United States and United Kingdom have been able to exert on international organizations such as the WHO, and in setting the global health agenda (for example, see Ingram 2005). Even so, in more recent years a number of emerging economies have begun to openly challenge the former status quo in global health. Significantly, the majority of these actors are from what has been described as the 'global South' and include countries such as Brazil, Russia, India, China and South Africa (more commonly referred to as 'BRICS') as well as countries such as Indonesia, South Korea, Thailand, Argentina and Mexico (Flemes 2009). The effect of these emerging economies – both in terms of forming new South–South coalitions and challenging the dominance of the global North – has been felt in a variety of contexts and issue areas such as access to medicines and intellectual property, biotechnology, medical tourism, and even the provision of medical services and other technical assistance (see Case study 8.1).

For example, the emergence of large generic manufacturing industries in Brazil and India has served to increasingly challenge existing intellectual property and patent protection laws, allowing for greater access to medicines. In the context of the WTO, India and Brazil have forcefully argued for greater use of the public health-related flexibilities under the Trade-Related Intellectual Property Rights (TRIPs) – moves that have been resisted by more powerful actors such as the United States, the European Union and China due to economic interests (Bliss 2010). India has subsequently been described as 'the pharmacy of the developing world' for the impact its industries have had on lowering the cost of life-saving medicines (Oxfam 2012); and yet India's generic pharmaceutical industry has been targeted for tighter regulation under a proposed Free Trade Agreement with the European Union (Kamradt-Scott 2012).

For many, the rise of these new economies and their influence in reshaping global health priorities has been welcomed as a countervailing force against high-income countries of the global North, but as Ruger and Ng (2010: 277) have also observed:

> The growth of emerging countries as major new international players with political and financial clout to influence global and domestic health agendas adds to the global health architecture's pluralism and fragmentation, possibly exacerbating the lack of coordination and the often ad hoc nature of the global health agenda.

> **Case study 8.1 Indonesia, H5N1 and virus sharing**
>
> The Global Influenza Surveillance Network (now Global Influenza Surveillance and Response Network) was established in 1952 under the auspices of the WHO to facilitate international cooperation in the collection and sharing of influenza surveillance information and samples. In 2007 Indonesia announced that it would no longer share information and samples of the highly lethal H5N1 influenza virus with the WHO network due to several alleged breaches of protocol. At the heart of Indonesia's concern was the network's practice of forwarding influenza virus samples and information to pharmaceutical manufacturers to develop influenza vaccines, which they would then patent and attempt to sell back to countries at elevated prices. Indonesia, which remains the country most severely affected by the H5N1 virus, had attempted to purchase vaccines to protect its population but was unable to secure access to the medications due to limited global production capacity and the fact that many wealthy nations had signed contracts with pharmaceutical companies to supply them first. In an attempt to resolve the impasse that developed, the WHO announced the immediate creation of a global stockpile of pandemic vaccines that all low-income countries could access based on demonstrated need. In addition, a series of meetings were held between 2007 and 2011 to develop a new Pandemic Influenza Preparedness Framework (PIPF) to facilitate greater access to influenza vaccines and a more equitable distribution of benefits for low-income countries.

Importantly, however, it is not only the rise of newly emerging economies that has been responsible for reshaping GHG processes and practices. In their work, Buse and Harmer (2004) have traced the rise of public–private partnerships (PPPs) (also described as GHPs) that have now become a well-established feature of contemporary GHG. Although many variations in their structure, purpose and function exist, PPPs can be broadly described as entities that have been jointly created by government and the private sector to provide public infrastructure, facilities and/or services (Schaeffer and Loveridge 2002). GHPs in health first appeared in the early 1980s, but following the appointment of Gro Harlem Brundtland as Director-General of the WHO in 1998, these initiatives have grown significantly in both number and strength (Brown *et al.* 2006). Moreover, despite ongoing questions over the legitimacy, accountability and transparency of these entities, in issue-specific areas PPPs such as the Global Alliance for Vaccines and Immunization (GAVI) have often surpassed the role and influence of traditional health International Organizations (IOs) such as the WHO due to considerable financial resources they wield (see Case study 8.2). In large part, this financial power can be attributed to two key factors: the increase of health-related official development assistance (ODA), and the involvement and participation of the for-profit corporate sector.

As Reich (2000: 617–18) has noted, for example, particularly since the mid-1990s, a number of pharmaceutical companies 'have become involved in a number of high-visibility drug donation programs based on partnerships'. Pharmaceutical manufacturers have also served in various advisory positions in PPPs on committees and boards of such projects as the Medicines for Malaria Venture (MMV) and the Global Programme to Eliminate Filariasis (GPEF) (MMV 2012, Buse and Walt 2000).

Case study 8.2 The Global Alliance for Vaccines and Immunization

The Global Alliance for Vaccines and Immunization (GAVI) was founded in 2000 as a public–private partnership to:

- accelerate the uptake and use of underused and new vaccines
- strengthen capacity of integrated health systems to deliver immunization
- increase predictability and sustainability of financing for immunization
- shape vaccine markets to provide appropriate and affordable vaccines.

In this role, and through its networks and financial resources, GAVI has successfully overseen the creation of various new vaccines (e.g. pneumococcal) as well as encouraged the uptake of underutilized vaccines (e.g. rotavirus) to improve the health and well-being of the most vulnerable (GAVI 2012a). The partnership's activities are overseen by a governing board that comprises 18 representatives drawn from the major donor countries, the private sector, philanthropic foundations, civil society organizations and research institutes (Harman 2012b; GAVI 2012b). The majority of the organization's work since it was founded has been on contributing to achieving the health-related Millennium Development Goals (MDGs) that focus particularly on child and maternal health, as well as targeting specific diseases such as HIV/AIDS, tuberculosis and malaria. One of the key accomplishments of GAVI has been the promotion and creation of innovative funding mechanisms such as advance market commitments (AMC) that secure financial commitments from donors to guarantee the price of new vaccines when they are developed, thereby incentivizing pharmaceutical manufacturers to invest in new research and development, and expand their manufacturing capacity (GAVI 2012c). In addition, as a result of the strong financial backing of organizations such as the Bill and Melinda Gates Foundation, the World Bank, the United Nations Children's Fund (UNICEF) and WHO, the partnership has also been able to leverage sovereign pledges to raise additional capital from financial markets to support its activities and programmes (Harman 2012b).

> Accordingly, as a result of this activity GAVI has subsequently committed some US$7.2 billion in programme support to low-income countries to 2016, helped immunize over 124 million children with the Haemophilus influenza type b vaccine and 267 million children with the hepatitis B vaccine, and is estimated to have helped avert approximately 5.5 million future deaths (GAVI 2012d).

The underlying premise behind these endeavours has been that by co-opting corporate actors and directly involving them in decision-making processes, companies would be more inclined to make financial or in-kind contributions to address a specific area or health issue that would, otherwise, receive minimal attention. Attempts to quantify private sector contributions have historically proven difficult, however (Kettler and White 2003); and, as Buse and Walt (2000: 706) have concluded, several questionable out-comes have emerged from corporate sector participation in GHG:

> For the private sector, partnerships have (1) increased corporate influence in global policy-making and at the national level; (2) brought direct financial returns, such as tax breaks and market penetration, as well as indirect financial benefits through brand and image promotion; and (3) enhanced corporate authority and legitimacy through associa-tion with UN and other bodies.

Yet, even despite these acknowledged risks, the perceived impact of entities like the GAVI and other PPPs like the Global Fund to Fight AIDS, Tuberculosis and Malaria have been so successful that, as Williams and Rushton (2011: 2) have observed, 'it is likely that the shift to private forms of authority which has characterized the last decade of global health will become further entrenched rather than scaled back'.

Another group of actors that have made particularly strong inroads into GHG has been Civil Society Organizations (CSOs) and philanthropic foundations. Although both groups have a long pedigree of involvement in global health issues (Berridge et al. 2009), the influence of CSOs engaged in global health has grown considerably over the past few decades (Doyle and Patel 2008). CSOs have subsequently become engaged in a variety of health-related activities, mobilizing public opinion, contributing technical expertise, and even raising money to address a range of issues from the use of breast milk substitutes to tobacco control and access to medicines. In some instances, governments have even been observed to channel ODA through CSOs in order to circumvent the potential misappropriation or diversion of funds by corrupt regimes (McCoy et al. 2009). Added to this, the emergence of new philanthropic entities such as the Bill and Melinda Gates Foundation ('Gates Foundation') have joined with other notable foundations dedicated to global health such as the Rockefeller, W.K.

Kellogg, Aga Khan and Ford foundations. Importantly, the impact of these institu-tions – and particularly the recent arrival of the Gates Foundation – has been significant given their distribution of financial resources. As McCoy et al. (2009: 410) have recently noted:

> the entry of the Bill and Melinda Gates Foundation into the global health landscape (bringing with it also the donation of US$30 million by Warren Buffett) has taken private, philanthropic funding for international development, especially for health, to new and unprecedented heights. One estimate of the amount of private foundation spending on global health in 2005 was US$1.6 billion, much of it coming from the Gates Foundation.

Since the beginning of the twenty-first century global health has garnered considerable political attention that has also been accompanied by significant financial resources. In their work, Ravinshankar et al. (2009) have traced the increase in health-related ODA between 1990 and 2007, noting that there was an increase from US$5–6 billion in 1990 to some US$21.8 billion in 2007. In another study that examined the period between 2000 and 2004, it was noted that health ODA rose at an annual rate of 7.7 per cent from US$8.5 billion in 2000 to US$13.5 billion just four years later (Kates et al. 2006). Following several H5N1 influenza outbreaks in 2005, by 2009 the World Bank recorded new pledges of some US$4.3 billion to strengthen global pandemic preparedness (UNSIC and World Bank 2010), whereas between 2003 and 2006 disbursements for the maternal and child health MDGs (see below) increased by 64 per cent from US$2.12 billion to US$3.48 billion (Schäferhoff et al. 2010). These statistics evidence the importance accorded to global health in recent years, while it has also raised several inter-related challenges in terms of ensuring 'good' health governance.

The challenge of GHG processes, forums and mechanisms

Indeed, one of the inherent challenges associated with the expansion of contemporary GHG actors has been how to ensure better coordination, both in terms of technical assistance and how it is delivered, as well as in the allocation of financial resources. This is important not only to avoid unnecessary duplication of effort, but also to prevent valuable (and often limited) resources from being wasted. Moreover, as Szlezák et al. (2010: 1) have argued, there are also several associated questions 'about the roles various organizations should play, the rules by which they play, and who sets those rules'. By and large, however, the international community has been particularly slow to embrace new health governance processes, forums and mechanisms or amend existing ones.

Historically, the traditional forum where global health policies have been developed and agreed has been within the United Nations organizations such as the WHO and UNICEF (Moon *et al.* 2010). Here, policies would be tabled by governments in the form of resolutions at an annual meeting comprised solely of member states – such as the World Health Assembly (WHA) – where they would be voted on. If sufficient numbers agreed (e.g. in the context of the WHO, a two-thirds majority of member states is required to pass a resolution) the policy would be endorsed and the Secretariat or staff would then be tasked with responsibility for implementing the policy. Governments would frequently be encouraged to comply with the resolution/policy, and provide either financial or in-kind technical support as needed, but compliance is usually on a voluntary basis, leaving governments to pick and choose what policies they will, and which ones they will not, support.

Accompanying the influx of new actors, however, has been a demand for new processes, forums and mechanisms to facilitate more effective forms of GHG. Central to these demands have been calls for greater accountability, transparency and democratization of decision-making processes; and several albeit small changes have begun to emerge. For example, traditional forums such as the WHA have previously tended to sideline CSOs, either excluding them entirely from proceedings or resigning them to observer status with no voting rights. In response to the growing number of CSOs engaged in global health work, momentum began to build for alternative forums. In 2000, the People's Health Movement (PHM) was formed to pursue 'the revitalization of the principles of the Alma-Ata Declaration which promised Health for All by the year 2000 and complete revision of international and domestic policy that has shown to impact negatively on health status and systems' (PHM 2012). Concurrent to the creation of the PHM has also been the 'People's Health Assembly' (PHA), which is intended to serve as an alternative forum to the WHA, to debate contemporary health policies and priorities, and advocate for change. Importantly, although the WHO had initially avoided interacting with the PHM, in 2004 it reversed this policy and sent a delegation to the PHA. Later, members of the PHM were invited by the WHO to contribute to the WHO Commission on Social Determinants of Health and the WHO Task Force on Health Systems Research (Narayan 2006), thereby expanding the consultation process beyond the standard intergovernmental approach.

Likewise, despite ongoing questions as to the legitimacy of public–private partnerships (PPPs) (or GHPs) it can be argued that their creation reflects a genuine attempt to move towards a more inclusive form of governance. Indeed, it is now common practice for PPPs such as GAVI to include representation from CSOs and/or philanthropic foundations on governing boards and key decision-making committees (see Case study 8.2). These positions, which often provide the organizations with the ability to vote on policies and planned expenditures, permit CSOs and philanthropic foundations greater ability to participate in, and directly shape, the global health agenda.

Ironically, in some quarters it has been the very inclusion of these organizations that has added to concerns over the legitimacy of PPPs. This is principally because, as Doyle and Patel (2008: 1932) have highlighted, the 'rhetoric about the "representative" role of global civil society assumes a consensus between CSOs that does not always exist'. Critics have also correctly underlined that whereas (democratic) governments can be held to account by their populations via periodic general elections, oftentimes CSOs and philanthropic foundations lack equivalent accountability mechanisms (Batliwala 2002; Doyle and Patel 2008). This understandably raises legitimate questions about the role and influence of these organizations within GHG forums, given the 'profound' impact entities such as the Gates Foundation have had in shaping global health priorities (McCoy *et al.* 2009; Stuckler *et al.* 2011).

At the same time, attempts to reform the WHO to make it a more effective and inclusive organization have habitually failed to materialize. Various proposals have been tabled for how the organization could conceivably be restructured, such as lessening the influence of its regional offices (Ermakov 1996) or forming a new 'Committee C' that would include both state and non-state actors in decision-making processes and priority-setting activities (Kickbusch *et al.* 2010). Yet other proposals have included the creation of a 'Framework Convention on Global Health' (Burris and Anderson 2010), but to date, member states have repeatedly failed to demonstrate their commitment to reforming the institution, preferring instead to maintain the status quo.

Within the context of GHG mechanisms, despite its serious limitations, international law has long served as the primary means to encourage government cooperation. International treaties to control the spread of infectious diseases can, for example, be traced back to Sanitary Conventions of the nineteenth century; similar regulatory frameworks such as the International Health Regulations (IHR) that are designed to prevent the spread of infectious disease while minimizing disruption to international traffic and trade have been regularly revised and updated, most recently in 2005. These efforts were notably joined in 2003 with the passage of the WHO's first treaty – the *Framework Convention on Tobacco Control* (FCTC) – and again in 2011 with the endorsement of the *2011 Pandemic Influenza Preparedness Framework* to facilitate influenza virus-sharing practices and the distribution of benefits.

Unfortunately, aside from the fact that the international legal system remains inherently state-centric, often completely ignoring or making no provision for non-state actors such as CSOs, international law has also been a very poor tool for encouraging equitable and effective GHG. As Gostin (2008: 57) observes,

> The overriding principle of sovereignty makes international law fundamentally different from domestic law. In particular, international law is largely voluntary: there is generally no supranational authority to develop and enforce law against sovereign states ... the drive to establish universal consensus in contemporary treaty negotiations often leads to the codification of fairly weak treaty commitments or what is known as 'lowest common denominator' standards.

It is in this regard that proposals such as the Framework Convention on Global Health, even if they were to be negotiated, are unlikely to affect considerable change, principally because governments are usually reluctant to agree to conditions that may further diminish their authority.

The combination of state-centric processes, the diversity of global health actors, an inability to reform multilateral organizations such as the WHO, and the limited tools by which to compel governments into fulfilling global health responsibilities, are having significant implications for achieving global health objectives and hindering meaningful progress. For example, it is now well documented that one of the inadvertent outcomes to have arisen from the considerable influx of health-related Official Development Assistance (ODA) and the multiplicity of donors has been to place overly burdensome reporting procedures on recipient countries (Schieber *et al.* 2007). In the same vein, the short-term nature of ODA, which can be subject to annual funding level changes at minimal notice, frequently prevents recipient countries from increasing their health budgets to improve health outcomes because such policies are inconsistent with the recommendations of the world's leading international financial institutions (Ooms *et al.* 2010). Critically, however, the governance challenges that have arisen with the changing nature of GHG and the multiplicity of global health actors are unlikely to diminish. Rather, for well into the foreseeable future they are probably inclined to intensify.

The realignment of global health priorities

Commensurate with the changes in global health actors and the inflow of global health funding has been a further transformation in global health priorities. Following the creation of the WHO in 1948, for a time the international community adopted a very disease-specific approach, investing substantial sums of money into vertical programmes that targeted one specific disease at a time. Although this approach had one particularly notable success with the elimination of smallpox, the majority of the WHO's vertical programmes (e.g. malaria eradication, tuberculosis, etc.) proved spectacularly unsuccessful while also creating duplicate health structures and bureaucracy (see Siddiqi 1995). The launch of the Primary Health Care (PHC) movement in 1978 and the promise of 'Health For All by the Year 2000' marked the official start of a broader 'horizontal' approach to healthcare financing, one that shifted focus to building and strengthening basic health services (Cueto 2004). The 'Health for All' target was not achieved; but the movement nevertheless had a fundamental impact on how global health priorities were viewed, and how financial resources were disbursed.

In 2000, the United Nations established the MDGs that identified eight priority areas for development assistance. Importantly, three of the eight targets to be achieved by the year 2015 were explicitly health-related – MDG 4, which aimed at reducing child mortality; MDG 5 on improving maternal health; and MDG 6 to combat HIV/AIDS, malaria and other diseases (UN 2012b). In many respects, for the better part of almost 15 years the MDGs have served as a focal point for the international community, both in terms of highlighting the plight and vulnerability of the world's poorest, as well as in providing the impetus for the distribution of billions of dollars in ODA. Even so, it is clear – at least at the time of writing in 2012 – that while significant improvements in health and other areas such as education have been made under the auspices of the MDGs, the majority of the MDG targets will not be met by 2015.

Arguably, there are several reasons why this is the case. Critics of MDGs have identified that despite the fact the targets have raised the profile of health-related development assistance, they have also inadvertently encouraged a return to a vertical programme-style approach. Certainly, the creation of the Global Fund and the US President's Emergency Plan for AIDS Relief (PEPFAR), which have channelled billions of dollars in aid relief for HIV/AIDS and malaria (while excluding multiple other equally legitimate diseases), would support such a conclusion (Sridhar and Batniji 2008; Piva and Dodd 2009). The implication of these criticisms is that by failing to take a broader, horizontal approach, the underlying social determinants of health continue to remain unaddressed and the MDG project was thereby doomed to failure.

Tempting as it may be, however, to ascribe the limited success of the MDGs solely to programme design issues, there is little question that the 2008 global financial downturn and related events have had a marked impact on health-related ODA disbursements. By 2006, considerable pressure had begun to mount on the world's wealthiest nations to do more to ensure the success of the MDGs. The G8 Gleneagles Summit proved particularly significant in this context (Payne 2006), but just as the international community was preparing to distribute billions of dollars in new aid, the financial crisis provoked by the meltdown of the US mortgage lending market understandably diverted attention away from the MDGs (and global health more generally) to the state of the global economy (Fidler 2009).

Further added to this, a paradigm shift was underway within global health from that of 'public health' to 'health security' – a shift that has had significant implications for global health priorities. Even before the September 2001 anthrax letter attacks in the United States, the WHO had been arguing for a change in the way the international community perceived and responded to disease-related events, reframing such activity as 'global health security' (Hardiman 2003). By 2007, in the wake of such events such as the 2003 SARS outbreak and the progressive global spread of the highly virulent H5N1 influenza virus, this new way of viewing the WHO's traditional mandate of disease control and prevention had become firmly entrenched. Governments subsequently began to invest heavily in strengthening global pandemic preparedness – which had been often portrayed as the most serious and imminent 'threat' – to the extent that by 2009 some US$4.3 billion in new ODA had been allocated to address the threat of pandemic influenza alone (UNSIC and World Bank 2010).

While the move towards global health security has been welcomed by many (WHO 2011), critics have nevertheless emerged, and importantly, some of the most vocal opponents have been global health's new players. In this, Brazil has been particularly strident in arguing against the framing of public health issues in the language of national or international security, but it has also been joined in its opposition by other countries such as Thailand, India and Indonesia (Aldis 2008). Much of this resistance appears to stem from the notion that the deployment of security language reflects the political priorities of high-income (largely Western) governments concerned about protecting their populations from the diseases of the world's poor (Rushton 2011). Intriguingly, while there may be a measure of veracity to this claim, in 2007 Indonesia used the concept of global health security to agitate for changes in GHG processes and systems relating to pandemic influenza and access to life-saving vaccines (see Case study 8.2). The fact that a low-income country such as Indonesia has since achieved limited success in this endeavour speaks to the strength with which the discourse of global health security currently resonates with the wider international community. Indeed, for all the criticisms that can be legitimately brought forth, there is no denying that the focus on health security has helped to elevate global health to the realm of 'high politics', placing it firmly on the foreign policy agenda. As a result, this alternative view of global health continues to reshape agendas. Indeed more broadly, retaining the WHO's explicit global health security focus has been identified as a priority in any future attempts to reform the organization, even though the security agenda has had a noticeable impact on existing global health priorities by elevating some (such as infectious diseases) while downplaying others (Rushton 2011).

Likewise, while welcomed by governments, the shift towards GHPs that integrate a range of corporate, private and/or philanthropic organizations has led to new tensions arising over global health priorities. This is principally because the creation of issue-specific GHPs has been observed to attract significant funding (Jones 2012), but this funding has also distorted priorities and agendas (Hill 2011), leading to legitimate questions over whose interests are really being served. It has been recognized, for instance, that 'an overarching goal on the part of many of the corporate partners is the desire to attain social legitimacy in markets where foreign multinationals are often viewed with suspicion and scepticism' (Dahan *et al.* 2010: 335). At the same time, as Sengupta (2011: 88) notes, 'the gross under-representation of Southern stakeholders in the governance arrangements of [GHPs], coupled with the Northern location of their secretariats, is reminiscent of imperial approaches to public health.' Duplication of services and the creation of parallel health structures that place additional administrative burdens on already stretched human and technical resources have been recognized as further 'downsides' of GHP programmes (Marchal *et al.* 2010). Although these new forms of governance are thus generally celebrated, they are also creating new and unanticipated problems, often adversely affecting the very people they were created to assist – namely, the world's poor and vulnerable.

Conclusion

This chapter has set out to examine some of the key challenges confronting global health governance in the twenty-first century. In so doing, the chapter has engaged with three key questions of 'who' are influencing the governance arrangements, 'how' that governance is occurring, and 'what' is being governed. It has examined the rise of global health issues on foreign policy agendas, and how this has been accompanied by the emergence and creation of multiple new global health actors ranging from conventional state-based to new forms of non-state and public–private actors. The chapter has also examined the challenges that currently exist around the type of mechanisms, processes and forums deployed to govern global health, and how many of them are inadequate to the task. It has discussed the limitations of international law, and how the emergence of new actors has contributed to new questions about the legitimacy, accountability and appropriateness of existing forums such as the World Health Assembly. Finally, the chapter has examined how global health priorities have continued to ebb and wane, and while the creation of the Millennium Development Goals and the reframing of health issues in the language and discourse of security have helped elevate global health issues further up the political agenda, events such as the 2008 global financial downturn have adversely affected the prospects for improving global health outcomes. For all of these reasons, global health governance remains highly contested and conceptually vague. Competing views and ideas will continue to emerge, and agendas and priorities will undoubtedly continue to shift. What remains to be seen is how well the international community can weather the current 'perfect storm' brought about by the multiplication of global health actors with diverging agendas to further improve the health and well-being of the world's most vulnerable. Only time will tell.

Recommended reading

Davies, S. (2009). *The Global Politics of Health*, Cambridge: Polity Press.
Fidler, D. (2007). 'Architecture amidst Anarchy: Global Health's Quest for Governance', *Global Health Governance*, 1(1): 1–17.
Harman, S. (2012). *Global Health Governance*, London: Routledge.
Williams, O. D. and Rushton, S. (2011). 'Are the "Good Times" Over? Looking to the Future of Global Health Governance', *Global Health Governance*, 5(1): 1–16.
Youde, J. (2012). *Global Health Governance*, Cambridge: Polity Press.

Recommended websites

Bill and Melinda Gates Foundation: http://www.gatesfoundation.org/Pages/home.aspx
The Global Fund to Fight AIDS, Tuberculosis and Malaria: http://www.theglobalfund.org/en/
Global Health Diplomacy Network: http://www.ghd-net.org/
People's Health Movement: http://www.phmovement.org/
World Health Organization: http://www.who.int/en/ (and in particular the Trade, Foreign Policy, Diplomacy and Health division accessible via http://www.who.int/trade/en/)

9 Governing climate change and the planetary environment

Carl Death

Human-induced changes to our planet's climate present one of the most fundamental challenges for contemporary global governance. Indeed, there could be few issues more obviously 'global' than changes to the Earth's atmosphere and climate: greenhouse gas emissions in all parts of world contribute to the problem (although not equally), and climatic changes will impact all parts of the world (although not equally). Climate change requires collective governance since actions by individuals, national governments and even regions will be ineffective unless other individuals, governments and regions also take action. However, the current focus on climate change can sometimes obscure other environmental issues from view, so this chapter will place climate change within the context of the rise of global environmental governance, and show how climate change is not a single issue but rather encapsulates and reframes a range of other environmental issues including food and water security, sustainable development, industrial pollution and biodiversity conservation. These issues are important because they are about how our species relates to other species on our planet, and the stakes are nothing less than what will become of us in the future.

The following section sets out what is being governed and why. It chronicles the emergence of 'modern environmentalism' in the 1960s in the form of awareness of environmental degradation and planetary limits, and the rise of global governance through international summits. The second section identifies some of the key actors and institutions involved at a variety of levels. The third section explores some of the key mechanisms of governance, focusing particularly on scientific monitoring, international legal and political regimes, and carbon markets, each of which have important consequences for power relations and the formation of political subjectivities. The fourth section considers some of the central problems and issues that arise in the governance of the environment, focusing particularly on the classic problem of 'the tragedy of the commons'. This framing of environmental politics also has important side effects, however, and the chapter concludes by considering alternative ways of mapping the rationalities that underpin environmental governance. The implications of the forms of governance discussed in this chapter have ramifications not only for the future of our and other species, but also for the very ways in which we imagine our relationship with the environment that surrounds us, and fundamental categories of modern thought such as the division between the natural and the social.

What is being governed and why?

Environmental concerns have been an issue for human societies ever since the earliest groups tried to shelter from the wind and rain, build fires to keep warm, collect and nurture edible plants and herd animals (Diamond 1997; McDonald 2010: 1). In this sense the earliest emergence of governance could be said to be large irrigation systems in Mesopotamia, with their structured division of labour and production of surplus food and water (Whitehead *et al.* 2007: 57). The emergence of genuinely *global* governance is a rather different issue, however, and is more usually seen as a product of the second half of the twentieth century. In particular, global governance relies upon a conception of the world as a singular and interconnected whole. In this respect few events are more significant than the 1968 Apollo 8 mission, whose pilots became the first humans ever to see the Earth as a whole planet. The famous photos of the small, apparently fragile blue planet hanging alone in space became known as 'Spaceship Earth' (Lövbrand *et al.* 2009: 9; Sachs 1999: 110–11).

These images coincided with the growth of environmental concern. In the 1960s and 1970s a whole range of popular movements in Europe and North America began to express their concerns about the impact of modern industrialisation on nature (Conca and Dalbelko 2004; Dryzek 2005). Groups such as the World Wildlife Fund (WWF), Greenpeace and Friends of the Earth were formed to lead campaigns promoting conservation, and against nuclear testing and the profligate use of natural resources. The term 'ecosystem' began to enter public discourse, referring to new approaches to biology and ecology that emphasised the interlinked and systemic character of particular environments and the plant and animal species they contained. Threats to one species, it was realised, were having effects on many other species that relied upon them. Our part within these ecosystems (rather than being separate from them), and the impact of our activities on them, was increasingly hard to ignore. A key publication here was Rachel Carson's angry and passionate *Silent Spring* (1969), which charted the effects of modern chemical pesticides on insects, bird populations, and the rest of the ecosystem, which she described as 'those chains of poisonings, this ever-widening wave of death that spreads out, like ripples when a pebble is dropped into a still pool' (1969: 105). Ecosystem research revealed the interconnectedness of nature and the complex 'web of life' that made our planet habitable, the air breathable, and provided every species with sources of food. These new forms of knowledge were one more way in which 'Nature' – the untameable, unknowable, elemental force of classical and medieval worldviews – was gradually being transformed into 'the environment': a discrete, calculable, manageable network of relationships which could be mapped and monitored (Luke 1999; Rutherford 1999).

Scientists from these disciplines who were starting to map, monitor and model environmental relationships in ever greater detail were producing some worrying findings. A decade after Carson's *Silent Spring* the so-called Club of Rome produced a report entitled *The Limits to Growth* (Meadows *et al.* 1972). The report sold more than 12 million copies in over 30 different languages, and proclaimed that population levels, industrialisation, pollution, food production and resource depletion rates would all grow exponentially, whilst the availability of resources would only grow linearly. It warned that continuing levels of economic growth would lead to spectacular overshoot and collapse – a warning that echoed the eighteenth-century thoughts of Reverend Thomas Malthus on the dangers of human population growth outstripping the ability of agriculture to provide sufficient food (Sachs 1999: 58).

Box 9.1 The growth of modern environmentalism

The first 'Earth Day' took place on 22 April 1970 in the US, when some 20 million Americans took part in massive rallies across the country, bolstered by the counter-cultural youth movements of the 1960s (Sachs 1999: 153). Groups such as Friends of the Earth and Greenpeace were emerging to radicalise older conservation organisations like the Sierra Club and the Wildlife Conservation Society in the USA, and the Royal Society for the Protection of Birds (RSPB) in the UK. In other parts of the world other movements were also beginning to frame their struggles in explicitly environmental terms. Examples include the Chipko movement in India which practised Gandhian forms of struggle, including hugging trees, to prevent deforestation in India; the Green Belt Movement of Kenya which planted trees and empowered women in their communities; and the Movement for the Survival of the Ogoni People (MOSOP) who campaigned against oil-induced exploitation of their land and peoples (Haynes 1999; Martinez-Alier 2002).

Environmental movements around the world were also motivated by disasters such as the crash off the coast of Cornwall of the *Torrey Canyon* oil supertanker, carrying 120,000 tonnes of crude oil, in 1967; the 1979 central core meltdown at the Three Mile Island nuclear facility in Pennsylvania; the gas explosion at the Union Carbide pesticide plant in Bhopal, India, which killed thousands in 1984; and the 1987 Chernobyl nuclear meltdown. Environmentalist messages were reinforced by the global oil and energy crises in the 1970s, plummeting fish stocks, acid rain produced by pollution from UK factories decimating Scandinavian forests, images of famine and desertification in the Sahel and the Horn of Africa, and a litany of scares about chemical products from asbestos to ozone-depleting chemicals (CFCs), and from pesticides (such as DDT) to leaded petrol (Beck 1992; Dryzek 2005; McDonald 2010).

These concerns were given a global political platform in 1972 when the UN Conference on the Human Environment was held in Stockholm. It was attended by representatives of 113 governments, and debates centred on the apparently conflicting priorities of economic development and the protection of the environment (Haas 2002: 79). Whilst environmental activists from Europe and North America were urging their politicians to protect and conserve ecosystems, representatives from developing countries were unwilling to accept environmental limits on their development. 'Poverty is the worst form of pollution', Indian Prime Minister Indira Gandhi famously told the conference (Dresner 2002: 28). Despite these deep disagreements, the conference did agree that global environmental issues required some kind of global management, and the conference led to the creation of the UN Environment Programme (UNEP) based in Nairobi (Ivanova 2012).

The apparent tension between environmental degradation and the need for economic growth and development, especially in the world's poorest countries, was the subject of the World Commission on Environment and Development, which became known as the Brundtland Commission after its chair, Gro Harlem Brundtland, Norwegian Prime Minister and Minister for Environmental Affairs (Dresner 2002; Dryzek 2005; Sachs 1999). The 22-person Brundtland Commission was convened at the request of the UN Secretary-General in 1983. The commission spent four years travelling worldwide, hearing from scientists, communities, politicians, teachers, industrialists and many others. They produced their report, *Our Common Future*, in 1987. It became a landmark text for the concept of sustainable development, which it defined as 'development which meets the needs of the present, without compromising the ability of future generations to meet their own needs' (Brundtland 1987: 43). The stakes of environmental governance had never been clearer: as the title of the report indicated, this was about our common future.

In terms of the evolution of global environmental governance, the Brundtland Report urged that 'the unity of human needs requires a functioning multilateral system that respects the democratic principle of consent and accepts that not only the Earth but also the world is one' (Brundtland 1987: 51–2). This made the case for a more coordinated system of global environmental governance. Although many countries had begun to enact environmental protections and regulations as a result of social movement pressures in the 1970s and 1980s, it was becoming obvious that many environmental issues – such as acid rain, declining fish stocks and climate change – were transboundary or global, and required coordinated action by many or all states. For this reason another global summit was needed.

The Rio Earth Summit was held twenty years after Stockholm, and dwarfed it in size and public attention (Dresner 2002; Dryzek 2005; Haas 2002; Sachs 1999). Coming in 1992, just after the end of the Cold War and at a time of huge enthusiasm about the future of global cooperation and the 'victory' of liberal democracy, it seemed to be the best chance in a generation to secure substantive progress on building a coherent architecture of global environmental governance.

It was attended by 108 heads of state or government, and representatives of 172 governments. Over 17,000 people attended the parallel NGO forum. After months of pre-conference diplomacy and heated disagreements, delegates finally signed up to a lengthy blueprint for sustainable development known as *Agenda 21* (UN 1992) and the Rio Declaration on Environment and Development. Governments also used the conference to promote two legally binding conventions on biodiversity and climate change, and a declaration on forests. The Global Environmental Facility (GEF) was also established at Rio as a funding mechanism for these agreements. Rio was therefore a key moment in the development of global environmental governance.

Rio was also a key moment for the global governance of climate change. Climate change had become an increasingly significant issue for the scientific community in the 1980s, with the formation of the Intergovernmental Panel on Climate Change (IPCC) in 1988, a panel of scientists convened by governments to provide independent and objective advice on the state of scientific research on climate change (Bulkeley and Newell 2010: 26–8). It was during the 1990s, however, that climate change became a political issue, and negotiations for the UN Framework Convention on Climate Change (UNFCCC) and the Kyoto Protocol (which was agreed in 1997 and entered into force in 2005) began to construct the architecture of global climate governance (Bäckstrand and Lövbrand 2006; Bulkeley and Newell 2010; Lohmann 2006; Oels 2005). It was at this point that the political implications of such agreements began to emerge: anthropogenic climate change required countries to cut their greenhouse gas emissions, and that meant limits on economic growth. The central dilemma of sustainable development – environmental protection versus economic growth – was therefore played out again through the climate change negotiations, with the result that developing countries (Annex II countries, in the language of Kyoto) were excluded from binding emission cuts, and the world's largest emitter, the USA, was unable to ratify the agreement due to domestic opposition (Bulkeley and Newell 2010: 30).

The political trade-offs and power relations at stake in global environmental governance are therefore considerable. Some perspectives on global governance – such as liberal institutionalist attempts to design better regimes, regulations and institutions (e.g. Keohane *et al.* 1993) – sometimes seem to neglect the central role of political power in governance. Importantly, power is not only a question of competing interests between actors (distributive questions) but also a matter of which actors are seen as legitimate participants in governance at all (constitutive questions) (Okereke *et al.* 2009: 64). In other words – who are the 'we' that participate in environmental governance and have responsibility for environmental issues? The next section considers these questions.

Who are the key actors involved?

The UN and its family of departments, agencies and programmes have been central actors in global environmental governance. Far more than merely providing a venue for governments to talk to each other through the General Assembly and Security Council, institutions like UNEP, as well as the Commission for Sustainable Development (CSD), and other related bodies such as the UN Development Programme (UNDP), Food and Agriculture Organisation (FAO), World Health Organisation (WHO), UN Educational, Scientific and Cultural Organisation (UNESCO) as well as many others have taken an active stance on issues of environmental governance and sustainable development, pushing their own agendas sometimes in the face of considerable opposition (Bulkeley and Newell 2010; Haas 2002; Imber 1996; Young 1994). The scope of environmental governance is indicated by the diverse nature of these organisations: the UNDP concentrates on the effects of environmental degradation on poverty and inequality, whilst the FAO and the WHO are concerned with the links between environmental degradation and food security and health, respectively. UNESCO regards part of its mission as teaching society how to behave responsibly towards the environment. The imperative of international cooperation in the face of environmental dangers means that the UN family has enthusiastically adopted environmental and sustainable development issues as providing 'a definitive post-Cold War purpose for the organisation' (Imber 1996: 138), and since Rio in 1992 the CSD has been responsible for trying to coordinate action on sustainable development within the UN and its agencies and programmes. Reform of UNEP has been a recurrent topic of negotiations on global environmental governance, with proposals including the creation of a stronger World Environment Organisation (Ivanova 2012). These debates resurfaced at the Rio+20 conference in 2012.

UN conferences and summits have to a significant extent determined the landscape and pace of global environmental governance (Death 2010: 2–3; Haas 2002). It was Stockholm in 1972 that first recognised the environment as a global political issue, and Rio in 1992 that created many of the principles, institutions and legal regimes that now constitute global environmental governance. Ten years later heads of state met again in Johannesburg for the World Summit on Sustainable Development (WSSD), or Rio+10. Intended to review progress since Rio as well as identify new areas for action, the summit became embroiled in debates over implementation mechanisms and clashes between trade and environmental law, and did not produce any new international agreements of substance (Dresner 2002: 59; Dryzek 2005: 149). The attendance of over 100 heads of state and representatives of over 190 governments was at least partially overshadowed by the notable absence of US President George W. Bush. This apparent snub was reflected in the public booing of Secretary of State Colin Powell during a plenary session (Death 2010: 96). It is revealing, therefore, that there was little enthusiasm for large sustainable development conferences post-Johannesburg. In June 2012 'Rio+20' returned to Brazil and was a much smaller event lasting only three days.

The UN system has also played a key role in governing climate change. The UNFCCC and the Kyoto Protocol are the primary instruments for managing international commitments and cooperation on climate change. These have been dogged by political differences at every stage, from the fraught negotiation of Kyoto in the 1990s to efforts to get it ratified in the early 2000s, to attempts to negotiate a follow-up treaty after it expires in 2012 (Bulkeley and Newell 2010; Christoff 2010; Dimitrov 2010). Serious differences remain between countries reluctant to jeopardise their economic growth (such as the USA, Canada and Japan, for example), as well as major emerging economies which refuse to submit to binding legal restraints on a problem which they argue they played no role in creating (such as India, Brazil and China). On the other hand, representatives of many African states and the Small Island Developing States (SIDS) have urged the international community that their very survival is at stake if greater action to mitigate climate change is not taken, and more resources to enable countries to adapt to climate change are not made available.

These issues have dominated negotiations and debates at the annual Conferences of the Parties (CoPs) to the UNFCCC and Kyoto Protocol, such as the high-profile meeting in Copenhagen in 2009 which turned into an unexpected summit when the world's leaders descended in an attempt to rescue climate governance. Despite the presence of world leaders and a vocal civil society protest outside, the conference was able to do little more than agree that states would make voluntary commitments to reduce emissions (Christoff 2010). The emphasis on voluntary rather than binding commitments is illustrative of a broader trend in environmental governance towards multi-stakeholder partnerships and flexible market mechanisms (Bäckstrand and Lövbrand 2006; Bulkeley and Newell 2010; Death 2010; Lohmann 2006), and it was also significant that the architects of the 'Copenhagen Accord' were the USA together with emerging powers such as China, Brazil, India and South Africa. For some observers this indicated a major shift in the topography of power within global environmental governance. For others, the message of the conference was more bluntly that it 'was a failure whose magnitude exceeded our worst fears, and the resulting Copenhagen Accord was a desperate attempt to mask that failure' (Dimitrov 2010: 18).

As well as the UN family, many other international organisations and institutions have found their purpose and role reinvigorated by the need for international cooperation on environmental issues and climate change. The World Bank has been reinvented as a principal agent of sustainable development, establishing its own Environment Department in 1987 and a Vice Presidency for Environmentally Sustainable Development in 1993 (Young 2002). Between 2005 and 2010 'Environment and Natural Resource Management' projects accounted for around nine per cent of new Bank lending, and close to 90 per cent of country assistance and partnership strategies in 2010 emphasised climate action. The World Bank now sees itself as one of the major repositories for environmental knowledge on the planet: a global 'knowledge Bank' (Luke 1999; Young 2002: 205). Major World Bank projects must include environmental and social impact assessments which seek to predict and address the negative side effects of development schemes such as dams or power stations, in no small part as a reaction to the delays or cancellations caused by environmental objections to big projects in the past – most famously the Narmada Dam project in India (Haynes 1999: 228–9). This has led to a profusion of 'green' projects involving biodiversity zones, green development corridors, sustainable livelihood programmes and resource management initiatives, all in order to promote environmentally sustainable development rather than environmentally destructive development. Yet there are suspicions that many within the World Bank still view environmental concerns as a potential constraint upon development, and an irritating side issue that must be addressed to placate vocal civil society groups. For this reason, as well as the USA's status as largest funder of the World Bank, there is some resentment of the organisation's influence over environmental issues through bodies like the GEF and the new Green Climate Fund. The World Bank is the trustee of GEF funds, and thus is able to exercise substantial influence over which projects get funding. Through the GEF, Zoe Young argues, 'the World Bank has been able to bring its economistic vision of development into what was previously UN territory of global environmental protection' (2002: 8).

The complex and multi-centric nature of global governance does not mean, however, that states have been displaced or sidelined, and they continue to play a central role in environmental governance (Conca 2005; Keohane et al. 1993: 17; Whitehead et al. 2007). Indeed, one of the most significant effects of the rise of environmental concerns over the past half-century has been the widespread recognition that a central function of the modern state is to manage environmental changes. This is reflected both in national legislation such as the UK Clean Air Act of 1956, and in the rise of environmental departments and ministries within national governments, such as in Germany in 1969, the US Environmental Protection Agency in 1970, and the UK in 1987 (Dryzek 2005: 78; Whitehead et al. 2007: 122–9). More recently, in 2009, 106 UN member states were implementing a National Sustainable Development Strategy. Indeed, despite the emphasis on global environmental governance and new actors and coalitions, the actual and potential role of 'green states' remains at the heart of global environmental governance, and is evidence of the ways in which this governance is constitutive of political identities and subjectivities.

Yet states are no longer (if they ever were) the sole actors in global governance. Indeed, it was civil society organisations and social movements that drove the construction of a new architecture of global governance (Bryant 2002; Bulkeley and Newell 2010; Epstein 2008; Wapner 2002). The older conservation organisations – such as the Sierra Club and the Wildlife Conservation Society – pre-date the emergence of modern global environmental governance, but since the 1960s and 1970s they have played an increased role lobbying states and international organisations, conducting scientific work, implementing projects on the ground, and spreading information and awareness to broader publics. Since the 1960s newer waves of more radical movements and international NGOs have also become central players in environmental politics. Activist groups like Greenpeace and Friends of the Earth, as well as more research-orientated groups like the International Institute for Sustainable Development (IISD), the International Institute for Environment and Development (IIED), WorldWatch, and the World Resources Institute are now ever-present at the institutions and conferences of global environmental governance – whether in the negotiating rooms and corridors lobbying and advising, or outside on the streets waving banners (Death

2010: 100–103; Haas 2002). These have been joined by a wide range of organisations from outside the Western world – the Third World Network, Eco-Equity, the Green Belt movement, Via Campesina, and many others associated with the World Social Forum – which, despite continuing obstacles to access including funding, personnel, governmental obstruction and hegemonic discourses of knowledge and acceptable science, have increasingly put their stamp on environmental governance (Haynes 1999). This has had the result that issues of environmental justice and racism have received more attention, alongside sensitivity to questions of gender, class, religion and the rights of indigenous peoples. Furthermore, they have also forced processes of environmental governance to become more open, transparent, consultative and participatory.

Accordingly, international institutions and governments have been required to allow non-state actors access to deliberations on environmental governance. Agenda 21 argued that these actors would be 'critical to the effective implementation of the objectives, policies and mechanisms agreed to by states' (UN 1992: 23.1), and the participation of nine major groups (business and industry, children and youth, farmers, indigenous people, local authorities, NGOs, the scientific and technological community, women, and workers and trade unions) is now a requirement at all levels of environmental governance. Of course, access does not necessarily mean greater influence, and the ability of non-state actors to determine the substance of environmental policies remains severely limited. Moreover, not all major groups have equal influence.

One major group which has emerged as a central actor in delivering environmental partnerships and sustainable development is the private sector (Bulkeley and Newell 2010: 87–104; Death 2010: 50; Dryzek 2005: 167–8). Environmental protection has been a crucial area in which greater private sector participation in global governance has occurred, reflected in the rise of discourses of corporate social responsibility in the 1990s and 2000s. These were exemplified by the launch of the UN's Global Compact in July 2000, and the visibility of major transnational corporations at the Johannesburg Summit in 2002, where 251 public–private partnerships were listed as recognised outcomes of the conference (Death 2010: 70–86). One of the major themes of the Rio+20 conference in 2012 was the 'green economy' – or the ability of clean and green technologies and innovation to produce economic growth and sustainable development. There has also been a similar shift in climate governance towards market mechanisms, and the UN estimated in 2007 that more than 87 per cent of the financial flows and investment needed to tackle climate change will need to come from the private sector (Bulkeley and Newell 2010: 88).

The private sector has been brought within global environmental governance not only in the form of major multinational corporations, but also in terms of the lives, values and consumption patterns of individuals. What we eat and drink, where we live, how we travel, and our values and beliefs are all potential objects of environmental governance. Whilst the origins of this individualisation can perhaps be located in the environmental movement itself – with the 1960s emphasis on alternative lifestyles, new age beliefs and personal sacrifice – in the early twenty-first century this has been a project of broader social and cultural change by governance institutions (Bryant 2002; Wapner 2002). Agenda 21 proclaimed that 'one of the fundamental prerequisites for the achievement of sustainable development is broad public participation in decision-making' (UN 1992), and *Our Common Future* asserted that sustainable development 'will also require promoting citizens' initiatives, empowering peoples' organisations, and strengthening local democracy' (Brundtland 1987: 63–5). Environmental education programmes and good citizenship initiatives accordingly sought to produce responsible individuals who had internalised environmental self-governance, and who would recycle, take public transport to work, and count their carbon consumption. New techniques of producing self-governing individuals have emerged in recent years, including personal carbon allowances, carbon-offsetting, 'nudge' behavioural economics, cash transfers and many others (Bulkeley and Newell 2010: 70–86; Jones *et al.* 2011; Paterson and Stripple 2010). Through such mechanisms individuals themselves have become important actors within global environmental governance, and the degree to which such incorporation happens under a market rationality – or a rights-based rationality, or a technical–scientific rationality, for example – all have significant implications for power relations.

The diversity of actors involved in global environmental governance perhaps exceeds many other areas of global governance. A key question both for the future design of global environmental governance networks and institutions, and for critical research into their implications, is how the relationships between these actors develop, and where the priorities, rights and responsibilities lie. This question is closely related to, and indeed underpins, the more practical issue of what mechanisms are at work in global environmental governance.

What are the key mechanisms of government?

The many different types of mechanism employed in the field of global environmental governance reflect the diversity both of the actors involved and of the issues. Mechanisms include legal regulation, voluntary codes and standards (such as the ISO 14000 series on environmental management and ISO 26000 on social responsibility), markets and trading schemes for pollution, geo-engineering of local or even planetary ecosystems, end-of-pipe technical solutions, clean or 'green' technologies, education campaigns, best practice examples, national strategies and planning, environmental and social impact assessments, conservation parks and biodiversity corridors, and countless more.

Rather than attempt to give a (necessarily partial) overview of all these different mechanisms, this section focuses on three types of mechanism which are particularly significant. These are global scientific monitoring, international regimes and legal agreements, and carbon markets. In almost every area of global environmental governance – from climate change to water pollution, food security to species conservation – these three mechanisms (or some permutation or combination of them) are present.

Global scientific monitoring

Without scientific monitoring and the natural sciences there would be no global environmental governance. Indeed, we would not even be aware of the existence of many environmental problems. Whilst we might notice seasonal changes in the weather, or higher frequencies of skin cancer, we would not be able to link them to human-induced climate change or CFC-induced holes in the ozone layer without scientific monitoring (Beck 1992; Litfin 1994). The first part of this chapter emphasised the role of ecosystems science and modelling in the growth of environmental concern in the 1960s and 1970s, and the significance of the IPCC in drawing attention to climate change since 1988. An important body of literature focusing on these 'epistemic communities' has drawn attention to the constitutive role of science in producing environmental politics (Bulkeley and Newell 2010: 8; Epstein 2008: 61; Keohane *et al.* 1993: 21–22; Litfin 1994).

Mainstream approaches to global environmental governance are characterised by the fundamental optimism of the scientific outlook. Whilst scientists can tell us how bad the problem really is, the scientific outlook is also generally optimistic that human ingenuity and technological progress will deliver solutions. *Our Common Future* captured this dynamic between environmental dangers and technological optimism in its opening paragraphs:

> From space, we see a small and fragile ball dominated not by human activity and edifice but by a pattern of clouds, oceans, greenery and soils. Humanity's inability to fit its doings into that pattern is changing planetary systems, fundamentally. Many such changes are accompanied by life-threatening hazards. This new reality, from which there is no escape, must be recognised – and managed. Fortunately, the new reality coincides with more positive developments new to this century ... our technology and science gives us at least the potential to look deeper into and better understand natural systems.
> (Brundtland 1987: 1)

Accordingly, *Our Common Future* recognised the 'indispensable role' of the scientific community in 'identifying risks, in assessing environmental impacts and in designing and implementing measures to deal with them' (Brundtland 1987: 326).

The tools and concepts available to scientists have largely determined the manner in which environmental problems have been tackled. Concepts such as the 'maximum sustainable yield' of a renewable resource (such as fish stocks or forest timber) have been used to calculate the rate at which resources could be consumed without depleting the capital stock, and through careful measurement and modelling of these ecosystems usage quotas have been negotiated (Dryzek 2005: 76).

The rise of Earth Systems Science has involved the scaling up of these older concepts to incorporate far more complex factors and relationships, such as 'global models of atmospheric, hydrological and terrestrial systems' (Bäckstrand 2003: 29; see also Lövbrand *et al.* 2009). Global scientific assessments include the WorldWatch Institute's *State of the World* and *Vital Signs* reports, the World

Resources Institute's Earthtrends programme, the UN Earthwatch initiative, and the UNEP's World Conservation Monitoring Centre and *Global Environmental Outlook* reports. In the field of food security the Codex Alimentarius, Food and Agriculture Organisation, World Health Organisation, World Food Programme, USAID's Famine Early Warning System and others track levels of hunger, food supplies and prices, pests, weather, diseases, fuel prices, droughts and many other indicators (McDonald 2010: 159). It is only through the work of these institutions and monitoring networks that the prospect of global environmental governance is even possible (Bäckstrand and Lövbrand 2006; Lövbrand *et al.* 2009; Luke 1999; Rutherford 1999).

International regimes and legal agreements

Early conservation and natural resource policies were associated with a 'command and control' style of government (Haynes 1999: 231). National governments – both at home and in the colonies – would take advice from scientists and interest groups, and then enact and enforce new laws and regulations in accordance with their policy goals. Since the 1980s and 1990s it is often claimed that this era has gone, and that the function of government is now better described in terms of 'steering rather than rowing' – setting the broad framework but not micro-managing particular issue areas (Oels 2005). This does not mean, however, that legal agreements and regulations are no longer part of environmental governance. In contrast, they have proliferated. According to the WTO there are over 250 multilateral environmental treaties (MEAs) currently in force, and Conca and Dalbelko calculated in 2004 that there are over 1,000 international environmental agreements (Conca and Dalbelko 2004: 5–6). These cover a huge range of environmental issues, including trade in endangered species (CITES 1975), hazardous waste (Basel Convention 1989), ozone depletion (Montreal Protocol 1989), climate change (UNFCCC 1992), desertification (CCD 1994), access to information, public participation in decision-making and access to justice in environmental matters (Aarhus Convention 1998), persistent organic pollutants (Stockholm Convention 2001) and biosafety (Cartagena Protocol 2003).

These legal agreements are one part of what are known as 'international regimes' or institutions, usually defined as comprising both formal and informal bundles of rules, roles, principles, norms and decision-making procedures that define and regulate the social practices of states and non-state actors (Bulkeley and Newell 2010: 6–10; Haas 2002: 73; Okereke *et al.* 2009). For regime theorists, it is the potential of human societies to design institutions to deal with collective action problems which is our best – perhaps only – hope of resolving the environmental threats we face. This is captured by Keohane *et al.*: 'the international community's ability to protect the quality of the planet for future generations depends upon international cooperation. Successful cooperation, in turn, requires effective international institutions to guide international behaviour along a path of sustainable development' (1993: 4). Yet in many areas of global environmental governance this has not happened. Oran Young's work has looked at why effective regimes have formed in the areas of ozone depletion and Antarctic protection, for example, but not for biodiversity protection or climate change (Young 1994).

To take the latter case, it is clear that a coherent and effective 'climate change regime' does not yet exist. However, Keohane and Victor have argued that instead what we see is a 'climate change regime complex', in the sense of 'loosely coupled sets of specific regimes' (Keohane and Victor 2011: 7). The inherent diversity of the issues related to climate change means that it incorporates a whole range of other regimes: such as the Montreal Protocol on ozone-depleting gases (which also affect climate change), bilateral agreements and initiatives between states, scientific assessments and panels (such as the IPCC), adaptation initiatives (such as the Green Climate Fund), initiatives by other international 'clubs' (G8, G20, G8+5, etc.), multilateral development assistance (World Bank and UNDP programmes), carbon markets and carbon trading schemes (the Clean Development Mechanism [CDM], Joint Implementation, the European Trading Scheme, and the Reducing Emissions from Degradation and Deforestation [REDD] programme), as well as the central legal agreements of the UNFCCC and the Kyoto Protocol (Bernstein *et al.* 2010; Bulkeley and Newell 2010; Keohane and Victor 2011: 10; Lohmann 2010). Many other fields of governance – such as migration, trade, health, urbanisation, conflict and peacekeeping – also have particular ramifications for climate change.

Carbon markets

The complexity of the climate change regime complex is encapsulated in the presence of a whole range of carbon markets that transcend public–private divisions. Carbon markets are used here as shorthand to refer to a range of market mechanisms that allow trading of pollution permits. They have become most commonly associated with permits to emit carbon dioxide (CO_2) but markets also exist for other greenhouse gases and industrial pollutants (Lohmann 2006: 47–8). The most well-known carbon markets are those created under the Kyoto Protocol, in which three mechanisms were established to allow the 38 'Annex I' states to achieve their agreed emissions reductions of an average of 5.2 per cent by 2012. These mechanisms are emissions trading, Joint Implementation, and the CDM (Bulkeley and Newell 2010: 24–5). The mechanisms work by issuing permits to polluters to emit CO_2, and those who emit less than they are permitted can sell their excess to those who need more permits. Special mechanisms exist to generate new permits from emission reduction projects (typically end-of-pipe industrial improvements, but also clean energy schemes, etc.) in other Annex I countries (through Joint Implementation) or in the developing world (through the CDM).

Other carbon markets have also sprung up. In 2005 the EU Emissions Trading Scheme (ETS) was launched to help meet European targets under Kyoto. Some corporations and industry sectors have launched their own emissions trading schemes, either within the corporation or through organisations like the Chicago

Climate Exchange (Bulkeley and Newell 2010: 95). There are also many companies offering voluntary credits to private buyers who want to offset their emissions – for example when you buy airline tickets or order groceries online. The rationale behind all these schemes is two-fold: emissions trading is designed to let the market find the cheapest and most efficient place to cut emissions, and project-based emissions credits represent a potential source of development funding for poorer countries, where the 'carbon savings' achieved through halting deforestation or installing solar heaters can be sold to wealthier states, industries and individuals who want to offset their own emissions (Keohane and Victor 2011: 17–18).

However, carbon markets have received a great many criticisms, and entail significant disadvantages as well as advantages (Bäckstrand and Lövbrand 2006; Bernstein *et al.* 2010; Lohmann 2006; Paterson and Stripple 2010). Critics have warned they are potentially unfair and unjust, with some even labelling them 'carbon colonialism' as they mean rich polluters can continue business as usual whilst poorer countries are treated as 'carbon reserves'. Murky deals, forced removals of local populations and under-priced land deals in places such as Uganda have contributed to concerns over the political implications of carbon markets (Lohmann 2006: 237–46). Moreover, the scientific basis of calculations of carbon storage and avoided emissions are complex and often highly debatable. Finally, critics argue that these markets are unlikely to facilitate transitions to a greener economy. They still require politicians to make the hard decisions to impose emissions reductions, and market mechanisms may even impede investment in cleaner technologies. Lohmann's verdict is that 'emissions trading may coax a bit more out of the fossil economy, but it is not going to help the world get past it' (2006: 110).

What are the problems and issues that arise in this area?

The mechanisms discussed in the previous section – scientific monitoring, international regimes and carbon markets – are all significant and interesting areas of academic research. Better science, more effective regimes and more efficient markets may all lead to better global environmental governance (Keohane *et al.* 1993: 6). Yet merely to focus on better technical solutions to these problems runs the risk of leaving some of the underlying social, political and structural causes of environmental degradation unexamined (Okereke *et al.* 2009).

This can be illustrated through a discussion of one of the most influential ways of framing environmental problems and justifying the need for global environmental governance: Garrett Hardin's 'tragedy of the commons' (1968). Hardin was an American ecologist who published one of the most reprinted and widely cited essays in environmental governance. Based on the analogy of grazing land held in common – meaning free access of all – in medieval and early modern England, he argued that population growth would inevitably and tragically lead to the degradation of shared resources such as land, water, fish stocks, timber and so on. The basic principle he set out was that each herdsman has a rational incentive to increase the size of their herd. All the benefits of an extra animal in the herd accrue to the herdsman, whilst the costs (land erosion, water depletion, overgrazing) are shared between them all.

> Therein is the tragedy. Each man is locked into a system that compels him to increase his herd without limit – in a world that is limited. Ruin is the destruction to which all men rush, each pursuing his own best interest in a society that believes in the freedom of the commons. Freedom in a commons brings ruin to all.
>
> (Hardin 1968: 1244)

The solution for Hardin was to enclose the commons – in other words to restrict usage of common access goods, impose private ownership and regulate freedoms. Controversially he concluded with a call for 'relinquishing the freedom to breed', as unlimited population growth in a finite world of limits would lead to 'the misery of overpopulation' (Hardin 1968: 1248). Similar principles could be argued to apply in the area of climate politics: in the absence of a binding international regime, each individual country is rationally incentivised to increase CO_2 emissions (i.e. increase economic output) despite the collective damage to the atmosphere and climate, thereby requiring more coercive or authoritarian global governance.

There are a number of problematic assumptions and implications that stem from framing the problem of environmental governance in this manner – even beyond the historical observation that this rather crude model of land use probably never existed (Dryzek 2005: 29). Elinor Ostrom has shown how designing public policy or governance mechanisms based around the metaphor of the tragedy of the commons assumes (i) that individuals are rational self-interested 'norm-free maximisers of immediate gains', whereas government officials are public servants able to analyse long-term patterns; (ii) that designing new rules or enclosing commons is relatively easy and straightforward and can be accomplished by officials working in the public interest; and (iii) that the organisation itself requires central direction and hierarchical coordination (Ostrom 1999: 496). These assumptions are actually all deeply problematic and contested. Whereas a simplistic assumption of the tragedy of the commons tends to be used to argue for centralised, coercive, restrictive types of environmental governance (Dryzek 2005: 36–7), it is possible to demonstrate that in many cases local users of irrigation systems, fisheries and forests are capable of self-organising to find solutions to commons dilemmas, and that 'polycentric governance systems' and 'complex adaptive systems' are able 'to cope more effectively with tragedies of the commons and many of the other problems facing modern societies' (Ostrom 1999: 497).

In order to understand how and why environmental degradation takes place and what might be done to govern environmental issues differently and better, a number of alternative theoretical approaches have drawn attention to important issues missing from Hardin's model of the tragedy of the commons. Two worth drawing particular attention to here highlight the role of ideas, norms and discourses, as well as more nuanced appreciations of the power/knowledge relations that constitute environmental politics.

Ideas, norms and discourses

A considerable body of constructivist and post-positivist work has highlighted the important role of ideas, norms and discourses in environmental politics in recent decades (Haas 2002; Hajer and Versteeg 2005; Litfin 1994; Wapner 2002). This work spans a considerable range of arguments and theoretical approaches, but centrally emphasises the importance of social values and perceptions in determining what environmental issues are considered important, what forms of conflict and cooperation are considered appropriate in responding to them, and which actors are regarded as legitimate participants in environmental governance. Ostrom has contested the image of the rational, objective, self-interested individual, instead describing humans as 'fallible, boundedly rational, and norm-using' (1999: 496). Charlotte Epstein emphasises the role of discourses as 'sense-making practices' in explaining how whales shifted from being a resource to be harvested, to a majestic being in need of conservation and protection (2008: 4). John Dryzek's accessible survey of environmental thought and practice starts from the premise that language matters, and that environmental issues 'are interlaced with a range of moral and aesthetic questions about human livelihoods, public attitudes, and our proper relation to other entities on the planet' (2005: 3). All these show how different cultural contexts can mitigate or reframe the so-called tragedy of the commons in important ways.

These approaches concentrate upon framing: how certain problems are framed as needing governance, and what solutions are made necessary and reasonable. As Hajer and Versteeg put it, this allows the analyst 'to see how a diversity of actors actively try to influence the definition of the problem' (2005: 177). In terms of climate governance, US negotiators successfully framed the problem in terms of environmental externalities and inefficiency during the Kyoto negotiations, leading to a set of mechanisms reliant upon carbon markets (Bulkeley and Newell 2010: 31–2), whereas others predict future climate change conflicts as a consequence of the unfolding of the tragedy of the climate commons (Christoff 2010; Dimitrov 2010). Such framings can easily obscure issues of human rights, climate justice and environmental racism.

Power/knowledge relations

A related body of literature has taken a slightly different direction and used a different theoretical tool-kit to explore the politics of global environmental governance. This has drawn upon the work of French political theorist Michel Foucault, and particularly the concept of eco-governmentality, to investigate the power relations bound up within modern ways of thinking and knowing environmental issues (Foucault 1998). Whilst many of the constructivists mentioned above also draw inspiration from Foucauldian notions of power and discourse (Dryzek 2005; Epstein 2008; Litfin 1994), the eco-governmentality literature is now emerging as a distinct approach to global environmental governance (Bäckstrand and Lövbrand 2006; Bryant 2002; Death 2010; Lövbrand *et al.* 2009; Luke 1999; Okereke *et al.* 2009; Paterson and Stripple 2010; Rutherford 1999; Whitehead *et al.* 2007).

The central premise of this work is that debates between those emphasising power and conflict in a struggle for resources (Hardin 1968) and those emphasising freedom, cooperation and shared institutions (Haas *et al.* 1993; Ostrom 1999) both miss the fact that the power of environmental governance works *through* the production of particular types of freedom. The work of eco-governmentality scholars has therefore been to show the ways in which free, sovereign states have been produced by discourses and concrete practices of proper environmental management and responsibility (Whitehead *et al* 2007); or how civil society organisations and NGOs have been produced as watchdogs for environmental policymakers and the stewards of shared or endangered wildlife (Bryant 2002); or how free and rational individuals with carbon footprints and carbon allowances have been produced (Paterson and Stripple 2010). These actors are not timeless pre-existing entities but have been brought into being – or constituted – through new forms of governance. Similarly, particular regimes of climate knowledge and science, and mechanisms that work through surveillance, legal regimes or market trading, are not neutral and objective tools but deeply political forms of power with particular consequences for who we are and how we relate to other species. Even the construction of 'the climate' as a field of governance is deeply political rather than self-evident, with consequences for other areas of environmental politics – such as biodiversity conservation or food and water security – which are now less visible, or must be viewed through the prism of climate change.

This attention to eco-governmentalities is part of a broader critical environmental politics, but it is not necessarily condemnatory of all existing forms of environmental governance. For example, Paterson and Stripple conclude their discussion of techniques of individualisation with the thought that 'in a climate change context, it is difficult to envisage how limiting global warming to 2.8°C … might be achieved without such an intensive, managerial (and self-managerial) effort' (2010: 359). Forms of eco-govermentality may be used to foster docile and responsible individuals, or neoliberal economic rationalities, but they could also be used to ferment more socially just and ecologically sustainable forms of behaviour (Death 2010: 165). Perhaps we do need to try to change human behaviour and identities in order to avert environmental disaster?

It is here that some of the most profound implications of environmental governance are made clear: environmental governance is about our species and our relationships with other species – it is about who we are and how we understand and shape our society. New forms of environmental governance are capable of reshaping how we conceive ourselves and our relationship with nature, and work to reinforce or complicate fundamental categories of modern thought such as the natural and the social. Foucault famously claimed that 'what might be called a society's "threshold of modernity" has been reached when the life of the species is wagered on its own political strategies' (Foucault 1998: 143). What is at stake in debates over the principles, mechanisms and roles of environmental governance is nothing less than the future of our species, and indeed the very way in which we understand our species as living within a wider environment.

Conclusion

Global environmental governance is one of the most extensive and ambitious areas of global governance, as it literally attempts to bring the entire planet – and all life on the planet – into the sphere of human management and control. In so doing it has managed to mobilise a broad range of actors and a diversity of mechanisms. Much scientific energy and academic research has been devoted to better ways to organise this governance, as well as exploring the political implications of these forms of governance. The stakes here are quite terrifyingly high, and our attempts to govern natural environments have only ever met with, at best, partial success. It seems inevitable that 'Nature' will have a few more tricks up her sleeve for us in the future, as we try to govern, regulate, manage and plan our impact on the planet's climate and the diverse ecosystems on which human life depends. How our societies respond will shape what both we, and our world, will become in the future.

Recommended reading

Barry, J. and Eckersley, R. (eds) (2005). *The State and the Global Ecological Crisis*, Cambridge, MA: MIT Press.
Beck, U. (1992). *Risk Society: Towards a New Modernity*, London: Sage.
Bulkeley, H. and Newell, P. (2010). *Governing Climate Change*, Abingdon: Routledge.
Lohmann, L. (2006). *Carbon Trading: A Critical Conversation on Climate Change, Privatisation and Power*, Uppsala: Dag Hammarskjold Centre and Corner House.
Sachs, W. (1999). *Planet Dialectics: Explorations in Environment and Development*, London: Zed.

Recommended websites

Climate Justice Action: http://www.climate-justice-action.org/
Climate scientists comment on climate science: http://www.realclimate.org/
Earth System Governance Project: http://www.earthsystemgovernance.org/
EcoEquity (social justice NGO): http://www.ecoequity.org/
Worldwatch Institute: http://www.worldwatch.org/

10 Governing human rights
Rendition, secret detention and torture in the 'War on Terror'

Ruth Blakeley and Sam Raphael

In response to the horrors of the two World Wars, considerable effort was made in the latter half of the twentieth century to establish governance regimes aimed at ensuring the universal realisation of human rights. Yet the governance of human rights is hampered considerably by the absence of robust enforcement mechanisms. Therefore, human rights governance has tended to involve the monitoring of human rights by a range of bodies, and the subsequent application of varying degrees of diplomatic pressure on states to improve their human rights performance. Despite the lack of enforcement options, these monitoring processes have gone some considerable way to mitigating some of the most serious abuses of human rights in the modern world, especially by states.

The first part of this chapter provides an overview of the international human rights regime, and examines the various human rights governance mechanisms that have been established by the international community. It then explores the various ways in which human rights monitoring is undertaken, and how pressure is exerted by a variety of agents to bring about improved compliance with human rights. The second half of this chapter explores these themes in more depth, by examining a particular case study: the use by the United States and its allies of rendition, secret detention and torture in pursuit of the 'War on Terror'. This case demonstrates that, while the US has gone to considerable lengths to circumvent human rights law, at the same time the governance mechanisms in place have allowed for these practices to be challenged, both in the law courts and through the exercise of diplomatic and popular pressure. So while most would agree that human rights governance structures need strengthening at many levels, the case of rendition and secret detention demonstrates that, if nothing else, the world is a better place with these mechanisms in existence.

What is being governed and why?

Human rights, in their modern incarnation, and in the sense of a concept that is governed globally, can be understood as those rights which all people, in every region in the world, share under international law. There are several key principles which underpin this particular notion of human rights. First is the principle of *universality*: the rights enshrined in international law are applicable throughout the world, and reach into all political, cultural and religious systems. This principle has been highly controversial, with some arguing that the framework of universal human rights is not much more than an imposition of Western values. Without doubt, however, universality underpins the framework of human rights, and finds expression in all human rights instruments. Second, human rights as expressed at the global level are *inalienable*. That is, they are 'given' to us as humans by virtue of the fact that we are human, and cannot be taken away from us, except for some rights in particular contexts which are themselves governed by 'due process' and the rule of law. For example, while all people have the 'right to liberty', this can be curtailed in individual cases through imprisonment, as long as such curtailments are exercised in accordance with due process (including the right for the individual to appeal to a judicial authority). While the notion of international human rights applies both in peacetime and during times of armed conflict, in practice the *exact* rights laid down for enjoyment during wars are in many cases different from (and less than) those rights enjoyed outside of conflict and times of national emergency. There are, however, some rights which are cast as 'non-derogable'. That is, there are no circumstances whatsoever which would allow for these rights to be curtailed; everyone, for example, is granted the right to life and to be free from torture and slavery, at all times.

Third, and related to the principle of inalienability, human rights are applicable in a completely equal and non-discriminatory manner, regardless of the individual's race, sex, colour, nationality, sexuality, religion and so forth. Last, human rights under international law are conceived as *interdependent and indivisible*: they are not simply a list of separate rights, but come together to form a dense network of rights which are, in many ways, reliant upon each other. The undermining of one particular right would weaken the entire architecture of rights, through the knock-on effect that this weakening would have on interrelated rights.

The notion of human rights has its origin in a broader set of norms based on natural law, with the preceding notion that, by virtue of being human, certain universal moral standards exist in relation to our treatment of each other, and that we all have a duty to adhere to these. However, the contemporary understanding of human rights, and the associated attempt to govern rights at a global level, is a product of a desire to prevent a repeat of the horrors of the Second World War. With the establishment of the United Nations in 1945, the international community attempted to put in place mechanisms (enshrined in the UN Charter) to avoid wars between states. Crucially, given the mass violence delivered by states on both sides against civilians during the Second World War, the international community through the UN also attempted to define a comprehensive framework of rights which all individuals hold, and which should be respected and protected by all states around the world, in both peacetime and during war. This historical moment was fundamental to the establishment of the contemporary framework, and to the extension and infusion of the notion of rights throughout the international community.

Human rights, initially enshrined in the Universal Declaration of Human Rights (UDHR) in 1948 and the Geneva Conventions in 1949, but added to over subsequent years, are generally articulated in relation to the state. That is, it is states which sign up to international human rights instruments, and which consequently assume obligations in relation to individuals. States are understood to be both the main threat to human rights and also best positioned to respect, protect and fulfil those rights. In this context, states have several reinforcing obligations: to refrain from curtailing people's rights (the duty to respect); to protect citizens against violations of human rights (the duty to protect); and to take a proactive stance in the promotion and emergence of a society wherein all rights are respected and enjoyed by all people (the duty to fulfil).

The core human rights governed at a global level, and sitting at the centre of International Human Rights Law, are enshrined in the International Bill of Rights. This consists of the UDHR, which sets forth general principles and standards, and two associated Covenants (treaties) which begin to translate these principles into legal concepts. The two Covenants were opened for signature at the same time, in December 1966, and are the International Covenant on Civil and Political Rights (ICCPR) and the International Covenant on Economic, Social and Cultural Rights (ICESCR).

Alongside the core rights enshrined in International Human Rights Law, the post-war era has witnessed a parallel acceleration in the development of human rights applicable in times of armed conflict. Embodied in a second body of international law, known as International Humanitarian Law (IHL), the protections are to be guaranteed by all armed actors (ICRC 2003). The Geneva Conventions and additional protocols, ratified in 1949, fall under IHL. These updated three prior treaties from 1864, 1906 and 1929, concerning the humanitarian treatment of victims of conflict, and added a fourth, which focused on the treatment of prisoners of war and established certain protections for civilians. Of particular note is Common Article 3, present in all four of the Geneva Conventions, which sets out minimum standards to guarantee the humane protection of specific groups caught up in armed conflict, including armed actors that have been detained:

> Persons taking no active part in the hostilities, including members of armed forces who have laid down their arms and those placed hors de combat by sickness, wounds, detention, or any other cause, shall in all circumstances be treated humanely, without any adverse distinction founded on race, colour, religion or faith, sex, birth or wealth, or any other similar criteria.

Box 10.1 Core Universal Human Rights

Together, the core documents of the International Bill of Rights lay down a range of rights which are to be enjoyed universally, including (but not limited to):

- The right to life, with no-one's life being deprived arbitrarily
- Freedom from death penalty for children and pregnant women
- Freedom from torture, or cruel, inhuman or degrading treatment or punishment
- Freedom from medical or scientific experimentation without consent
- Freedom from slavery and servitude
- Freedom from forced or compulsory labour (except as part of a punishment under law, or as part of military service)
- The right to liberty and security of the person, with freedom from arbitrary arrest and detention
- Freedom of movement within a territory (if that person is lawfully within the territory)
- The right to equality before the law, the presumption of innocence, and a free and fair trial
- Freedom from arbitrary interference in the family, home or correspondence
- Freedom of thought, conscience and religion
- Freedom of expression
- Freedom of peaceful assembly
- Freedom of association with others, including the formation of trade unions
- The right to form a family, and to marry
- The right to vote, and to stand for election
- The right to a nationality
- The right to work, including fair wages, safe conditions, the opportunity for promotion, and a reasonable limitation of working hours
- The right to strike
- The right to social security
- The right to an adequate standard of living, including adequate food, clothing and housing
- The right to the enjoyment of the highest attainable standard of physical and mental health
- The right to education.

Common Article 3 then prohibits certain acts at all times and in all places, including:

(a) violence to life and person, in particular murder of all kinds, mutilation, cruel treatment and torture;
(b) taking of hostages;
(c) outrages upon personal dignity, in particular humiliating and degrading treatment;
(d) the passing of sentences and the carrying out of executions without previous judgement pronounced by a regularly constituted court, affording all the judicial guarantees which are recognised as indispensable by civilised peoples.

Under the Geneva Conventions, the International Committee of the Red Cross (ICRC) is mandated to promote the laws that protect victims of war. One of its most important roles is to visit individuals that have been detained during armed conflict. These visits are intended to ensure that the detainees, whatever the reasons for their arrest, are treated with dignity and humanity, in accordance with international norms and standards.

Who are the key actors involved in the governance of human rights and what are the key mechanisms of governance?

The idea that human rights are 'governed' suggests the development of mechanisms for enforcing compliance with human rights norms. Yet there are very few enforcement mechanisms in place internationally. Instead, human rights governance tends to involve the monitoring of human rights violations by individuals, non-governmental organisations (NGOs), local networks, governments or intergovernmental organisations, and the subsequent application, to varying degrees, of diplomatic pressure on states to improve their human rights records.

The various rights covered by the UDHR and other declarations are enshrined – and made legally binding for signatory states – in a number of Conventions with global reach. This governance architecture at a global level has been complemented by parallel regional efforts. This is particularly the case in Europe, where the Convention for the Protection of Human Rights and Fundamental Freedoms (commonly known as the European Convention on Human Rights, or ECHR) came into force in 1953. All member states of the Council of Europe are party to the ECHR, which codifies many of the rights and duties set out at the UN level. Other regional organisations that have been established with a mandate, among other things, to monitor and ensure compliance with human rights norms include the Organisation of American States and the Organisation of African Unity. Both have their own separate human rights codes and have taken steps to establish Human Rights Courts.

Box 10.2 Major global instruments of human rights law (1945–)

(Numbers in brackets = number of state parties, as of July 2012)

International human rights law

- International Convention on the Elimination of All Forms of Racial Discrimination, March 1966 (175)
- International Covenant on Economic, Social and Cultural Rights, December 1966 (160)
- International Covenant on Civil and Political Rights, December 1966 (167)
- International Convention on the Suppression and Punishment of the Crime of Apartheid, November 1973 (108)
- Convention on the Elimination of All Forms of Discrimination against Women, December 1979 (187)
- Convention against Torture and Other Cruel, Inhuman or Degrading Treatment or Punishment, December 1984 (150)
- International Convention against Apartheid in Sports, December 1985 (60)
- Convention on the Rights of the Child, November 1989 (193)
- International Convention on the Protection of the Rights of All Migrant Workers and Members of their Families, December 1990 (46)
- Convention on the Rights of Persons with Disabilities, December 2006 (117)
- International Convention for the Protection of All Persons from Enforced Disappearance, December 2006 (34).

International humanitarian law

- Convention on the Prevention and Punishment of the Crime of Genocide, December 1948 (142)
- Geneva Convention (I) for the Amelioration of the Condition of the Wounded and Sick in Armed Forces in the Field, August 1949 (194)
- Geneva Convention (II) for the Amelioration of the Condition of Wounded, Sick and Shipwrecked Members of Armed Forces at Sea, August 1949 (194)
- Geneva Convention (III) relative to the Treatment of Prisoners of War, August 1949 (194)
- Geneva Convention (IV) relative to the Protection of Civilian Persons in Time of War, August 1949 (194)

- Convention for the Protection of Cultural Property in the Event of Armed Conflict, May 1954 (125)
- Convention on the Prohibition of Military or any other Hostile Use of Environmental Modification Techniques, December 1976 (76)
- Convention on the Prohibition of the Development, Production and Stockpiling of Bacteriological (Biological) and Toxin Weapons and on their Destruction, April 1972 (165)
- Convention on Prohibitions or Restrictions on the Use of Certain Conventional Weapons which may be deemed to be Excessively Injurious or to have Indiscriminate Effects, October 1980 (114)
- Convention on the Prohibition of the Development, Production, Stockpiling and Use of Chemical Weapons and on their Destruction, January 1993 (188)
- Convention on the Prohibition of the Use, Stockpiling, Production and Transfer of Anti-Personnel Mines and on their Destruction, September 1997 (160)
- Convention on Cluster Munitions, 30 May 2008 (73).

Accompanying the various Conventions of IHL and IHRL, the major international organisations have established specific bodies to monitor states' compliance with the Conventions. At the UN, these include the Human Rights Committee, the Committee Against Torture and the Committee Against Enforced Disappearances. These Committees are empowered to establish fact-finding missions by special commission where appropriate, and can draw on the expertise of criminal investigators, military analysts or other experts. Reporting of such commissions plays an important role in highlighting non-compliance with human rights conventions. As well as monitoring by the UN and other external actors, the six main treaties of the UN human rights regime include within them mandatory reporting requirements for all signatory states, generally on a four- to five-year cycle, thereby causing states to review their performance in light of their human rights obligations on a regular basis.

Individual states also have their own strategies for monitoring compliance with human rights norms. The US Department of State, for example, produces annual reports on the human rights performance of all states that are members of the UN and all states in receipt of US foreign aid. Similarly, the European Parliament reports on the human rights records of its member states. Often human rights reporting of this nature is used to link benefits such as aid to the fulfilment of human rights obligations. Known as conditionality, this is a strategy that has been favoured by the EU in its efforts to promote human rights, democracy and the rule of law. Conditionality of course depends on monitoring mechanisms that have been put in place to evaluate states' compliance with the UDHR and other human rights conventions and treaties.

NGOs increasingly play an important role in holding states to account for their complicity in human rights violations. The 1980s saw a considerable increase in the numbers of human rights organisations that focused on human rights issues. NGOs are permitted to submit complaints to the various UN bodies, and can also report to the UN on compliance of states with human rights norms. Amnesty International and Human Rights Watch are among the most prominent NGOs involved in the systematic reporting of human rights violations.

Self-monitoring by states and external monitoring by international organisations or other external actors helps highlight non-compliance and can result in diplomatic pressure of various kinds being exerted on states whose human rights records fall short of expected standards. Increasingly, political legitimacy is understood and judged with reference to the human rights track record of political agents or states, and it is often argued that socialisation into and normalisation of human rights is an important vehicle for ensuring compliance with human rights. Thus it is argued that varying levels of diplomatic pressure, from gentle encouragement, urging and advising, to more robust forms of communicating, such as naming and shaming states for their harmful practices, are all important tools in encouraging states to fulfil their human rights obligations.

Human rights violations can also be addressed through international tribunals, such as the International Court of Justice in The Hague, or the International Criminal Court, or regional tribunals, such as the European Court of Human Rights. At the European level, the Parliamentary Assembly can choose to launch investigations into violations of the European Convention on Human Rights by member states. Any person who believes their human rights to be violated under the Convention can take a case to the European Court of Human Rights. Where judgements are made against member states, these judgements are binding.

On very rare occasions states might impose sanctions to try and force a change in state behaviour, as was the case with the imposition of sanctions against South Africa by numerous states, in a quest to force the regime to end apartheid. Even more rarely, states or coalitions of states might take military action to try and prevent human rights violations, or to force a regime change where states may have a notorious human rights record. Such actions are highly controversial; in such cases questions are raised about the motivations of intervening states, and while not the topic of this chapter, it is important to bear in mind that just because a state or coalition claims to be intervening on human rights grounds, this does not always mean this is the only (or even primary) motivation.

Human rights monitoring, and the subsequent pressure that can be put on states, can be effective in bringing about change. Yet the governance of human rights is hampered to a considerable degree by the lack of enforcement mechanisms. Furthermore, questions are regularly raised about the governance systems that are in place. UN processes are seen as overly bureaucratic and time-consuming. Only a small fraction of the complaints raised with the UN bodies are investigated. Little airtime is given to NGOs to report orally to the UN Commission. In addition, it is often argued that the Global North is quick to scrutinise the Global South, but much more reticent about having its own human rights records questioned.

Rendition, secret detention and torture in the 'War on Terror'

In the years after the declaration of the 'War on Terror' in September 2001, the United States Government led the way in constructing a global system of detention outside the law, illegal prisoner transfers between states (rendition), and interrogation and detainee treatment practices that were clearly cruel, inhuman and degrading, and that in some cases involved torture. Less than a week after the 9/11 terrorist attacks, on 17 September 2001, President George W. Bush authorised the Director of the CIA to engage in 'clandestine intelligence activity' as part of the counterterrorism campaign, including the formation of a 'terrorist detention and interrogation program'. Less than two months later, on 13 November 2001, President Bush issued an Executive Order on the Detention, Treatment, and Trial of Certain Non-Citizens in the War Against Terrorism, providing the Pentagon with the authority to detain *indefinitely* any non-American, in any place in the world, considered to pose a terrorist threat to US interests. Furthermore, within just three months of the second Executive Order, on 7 February 2002, President Bush issued a memo to his senior staff declaring that members of Al Qaeda and the Taliban were 'unlawful combatants', and as such did not qualify as 'prisoners of war' under the Geneva Conventions when detained. As well as denying prisoner of war status to the 'War on Terror' detainees, Bush determined that Common Article 3 of the Geneva Conventions did not apply to Al Qaeda or Taliban detainees. In doing so, he was denying that they should be guaranteed humane treatment in compliance with IHL.

This policy laid the foundations for the development of the global system of rendition and secret detention, as well as the official military detentions in Afghanistan and Guantánamo Bay, Cuba. It also paved the way for subsequent moves by the CIA to secure permission from the US Department of Justice for the use of so-called 'enhanced interrogation techniques', a euphemism for torture, to be used against certain 'High Value Detainees'. These were approved for use on 1 August 2002, in a move that opened the door to a range of aggressive techniques which most experts consider to fall within the definition of torture. What is more, in 2003 the CIA Inspector General was tasked with carrying out an investigation into the use of the so-called 'Enhanced Interrogation Techniques' (CIA 2004). His findings raised serious questions about the use of interrogation by the CIA, as he found that interrogators frequently deviated from the guidelines, using methods that had not been sanctioned, and using those that had been sanctioned in more prolonged and harsher ways than had been permitted. (For a full analysis of the CIA Inspector General's investigation, see Blakeley 2011.)

Box 10.3 The 'Enhanced Interrogation Techniques'

The ten approved techniques, along with a brief description provided by the CIA to the OLC, were:

The attention grasp	Consists of grasping the detainee with both hands, with one hand on each side of the collar opening, in a controlled and quick motion. In the same motion as the grasp, the detainee is drawn toward the interrogator.
Walling	The detainee is pulled forward and then quickly and firmly pushed into a flexible false wall so that their shoulder blades hit the wall. Their head and neck are supported with a rolled towel to prevent whiplash.
The facial hold	Used to hold the detainee's head immobile. The interrogator places an open palm on either side of the detainee's face and the interrogator's fingertips are kept well away from the detainee's eyes.
The facial insult or slap	The fingers are slightly spread apart. The interrogator's hand makes contact with the area between the tip of the detainee's chin and the bottom of the corresponding earlobe.
Cramped confinement	The detainee is placed in a confined space, typically a small or large box, which is usually dark. Confinement in the smaller space lasts no more than two hours and in the larger space it can last up to 18 hours.
Confinement with insects	Involves placing a harmless insect in the box with the detainee.
Wall standing	The detainee may stand about 4–5 feet from a wall with his feet spread approximately to their shoulder width. Their arms are stretched out in front of him and his fingers rest on the wall to support all of their body weight. The detainee is not allowed to reposition their hands or feet.
Stress positions	May include having the detainee sit on the floor with his legs extended straight out in front of him with their arms raised above his head or kneeling on the floor while leaning back at a 45-degree angle.
Sleep deprivation	Will not exceed 11 days at a time.
Waterboarding	Involves binding the detainee to a bench with their feet elevated above their head. The detainee's head is immobilised and an interrogator places a cloth over the detainee's mouth and nose while pouring water onto the cloth in a controlled manner. Airflow is restricted for 20–40 seconds and the technique produces the sensation of drowning and suffocation.

During the Bush administration, the secret detention of terror suspects took place within a complex 'network' of prisons. At its core was a set of US-run facilities, overseen by the Pentagon and CIA. These existed in several locations around the globe, including Iraq, Afghanistan, Thailand, Djibouti, Poland, Romania, Lithuania and Cuba (alongside the official prison at Guantánamo Bay). Supplementing these was a series of pre-existing detention sites, centred in North Africa and the Middle East, run by foreign security forces known to regularly use torture, but to which the CIA had direct access. Overall, this system has involved the detention, abuse and torture, in secret, of hundreds of detainees, in scores of detention sites around the world. Multiple and sustained human rights abuses have characterised the system, with violations of rights codified within both International Human Rights Law and International Humanitarian Law.

Such violations have come as a result of US practices, but also with the direct involvement of, or indirect complicity of, many states around the world. There is evidence (UN 2010; Seimas Committee 2009), for example, that states which hosted US-run secret prisons – such as Poland and Lithuania – knew about what was going on, and provided key logistical assistance and diplomatic cover to facilitate operations (through, for example, allowing the prisons to be constructed on their soil, and ensuring that aircraft carrying prisoners for detention and abuse were allowed to land without scrutiny). Other states played a key role in the capture of individual detainees, and their transfer to US forces for rendition, secret detention and abuse. These states included Canada, Italy, Macedonia, Sweden, Kenya, Tanzania, Malawi, Zambia, Sudan, Mauritania, The Gambia, Dubai, Yemen, Indonesia, Thailand and, most importantly, Pakistan. States across the Middle East and North Africa – including Jordan, Syria, Egypt, Libya and Morocco – have received, detained and interrogated suspects on behalf of the US. Indeed, this form of 'proxy detention' is central to the global system of detention outside the law, as the plausible deniability of the US and other Western involvement in torture is easier to maintain. Detainee accounts demonstrate that such proxy detentions often come with a more extreme form of abuse, and that severe beatings, electro-torture, genital mutilation and rape were experienced by those detained on behalf of the US.

Some Western democracies, often held up as key actors in the governance architecture of international human rights, have played a key role in the operation of this global system of detention outside the law, albeit often from an 'arm's length' position. Security forces from Canada, Sweden, Italy and the UK have facilitated the capture and transfer of terror suspects into the system of secret detention and torture. This has been either through involvement in the initial 'arrest' and handover to US forces, or through the passing of intelligence to friendly security forces to locate suspects and facilitate their capture. Canadian and British intelligence agencies, along with their German and Australian counterparts, have also been accused of direct involvement in the interrogation of suspects in secret prisons, or else being complicit in their mistreatment through sending questions for interrogators and receiving intelligence derived from torture.

Rendition, secret detention and torture as violations of IHL and IHRL

The global rendition system has, at its core, three interrelated practices which violate both IHL and International Human Rights Law (IHRL). The first is the *secret detention* of terror suspects, where the US and its allies have held people in undisclosed locations around the world. Not all detainees held in the 'War on Terror' have been held in secret, but those that have were denied access by third parties (such as lawyers, family members, or the International Committee of the Red Cross/Crescent), with their fate and whereabouts, and even the very fact of their detention, remaining unacknowledged by the detaining authorities. The second practice is the *rendition* of terror suspects between detention facilities in different parts of the world, where rendition refers to the extra-legal transfer of suspects across state borders. The third involves the cruel, inhuman and degrading treatment of suspects during detention and transfer, including the use by US and allied forces of practices that amount to *torture*. The processes involved in the rendition and secret detention of individuals in the 'War on Terror' violate the following laws, as set out in the various human rights conventions:

- the prohibition of arbitrary detention;
- the right to a fair trial; and
- the prohibition of torture and other cruel, inhuman and degrading treatment of punishment.

In addition, under international laws concerning non-refoulement, states have a responsibility to ensure that they are in no way accessories to human rights violations. Indeed they have certain responsibilities to prevent those violations.

The prohibition of arbitrary detention and the right to a fair trial

In the 'War on Terror' the US has arbitrarily detained individuals in a number of ways. This includes secretly holding people in Department of Defense facilities or in secret CIA prisons or 'black sites', detention by proxy, where third-party states provide the detention facilities for the detainees, and indefinite non-secret military detention, for example in the Guantánamo Bay detention facility.

Under international law, individuals that are detained during an armed conflict must be formally registered by the detaining authorities, and granted access to the ICRC (and through them to their families). Indeed, one of the most important roles of the ICRC is to visit individuals detained during armed conflict. In the wars in Afghanistan and Iraq, while the majority of prisoners have been registered with the ICRC, many have been held in secret.

Secret detentions occur when detainees are held incommunicado (i.e., when they are not permitted any contact with the outside world, including their families, lawyers or the ICRC), and when the detaining authorities refuse to acknowledge either the fact of the detention, or the fate and whereabouts of the detainee. The detention site itself does not have to be secret for the detention to be secret. This means that officially recognised detention facilities, and even secret wings within officially recognised detention facilities, can be used for secret detentions.

Those who were held in secret by the US include detainees which the US Government denied it held, or about which it refused to discuss. They also include those which the US Government admitted to holding, where it then refused to disclose their exact whereabouts and their current status of well-being. All of these detainees were fully cut off from the outside world, with no third party granted access to monitor the detention or speak to the detainee.

The UN Working Group on Arbitrary Detention has defined secret detention as a 'Category I' form of arbitrary detention, where it is 'clearly impossible to involve any legal basis justifying the deprivation of liberty'. The UN Working Group has also directly concluded that detainees held secretly within CIA prisons were victims of Category I arbitrary detention. In this sense, secret detention necessarily violates the rights to liberty and freedom from arbitrary detention guaranteed by Articles 9 and 14 of the ICCPR. Together, these articles set out the rights of each detainee to a fair trial before the courts.

The prohibition of torture

The US is a signatory to the Geneva Conventions, the UN Convention Against Torture and Other Cruel, Inhuman or Degrading Treatment or Punishment and the ICCPR. Torture and cruel, inhuman or degrading treatment or punishment are all prohibited under each of these Conventions. There is no derogation from this prohibition, even in times of war. Torture is defined by Article 1 of the UN Convention Against Torture as:

> Any act by which severe pain or suffering, whether physical or mental, is intentionally inflicted on a person for such purposes as obtaining from him or a third person information or a confession, punishing him for an act he or a third person has committed or is suspected of having committed, or intimidating or coercing him or a third person, or for any reason based on discrimination of any kind, when such pain or suffering is inflicted by or at the instigation of or with the consent or acquiescence of a public official or other person acting in an official capacity. It does not include pain or suffering arising only from, inherent in or incidental to lawful sanctions.

Despite this, the rendition and illicit detention of terror suspects in the 'War on Terror' has led to the torture, cruel, inhuman and degrading treatment and punishment of many detainees, either while held and interrogated by the CIA or by US Department of Defense personnel, or by states acting in conjunction with the US. A range of torture methods have been employed to cause pain and suffering, including beatings, mock drowning (waterboarding), mock executions, electrocutions, stress positions, sensory overload and sensory deprivation. In particular, secret detention has been found to be a primary facilitator in the commission of acts of torture and can *itself* constitute an act of cruel, inhuman or degrading treatment – and even in some cases an act of torture. As such, the UN's Human Rights Council have found many such cases to be in violation of Articles 7 and 10 of the ICCPR.

Non-refoulement

As well as violating various international human rights norms and laws, rendition and secret detention result in important questions about whether states have also violated their obligations to take measures to prevent such human rights violations. For example, under Article 3 of the Convention Against Torture, states have obligations to try to prevent torture by other parties. The transfer of an individual to another state where there is a risk that the individual faces torture is prohibited. The 2010 Joint Study on Global Practices in Relation to Secret Detention in the Context of Countering Terrorism (UN 2010c) found that numerous states had been complicit in a variety of ways in rendition and secret detention.

Despite the myriad violations of human rights as a result of the US-led rendition and torture of terror suspects, the governance architecture of human rights has provided a means by which a range of actors have attempted to hold the US and its allies accountable, and to seek redress for the injustices committed. Those involved in challenging the human rights violations associated with the global rendition system have drawn on IHL and IHRL, and have used the mechanisms established at the national, regional and international levels for seeking redress for human rights violations.

What are the issues that have arisen in relation to the governance of human rights with respect to the global rendition system?

Despite the attempts by the Bush administration to hold detainees beyond the law in the 'War on Terror', legal experts from around the world are overwhelmingly of the opinion that rendition, secret detention and torture, as sanctioned by the Bush administration, are illegal. In some cases they may even constitute 'war crimes' and 'crimes against humanity'. With recourse to IHL and IHRL, and the various national, regional and international mechanisms concerned with upholding human rights, the international human rights community has challenged the Bush administration's attempts to place detainees beyond the law.

Exerting pressure to comply with IHL and IHRL

Various organisations have exerted pressure on the US and allied states to comply with IHL and IHRL. The ICRC has played a significant role in this regard. One of the ICRC's most important remits is to visit those individuals detained during armed conflict. These visits are intended to ensure that the detainees, whatever the reasons for their arrest, are treated with dignity and humanity, in accordance with

IHL and IHRL. The ICRC has repeatedly expressed concern at the legal status of the detainees, arguing that the US has placed them beyond the law by refusing to recognise them as prisoners of war. The ICRC does not publish its findings on the compliance of states with IHL and IHRL. Instead, it tends to communicate privately with state officials to point out where IHL and IHRL are not being upheld. However, a confidential report (ICRC 2007), leaked in 2009, was highly critical of the involvement of medical professionals in the torture of detainees, and the systematic nature of the torture inflicted on the so-called 'high value detainees'. The fact that the ICRC rarely makes public is findings, but that a decision was made within the ICRC to leak the 2007 report, illustrates how seriously the ICRC took these human rights violations. It attracted considerable media coverage because it was such an unusual move, and was an important moment in calling the US to account for its illegal actions.

Legal challenges in the US courts

From February 2002 onwards, dozens of cases were brought before the US District Court for the District of Columbia to claim the habeas corpus rights of the detainees, that is, the right to challenge the basis for detention. Central to these cases was the aim of making explicit the ways in which the Bush administration had sought to curtail human rights through its framing of terror suspects as 'enemy combatants', rather than prisoners of war. Numerous articles of both US and international law have been invoked, including Title 18 of the US Code on Crimes and Criminal Procedure, Title 28 of the US Code on the Judiciary and Judicial Procedure, especially chapter 153 on Habeas Corpus rights, Articles I, II, III and IV and Amendments III, IV, V and VIII of the US Constitution, the UN Convention Against Torture, the Universal Declaration of Human Rights and the Geneva Conventions. The strategy of those representing the detainees was to show how Bush's Executive Orders and accompanying practices violate the principles at the heart of the US Constitution and international law.

What followed was a complex legal battle between the detainees' lawyers, the courts and the US Government. In June 2004, the Supreme Court held in *Rasul v. Bush* that the 600 Guantánamo Bay detainees had a right to access the US federal courts 'via habeas corpus and otherwise, to challenge their detention and conditions of confinement' (CCR 2008). However, within a week of this ruling the US Government authorised the establishment of the Combatant Status Review Tribunals (CSRTs) at Guantánamo (Wolfowitz 2004). These were deliberately intended to avoid providing Guantánamo detainees any access to the US courts, despite the ruling of the Supreme Court (CCR 2008). It was up to military officers to review each detainee's enemy combatant status without legal representation for the detainees, evidence was permitted that had been obtained under coercion or torture, and detainees were denied access to classified evidence, which in many cases comprised the majority of the evidence against the detainee (CCR 2008). Numerous challenges were brought in both the District and Supreme Courts to these tribunals, again invoking the habeas corpus rights of the detainees. And in turn, to try and halt these various petitions, the Bush administration and Congress passed the Detainee Treatment Act in December 2005. This purported to strip the US courts of their jurisdiction over the various habeas corpus petitions filed on behalf of the Guantánamo detainees, vesting exclusive review of the final decisions of the CSRTs and military commissions into the District of Columbia Circuit Court.

Yet within the Geneva Conventions themselves, provisions are made to halt states from holding detainees outside of the law. Article 5 of the Third Geneva Convention expressly states that in cases where an individual's status as a prisoner of war is in dispute, 'such persons shall enjoy the protection of the present Convention until such time as their status has been determined by a competent tribunal'. The Commentary on the Fourth Geneva Convention states that 'every person in enemy hands must have some status under international law: he is either a prisoner of war and, as such, covered by the Third Convention, a civilian covered by the Fourth Convention, or again, a member of the medical personnel covered by the First Convention. *There is no* intermediate status; nobody in enemy hands can be outside the law'. Indeed, this was the conclusion reached by the US Supreme Court, which ruled in *Hamdan v. Rumsfeld* in June 2006 that detainees did have the right to pursue habeas corpus cases in civilian courts. Despite this ruling, the Bush administration passed the Military Commission Act in October 2006 (Congress 2006), aimed at bypassing the Supreme Court's judgement through ratifying the severely limited CSRT review process as a substitute for habeas corpus. Further legal battles ensued, with the Supreme Court eventually ruling 5–4 in favour of the detainees in June 2008, granting the writ of habeas corpus. While this has been a game of cat and mouse, it highlights the importance of the independent judicial systems as mechanisms through which redress can be sought for victims of human rights violations, even when states are determined to circumvent the law.

Official inquiries

A number of investigations have been undertaken by international organisations, as well as by individual states, into rendition, secret detention and torture. Alongside the endeavours of human rights organisations and lawyers seeking redress for victims, these have had a significant impact. Two important inquiries into the involvement of European states in the global rendition system have caused a number of individual states to carry out their own investigations, and in one case, this led to charges against a senior official. These inquiries also raised concern among US policymakers about the impact of the global rendition programme on the global reputation of the US and its relations with European states. In January 2006, the European Parliament set up a Temporary Committee on the alleged use of European countries by the CIA for the transport and illegal detention of prisoners. The purpose of the investigation was to determine whether the CIA or other US agencies or the intelligence agencies of other third countries had carried out rendition, secret detention or torture and other cruel, inhuman and degrading treatment of prisoners on the territory of European Union member states. The interim reports (EU 2006) set out the nature of the 'global spider's web' of rendition and secret detention, and provided substantial new evidence of individual rendition operations. The final report (EU 2007) found that more than 1200 CIA-operated flights had used European airspace between 2001 and 2005. When the findings were reported by Giovanni Claudio Fava in January 2007, the European Parliament passed two key resolutions as a result, urging member states that had been complicit to act immediately to halt such practices, to investigate them fully, and to compensate victims.

The Fava report had repercussions beyond Europe. It raised considerable concerns in US policy circles, such that in April 2007, two subcommittees of the Committee on Foreign Affairs for the House of Representatives held a joint hearing to examine the impact of the US-led extraordinary rendition programme on transatlantic relations. Testimony was given by various experts and policymakers, and submissions were received from organisations such as Amnesty International. The transcript of the hearing demonstrates how concerned US officials were by the European Parliament's investigation, particularly as an indicator of the erosion of relations with some of its most important friends in the international community. Indeed, many of those giving testimony called for a reversal of those policies that so flagrantly violate US and international law on human rights, because of the damage that these policies were doing to the US' capacity to cooperate with important allies.

A second official investigation was launched in Europe, following allegations by Human Rights Watch in 2005 that secret CIA prisons were operating on the territory of member states of the Council of Europe. The Parliamentary Assembly of the Council of Europe (PACE) launched the investigation to examine the complicity of its member states. The final report, published in June 2007 (Marty 2007), concluded there was 'now enough evidence to state that secret detention facilities run by the CIA did exist in Europe from 2003 to 2005, in particular Poland and Romania', and also that governments of these countries were aware and may have authorized the facilities. The impact of this inquiry has been significant. Following publication of the report, Swiss Senator and PACE member Dick Marty confirmed that he had independently verified that a detention facility for rendition victims had operated on Lithuanian soil. This, along with reports in the Lithuanian press, caused the Lithuanian government to launch a confidential investigation into Lithuanian state complicity. It also paved the way for investigations and the subsequent arrest in Poland of the former intelligence chief on charges of allegedly exceeding his powers, depriving prisoners of their freedom and allowing corporal punishment of individuals detained in a secret prison operated on behalf of the CIA on Polish soil.

Most recently, a high-profile investigation was conducted by the UN Special Rapporteur on the Promotion and Protection of Human Rights and Fundamental Freedoms while Countering Terrorism, in collaboration with other UN committees.

The Joint Study on Global Practices in Relation to Secret Detention in the Context of Countering Terrorism was published in February 2010. It singled out numerous states for their involvement, either by supplying intelligence that led to renditions and secret detentions, or by seizing suspects, including the UK, Bosnia and Herzegovina, Canada, Croatia, Georgia, Indonesia, Kenya, Macedonia and Pakistan. It also stated that UK intelligence agents had been involved in interrogations of suspects in Pakistan, Afghanistan, Iraq and at Guantánamo Bay. While the UK Foreign Office responded by claiming that it does not solicit, encourage, condone or participate in torture (UN 2010), various MPs called for a judicial inquiry into the UK's role. Such calls continue to be voiced, especially following the emergence of evidence that MI6 officers were involved in the rendition of British residents, Abdel Hakim Belhadj and his pregnant wife, Fatima Bouchar, from Thailand to Libya, where they were illegally detained and mistreated by Colonel Gadaffi's regime. Lawyers acting for the couple have begun legal proceedings against then Foreign Secretary Jack Straw, who allegedly signed off on their rendition. At the time of writing, the case is on-going. Another Libyan, Sami al-Saadi, who was abducted with his wife and four children in Hong Kong and secretly flown to Libya in a joint US–UK operation, has accepted £2.23 million from the UK government in compensation in an out of court settlement in December 2012 (Norton-Taylor 2012). MI6 agents facilitated the rendition of the family, which led to the imprisonment of the entire family, initially, and the detention and torture of al-Saadi for four years by Colonel Gaddafi's regime. The UK government refused to accept any liability, even though evidence obtained by Human Rights Watch (HRW 2012) clearly demonstrates the complicity of MI6. Al-Saadi stated that he had accepted the compensation to avoid putting his family through further suffering, and because he lacked faith that the truth would come out through the courts (Norton-Taylor 2012). Investigations by international organisations thus play an important role in bringing to public attention state complicity. They can also help facilitate subsequent efforts to seek redress against complicit states by human rights organisations and lawyers, on behalf of victims.

There have been some successes in the struggle to reverse the most egregious of human rights violations that stemmed from the establishment of the global rendition system. Indeed, with recourse to IHL and IHRL, the international human rights community has succeeded in exposing many of those states that were secretly involved, and has pushed for states to investigate and, where necessary, compensate victims. Struggles on behalf of the Guantánamo detainees have led to the release of the majority of those held, although some 180 remain in detention. And as a result of the pressure from the international human rights community, both the Bush and Obama administrations had to bring an end to the use of secret CIA prisons and torture by CIA agents. Immediately upon entering office in 2009, President Obama passed three Executive Orders which significantly changed the legal parameters within which the US military and intelligence communities could detain and interrogate terror suspects. The CIA was no longer allowed to operate its own detention facilities, and secret detention was outlawed for all detainees in all armed conflicts, who find themselves in

US custody. 'Enhanced interrogation techniques' were also prohibited, with US interrogations now constrained by the guidelines found in Army Field Manual 2–22.3. Extraordinary renditions for the purposes of torture were also banned.

These Orders represented the formalisation of shifts in the rendition and secret detention programme witnessed during the final years of the Bush administration. These changes were largely achieved through the struggles in the US courts during the Bush years, as well as international pressure from international organizations and NGOs. The struggles are ongoing however, because the Military Commissions Act has enshrined into US law the processes that deny the rights of detainees to habeas corpus review and, without a change to the law, detainees can still be denied their rights. Furthermore, many thousands of detainees in the 'War on Terror' continue to be held beyond the bounds of US and international law. While a message by CIA Director Leon Panetta in April 2009 confirmed that the black sites had been closed, and that enhanced interrogation techniques were no longer employed, rendition and proxy detention by third party states known to regularly use torture have not been ruled out by the US Government, and may still form a central plank of counterterrorism policy (Panetta 2009).

Conclusion

Ensuring compliance with the laws intended to protect human rights has always been a challenge. The attempts by the Bush administration to place 'War on Terror' detainees beyond the law were materially different from cases where states simply flout the law. In this case the most powerful state in the world attempted to re-write the law.

While the governance of human rights tends to be based on monitoring and diplomacy, rather than enforcement, such monitoring can help mitigate serious violations of human rights. It is through monitoring the human rights performance of states that those states can be called to account within the international organisations that have a global governance remit. Documenting the abuse of human rights can facilitate those involved in seeking redress for victims. Where cases for redress are brought to the courts, this can have a significant effect on challenging state practices, certainly where there is an independent judiciary prepared to scrutinise the actions of states in light of their human rights obligations. The fact that human rights abuses are still a common occurrence in international affairs underlines the fact that human rights governance structures need strengthening; the world would surely be a bleaker place, however, without such attempts to provide global governance of human rights.

Recommended reading

Blakeley, R. (2011). 'Dirty Hands, Clean Conscience? The CIA Inspector General's Investigation of "Enhanced Interrogation Techniques" in the "War on Terror" and the Torture Debate', *Journal of Human Rights*, 10 (4), 544–61.
Donnelly, J. (2007). *International Human Rights*, 3rd edn. Cambridge, MA: Westview Press.
Forsythe, D. (2006). *Human Rights in International Relations*, 2nd edn. Cambridge: Cambridge University Press.
Greenberg, K. and Dratel, J. (eds) (2005). *The Torture Papers: The Road to Abu Ghraib*, Cambridge: Cambridge University Press.
Ishay, M. (2004). *The History of Human Rights: From Ancient Times to the Globalization Era*, London: University of California Press.
UN (2010). 'Joint Study on Global Practices in Relation to Secret Detention in the Context of Countering Terrorism', A/HRC/13/42 (20 May). Online: http://www.unhcr.org/refworld/pdfid/4d8720092.pdf (accessed 26 March 2011).

Recommended websites

Alleged Secret Detentions in Council of Europe Member States (Marty investigation): http://www.coe.int/T/E/Com/Files/Events/2006-cia/
European Parliament: Temporary Committee on the alleged use of European countries by the CIA for the transport and illegal detention of prisoners (Fava Investigation): http://www.europarl.europa.eu/comparl/tempcom/tdip/default_en.htm
Human Rights Watch World Report 2012: http://www.hrw.org/world-report-2012
Reprieve – Secret Prisons and Renditions: http://www.reprieve.org.uk/secretprisons/
The Rendition Project: www.therenditionproject.org.uk
The Torture Archive (National Security Archive, George Washington University): http://www.gwu.edu/~nsarchiv/torture_archive/index.htm
The United Nations Treaty Collection: http://treaties.un.org/
US Department of State: Human Rights reports: http://www.state.gov/j/drl/rls/hrrpt/

11 Governing forced migration

Phil Orchard

Forced migration is a significant problem for states in the international system. One reason is its scale. In 2010, there were almost 43 million people across the globe who had been forced to flee their homes. Equally important, different *forms* of displacement trigger different international responses. Because refugees, who number some 15 million, have had to flee their own state, and are without its protection, they are protected instead by an international regime composed of two parts: international law (particularly the 1951 Refugee Convention) and a formal international organization, the United Nations High Commissioner for Refugees (UNHCR), which has a legal mandate to provide international protection to refugees. While most refugees fall under the protection of UNHCR, some 4.8 million Palestinian refugees fall under the mandate of a separate UN agency, the UN Relief Works Agency, because the main cause of their displacement was the creation of the state of Israel in 1948 which predateed the creation of UNHCR. Refugees represent a transterritorial problem because the Westphalian state system created a linkage between the state and the population within its borders (see Ruggie 1998: 191; Philpott 1999: 570). Refugees who flee outside these borders become anomalies in the state system – because they can no longer count on the protection of their own state, they need some other form of protection which can only be provided through international cooperation (Haddad 2008: 69). At the same time, an international response is needed due to our common humanity. As Helton put it (2002: 7), 'we care about refugees because of the seed of fear that lurks in all of us that can be stated so simply: it could be me.'

By contrast, internally displaced persons (IDPs), who number some 27 million and are in a similar situation to that of refugees, remain within their own state. This means that the state is expected to take care of them (as citizens). Further, because the principle of sovereignty establishes that the international community can take only limited actions in matters which are within the state's domestic jurisdiction, the international community also has only a limited responsibility towards IDPs. Rather than an international convention, IDPs are protected only by a legally non-binding set of Guiding Principles on Internal Displacement and by an ad hoc framework of international and non-governmental organizations.

Thus, the central question that animates the issue of governing forced migration is how does the international community respond to people who have fled their own state, or fled within it? While the international response may vary, both groups flee for similar reasons. In a pioneering work, Zolberg *et al.* (1989) argued that flight occurs for three main reasons. The first is *individualized persecution*. This sees the refugee as an activist, engaged in political activities their state seeks to extinguish. These people may flee from a wide range of human rights abuses, including imprisonment, torture and murder. The second is situations of *generalized violence*. Here, the refugee is simply a victim seeking safety, as in a civil war. Finally the third is when refugees are systematically targeted by the state not because of their own actions or opinions, but because of the *social or cultural group* they belong to. At the extreme, such actions result in cases of ethnic cleansing and genocide.

When a person's own state is unable or unwilling to protect them, it is the goal of actors within two separate international regimes – relating to refugees and to internally displaced persons – to replicate this bond. At the heart of the global forced migration for the past sixty years has been UNHCR as the legal protector of refugees. But while UNHCR is an authoritative actor, throughout its history the agency has had to work closely with states (either as refugee producers, receivers and/or donors) and with a diverse mix of other UN agencies and non-governmental organizations. Therefore, this chapter explores how these various actors have sought to 'govern' the problem of forced migration, focusing on international efforts to protect both refugees and internally displaced persons. It begins by focusing on the legal protections offered to refugees and IDPs, and the limitations of existing international law. It then explores the historical origins of the current international refugee regime before focusing on the role of UNHCR as a protector of refugee rights, and the role of states, who seek to limit their obligations to the current regime. The chapter ends with a focus on the separate issues that IDPs face, in particular the challenge of providing them with protection when their own state is unable or unwilling to protect them, or is even complicit in their displacement.

The legal foundations of forced migrant protection

When we talk about refugee protection, Helton has argued, 'we mean legal protection. The concept must be associated with entitlements under law and, for effective redress of grievances, mechanisms to vindicate claims in respect of those entitlements' (2003: 20). Hence, the cornerstone of refugee protection is the 1951 Convention Relating to the Status of Refugees (or Refugee Convention) which defines a refugee as:

> Any person who owing to well-founded fear of being persecuted for reasons of race, religion, nationality, membership of a particular social group or political opinion, is outside the country of his nationality and is unable or, owing to such fear, unwilling to avail himself of the protection of that country; or who, not having a nationality and being outside the country of his former habitual residence as a result of such events, is unable or, owing to such fear, unwilling to return to it.
> (UN General Assembly 1951: Article 1A (2))

The Refugee Convention is one of the most widely adopted international conventions, with 144 State Parties, and 144 are parties to the 1967 Protocol. 147 states are party to one or the other (UNHCR 2011).

The Convention does three things. First, it consolidates all previous instruments to provide a comprehensive codification of refugee rights. Second, it provides basic minimum standards for the treatment of refugees. These rights include a right to property, to access the court system, of association, to employment, to housing, to education, to support and assistance, to freedom of movement, to identity papers, and to travel documents. Most importantly, refugees cannot be prosecuted for illegal entry into the country of refuge, and the Convention introduces a right to *non-refoulement* or non-return:

> No Contracting State shall expel or return ('refouler') a refugee in any manner whatsoever to the frontiers of territories where his life or freedom would be threatened on account of his race, religion, nationality, membership of a particular social group or political opinion.
> (UN General Assembly 1951: Article 33 (1))

Third, the Convention provides for non-discriminatory treatment of refugees (though in some cases the rights of refugees match those of citizens, while in others they only match the level accorded to nationals of other countries) and provides provisions for documentation.

The Convention's definition of refugee status is *universal*, in that it applies equally to all people around the world. This was not the case when the Convention first entered into force – then, it included language that people qualified as refugees only 'as a result of events occurring before 1 January 1951'. Further, signatory countries could decide if those events applied only to Europe, or Europe and elsewhere. And, just to add further complications, UNHCR's own Statute placed no geographical limitations on it so new refugees would fall under UNHCR's mandate but not receive the protections in the Convention. This was finally changed in 1967, when states adopted a Refugee Protocol (UN General Assembly 1967) which removed the time and geographic restrictions.

But the Convention remains limited in other ways. First, it lacks a duty on states to provide asylum; refugees rather only have the right to seek it, something that is echoed in the Universal Declaration of Human Rights (Roberts 1998: 381). This means that the only refugees that states need to accept are those within their territory or at their border. Hence, states in the developed world have 'a perverse incentive to allocate resources towards border control to prevent refugees and asylum seekers from reaching their territory instead of supporting protection' in the developing world (Betts 2009: 14). Second, it is focused on individualized state-based persecution, reflecting its origins in the early 1950s when the main concerns were the recent Nazi atrocities and then-ongoing Communist persecution. Under the Convention definition,

> [I]t's not enough to be the victim or potential victim of generalized violence. The violence must be directed at the claimant … the notion of persecution implies that refugees must be victimized by governments. A person victimized by the opposition is not legally considered to be within the refugee definition.
> (Matas 1989: 42)

Some regional Conventions do take into account these issues. For example, the Refugee Convention adopted by the Organization for African Unity (now the African Union, AU) in 1969 includes 'events seriously disturbing public order' in its refugee definition, thereby encompassing such problems as generalized violence. Because it is regional law, however, a person may be a refugee within the African Union, but lose that status as soon as they leave the continent.

In addition, the refugee convention is exclusive – no new reasons for refugee status can be included within it. New forms of persecution, instead, are left to the determination of individual states. For example, gender is not included within the refugee definition. But this raises the issue of how states should respond to people fleeing sexual violence when the state fails to protect the victim. A number of European states follow a European Parliament recommendation that 'gender' does fall within the broader category of 'social groups', and hence within the Convention definition, but states are not bound by this (Martin 2010). Finally, many people who do not qualify as refugees under the 1951 Convention still receive protection on humanitarian grounds. Thus between 1996 and 2005, the United Kingdom accorded Convention status to 17 per cent of asylum claimants, but humanitarian status to an additional 33 per cent of claimants. In other words the UK government decided that half of all asylum seekers during this period required some form of protection (UNHCR 2006a: 161–2).

IDPs, though displaced for similar reasons, do not have the same legal protections since they remain within their own state (Cohen and Deng 1998: 275). And yet, the state may either be unable or unwilling to protect them, and in some cases it is the state that deliberately displaces its own people for ethnic, religious or political reasons, or as a means of counterinsurgency. Because of this, IDPs frequently find themselves in worse conditions than other groups, not only being deprived of their rights, but also basic necessities including food and shelter (Mooney 2005: 14–16). To deal with these issues, a set of non-binding Guiding Principles on Internal Displacement were introduced in 1998. These provide a definition of IDPs as

> persons or groups of persons who have been forced or obliged to flee or to leave their homes or places of habitual residence, in particular as a result of or in order to avoid the effects of armed conflict, situations of generalized violence, violations of human rights or natural or human-made disasters, and who have not crossed an internationally recognized State border.
> (Office for the Coordination of Humanitarian Affairs 1999: 1)

The Principles use as their foundation existing international human rights law (including the UN Charter, the Universal Declaration of Human Rights and the International Covenants on Civil and Political Rights and on Economic, Social and Cultural Rights), humanitarian law (including the four Geneva Conventions of 1949, as well as Protocols I and II of 1977) and refugee law (including the Refugee Convention of 1951 and the Refugee Protocol of 1967) to lay out the protections that IDPs are entitled to as citizens of their own state and as human beings. As Walter Kälin, the former Representative of the Secretary-General for the human rights of internally displaced persons, has argued:

> It is possible to cite a multitude of legal provisions for almost every principle ... Because of that solid foundation, as well as the breadth of rights covered and the wide acceptance the Guiding Principles have found, it can persuasively be argued that they are the minimum international standard for the protection of internally displaced persons.
> (Kälin 2005: 29–30)

Thus, according to the Principles, IDPs shall not be subject to discrimination; they shall be free from arbitrary displacement; and they should enjoy a broad range of civil, political, economic, social and cultural rights. These include the right to life, to freedom of movement including against forcible return and to seek asylum, an adequate standard of living including safe access to essential materials, to personal documentation, to respect for family life, to education and training, to employment, and to vote and participate in government. They should also have access to a durable solution to displacement, including safe return, resettlement, or reintegration (Office for the Coordination of Humanitarian Affairs 1999; Kälin 2008). The Principles also establish that 'national authorities have the primary duty and responsibility to provide protection and humanitarian assistance to internally displaced persons within their jurisdiction' but that:

> International humanitarian organizations and other appropriate actors have the right to offer their services in support of the internally displaced ... Consent thereto shall not be arbitrarily withheld, particularly when authorities concerned are unable or unwilling to provide the required humanitarian assistance.
> (Office for the Coordination of Humanitarian Affairs 1999: 13)

The Principles, therefore, enshrine rights for the international community to take action to assist IDPs in spite of the fact that they remain within their own state. However, these rights are limited and require the consent of the host state.

There are moves to make the soft law Guiding Principles into hard law. In 2006, a Protocol on Protection and Assistance to Internally Displaced Persons was adopted by the eleven member states of the African International Conference on the Great Lakes Region which obliges those states to accept the Principles and incorporate them into domestic law (Beyani 2006: 187–97). In October 2009, the African Union Special Summit of Heads of State adopted the Convention for the Protection and Assistance of Internally Displaced Persons in Africa (the Kampala Convention). The Convention, which came into force in December 2012, replicates the rights introduced by the Guiding Principles and introduce both a monitoring provision to ensure states abide by the Convention and allow for disputes between state parties to be referred to the African Court of Justice and Human Rights.

Consequently, while refugees and IDPs flee for similar reasons, they receive very different protections: refugees are protected by a 60-year-old international legal treaty, while IDPs receive protections through soft law and based on their status as citizens and human beings. But, with the guiding principles and the Kampala Convention, we can observe moves at the international level to introduce a legal regime for the internally displaced similar to that which refugees already have.

The historical evolution of the international refugee regime

The roots of refugee protection stretch back three centuries. When Louis XIV of France revoked the Edict of Nantes in 1685, which had ended a long-running civil war between French Catholics and Protestants, or Huguenots, some 200,000 Huguenots fled the country. These people, the first to be called 'refugees', were quickly accommodated by other European states and were granted broad domestic legal protections for the first time. These informal protections continued over the next two centuries, and were extended to political refugees following the French Revolution in 1789. By the mid-nineteenth century, Lord Palmerston, then Britain's Foreign Secretary, could argue that the return of refugees was forbidden by 'the laws of hospitality, the dictates of humanity, the general feelings of humankind ... and any independent government which of its own free will were to make such a surrender would be universally and deservedly stigmatised as degraded and dishonoured' (cited in Schuster 2003: 95 fn. 66).

But an informal regime, which only reflected state practice rather than binding international law, could not survive rising immigration restrictionism in the United States, Britain and other countries from the late nineteenth century onwards. Nor could it deal with the enormous flows of refugees created by the First World War and the Russian Revolution, which displaced over a million people. Even governments who were open to receiving refugees faced their own reconstruction problems, and 'were ill-equipped for an influx of destitute people whose attitudes and dubious legal status made them a political problem ...' (Holborn 1975: 4–5). Instead, a mixture of wartime voluntary organizations (including the Red Cross and the Save the Children Fund) sought to provide assistance to these refugees (Marrus 2002: 82–4). But assistance was only a temporary response – by 1921, the problem had grown too large and needed some form of longer-term action. Bilateral negotiations between states failed. Instead, a network of these voluntary organizations led by Gustave Ador, the President of the ICRC, argued that only the League of Nations could solve the problem by providing not only relief but also longer-term employment or repatriation activities and by providing refugees with a clear international legal status (Ador 1921). Ador not only convinced the League Secretariat to take on this role, but also successfully lobbied its member states.

As a result, the League of Nations created the first international organization to protect refugees. Fridthof Nansen, the first League of Nations High Commissioner for Refugees (LNHCR), was tasked with creating a solution to the Russian refugees' legal status. He did this by creating a series of legal Arrangements which provided individual refugee groups with passports issued by the League. These 'Nansen Passports' not only granted to the refugees a legal identity but also marked the beginnings of international refugee law. This was an ad hoc system – new arrangements had to be negotiated for each new refugee group – and states could still refuse to grant entry to refugees. Attempts to create more binding international law, including a Refugee Convention in 1933 and a 1938 Convention on Refugees Coming from Germany, failed to gain much support from states (Skran 1995).

Providing refugees with assistance was also an issue. Nansen found that few governments were willing to offer the LNHCR funds. Instead, he created a special joint committee to work directly with voluntary organizations on the issue. He used these organizations both to provide funds to the LNHCR which could then be used for refugee assistance, but also to lobby – and indirectly criticize – their own governments for not doing more (Holborn 1975: 7; Johnson 1938: 159).

Because of these limitations, shifts in the broader political environment, and a new refugee crisis looming – that of Jews seeking to flee from Nazi Germany – the League was widely seen as a failed organization. Alternatives were also unsuccessful: the United States organized the 1938 Evian Conference following the Austrian Anschluss to search for a solution, but due to domestic politics the Americans were neither willing to provide financial support to help the refugees nor prepared to accept in more refugees than permitted by their existing legislation. Between 160,000 and 180,000 German Jews (out of a population of 522,000 in 1933) were unable to leave Germany and died in the Holocaust (United States Holocaust Memorial Museum 2012). In addition, however, the unwillingness of states to accept in refugees from Germany, which otherwise would have provided a form of exit, may 'ultimately have helped to push the Nazis toward extermination as the "final solution" of the "Jewish problem"' (Torpey 2000: 135–6).

The discourse that had limited refugee migration changed substantially following the Second World War, particularly as governments realized the magnitude of the Holocaust as well as the scale of displacement brought about by the war: as many as 65 million people were displaced throughout Europe (Cronin 2003: 164 fn). States became more attuned to the plight of the refugee population, to the entails of the voluntary organizations, and to the concerns of their own population. As Eleanor Roosevelt argued at the United Nations, international action to help refugees was needed 'in the interest of humanity and social stability' (Holborn 1956: 31). A succession of temporary international organizations helped to resettle or return the vast majority of these people, but by 1950, some 200,000 refugees remained in camps, primarily in Germany. Further, peace had not stopped new refugee flows. New flows in the millions were generated by the partition of India, the creation of Israel and the Korean War. And by 1950 refugees were fleeing across the Iron Curtain into West Germany at a rate of 15,000 per month, a continuous refugee flow with little prospect of ending. Therefore, states agreed to create the Refugee Convention – to provide refugees with legal assistance – and for UNHCR to administer it.

UNHCR, however, began its existence with little authority. It was a temporary body destined to be reviewed in three years' time, with only US$300,000 of funding, no operational budget or ability to provide material assistance, and a limited staff (UNHCR 1971: 13, 17). Its main focus was to provide international protection to refugees who fell within its mandate and to seek permanent solutions to the refugee problem, either through voluntary repatriation or by promoting assimilation through local integration or resettlement (UNHCR 1971: 16–17).

This weakness reflected the tensions of the emerging Cold War. The US government was concerned that through the United Nations, the Soviet Union would have too much of a say (Acheson 1969: 231). Instead, they funded a separate organization, the Intergovernmental Committee on Migration (now the International Organization on Migration, IOM) to help states to manage and structure their migration flows. The organization was deliberately 'established as a multilateral institution outside of the United Nations, with an American Director, and a board composed entirely of democratic nations friendly to the United States' (Loescher 2001: 59).

UNHCR, however, succeeded in making itself invaluable as an authoritative international actor which could quickly respond to new refugee situations, ensure refugee protection and coordinate assistance. Moreover, as an impartial UN agency, it was able to act in areas where individual states would be unable to do so because of the politics of the Cold War. For example, when refugees fled the Soviet overthrow of the Hungarian government in 1956, UNHCR successfully resettled over 150,000 refugees. The agency also served as the lead agency to organize the international relief effort. As such, it established a role as a gatekeeper for other intergovernmental organizations and NGOs by managing the assistance operation (Loescher 2001: 83–4; UNHCR 1971: 69–71). Thus, over the ensuing decades, UNHCR played a pivotal role in providing refugee protection, but also in coordinating the international response to new refugee flows. Through its activities, the agency 'developed a degree of independence and credibility it had not enjoyed before. Its autonomy and authority derived from its status as the guardian of international refugee norms and as the holder of specialized knowledge and expertise on refugee issues' (Loescher 2001: 140).

Refugee protection has been subject to considerable change and evolution over the past three centuries, from legal protection anchored at the domestic level to a full-fledged international regime anchored in international law and a formal international organization. However, while UNHCR was critical for refugee protection during the Cold War, since its end the agency has found itself in a more contested terrain as states assert their own sovereignty over refugee flows while at the same time the numbers of internally displaced persons have increased dramatically.

Refugee policy in the post-Cold War world

With the end of the Cold War, how refugees received protection changed dramatically. Whereas previously UNHCR's activities were widely supported, major growth in the numbers of both refugees (which peaked in 1992 at 17.8 million, see Figure 11.1) and asylum seekers (which peaked in the same year at 690,000) caused states to curtail the agency's independence, even as states themselves introduced new restrictionist policies designed to keep refugees in their regions and countries of origin. At the same time, the end of the Cold War meant that UNHCR could focus on refugee repatriation, a policy shift which led to its increased involvement within countries of origin.

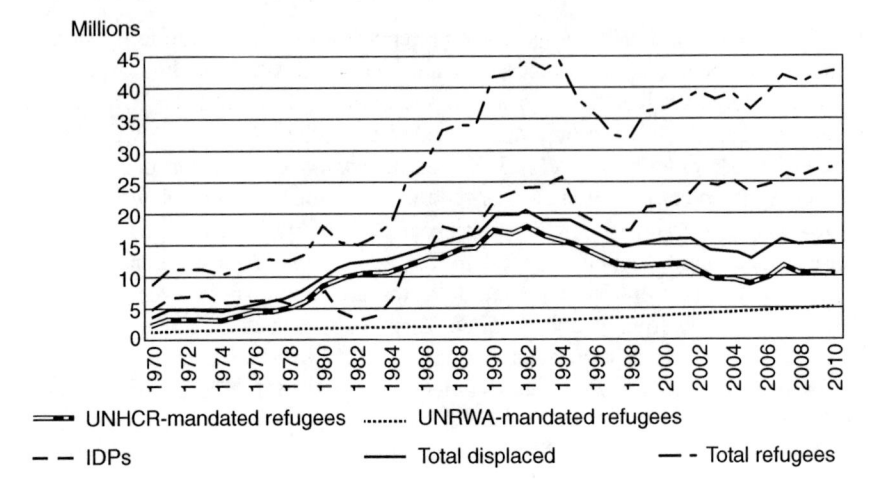

Figure 11.1 Total displaced persons, 1970–2010

Source: Adapted from Orchard 2010.

UNHCR's shifting role

While UNHCR flourished through much of the Cold War, from the 1980s it has been increasingly constrained by states in two ways. The first has been the decline of its financial autonomy and independence as states have increasingly sought to control their own borders (Loescher 2001: 238; Vayrynen 2001: 150). At the same time, NGOs have played a growing role in providing aid to refugees and IDPs. Many of UNHCR's own programmes are implemented through NGOs – in 1999, UNHCR channelled US$295 million through 545 NGOs (Ferris 2003: 125). But states have also increasingly funded NGOs directly, both because they are cheaper and more flexible but also because they are perceived to be more malleable than the agency (Raper 2003: 355).

The second source of constraint has been a shift in the agency, driven both by donor states and by its own internal dynamics, away from a resettlement- and protection-oriented mandate in host countries to one focused on activities within countries of origin (Barnett 2001: 246; Gorlick 2003: 86). The end of the Cold War meant that UNHCR could prioritize the repatriation of refugees. Between 1991 and 1996, UNHCR estimates that more than nine million refugees were returned to their own countries (UNHCR 1997: 143). But this shift brought about two major problems. First, while the choice to return home to their own countries should always be a refugee's choice, increasingly the 'voluntariness' of it became a relative attribute subject to reinterpretation (Barnett 2001: 261). In extreme cases – such as Rohingya refugees from Myanmar – UNHCR manipulated information provided to refugees to convince them to return, exaggerating the improved security situation while also offering the refugees increased financial assistance to return (Loescher 2001: 285–6). Second, the agency increasingly operated within countries of origin, first to assist returning refugees, then also to protect internally displaced persons and the broader civilian population in war zones ranging from Northern Iraq in 1991 to Bosnia (see Box 11.1).

Box 11.1 Helping the displaced in Bosnia, 1992–5

During the Bosnian War, UNHCR moved away from its traditional role and provided humanitarian assistance not only to refugees but also to IDPs and the broader civilian population of Bosnia, who accounted for over 40 per cent of their case load (Weiss and Pasic 1997: 47). By serving as the lead agency, a role endorsed by its donors, Sadako Ogata, the UN High Commissioner for Refugees, cast UNHCR as providing both assistance and protection to the Bosnian population. But this shift was problematic in several ways. The first was how it altered the role that UNHCR played vis-à-vis the displaced. While Ogata may have felt that assistance and protection could be combined, too often assistance was prioritized over protection. As one UNHCR field officer was quoted, 'it would compromise food deliveries if I made a *démarche*' on human rights violations against minorities (Minear *et al.* 1994: 24–5).

The second was that UNHCR's role was seen as a way for the international community to avoid other, more decisive, forms of action (Andreas 2008: 13). As Keen has argued, '[i]n line with major donors' priorities, UNHCR assumed a "preventive" protection responsibility inside the former Yugoslavia, without having the number of staff or the influence over armed groups to fulfil this task' (Keen 2008: 139). Thus François Fouinat, the Coordinator of the UNHCR Task Force, stated that 'it is not simply that the UN's humanitarian efforts have become politicized; it is rather that we have been transformed into the only manifestation of international political will' (UNHCR 2000: 220).

The most extreme example of how such a policy can fail was in the Bosnian town of Srebrenica, which the UN Security Council established as a 'safe area'. While UN Secretary-General Boutros Boutros-Ghali had requested an additional 35,000 troops to protect the safe areas, by 1995 the Srebrenica safe area was protected by only 450 Dutch peacekeepers. These troops were unable to stop the Bosnian Serb Army which overran the safe area on 11 July 1995 and killed over 7,000 internally displaced Muslim civilians. As Secretary-General Kofi Annan noted in a 1999 report,

> when the international community makes a solemn promise to safeguard and protect innocent civilians from massacre, then it must be willing to back its promise with the necessary means. Otherwise, it is surely better not to raise hopes and expectations in the first place, and not to impede whatever capability they may be able to muster in their own defence.
>
> (cited in UNHCR 2000: 224)

The state response

At the same time as UNHCR's role towards refugees has been changing, states in the developed world have sought to curtail their responsibilities towards asylum seekers in a direct challenge to the foundations of the refugee regime. As Gibney comments, 'if the provision of protection for refugees is its central goal, then the system of asylum offered by Western states is currently in deep crisis' (2004: 229). Instead of an exile-bias focused around resettlement, these states have focused on repatriation and containment of refugees to the developing world (Shacknove 1993: 523). Thus, most refugees remain within the developing world and long-term encampment of refugees has become a de facto durable solution (Loescher and Milner 2005: 15–16). In fact, the average length of major refugee situations is now seventeen years, and two-thirds of refugees are trapped in such protracted refugee situations.

States in the developed world justify limiting refugee acceptance for two reasons: because of the financial support that they provide to UNHCR, and because of the resettlement opportunities they offer to refugees. Governments do make considerable contributions to UNHCR – in 2011, when the agency had a budget of roughly US$2 billion, all of the top ten state donors were from the developed world. But these contributions are not enough to help all refugees; rather UNHCR has to make the decisions as to how to allocate its budget to best help those in need. As Antonio Guterres noted upon becoming High Commissioner in 2005,

> the biggest shock I have received in the past few days was when reading in a protection report that food rations in many of our camps are substantially below what is needed. I must tell you I feel devastated, sitting here with you today, knowing that refugees we care for are not getting enough food.
> (Guterres 2005)

In addition, these contributions are year to year, which means UNHCR has no firm idea of what its total budget is going to be year to year (Vayrynen 2001: 164). Moreover, governments can directly control where their contributions go through the process of earmarking in which contributions are assigned to specific programmes or priorities (Loescher *et al.* 2008: 92–3).

Resettlement opportunities are also limited. In 2010, only 98,800 refugees were resettled to the developed world, less than 1 per cent of the total refugee population. Moreover, five countries were responsible for almost all of this resettlement: the United States (71,400), Canada (12,100), Australia (8,500), Sweden (1,800) and Norway (1,100). No other country accepted more than a thousand refugees, and only 17 other countries accepted any resettled refugees at all (UNHCR 2011a: 3, 19). States legitimate practices which restrict the ability of refugees to receive asylum by pointing to 'the need to distinguish between "genuine" and "bogus" asylum seekers and, second, the importance of not carrying a disproportionally high portion of the European "asylum burden"' (Vink and Meijerink 2003: 300), as well as by arguing that these policies lead to a more efficient asylum system that helps 'genuine asylum seekers and deters abusive claimants' (Home Office 1998: 1.8). More bleakly, these policies are also designed to save money, criminalize migrants and 'to convince the electorate that the government is dealing effectively with the "refugee problem"' (Hassan 2002: 185).

Deterrent measures play two important roles: they enable governments to control borders while providing plausible justifications and also provide an alternative discourse in which refugees are reframed as 'illegal migrants' and therefore should not be accorded protection or even hospitality. One set of measures is designed to make the costs of entry arbitrarily high and to discourage potential asylum seekers from attempting entry. These mechanisms include limitations on employment for asylum seekers while their claims are processed, limitations on access to welfare or payment through in-kind benefits and, at the extreme, policies of detention. In most cases, these policies are reversed once the refugee proves their bona fide status (Gibney and Hansen 2003: 7–8).

At the same time, a number of extraterritorial measures are designed to prevent asylum seekers from being able to access refugee determination processes and thereby asylum at all (Gibney 2005: 4). One mechanism used by all Western countries is visa controls, which are designed to act as deterrents in two ways: the additional cost, hassle and time of applying for a visa, and as a mechanism to deny entry to those who might seek asylum (Neumayer 2005: 4). Even if an individual qualifies for a visa, the action of going to apply at embassies in their own country may be risky in and of itself (Schuster 2003: 144). All European Union countries except for Ireland and Great Britain refer to an identical list of countries whose inhabitants require a valid visa to cross external borders, a list which included 132 countries in the 2001 regulation (Neumayer 2005: 5). In the United States, countries are added to the list of those requiring visas if their disqualification rate, the percentage of individuals who violate conditions of entry or are rejected or withdraw their application, is above 2 per cent (Siskin 2004).

In addition, there are a number of measures which directly affect the travel process. Through so-called 'carrier sanctions', states levy fines on air, land and sea carriers that bring foreign nationals without proper documentation to state territory, and include both a financial penalty (which can range as high as €10,000) as well as the ancillary costs of return (UNHCR 2006b: 35). The issue with such policies is that they do not take into account whether or not the individual is a refugee: there is little capacity within these systems to claim refugee status and, particularly with carrier sanctions, the asylum seeker will be dealing with a third-party company employee who may have little or no immigration training (Gibney and Hansen 2003: 5–7).

Finally, Safe Third Country (STC) agreements allow governments to send back asylum seekers to other countries through which they had travelled en route. The UNHCR has argued these practices are 'clearly contrary to basic protection principles', in particular because they may trigger chain deportations, with asylum seekers being passed from one state to another (UNHCR 2000: 161). Within the European Union, for example, all member states are considered safe even though they have widely variable refugee acceptance rates. On first application, for example, the UK had a Convention acceptance rate of 17.5 per cent in 2010, while Greece had a rate of only 1.7 per cent (UNHCR 2011b: 90, 92).

Box 11.2 Interdiction at sea and Australia's refugee policy

The government of Australia represents an interesting case of how governments can respond to the dilemmas created by the global refugee regime. On the one hand, the government has made a strong committee to refugee resettlement. As Chris Bowen, the Minister for Immigration and Citizenship, has argued: '[f]or decades Australia has offered a generous resettlement programme – the highest in the world on a per capita basis – even though, of course, the Convention imposes no requirement for us to do so. We do it not because we have to; we do it because we are a humanitarian nation' (Bowen 2012).

Since 2001, however, the government has deliberately sought to limit asylum seekers reaching its territory. This followed the MV *Tampa* incident, when a Norwegian freighter rescued 438 Afghan asylum seekers from a sinking ship in international waters and sought to dock the ship at Christmas Island, part of Australia's territory. The Australian government ordered him to not enter Australia's territorial waters and, following his refusal, boarded and seized the ship. Prime Minister John Howard argued that 'we simply cannot allow a situation where Australia is seen around the world as a country of easy destination' (Gibney 2004: 189).

Instead, the government transported the asylum seekers to Papua New Guinea and the Pacific Island of Nauru, providing both countries with significant financial support for holding the asylum seekers until a third resettlement country could be arranged (Gibney 2004: 188–9). This arrangement, known as the Pacific Solution, operated until 2008. Legislation excised large areas of the Australian coast and outer island for immigration purposes. Asylum seekers who reached these areas, or whose ships were intercepted by the Australian Navy, were treated as an 'offshore entry person', had no guarantee of resettlement and they were 'prohibited from bringing legal proceedings to challenge their detention and transfer' (Kneebone 2006: 697; Phillips and Spinks 2012: 13–14).

How effective this policy was in deterring asylum seekers is unclear. While the number of boat arrivals declined considerably after 2001, falling from 5,561 people to only one person the following year, asylum claims across the developed world fell over the same period – in 2005, the 15-member European Union received 212,709 asylum applications, half the number received in 2002 (394,973) (Phillips and Spinks 2012: 18; UNHCR 2006c: 149). Further, between 2002 and June 2007, the Pacific Solution dealt with 1,547 asylum seekers, of which over 60 per cent were found to be refugees and resettled, with 40 per cent of the total going to Australia (Bem *et al.* 2007: 55). As a report commissioned by Just Australia and Oxfam Australia argues, the cost of the Pacific Solution for this period is over AUS$1 billion over the same period (Bem *et al.* 2007: 4).

While the Pacific Solution was ended with the election of Kevin Rudd's government in 2008, 'unauthorized' asylum seekers continued to be processed on Christmas Island and are subject to mandatory detention while their claims are processed. Under Prime Minister Julia Gillard, Rudd's successor, the Australian government proposed in 2011 to re-introduce a regional processing arrangement following a steady increase of asylum seekers arriving by boat (from 2,726 in 2009 to 4,565 in 2011) by transferring 800 asylum seekers to Malaysia in exchange for 4,000 UNHCR-recognized refugees. However, in this case, the government found it could not operate unilaterally – the proposal was blocked after an August 2011 Australian High Court decision ruled that the arrangement violated Australian law, as Malaysia had not signed the 1951 Refugee Convention and the asylum seekers could thereby be refouled to their own countries (Lowes 2012).

The result of these two measures is that asylum seekers and refugees today face new challenges in reaching countries where they can apply for asylum. This has meant that the vast majority of refugees remain within the developed world; at the same time, it has also triggered a dramatic increase in the number of internally displaced persons, a group effectively ignored during the Cold War.

The international protection of Internally Displaced Persons

The event that dramatically raised the profile of the IDP issue was the Gulf War and its aftermath in 1991. Following the war, Saddam Hussein crushed an uprising among Iraqi Kurds in the north of the country. One and a half million Kurds fled across the border into Iran and Turkey, while another million remained trapped in Iraq after Turkey closed its border. The American and British governments then led an intervention into northern Iraq in order to defuse the humanitarian crisis, and subsequently UNHCR took over the job of providing assistance to the IDPs and returning refugees. The scale of this crisis meant the UN could no longer ignore the IDP issue (Orchard 2010c: 108–13). Thus, in 1992, Dr Francis Deng, a former Sudanese diplomat, was appointed as the first Representative of the UN Secretary-General on IDPs.

Deng's role as a norm entrepreneur around this issue was critical. As an academic, he had coined the notion of 'sovereignty as responsibility' – that in order to be legitimate, governments must provide protection to their own people (Deng 1998: 3). As a career diplomat, he was also able to work closely with states, with high officials within the UN system, and with a number of critical NGOs including the United States Committee on Refugees and the Norwegian Refugee Council (Orchard 2010b: 291). The first major change that Deng introduced was a review of international law as it related to IDPs which led to the creation of the Guiding Principles. The second major change was to consider how the international community could help IDPs. Beyond law, however, Deng's office itself was small with no capacity in the field. Therefore he suggested two options to better protect IDPs. The first was to create a new UN agency to assist IDPs modelled on UNHCR. But this was disputed both because of costs and concerns that it duplicated existing arrangements within the UN (Cohen and Deng 1998: 169). The second was to assign responsibility for IDPs to an existing agency, most likely UNHCR. But this idea triggered 'a turf war among UN agencies unwilling to yield more power and responsibility to UNHCR' (Cohen 2002: 40–3).

Instead, an ad hoc collaborative system was introduced in 1998 which had UN's Emergency Relief Coordinator (who also serves as the head of the UN Office for the Coordination of Humanitarian Affairs) work closely with other UN agencies. But this approach did not work well, with a 2004 report finding that 'the UN's approach to the protection of [IDPs] is still largely ad hoc and driven more by the personalities and convictions of individuals on the ground than by an institutional, system-wide agenda' (Bagshaw and Paul 2004: 5). Because of these problems, the UN introduced the 'cluster approach' in 2006, in which specific agencies within the UN system and other key NGOs were made accountable for specific problem sectors or 'clusters'. UNHCR has been assigned the role as cluster lead for IDP protection, emergency shelter, camp management and coordination in a progressively expanding number of states.

This reflects the fact that getting assistance to the internally displaced is often the first critical issue. As Cohen (2006: 89) notes: 'The highest mortality rates ever recorded during humanitarian emergencies involved the internally displaced. They were often more deprived of food, shelter and health services than other members of the population and more vulnerable to assault and human rights abuse'. Thus, in addition to UNHCR, NGOs are crucial in providing assistance to IDPs, particularly in conflict areas. In practice, most international humanitarian NGOs operate within a country under the forebearance of the national authorities which produces a complex set of problems mollified partially by a commitment to neutrality and impartially in theory if not in practice (Terry 2002: 19).

Assistance is not a permanent solution. As Michael Barnett notes, 'humanitarianism provides relief; it offers to save individuals, but not to eliminate the underlying causes that placed them at risk' (Barnett 2005: 724). Humanitarian actors have little capacity to protect the displaced, particularly when they continue to be targeted. In conflict zones, these organizations can find themselves working in 'essentially lawless environments', where humanitarian organizations can do little without the use of military and police personnel (McNamara 2009: 5, 12; Orchard 2010a).

These problems are clear in the case of Darfur, Sudan. In this crisis, the bulk of displacement occurred between May 2003 and June 2004, with some 1.5 million people being internally displaced and 180,000 seeking refugee status during this time. The international humanitarian and political responses were disconnected – humanitarian actors were the first to deploy, yet they were slow to do so with one report noting that the distinguishing feature of the crisis in its first two years was 'the lateness and inadequacy of the humanitarian response. It has been so serious that it amounted to "systemic failure"' (Report by MSF-Holland, cited in Minear 2005: 77). Even once a range of humanitarian actors were providing assistance, however, aid was frequently driven by 'circumstances on the ground, reinforced by government policy and pressure' (Minear 2005: 104). Even the provision of peacekeepers – first under AU auspices, then under the UN – failed to improve the situation on the ground for the majority of the displaced (Orchard 2010c).

Conclusions

Forced migration reflects clearly the challenges that face the actors of global governance. The core dilemma here is created by state sovereignty, which leads to discrete responses towards people not due to what they have experienced, or the problems they have, but rather whether they have crossed an international border. The international refugee regime as currently constituted only creates a limited responsibility for individual states: they must process the claims of any asylum seekers who reach their borders. It is up to individual states to determine if they wish to resettle additional refugees or provide support to UNHCR or other actors assisting and protecting refugees, decisions too often subject to domestic political pressure and restrictionist arguments. At the same time, sovereignty means that states can restrict the international response to internally displaced persons, effectively limiting their legal rights and ability to receive assistance.

But the role of history is important here. Strong legal protections for refugees evolved because states were convinced it was in their collective interests to do so. This led to the creation of international organizations tasked to protect them, first under the auspices of the League of Nations, then under the UN. UNHCR has been an active international organization with refugee protection as its core mandate for 60 years. The agency has been able to operate in a space constrained in many ways by other actors, particularly states. While states themselves have faced growing numbers of asylum seekers over the past decades and have sought to limit their responsibilities, no state has sought to leave the Refugee Convention and they continue to acknowledge commitments to refugee protection and asylum in general.

And while states have sought to restrict asylum, they have also broadly sought to improve the rights of IDPs which in turn challenges basic assumptions around sovereignty. While this group was unrecognized even 20 years ago, the idea of *sovereignty as responsibility* has meant that international actors are able to play an increased role in protecting and assisting them, albeit in most cases with the consent of the state concerned. Increasingly, IDPs receive the assistance and protection they need either through UN agencies or through NGOs. In particular, the cluster approach has created a set of international actors (most notably UNHCR) with clearly defined responsibilities, while the Guiding Principles (and steps such as the Kampala Convention) clearly restate their existing rights in international law.

Forced migration is an oft-forgotten problem in terms of global governance. States, growing leery of refugee numbers, have prioritized their domestic interests over needed – and necessary – international cooperation. But this shift is one of the primary causes for the growth of IDPs; for the creation of a new problem now too requiring an international response. As states in particular wrestle with the problems of responding to internal displacement, the refugee regime and the right to seek asylum may be granted new life.

Recommended reading

Barnett, M. and Weiss, T. (2008). *Humanitarianism in Question: Politics, Power, Ethics*, Ithaca, NY: Cornell University Press.

Betts, A. (2009). *Protection by Persuasion: International Cooperation in the Refugee Regime*, Ithaca, NY: Cornell University Press.

Gibney, M. (2004). *The Ethics and Politics of Asylum: Liberal Democracy and the Response to Refugees*, Cambridge: Cambridge University Press.

Orchard, P. (2010). 'Protection of Internally Displaced Persons: Soft Law as a Norm-Generating Mechanism', *Review of International Studies*, 36(2): 281–303.

Recommended websites

Brookings–London School of Economics Project on Internal Displacement – an NGO project affiliated with the Special Rapporteur for the Human Rights of IDPs: http://www.brookings.edu/projects/idp.aspx

Forced Migration Online – a database on all aspects of forced migration, based at the University of Oxford: http://www.forcedmigration.org/

The Internal Displacement Monitoring Centre – an NGO which monitors internal displacement worldwide and provides the most reliable statistics: http://www.internal-displacement.org/

The United Nations High Commissioner for Refugees: www.unhcr.org and their Refworld online database: http://www.unhcr.org/cgi-bin/texis/vtx/refworld/rwmain

United Nations Reliefweb – a UN database which provides comprehensive information on current humanitarian and natural disasters: http://reliefweb.int/

Conclusion

Governing the world?

Sophie Harman and David Williams

By posing a set of questions to each of the contributors to this book – what is being governed? What are the key mechanisms and actors involved in governing? And what are the issues and problems associated with governance? – the chapters have highlighted an array of actors, political processes and domains that fall under the umbrella of global governance. This conclusion draws together the main findings of the book in response to these core questions. In so doing it does not provide a handy definition of global governance; as the Introduction outlined this is not the aim of the book and in many ways can be a fruitless endeavour as one key aspect of the concept is its elasticity and nebulous nature. Instead this chapter highlights common themes, practices and issues that help further our understanding of global governance.

What is governed and why?

Almost all aspects of everyday life around the world are now subject to some form of global governance or regulation – whether regulation by a regional body such as the European Union, a form of international law such as the international health regulations, or the demands of convention or norms such as the responsibility to protect. Even if these institutions, laws, norms or ideas are ignored, those that breach them are held to account through their existence. Hence in response to the question of what is regulated and why, it is clear that most aspects of everyday life are now subject to some form of global governance, the degree of which depends on the issue and where you live.

One way of thinking about the proliferation of regimes of governance has been to focus on the management, supply and regulation of global public goods such as the environment and water. Public goods are generally understood to be those goods which are non-excludable and non-rivalrous in consumption; in other words everyone can access them and in so doing one's access should not prevent another person from accessing the same good. The regulation of such goods is seen to require *global* governance because of their global nature. Though some of these goods can be sourced from different parts of the world, as the politics of water provision attests, there are questions over which public actors – for example states or private actors such as water companies – can lay claim to owning such goods.

Hence there is a need for co-ordination and attempts at management between public and private actors all of which have a stake in the provision of such goods at a global level. A problem arises when public goods become private goods: certain public goods and how they are provided for are becoming increasingly private goods, in that they do exclude people and are rivalrous in consumption. This is evident in the global governance of the patents on pharmaceutical products, an issue that cuts through both the public good of health and the private good of trade where the cost of such treatment makes the public good of health both excludable and rivalrous in consumption. What is to be governed thus includes those goods that are public, increasingly those that are private, and those that are somewhere in between.

The most difficult question to unravel when thinking about global governance is why a specific issue is seen to require governing in the first place. Part of the difficulty of this is it points to how specific issues are understood by the varied actors involved, and the degree to which they are willing to act towards addressing these issues. This can be a collective problem of governments attempting to generate public will in support of measures requiring co-ordinated action and behaviour change from various aspects of society. For example on an issue such as corruption this may require changes to government accountability and transparency mechanisms, to oversight and regulation of business practice, and to individual perceptions and tolerance. This can be an individual problem of how people perceive threats to their own lives and lifestyles and whether such a threat requires action or governance of some kind. This can be a problem of competing (at times expert) opinion of what actually necessitates a threat to an individual's human rights or a state's security for example, and thus requires the generation of a particular consensus in support of one opinion. The problem of identifying what is governed and why is thus inherently an area of political contestation where competing claims to what should be prioritised and the nature and legitimacy of such claims are questioned or accepted by the individuals, states, public bodies and private agencies involved in the governance of the issue.

The degree to which governance resembles an area of political contestation depends on the issue. For many case studies in this volume, politics is often something implicit in the process of governing but rarely acknowledged in practice. What is governed and why is often seen as functional and in many cases reactionary rather than preventative. Governance arrangements have often sprung up or been reinvigorated in response to the need or emergent necessity to regulate a specific issue, whether financial crisis or increased trade liberalisation. The underlying assumption is that specific issues such as labour, for example, both should be and can be governed globally. Moreover such governance necessitates a combination of public actors such as government bodies and expertise drawn from the private sector (such as financial regulators) or the public sector (such as university researchers) to draw together effective ways of managing issues. Thus the focus is on management and solution-orientated practice. What becomes tricky is the politics of what constitutes the right solutions or the most effective means of management that is not only linked to what is to be governed but who is best positioned to do the governing.

Who does the governing?

A common feature of governance reports, recommendations and progress measurements is collective words such as 'we' and 'our' ('Our Common Neighbourhood') that deliberately position global problems and their governance as something that affects us all. The majority of who does the governing in practice, however, comes down to a broad range of states, civil society organisations, private companies and authorities, knowledge leaders, intergovernmental organisations and partnerships. And the relationship between these and some common 'we' is a central theme in debates about global governance – do they really represent 'our' interests and concerns? How can 'we' shape what these collective agents do?

It is clear from this collection of case studies that the state is still very much a central part of global governance. States remain the signatories to key forms of international law, are held to account for shortcomings or a lack of will to address problems, and are seen as key sites of legitimacy for global commitments. However the influence of the state in global governance is also dependent on the issue and the state. In some instances individual leaders or political parties tend to be criticised for their role in governing specific issues – whether George W. Bush and rendition and the environment, or Tony Blair and security – rather than the state itself. In other cases it is governments or states as a whole that are the contentious actors – for example, in the case of Australian refugee policy outlined by Orchard (Chapter 11), it is not individual members of the government or a political party but Australia as a whole that takes this stance on migrants. With cases such as the governance of finance the state is seen to have a role but its ability to exert such a role is constrained by market forces and the role of private actors such as credit-rating agencies. How states operate in global governance also depends on two distinct factors: (i) whether the issue serves their domestic political interests and foreign policy agenda, and (ii) whether they are able to exert such an interest in the wider institutions and partnerships of global governance.

Global governance is sometimes seen as the process of the global North governing arrangements in the global South. This case can be argued when looking at how aid money is given to govern global poverty through goal-setting and reform of country systems and political and social structures or how the global trade agenda seems to disadvantage farmers predominantly in the global South. However this binary does not apply to all issues of contemporary global governance. As case studies such as that of extraordinary rendition show, governance mechanisms are also used to hold states in the global North to account for their actions. Such a North–South divide also overlooks the blurriness of processes of global governance and the agency of actors involved in it. While in some aspects a North–South distinction is clear, in others a more East–West distinction can be made, and in some cases such a distinction does not exist or is in a process of change.

One of the most common arenas for states and non-state actors to exert influence is in intergovernmental organisations, usually falling somewhere under the umbrella of the United Nations. Each of the chapters herein has highlighted at least one UN agency as the cornerstone of global governance. What is clear from the chapters is that the ability of UN agencies to promote co-operation or provide solutions to collective security problems is often wanting. UN directives in the form of guidelines, resolutions or in-country operations all serve to establish a general framework of governance for multiple issues. However, the degree to which these frameworks are integrated into domestic contexts, seen as legitimate or adhered to remains questionable. In some issues such as security, the UN remains hampered by the dominance of the permanent five members of the Security Council (China, France, Russia, the UK and the USA). In other areas such as climate change the UN is limited by divisions between country concerns in the North and South and with regard to issues such as health the institution is overcrowded by other bilateral and multilateral agencies with bigger budgets and greater expertise.

A common finding across the chapters has been the lack of influence and presence UN agencies have in comparison to international financial institutions such as the World Bank and private agencies. International financial institutions play a key role in the process of governing in perhaps obvious areas such as labour, corruption and trade as well as less obvious areas such as health and the environment. This has been a growing phenomenon of the past 30 years and has been an intrinsic part of the growth of market-based principles in the process of governing. The growth of economism is evident in the application of market-based principles of goal-orientated strategies and targets in areas such as governing poverty, markets and trading schemes for pollution reduction, the focus on economic growth over labour standards, and the stated benefits of free trade with minimal public sector intervention or barriers. These principles are not only applied to how problems of governance are understood and addressed, but are also relevant to the type of actors that are seen to be required to implement the process. For some, market principles are best implemented by those who know how markets work, i.e. the private sector, rather than those who want to limit or regulate markets for a variety of reasons but most commonly taxation, i.e. the state (depending of course on the type of state). In other areas the private sector seeks to create governance arrangements as a means of self-regulation to prevent the emergence of state regulation. Hence governance when linked to markets requires a degree of private sector participation.

Public–private partnerships are not necessarily a new phenomenon in governance. What is pertinent about partnerships today is their ubiquity across multiple areas of governance. Partnerships are seen as a key way to widen participation in governance and bring in expertise, dialogue and crucially money from the private sector into public forums of governance. In the main such partnerships are a one-way street, the bringing of the private sector into the public sector rather than the other way around. The private sector is subject to public regulation and the private sector does consult aspects of the public sector, however partnerships bringing the public into the private are seen as a rarity or, at the extreme, an example of corrupt practice. Either way these publicly based partnerships are central actors in global governance whether in the provision of security, health or labour standards.

The prominence of state-led and market-based approaches to multiple areas of governance often means that civil society organisations are overlooked. The term 'civil society organisations' can refer to a broad range of highly professionalised international non-governmental organisations (NGOs), transnational advocacy groups, community groups, activists and faith-based organisations. Many of the chapters highlight the role that these organisations have played in bringing key issues to the global agenda. They boost collaboration and provide channels of advocacy for those seen to be detached from the decision-making forums of global governance and are often important interlocutors between the international and local by their members and donor partners. These actors are not only involved in the framing and profile-raising of particular issues, but are also intrinsic to the implementation of global projects and agendas and form the basis of service delivery and partnerships in-country. They are contentious for the campaigns they promote and their claims to representation and legitimacy, yet they fill a gap by making global governance more transparent and more accountable to people, at least to some degree.

The final key actor with regard to who does the governing is that of experts or knowledge sources. Networks of experts cluster around all of the issues examined in this book, and they have become key opinion formers and influential contributors to how states, civil society organisations, business and intergovernmental organisations think about global problems and how to address them. The complexities of specific issues in global governance and the demands on the time of employees of various institutions has given rise to an expert network of consultants that offer advice and knowledge on a range of issues, from how to harness social media to how to break the trade deadlock in Doha, to how to best eradicate malaria. These networks stress the technocratic aspect of global governance in providing scientific- or knowledge-based responses to global problems. The growth of such actors into a culture of consultancy in global governance has to an extent shifted the focus of governance away from the political to the technocratic.

In the regimes of governance examined in this book there are, then, a complex set of agents involved, relating in often complex ways. These relationships are sometimes co-operative, at other times antagonistic, and it is through this that the politics of global governance becomes visible. Different agents often have different interests, commitments and sources of legitimacy, and have different abilities to influence the construction and development of regimes of governance. This is one reason why global governance is often such a messy, contentious and ultimately open-ended process.

What are the main mechanisms of governance?

Governance operates through a range of mechanisms. Binding or non-binding forms of international law have provided the main framework for the practice of global governance across the chapters. This is evident when looking at the United Nations Convention Against Corruption, the Universal Declaration of Human Rights, or the Convention Relating to the Status of Refugees. The central purpose of such international law is protection, guidance, adherence and standard-setting for all actors involved in global governance. Legitimacy for such legal frameworks is derived from the number of signatories a specific law may have, what the law regulates and the origin of the law. There are extensive debates about the status and significance of international law; however, as these chapters have shown, its very existence, as vague as some aspects may be, provides a benchmark for governance and the behaviour of states and other actors. International law with regard to global governance traditionally focuses on sources of public law; however, the increasingly privatised nature of governance, and problems of trade and finance, see an increased blurring of public and private international law.

One form of soft international law or soft regulation is voluntary standards and codes of conduct. Labour standards, financial regulation or corruption monitoring are all examples of voluntary conduct established by partnerships between the private and public sector as a means of self-regulation and standard-setting. Such standards are often established at the global level through initiatives such as the Global Compact and the International Organisation for Standardisation (ISO) but impact on national behaviour through their adoption at state level. The purpose of such standards is regulation, crucially either in partnership with the state or somehow separate from the state. Standardisation is perhaps one of the less recognised mechanisms of global governance but perhaps the most all-pervasive when considering the informal behaviour and codes of conduct private companies do or do not adhere to, how they become the basis for domestic law, and how they impact on the everyday lives of people around the world, the products we buy and how we work.

One way in which international law shapes the conduct of states is through the creation and codification of norms. Norms of behaviour, conduct and governance also emerge from entrepreneurs (whether states, individuals, civil society organisations or private businesses), and through processes of repetition, practice and consolidation can become entrenched within domestic and international systems as operating principles of governance. Norms can take on different forms and expressions and can be generated by a range of actors. Civil society organisations for example have been particularly influential in the creation of key human rights norms. The extent to which norms actually operate to constrain actors varies from issue to issue, and like almost everything else involved in global governance, is subject to contestation and interpretation.

Ideas and knowledge or claims to knowledge are another key mechanism of global governance. As Death highlights (Chapter 9), competing rationalities or ideas about the problems of the planetary environment lead to very different outcomes or justifications for action and inaction. Ideas or claims to knowledge can be used as a source of 'evidence' by which to generate political will or engender fear or the need to act on specific issues. Knowledge can thus be used as a mechanism of governance in two main ways. First, it can be used to frame an issue in a specific manner so as to elicit wider support or suppress the collective need for action. Claims to expertise can here refute widespread political opinion with the assertion that somehow the 'facts' or 'evidence' are incorrect and thus the need for governance is wrong, misunderstood or somehow different to what was first thought. The second use of knowledge can be in establishing and maintaining a dominant paradigm of how we think about the world and solutions to specific problems. A common factor in many of the chapters has been the liberal manner in which problems ranging from migration to labour to trade have been framed and responded to. This liberal approach to governance issues is supported by knowledge claims about effective policies that promote good governance or market-based reform and to an extent narrows the scope for alternative paradigms or claims to knowledge. Thus as a mechanism of governance, specific kinds of knowledge are intrinsic to how issues are understood, approached and governed; and when adopted at the global level can be applied in ways that squeeze the space for alternative means of thinking about problems.

A central mechanism associated with the role of norms and knowledge in global governance is that of issue framing. Incidents of framing issues as security threats, human rights concerns, emergencies or crises can be seen throughout the chapters. The purpose of such framing is to get attention for an issue, galvanise political and monetary support, and precipitate action on a competing international stage. Issue framing that targets key international civil servants, political leaders and public opinion that generates associated campaigns and leverage can elevate specific issues to areas of high importance in global governance. As Kamradt-Scott's chapter shows (Chapter 8) this has been a key source of financial support for global health strategies, particularly HIV/AIDS. However such framing can also lead to threat or crisis fatigue that has the opposite effect of reducing an issue's pertinence in global governance.

Issue framing, voluntary standards and norms are limited as mechanisms of global governance without transnational political campaigns to support them. The sources of such campaigns can be from civil society, key states, the private sector, intergovernmental organisations, or the combination of all four. Campaigns elevate particular ideas or issues and galvanise widespread political support for their governance. Moreover campaigns are intrinsic to adherence to international law with regard to the public ability to name and shame key actors that fall short of commonly accepted standards. Such naming and shaming can have little immediate effect in some instances, as Blakeley and Raphael's case study on human rights and rendition suggests (Case study 10.1), but can have a longer implicit effect on the reputation of a state, person or company. Global campaigns elevate issues of concern, police breaks from key standards or norms, and can act as markers of progress.

Measurement, goal setting and performance have increasingly become mechanisms of global governance used by intergovernmental organisations, states and civil society organisations to measure progress in response to issues. This is most evident in the case of the Millennium Development Goals. Measurement and goal setting suggest global governance is a project that can be measured and monitored. In this sense global governance could be interpreted as something that has an end project or goal or specific aims. The content of such aims, however, remains precarious and hard to identify. As with the section on what is to be governed, this can depend on the issue, the actors involved and the ideas popular or dominant at the time. Hence global governance is not a static entity but a process always in flux.

Governing the world? The practice and problems of global governance

What is clear from the foregoing chapters is that while governance regimes exist to regulate global issues and promote greater co-operation between varied agents, there are several tensions and problems within the current forms of global governance. On the one hand the process of governing issues can be seen to be working: there are multiple different configurations of actors, processes and ideas established to respond to both contemporary and traditional issues. This shows the existence of political will, support and commitment to at least some form of global management. However the type of will, support and commitment often remains limited and there are significant problems with how global issues and processes are identified and understood. Some issues, such as labour and poverty for example, are seen as inherently feminised problems, yet gendered frames for understanding them or addressing them are not forthcoming. Some ideas or concerns about security threats supersede wider concerns of human rights and protection of migrants. Some regulation and standardisation in areas such as trade have an adverse impact on aspects of health. Hence the case studies included in this book show that no aspect of governance operates in isolation of wider processes of global governance, thus leading to tensions over what should be governed and what forms or issues of global governance take priority and why.

Competition for political attention in global governance can in part stem from a lack of leadership. In many of the case studies leadership mainly comes from dominant states, the odd civil society campaign, or in some instances the private sector. What is lacking is leadership in intergovernmental organisations, which culminates in many state and non-state actors operating at multiple levels of governance with only directives, statements and rhetoric to guide them. Directives, agreements and goals are all set but there is little leadership in seeing them through. Problems of leadership and commitment to some of the regulatory frameworks of global governance have in some instances led to the generation of new institutions, partnerships and frameworks for action. Some of these new actors and processes have been successful in generating money to support an issue and providing new ideas; however in other areas they have added to an overcrowded space in which governance is defined by many different acronyms rather than activity or function.

Different understandings, rationalities or paradigms in which various issues of global governance are understood can generate inertia and lack of progress. This is evident in aspects of governing climate change, poverty and human rights. What to prioritise and how to do so can generate competing approaches to an issue that can counteract each other and undermine co-ordination. Global events and state priorities can skew agendas towards self-interest or alignment with other areas or efforts.

However this is not just the action of states: intergovernmental organisations can also align issues and mechanisms of governance with their own interests or that which they think will gain greater traction in the international system. Thus the merits or normative arguments for why specific issues become politically relevant or important in the international system are often second to or intertwined with domestic interests or the money available to implement processes of governance.

Money and structures of capital overwhelmingly frame the space and options that processes of governance operate in. Nesvetailova and Belli's chapter on governing finance shows how governance structures failed to address or foresee the 2007 financial crisis, and have since failed to establish some form of regulation or control of capital and money around the world. Langan's chapter on trade shows how the wealth of rich countries and the lack of wealth in developing countries limit progress in consolidating a global system of liberalised trade. Capital is increasingly subject to voluntary standards and private forms of regulation and international law. However public regulation and *global* public regulation are seen as somehow wanting. This is in part because of a lack of political will and part a lack of ability. The lack of such will and perceptions of an unregulated system of finance however are changing in public opinion, particularly within Europe. This may, in turn, generate wider debates on how money can or should be regulated globally within existing and new models of governance; or, it may see a shift of European ideas and control of mechanisms of governance decline.

These problems suggest that global governance is somehow not working as well as it might, and that governing issues is and always will be somewhat problematic. However, this only holds if governance or governing is seen as a static entity that is not capable of evolution or change. Moreover, it also suggests that governance is somehow separate from and not a space for politics – namely contestation, discussion, and debates over what the best course of action is, who is best to lead it, and what mechanisms are available to do so from the broad spectrum of options available. Global governance is messy, ambiguous and only vaguely cohesive, as it involves a myriad of ideas, people and social forces. What the problems inherent to the practice of global governance really suggest is that governing is not just about the process of managing a broad array of actors and ideas; it is also an area of political contestation and negotiation. Hence the problems of global governance are in part directly attributable to the process, mechanisms and actors involved, but also reflect the core dynamics of the politics of international relations. Global governance is thus in many ways the technocratic, multi-participant way in which international relations is operationalised in practice. It is thus not separate to or somehow different from the tensions of, say, diplomacy and foreign policy, but is an intrinsic and vital part of how we understand the management of international relations.

Bibliography

ABC News (2008). *Trade Talks Failure Prompts Claims of Neocolonialism.* ABC News, 30 July 2008. Available at: http://www.abc.net.au/news/2008-07-30/trade-talks-failure-prompts-claims-of-neo/457786 (accessed 21 October 2012).
Acheson, D. (1969). *Present at the Creation: My Years in the State Department*, 1st edn. New York: W. W. Norton.
Ador, G. (1921). 'Letter from Gustave Ador to the President of the Council of the League of Nations,' 15 June 1921. League of Nations Archives. Geneva, R1713/13314 (Dossier 12319).
African Union (2012). *Convention for the Protection and Assistance of Internally Displaced Persons in Africa (Kampala Convention).* Available at: http://www.unhcr.org/4ae9bede9.html (accessed 12 February 2013).
Aginam, O. (2004). 'Salvaging Our Global Neighbourhood: Critical Reflections on the G8 Summit and Global Health Governance in an Interdependent World', *Law, Social Justice & Global Development Journal*, 24(1). Available at: http://elj.warwick.ac.uk/global/04-1/aginam.html (accessed 24 January 2012).
Aikman, S., Unterhalter, E. and Challender, C. (2005). 'The Education MDGs: Achieving Gender Equality through Curriculum and Pedagogy Change', *Gender and Development*, 13(1): 44–55.
Alben, E. (2001). 'GATT and the Fair Wage: A Historical Perspective on the Labour–Trade Link', *Columbia Law Review*, 101(6): 1410–16.
Aldis, W. (2008). 'Health Security as a Public Health Concept: A Critical Analysis', *Health Policy and Planning*, 23(6): 369–75.
Alston, P. (2004). '"Core Labour Standards" and the Transformation of the International Labour Rights Regime', *European Journal of International Law*, 15(3): 417–56.
Alston, P. and Heenan, J. (2004). 'Shrinking the International Labour Code: An Unintended Consequence of the 1998 ILO Declaration on Fundamental Principles and Rights at Work?' *New York University Journal of International Law and Politics*, 36(2/3): 221–264.
Alvestrand, H. and Lie, H. W. (2009). 'Development of Core Internet Standards: The Work of IETF and W3C', in L. Bygrave and J. Bing (eds), *Internet Governance: Infrastructure and Institutions*, Oxford: Oxford University Press, pp. 126–46.
Amato, M. and Fantacci, L. (2011). *The End of Finance*, Cambridge: Polity Press.
Amnesty (2012). 'Amnesty International Report 2012: No longer business as usual for tyranny and injustice', Press release, 24 May. Available at: http://www.amnesty.org.uk/news_details.asp?NewsID=20135.
Amoore, L. (2006). 'Invisible Subject(s): Work and Workers in the Global Political Economy', in M. Davies and M. Ryner (eds), *Poverty and the Production of World*

Politics: Unprotected Workers in the Global Economy, Basingstoke: Palgrave Macmillan, pp. 89–112.

Anderson, S. and Heywood, P. M. (2009). 'The Use and Abuse of Transparency International's Approach to Measuring Corruption', *Political Studies*, 57(4): 746–67.

Andreas, P. (2008). *Blue Helmets and Black Markets: The Business of Survival in the Seige of Sarajevo*, Ithaca, NY: Cornell University Press.

Annan, K. A. (2000). *We the Peoples: The Role of the United Nations in the 21st Century*, New York: United Nations Department of Public Information.

APWG (Anti-Phishing Working Group) (2012), 'Anti-Phishing Working Group'. Available at: http://www.antiphishing.org/index.html (accessed 1 August 2012).

Arevalo, J. and Fallon, F. (2008). 'Assessing Corporate Responsibility as a Contribution to Global Governance: The Case of the UN Global Compact', *Corporate Governance*, 8(4): 456–70.

Austrian Foreign Ministry website. (2012). Available at: http://www.bmeia.gv.at/en/foreign-ministry/foreign-policy/human-rights/human-security-network.html.

Awofeso, N. (2005). 'Re-defining "Health"', *Bulletin of the World Health Organization*, 83(11): 802.

Ba, A. and Hoffman, M. (eds) (2005). *Contending Perspectives on Global Governance: Coherence, Contestation and World Order*, London: Routledge.

Bäckstrand, K. (2003). 'Civic Science for Sustainability: Reframing the Role of Experts, Policy-makers and Citizens in Environmental Governance', *Global Environmental Politics*, 3(4): 24–41.

Bäckstrand, K. and Lövbrand, E. (2006). 'Planting Trees to Mitigate Climate Change: Contested Discourses of Ecological Modernization, Green Governmentality, and Civic Environmentalism', *Global Environmental Politics*, 6(1): 50–75.

Bagshaw, S. and Paul, D. (2004). 'Protect or Neglect: Towards a More Effective United Nations Approach to the Protection of Internally Displaced Persons', New York: Brookings–SAIS Project on Internal Displacement; UN Office for the Coordination of Humanitarian Affairs.

Bair, J. and Werner, M. (2011). 'Commodity Chains and the Uneven Geographies of Global Capitalism: A Disarticulations Perspective', *Environment and Planning A*, 43(5): 988–9.

Baldwin, D. (2011). 'The Concept of Security', in C. Hughes and L. Meng (eds), *Security Studies: A Reader*, London: Routledge.

Barnett, M. N. (2005). 'Humanitarianism transformed', *Perspectives on Politics*, 3(4): 723–41.

Barnett, M. N. (2001). 'Humanitarianism with a Sovereign Face: UNHCR in the Global Undertow', *International Migration Review*, 35(1): 244–76.

Barrientos, S. and Smith, S. (2006). *The ETI Code of Labour Practice: Do Workers Really Benefit? Report on the ETI Impact Assessment 2006 – Summary*. Sussex: Institute of Development Studies.

—— (2007). 'Do Workers Benefit from Ethical Trade? Assessing Codes of Labour Practice in Global Production Systems', *Third World Quarterly*, 28(4): 713–29.

Barrientos, S., McClenaghan, S. and Orton, L. (1999). *Gender and Codes of Conduct: A Case Study from Horticulture in South Africa*, London: Christian Aid.

Batliwala, S. (2002). 'Grassroots Movements as Transnational Actors: Implications for Global Civil Society', *Voluntas: International Journal of Voluntary and Nonprofit Organizations*, 13(4): 393–409.

BBC (2005). 'Asia's tsunami death toll soars', 20 January. Available at: http://news.bbc.co.uk/1/hi/world/asia-pacific/4189883.stm.

—— (2012), 'US Resists Control of Internet Passing to UN Agency'. Available at: http://www.bbc.co.uk/news/technology-19106420 (accessed 3 August 2012).
Beck, U. (1992). *Risk Society: Towards a New Modernity*, London: Sage.
Beckett, C. with Ball, J. (2012). *WikiLeaks: News in the Networked Era*, Cambridge: Polity Press.
Bem, K., Field, N. and Maclellan, N. (2007). *A Price Too High: The Cost of Australia's Approach to Asylum Seekers*, Glebe: A Just Australia and Oxfam Australia.
Berridge, V., Loughlin, K. and Herring, R. (2009). 'Historical Dimensions of Global Health Governance', in K. Buse, W. Hein, and N. Drager (eds), *Making Sense of Global Health Governance: A Policy Perspective*, London: Palgrave Macmillan, pp. 28–46.
Bernstein, S., Betsill, M., Hoffmann, M. and Paterson, M. (2010). 'A Tale of Two Copenhagens: Carbon Markets and Climate Governance', *Millennium*, 39(1): 161–73.
Betsill, M. and Bulkeley, H. (2004). 'Transnational Networks and Global Environmental Governance: The Cities for Climate Protection Program', *International Studies Quarterly*, 48(2): 471–93.
Betts, A. (2009). *Protection by Persuasion: International Cooperation in the Refugee Regime*, Ithaca, NY: Cornell University Press.
Beyani, C. (2006). 'Recent Developments: The Elaboration of a Legal Framework for the Protection of Internally Displaced Persons in Africa', *Journal of African Law*, 50(2): 187–97.
Bieler, A. and Lindberg, I. (2011a). 'Globalisation and New Challenges for Transnational Solidarity: An Introduction', in A. Bieler and I. Lindberg (eds), *Global Restructuring, Labour and the Challenges for Transnational Solidarity*, London: Routledge, pp. 3–15.
Bieler, A. and Lindberg, I. (eds) (2011b). *Global Restructuring, Labour and the Challenges for Transnational Solidarity*, London: Routledge.
Blair, T. (1999). 'Doctrine of the International Community', speech to the Chicago Economic Club, Chicago, 22 April.
—— (2003a). 'Speech to the Foreign Office Conference', London, 7 January.
—— (2003b). 'Motion for War', House of Commons, London, 18 March.
Blakeley, R. (2011). 'Dirty Hands, Clean Conscience? The CIA Inspector General's Investigation of "Enhanced Interrogation Techniques" in the "War on Terror" and the Torture Debate', *Journal of Human Rights*, 10(4): 544–61.
Bliss, K. (2010). 'Introduction', in K. Bliss, X. Boynton, V. Cha and S. Chand (eds), *Key Players in Global Health: How Brazil, Russia, India, China, and South Africa are Influencing the Game*, Washington, DC: Center for International and Strategic Studies, pp. v–ix.
Booth, D. (1985). 'Marxism and Development Sociology: Interpreting the impasse', *World Development*, 13(7): 761–87.
Booth, K. (1991). 'Security and Emancipation', *Review of International Studies*, 17(4): 313–26.
Booth, S., Howarth, C., Persson, M. and Scarpetta, V. (2011) *Continental Shift: Safeguarding the UK's Financial Trade in a Changing Europe*, London: Open Europe.
Bowen, C. (2012). 'The Refugee Convention and Beyond', Canberra: Department of Immigration and Citizenship, Government of Australia.
Brasted, H. V. (2004). 'Women, Labour Standards, and Labour Organising', in A. Kaur (ed.), *Women Workers in Industrializing Asia: Costed not Valued*, Basingstoke: Palgrave Macmillan, pp. 218–40.
Brautigam, D. (2009). *The Dragon's Gift: The Real Story of China in Africa*, Oxford and New York: Oxford University Press.

Brenner, S. (2007). 'History of Computer Crime', in K. de Leeuw and J. Bergstra (eds), *The History of Information Security*, Amsterdam: Elsevier, pp. 705–21.

Bresser-Pereira, L. (2009). 'The Political Economy of Global Economic Disgovernance', in C. Gnos and L. Rochon (eds), *Monetary Policy and Financial Stability: A Post-Keynesian Agenda*, London: Edward Elgar, pp. 167–89.

—— (2010). 'The Global Financial Crisis, Neoclassical Economics, and the Neoliberal Years of Capitalism', Revue de la Régulation, no7, 1st semester. Available at: http://www.regulation.revues.org/index7729.html (accessed 4 February 2012).

Brill, L. (2002). 'Can Codes of Conduct Help Home Based Workers?' in R. Jenkins, R. Pearson and G. Seyfang (eds), *Corporate Responsibility and Labour Rights: Codes of Conduct in the Global Economy*, London: Earthscan, pp. 113–23.

Brinkerhoff, J., Smith, S. and Teegen, H. (eds) (2007). *NGOs and the Millennium Development Goals*, New York and Basingstoke: Palgrave Macmillan.

Brown, T., Cueto, M. and Fee, E. (2006). 'The World Health Organization and the Transition from "International" to "Global" Public Health', *American Journal of Public Health*, 96(1): 62–72.

Bruen, G. (2012). 'Our Internet Infrastructure at Risk', in M. Jakobsson (ed.), *The Death of the Internet*, Hoboken, NJ: Wiley, pp. 89–102.

Brundtland, G. (1987). *Our Common Future: World Commission on Environment and Development*, Oxford: Oxford University Press.

Brunnermeier, M. (2009). 'Deciphering the 2007–2008 Liquidity and Credit Crunch', *Journal of Economic Perspectives*, 23(1): 77–100.

Bryant, R. (2002). 'Non-governmental Organizations and Governmentality: "Consuming" Biodiversity and Indigenous People in the Philippines', *Political Studies*, 50(2): 268–92.

Bukovanksy, M. (2006). 'The Hollowness of Anti-Corruption Discourse', *Review of International Political Economy*, 13(2): 181–209.

Bulkeley, H. and Newell, P. (2010). *Governing Climate Change*, London: Routledge.

Bull, B. (2010). 'The global elite, public–private partnerships and multilateral governance', in J. Clapp and R. Wilkinson (eds), *Global Governance, Poverty and Inequality*, London and New York: Routledge, pp. 209–34.

Bull, H. (1977). *The Anarchical Society: A Study of Order in World Politics*, London: Macmillan.

Burn, G. (1999). 'The State, the City and the Euromarkets', *Review of International Political Economy*, 6(2): 225–61.

Burris, S. and Anderson, E. (2010). 'A Framework Convention on Global Health: Social Justice Lite, or a Light on Social Justice?' *Journal of Law, Medicine & Ethics*, 38(3): 580–93.

Buse, K. and Harmer, A. (2004). 'Power to the Partners? The Politics of Public–Private Partnerships', *Development*, 47(2): 49–56.

Buse, K. and Walt, G. (2000). 'Global Public–Private Partnerships: Part II – What are the Health Issues for Global Governance?' *Bulletin of the World Health Organization*, 78(5): 699–709.

Buzan, B. (1991). *People, States & Fear*, 2nd edn. London: Harvester Wheatsheaf.

Buzan, B., Waever, O. and de Wilde, J. (1998). *Security: A New Framework for Analysis*, London: Lynne Reinner.

Bybee, J. (2002). 'Memorandum for Alberto R Gonzales, Counsel to the President. Re: Standards of Conduct for Interrogation under 18 USC 2340-2340A', US Department of Justice, Office of Legal Counsel, Washington, DC.

Calkins, L. B. (2012). 'Ex-KBR CEO Stanley Gets 2 ½ Years in Prison for Foreign Bribes', Bloomberg, 24 February.
Cammack, P. (2004). 'What the World Bank Means by Poverty Reduction, and Why it Matters', *New Political Economy*, 9(2): 189–211.
Capturing the Gains (2012). Sector Overview: Mobile Telecommunications. Available at: http://www.capturingthegains.org/research/themes/sectors/mobile-telecoms/index.htm (accessed 21 October 2012).
Carr, M., Chen M. and Tate, J. (2000). 'Globalisation and Home Based Workers', *Feminist Economics*, 6(3): 123–42.
Carson, R. (1969). *Silent Spring*, Boston, MA: Houghton Mifflin.
CCR (Central Commission for the Navigation of the Rhine) (1815). 'Annexe 16B du 24 Mars 1815'. Available at: http://www.ccr-zkr.org/files/histoireCCNR/02_annexe-16-b-du-24-mars-1815.pdf (accessed 26 July 2012).
CCR (2008a). 'Boumediene v. Bush / Al Odah v. United States', *Center for Constitutional Rights*.
CCR (2008b). 'Hamdan v. Rumsfeld', *Center for Constitutional Rights*.
Cerny, P. G. (2008). 'Paradoxes of the Competition State: The Dynamics of Political Globalization', *Government and Opposition*, 32(2): 251–274.
Chang, H. (2003). *Kicking Away the Ladder*, London: Anthem Press.
Chatham House (2010). *British Attitudes Towards the UK's International Priorities: A Chatham House-YouGov Survey*, London: Chatham House.
Chen, M. (2005). *Progress of the World's Women 2005*, New York: United Nations Development Fund for Women.
Chen, S. and Ravallion, M. (2008). 'The Developing World is Poorer than we Thought, but No Less Successful in the Fight Against Poverty', *World Bank Policy Research Working Paper* No. 4703, Washington, DC: World Bank.
Chenery, H. B. (1961). 'Comparative advantage and development policy', *The American Economic Review*, 51(1), pp.18–51.
Chick, V. (2008). 'Could the Crisis at Northern Rock have been Predicted? An Evolutionary Approach', *Contributions to Political Economy*, 28(1): 115–124.
Chin, C. (1998). *In Service and Servitude: Foreign Female Domestic Workers and the Making of the Malaysian 'Modernity' Project*, New York: Columbia University Press.
Cholewinski, R. (2006). 'International Labour Law and the Protection of Migrant Workers: Revitalizing the Agenda in the Era of Globalization', in J. Craig and M. Lynk (eds), *Globalization and the Future of Labour Law*, Cambridge: Cambridge University Press, pp. 409–44.
Christoff, P. (2010). 'Cold Climate in Copenhagen: China and the United States at COP15', *Environmental Politics*, 19(4): 637–56.
Christou, G., Croft, S., Ceccorulli, M. and Lucarelli, S. (2010). 'European Union security governance: putting the "security" back in', *European Security*, 19(3): 341–59.
CIA (2004). 'CIA Inspector General Special Review: Counterterrorism, Detention and Interrogation Activities (September 2001–October 2003)', 7 May.
Cioc, M. (2002). *The Rhine: An Eco-Biography, 1815–2000*, Seattle, WA: University of Washington Press.
Clausen, B., Aart K. and Nyiri, Z. (2011). 'Corruption and Confidence in Public Institutions: Evidence from a Global Survey', *World Bank Economic Review*, 25(2): 212–249.
Clay, E., Geddes, M. and Natali, L. (2009) *Untying Aid: Is it working? An Evaluation of the Implementation of the Paris Declaration and of the 2001 DAC Recommendation of Untying ODA to the LDCs*, Copenhagen: Danish Institute for International Studies.

Clemens, M., Kenny, C. and Moss, T. J. (2007). 'The trouble with the MDGs: Confronting expectations of aid and development success', *World Development*, 35(5), 735–51.
Clover, J. (2003). 'Food Security in Sub-Saharan Africa', *African Security Review*, 12(1): 5–15.
Cohen, B. (1998). *The Geography of Money*, Ithaca, NY: Cornell University Press.
—— (2007). 'The Transatlantic Divide: Why are British and American IPE so different?' *Review of International Political Economy*, 14(2): 197–219.
—— (2008). 'Monetary Unions', in R. Whaples (2008), EH.Net Encyclopedia. Available at: http://eh.net/encyclopedia/article/cohen.monetary.unions (accessed 9 January 2012).
Cohen, R. (2002). 'Nowhere to Run, No Place to Hide', *Bulletin of the Atomic Scientists*, 58(6): 36–45.
—— (2006). 'Developing an International System for Internally Displaced Persons', *International Studies Perspectives*, 7(2): 87–101
Cohen, R. and Deng, F. (1998). *Masses in Flight: The Global Crisis of Internal Displacement*, Washington, DC: Brookings Institution Press.
Commission on Global Governance (1995). *Our Global Neighborhood*, Oxford: Oxford University Press.
Commission on Global Governance (2005). 'A New World', in R. Wilkinson (ed.), *The Global Governance Reader*, London: Routledge, pp.26–44.
Commission on Human Security (CHS) (2003). *Human Security Now*, New York: CHS.
Conca, K. (2005). 'Old States in New Bottles? The Hybridization of Authority in Global Environmental Governance', in J. Barry and R. Eckersley (eds), *The State and the Global Ecological Crisis*, Cambridge, MA: MIT Press, pp. 181–206.
Conca, K. and Dalbelko, G. D. (2004). 'Introduction: Three Decades of Global Environmental Politics', in K. Conca and G. D. Dalbelko (eds), *Green Planet Blues: Environmental Politics from Stockholm to Johannesburg*, Boulder, CO: Westview Press, pp. 1–23.
Congress, U.S. (2006). 'Military Commissions Act of 2006', *US Public Law 109–366: 109th Congress*, Boston, MA: Houghton Mifflin.
Cooney, S. (1999). 'Testing Times for the ILO: Institutional Reform for the New International Political Economy', *Comparative Labour Law and Policy Journal*, 20(3): 365–400.
CounterBalance (2010). *The Mopani Copper Mine, Zambia: How European Development Money Has Fed a Mining Scandal*, Brussels: CounterBalance.
Cox, R. (1977). 'Labour and Hegemony', *International Organisation*, 31(1): 385–424.
Craig, D. and Porter, D. (2003) 'Poverty Reduction Strategy Papers: A New Convergence', *World Development*, 31(1): 53–69.
—— (2006) *Development beyond Neoliberalism? Governance, Poverty Reduction and Political Economy*, London and New York: Routledge.
Croft, S. (2012) *Securitizing Islam: Identity and the Search for Security*, Cambridge: Cambridge University Press.
Cronin, B. (2003). *Institutions for the Common Good: International Protection Regimes in International Society*, Cambridge: Cambridge University Press.
Crotty, J. (2009). 'Structural Causes of the Global Financial Crisis: A Critical Assessment of the "New Financial Architecture"', *Cambridge Journal of Economics*, 33: 563–580.
Croucher, R. and Cotton, E. (2009). *Global Unions, Global Business: Global Union Federations and International Business*, London: Middlesex University Press.
Cueto, M. (2004). 'The Origins of Primary Health Care and Selective Primary Health Care', *American Journal of Public Health*, 94(11): 1864–74.
DAC (1996). *Shaping the 21st Century: The Contribution of Development Cooperation*, Paris: OECD.

Dahan, N., Doh, J., Oetzel, J. and Yaziji, M. (2010). 'Corporate–NGO Collaboration: Co-creating New Business Models for Developing Markets', *Long Range Planning* 43(2–3): 326–42.

Darrough, M. (2009). 'The FCPA and the OECD Convention: Some Lessons from the US Experience', *Journal of Business Ethics*, 93: 255–76.

Davies, T. (2013). *NGOs: A New History of Transnational Civil Society*, London: Hurst.

Davis, K. and Kingsbury, B. (2010). 'Obligation Overload: Adjusting the Obligations of Fragile or Failed States'. Available at: http://www.iilj.org/courses/documents/HC2010 Dec01.DavisKingsbury.pdf.

Death, C. (2010). *Governing Sustainable Development: Partnerships, Protests and Power at the World Summit*, London: Routledge.

Deaton, A., Banerjee, A., Lustig, N. and Rogoff, K. (2006) *An Evaluation of World Bank Research*, 1998–2005, Washington, DC: World Bank.

Deng, F. M. (1998). 'Promoting Responsible Sovereignty in Africa', in F. Deng and T. Lyons (eds), *African Reckoning: A Quest for Good Governance*, Washington, DC: The Brookings Institution, pp. 1–11.

Diamond, J. (1997). *Guns, Germs and Steel: The Fate of Human Societies*, London: Jonathan Cape.

Diess, J. (2011). 'Opening remarks at the Conference on "Global Governance and Security Council Reform"', Rome, 16 May.

Dimitrov, R. S. (2010). 'Inside Copenhagen: The State of Climate Governance', *Global Environmental Politics*, 10(2): 18–24.

Dingwerth, K. and Pattberg, P. (2006). 'Global Governance as a Perspective on World Politics', *Global Governance*, 12(2): 185–203.

DNDI. (2012) Board of Directors. Available at: http://www.dndi.org/our-people/board-of-directors.html?ids=1 (accessed 26 January 2012).

Dollar, D. and Kraay, A. (2002). 'Growth is Good for the Poor', *Journal of Economic Growth* 7(3): 195–225.

Doyle, C. and Patel, P. (2008). 'Civil Society Organisations and Global Health Initiatives: Problems of Legitimacy', *Social Science & Medicine*, 66(9): 1928–38.

Dresner, S. (2002). *The Principles of Sustainability*, London: Earthscan.

Dryzek, J. (2005). *The Politics of the Earth: Environmental Discourses*, Oxford: Oxford University Press.

Duffield, M. (2002). 'Social Reconstruction and the Radicalization of Development: Aid as a Relation of Global Liberal Government', *Development and Change*, 33(5): 1049–1071.

Dutton, W. H., and Palfrey, J. (2007). 'Deciphering the Codes of Internet Governance: Understanding the Hard Issues at Stake', OII/e-Horizons Forum Discussion Paper, Oxford: Oxford Internet Institute.

Easterly, W. (2006). *White Man's Burden: Why the West's Efforts to Aid the Rest Have Done So Much Ill and So Little Good*, Oxford: Oxford University Press.

—— (2009). 'How the Millennium Development Goals are unfair to Africa', *World Development*, 37(1): 26–35.

Eco, U. (1995). *The Search for the Perfect Language*, Oxford: Blackwell.

Elias, J. (2004). *Fashioning Inequality: The Multinational Corporation and Gendered Employment in a Globalizing World*, Aldershot: Ashgate.

—— (2008). 'Struggles over the Rights of Foreign Domestic Workers in Malaysia: The Possibilities and Limitations of "Rights Talk"', *Economy and Society*, 37(2): 282–303.

Elson, D. and R. Pearson (1981). '"Nimble Fingers Make Cheap Workers": An Analysis of Women's Employment in Third World Export Manufacturing', *Feminist Review*, 7: 87–107.

Emmerij, L., Jolly, R. and Weiss, T.G. (2001). *Ahead of the Curve? UN Ideas and Global Challenges*, Bloomington, IN: Indiana University Press.

Epstein, C. (2008). *The Power of Words in International Relations: Birth of an Anti-Whaling Discourse*, Cambridge, MA: MIT Press.

Ermakov, V. (1996). 'Reform of the World Health Organization', *Lancet*, 347(9014): 1536–7.

Ethical Trading Initiative (ETI) (2012) *About ETI*. Available at: http://www.ethicaltrade.org/about-eti/www.ifj.org (accessed 21 October2012).

Eurodad (2011). '"Boomerang aid": billions of development aid diverted to companies in rich countries', Brussels: Eurodad. Available at: http://eurodad.org/4640.

Export Processing Zones Authority (2005). *Kenya's Apparel and Textiles Industry 2005*, Nairobi: Export Processing Zones Authority.

European Commission (2007). *Contribution to an EU Aid for Trade Strategy*, Brussels: European Commission.

EU (2006). 'Interim Report on the Alleged Use of European Countries by the CIA for the Transportation and Illegal Detention of Prisoners (2006/2027(INI)) [A6-9999/2006]', 15 June, European Parliament. Available at: http://www.europarl.europa.eu/sides/getDoc.do?pub Ref=-//EP//NONSGML+REPORT+A6-2006-0213+0+DOC+PDF+V0//EN.

EU (2007). 'Report on the Alleged Use of European Countries by the CIA for the Transportation and Illegal Detention of Prisoners (2006/2200(INI)) [A-0020 /2007]', 30 January, European Parliament. Available at: http://www.europarl.europa.eu/sides/getDoc.do? pub Ref=-//EP//NONSGML+REPORT+A6 -2007 -0020+0+DOC+PDF+V0//EN.

Falk, R. (2000). 'Humane Governance for the World: Reviving the Quest', *Review of International Political Economy*, 7(2): 317–34.

Ferris, E. (2003). 'The Role of NGOs in the International Refugee Regime', in N. Steiner, M. Gibney and G. Loescher (eds), *Problems of Protection: The Unhcr, Refugees, and Human Rights*, New York: Routledge, pp. 117–37.

Fidler, D. (2009). 'After the Revolution: Global Health Politics in a Time of Economic Crisis and Threatening Future Trends', *Global Health Governance*, 2(2): 1–21.

Financial Action Task Force (2004), *FATF 40 Recommendations*, as amended up to October 2004.

—— (2008), *FATF IX Special Recommendations*, as amended up to February 2008.

Finkelstein, L. (1995). 'What is Global Governance?' *Global Governance*, 1(3): 367–72.

Flemes, D. (2009). 'India–Brazil–South Africa (IBSA) in the New Global Order: Interests, Strategies and Values of the Emerging Coalition', *International Studies*, 46(4): 401–21.

Ford, M. (2005). 'Migrant Labor NGOs and Trade Unions: A Partnership in Progress?' *Asian and Pacific Migration Journal*, 15(3): 299–312.

Foucault, M. (1998). *The Will to Knowledge: The History of Sexuality, Volume 1*, (trans. R. Hurley), London: Penguin.

Fransen, L. and Burgoon, B. (2012). 'A Market for Worker Rights: Explaining Business Support for Private Labour Regulation', *Review of International Political Economy*, 19(2): 236–66.

Frenkel, S. J and Scott, D. (2002), 'Compliance Collaboration and Codes of Labor Practice: The Adidas Connection', *California Journal of Management*, 45(1): 29–49.

Fukuda-Parr, S. and Hulme, D. (2011). 'International Norm Dynamics and the "End of Poverty": Understanding the Millennium Development Goals', *Global Governance* 17(1): 17–36.

Gall, G. (2006). *Sex Worker Organizing: An International Study*, London: Palgrave Macmillan.

GAVI (2012a). Global Alliance for Vaccines and Immunisation. *GAVI's strategy*. Available at: http://www.gavialliance.org/about/strategy/ (accessed 27 July 2012).

GAVI (2012b). *Board composition*. Available at: http://www.gavialliance.org/about/governance/gavi-board/composition/ (accessed 27 July 2012).

GAVI (2012c). *How the pneumococcal AMC works*. Available at: http://www.gavialliance.org/funding/pneumococcal-amc/how-the-pneumo coccal-amc-works/ (accessed 27 July 2012).

GAVI (2012d). *GAVI facts and figures*. Available at: http://www.gavialliance.org/advocacy-statistics/ (accessed 27 July 2012).

George, S. (2010). *The Truth About Trade: The Real Impact of Trade Liberalization*, London and New York: Zed Books.

Gephart, M. (2009). 'Contextualizing Conceptions of Corruption: Challenges for the International Anti-corruption Campaign', *GIGA Working Paper* 115, Leibniz: German Institute of Global and Area Studies.

Gibney, M. J. (2004). *The Ethics and Politics of Asylum: Liberal Democracy and the Response to Refugees*, Cambridge and New York: Cambridge University Press.

—— (2005). 'Beyond the Bounds of Responsibility: Western States and Measures to Prevent the Arrival of Refugees', *Global Migration Perspectives* 22, Geneva: Global Commission on International Migration.

Gibney, M. J. and Hansen, R. (2003). 'Asylum Policy in the West: Past Trends, Future Possibilities', *UNU-Wider Discussion paper 68/2003*, Helsinki: United Nations University, World Institute for Development Economics Research.

Gill, S. (2005). 'New Constitutionalism, Democratisation, and Global Political Economy', in R. Wilkinson (ed.) *The Global Governance Reader*, London: Routledge, 174–86.

Goertz, G. (2003). *International Norms and Decision-making: A Punctuated Equilibrium Model*, Lanham, Maryland: Rowman & Littlefield Publishers.

Goldsmith, J. and Wu, T (2006). *Who Controls the Internet? Illusions of a Borderless World*, New York: Oxford University Press.

Goldstein, J. (1998). 'International Institutions and Domestic Politics: GATT, WTO and the Liberalization of International Trade', in A. Krueger (ed.), *The WTO as an International Organization*, Chicago: University of Chicago Press, pp. 133–52.

Goodison, P. (2007) 'What is the Future for EU–Africa Agricultural Trade after CAP Reform?' *Review of African Political Economy*, 34(112): 279–95.

Gore, C. (2004). 'MDGs and PRSPs: Are Poor Countries Enmeshed in a Global–Local Double Bind?' *Global Social Policy*, 4: 277–83.

Gorlick, B. (2003). 'Refugee Protection in Troubled Times', in N. Steiner, M. Gibney and G. Loescher (eds), *Problems of Protection: The Unhcr, Refugees, and Human Rights*, New York: Routledge, pp. 79–100.

Gostin, L. (2008). 'Global Health Law: A Definition and Grand Challenges', *Public Health Ethics*, 1(1): 53–63.

Gostin, L. and Mok, E. (2009). 'Grand Challenges in Global Health Governance', *British Medical Bulletin*, 90(1): 7–18.

Graff, J. and Crumley, B. (2003). 'France Is Not a Pacifist Country', *Time Magazine*, Sunday 15 February, available at: http://www.time.com/time/magazine/article/0,9171,423466,00.html.

Greenberg, M. (1969). *British Trade and the Opening of China*, Birmingham: Carlyle Press.

Gurak, L. and Logie, J. (2003). 'Internet Protests, from Text to Web', in M. McCaughey and M. Ayers (eds), *Cyberactivism: Online Activism in Theory and Practice*, New York: Routledge, pp. 25–46.

Guterres, A. (2005). 'Remarks by Mr. António Guterres, United Nations High Commissioner for Refugees, to the 17 June Informal Meeting of the Executive Committee', Geneva: UNHCR.

Haas, P. (2002). 'UN Conferences and Constructivist Governance of the Environment', *Global Governance*, 8(1): 73–91.
Haddad, E. (2008). *The Refugee in International Society: Between Sovereigns*, Cambridge: Cambridge University Press.
Hajer, M. and Versteeg, W. (2005). 'A Decade of Discourse Analysis of Environmental Politics: Achievements, Challenges, Perspectives', *Journal of Environmental Policy and Planning*, 7(3): 175–84.
Hannay, D. (1999). 'Interview'. Available at: http://www.chu.cam.ac.uk/archives/collections/BDOHP/#g.
Hardin, G. (1968). 'The Tragedy of the Commons', *Science*, 162(13): 1243–8.
Hardiman, M. (2003). 'The Revised International Health Regulations: A Framework for Global Health Security', *International Journal of Antimicrobial Agents*, 21(2): 207–11.
Harman, S. (2012a). 'Women and the MDGs: Too Little, Too Late, Too Gendered', in R. Wilkinson and D. Hulme (eds), *The Millennium Development Goals and Beyond: Global Development after 2015*, London: Routledge.
—— (2012b). *Global Health Governance*, London: Routledge.
Harvey, D. (2005). *A Brief History of Neoliberalism*, Oxford: Oxford University Press.
Harvey, F. (2011). 'Extreme weather will strike as climate change takes hold, IPCC warns', The *Guardian*, 18 November. Available at: http://www.guardian.co.uk/environment/2011/nov/18/extreme-weather-climate-change-ipcc.
Hassan, L. (2002). 'Deterrence Measures and the Preservation of Asylum in the United Kingdom and United States', *Journal of Refugee Studies*, 13(2): 184–204.
Haynes, J. (1999). 'Power, Politics and Environmental Movements in the Third World', *Environmental Politics*, 8(1): 222–42.
Heineman, B. and Heimann, F. (2006). 'The Long War Against Corruption', *Foreign Affairs*, 85(3): 75–86.
Held, D. (1995). *Democracy and the Global Order: From the Modern State to Cosmopolitan Democracy*, Cambridge: Polity Press.
Helleiner, E. (1994). *States and the Re-emergence of Global Finance*, Ithaca and London: Cornell University Press.
—— (2003). *The Making of National Money: Territorial Currencies in Historical Perspective*, Ithaca, NY: Cornell University Press.
—— (2008). 'The Evolution of the International Monetary and Financial System', in J. Ravenhill (ed.), *Global Political Economy*, 2nd edn. New York: Oxford University Press, pp. 213–240.
Helton, A. C. (2002). *The Price of Indifference: Refugees and Humanitarian Action in the New Century*, Oxford and New York: Oxford University Press.
—— (2003). 'What is Refugee Protection? A Question Revisited', in N. Steiner, M. Gibney and G. Loescher (eds), *Problems of Protection: The Unhcr, Refugees, and Human Rights*, New York: Routledge, pp. 19–36.
Herlihy, D. (1997). *The Black Death and the Transformation of the West*, Cambridge, MA: Harvard University Press.
Hill, P. (2011). 'Understanding Global Health Governance as a Complex Adaptive System', *Global Public Health*, 6(6): 593–605.
Hobden, C. (2011). 'Reversing a History of Exclusion Through Labour Law', *International Feminist Journal of Politics*, 13(3): 437–461.
Hodges, T. (2004). *Angola: Anatomy of an Oil State*, Oxford: James Currey.
Hodgson, D. L. (2002). 'Introduction: Comparative perspectives on the indigenous rights movement in Africa and the Americas', *American Anthropologist*, 104(4): 1037–1049.

Holborn, L. (1956). *The International Refugee Organization: A Specialized Agency of the United Nations: Its History and Work, 1946–1952*, Oxford: Oxford University Press.
—— (1975) *Refugees, a Problem of Our Time: The Work of the United Nations High Commissioner for Refugees, 1951–1972*, Metuchen, NJ: Scarecrow Press.
Home Office (1998). *Fairer, Faster, and Firmer? A Modern Approach to Immigration and Asylum*, London: HMSO.
Howard-Hassmann, R. (2012). 'Human Security: Undermining Human Rights?' *Human Rights Quarterly*, 34(1): 88–112.
HTSPE (2003) *Assessment of the International Competitiveness and Value Adding Opportunities of the Kenyan Cotton Industry – Project No. Quince/14/2003/KE – Final Report*, London: HTSPE.
Hughes, S. and Haworth, N. (2010). *The International Labour Organization. Coming in from the Cold*, London: Routledge.
—— (2011). 'Decent Work and Poverty Reduction Strategies', *Relations Indusrielles/Industrial Relations*, 66(1): 34–53.
Hulme, D. (2007). 'The making of the Millennium Development Goals: Human development meets results-based management in an imperfect world', *BWPI Working Paper No. 16*, Manchester: University of Manchester.
—— (2009). 'Politics, ethics and the Millennium Development Goals: The case of reproductive health', *Brooks World Poverty Institute Working Paper No. 104*, Manchester: University of Manchester.
—— (2010). *Global Poverty: How global governance is failing the poor*, London and New York: Routledge.
Human Rights Watch (2004). *Help Wanted: Abuses against Female Domestic Workers in Indonesia and Malaysia*. Available at http://www.hrw.org/reports/2004/07/21/help-wanted (accessed 21 March 2012).
—— (2012). *Delivered Into Enemy Hands: US-Led Abuse and Rendition of Opponents to Gaddafi's Libya*. Available at: http://www.hrw.org/sites/default/files/reports/libya0912webwcover_1.pdf.
Hyman, R. (2011). 'Trade unions, global competition and options for solidarity', in A. Bieler and I. Lindberg (eds), *Global Restructuring, Labour and the Challenges for Transnational Solidarity*, London: Routledge, pp. 16–30.
IATA (International Air Transport Association) (2012). 'Membership'. Available at: http://www.iata.org/membership/Pages/Index.aspx (accessed 19 August 2012).
ICANN (Internet Corporation for Assigned Names and Numbers) (2011). *Annual Report 2011*, Marina del Rey, CA: ICANN.
ICISS (2001). *The Responsibility to Protect: Report of the International Commission on Intervention and State Sovereignty*, Ottawa: International Development Research Centre.
ICRC (2003). 'International Humanitarian Law and International Human Rights Law: Similarities and Differences', Geneva: ICRC Advisory Service.
—— (2007). 'ICRC Report on the Treatment of Fourteen "High Value Detainees" in CIA Custody', Geneva: ICRC.
IEO (Independent Evaluation Office) (2011). *IMF Performance in the Run-up to the Financial and Economic Crisis: IMF Surveillance in 2004–07*, Washington DC: International Monetary Fund.
IETF (Internet Engineering Task Force) (2004). 'A Mission Statement for the IETF', Available at: http://www.ietf.org/rfc/rfc3935.txt (accessed 2 August 2012).
IGF (Internet Governance Forum, 2012a). 'Dynamic Coalitions'. Available at: http://www.intgovforum.org/cms/dynamic-coalitions (accessed 1 August 2012).

—— (2012b). 'The Multi Stakeholder Advisory Group'. Available at: http://www.intgovforum.org/cms/magabout (accessed 1 August 2012).

Ikiara, M. and Ndirangu, L. (2002). 'Developing a Revival Strategy for the Kenyan Cotton Textile Industry: A Value Chain Approach', *KIPPRA Working Paper No. 8*, Nairobi: Kenya Institute for Public Policy Research and Analysis.

ILO (1919). *Constitution of the International Labour Organisation*. Available at http://www.ilo.org/ilolex/english/iloconst.htm (accessed 11 January 2012).

—— (1998). *Declaration on Fundamental Principles and Rights at Work*. Available at http://www.ilo.org/declaration/thedeclaration/textdeclaration/lang--en/index.htm (accessed 11 January 2012).

—— (2005). 'ILO Tsunami Response: ILO calls for integrated employment strategy', Press Release, 19 January. Available at: http://www.ilo.org/global/about-the-ilo/press-and-media-centre/news/WCMS_005169/lang--en/index.htm.

—— (2008). *Declaration on Social Justice for a Fair Globalisation*. Available at http://www.ilo.org/wcmsp5/groups/public/---dgreports/---cabinet/documents/publication/wcms_099766.pdf (accessed 11 January2012).

Imber, M. (1996). 'The Environment and the United Nations', in J. Vogler and M. Imber (eds), *The Environment and International Relations*, London: Routledge, pp. 138–53.

IMF (2002). 'Angola: Staff Report for the 2002 Article IV Consultation', Washington DC: International Monetary Fund.

—— (2003). 'Angola: Selected Issues and Statistical Appendix', IMF Country Report No. 03/292, Washington DC: International Monetary Fund.

—— (2005). *Guide on Resource Revenue Transparency*, Washington DC: International Monetary Fund.

—— (2007). *Global Financial Stability Report*, April. Washington, DC: International Monetary Fund.

Independent Inquiry Committee into the United Nations Oil-for-Food Programme (2005a). 'Report on the Manipulation of the Oil-for-Food Programme', New York: IIC-OFFP.

—— (2005b), Press Release, 27 October, New York: IIC-OFFP.

Ingram, A. (2005). 'Global Leadership and Global Health: Contenting Meta-narratives, Divergent Responses, Fatal Consequences', *International Relations*, 19(4): 381–402.

IPCC (2012). Available at: http://www.ipcc.ch/organization/organization_history.shtml.

Ismail, F. (2008). 'Aid for Trade: An Essential Component of the Multilateral Trading System and the WTO Doha Development Agenda', in D. Njinkeu and H. Cameron (eds), *Aid for Trade and Development*, New York: Cambridge University Press, pp.46–73.

ISOC (Internet Society) (2012). 'What is the Internet?' Available at: http://www.Internetsociety.org/Internet/what-Internet (accessed 30 July 2012).

Itaye, S. (2011). 'Aid for Trade: Success Stories and Lessons', *Trade Negotiations Insights*, 10(7). Available at: http://ictsd.org/i/a4t/115352/ (accessed 21 October 2012).

ITU (International Telecommunication Union, 2010). *ITU's History*. Available at: http://www.itu.int/en/history/overview/Pages/history.aspx (accessed 27 July 2012).

—— (2011a). 'ITU Membership Overview'. Available at: http://www.itu.int/en/membership/Pages/overview.aspx (accessed 31 July 2012).

—— (2011b). *Collection of the Basic Texts of the International Telecommunication Union adopted by the Plenipotentiary Conference*, Geneva: ITU.

—— (2012). 'What does ITU do?' Available at: http://www.itu.int/en/about/Pages/whatwedo.aspx (accessed 31 July 2012).

Ivanova, M. (2012). 'Institutional Design and UNEP Reform: Historical Insights on Form, Function and Financing', *International Affairs*, 88(3): 565–84.

Jawara, F. and Kwa, A. (2004). *Behind the Scenes at the WTO: The Real World of International Trade Negotiations*, London and New York: Zed Books.

Jenkins R., Pearson, R. and Seyfang, G. (2002). 'Introduction', in R. Jenkins, R. Pearson and G. Seyfang (eds), *Corporate Social Responsibility and Labour Rights: Codes of Conduct in the Global Economy*, London: Earthscan, pp. 1–12.

Johnson, T. (1938). *International Tramps: From Chaos to Permanent World Peace*, London: Hutchinson & Co.

Jones, R., Pykett, J. and Whitehead, M. (2011). 'The Geographies of Soft Paternalism in the UK: The Rise of the Avuncular State and Changing Behaviour after Neoliberalism', *Geography Compass*, 5(1): 50–62.

Jones, S. (2012). 'Innovating Foreign Aid – Progress and Problems', *Journal of International Development*, 24(1): 1–16.

Jreisat, J. (2004). 'Governance in a Globalizing World', *International Journal of Public Administration*, 27(13–14): 1003–1029.

Kabeer, N. (2005). 'Gender Equality and Women's Empowerment: A Critical Analysis of the Third Millennium Development Goal', *Gender and Development*, 13(1): 13–24.

Kahler, M. (2002). 'Bretton Woods and its Competitors: The Political Economy of Institutional Choice', in D. Andrews, C. Henning, and L. Pauly (eds), *Governing the World's Money*, Ithaca, NY: Cornell University Press, pp. 38–59.

Kälin, W. (2005). 'The Guiding Principles on Internal Displacement as International Minimum Standard and Protection Tool', *Refugee Survey Quarterly*, 24(3): 27–36.

—— (2008). *Guiding Principles on Internal Displacement: Annotations*, 2nd edn. Washington DC: The American Society of International Law.

Kamradt-Scott, A. (2011). 'The Evolving WHO: Implications for Global Health Security', *Global Public Health*, 6(8): 801–13.

—— (2012). 'EU–India Free Trade Agreement: Implications for Global Health', *Health Diplomacy Monitor*, 3(2): 6–8.

Kamradt-Scott, A. and Lee, K. (2011). 'The 2011 Pandemic Influenza Preparedness Framework: Global Health Secured or a Missed Opportunity?' *Political Studies*, 59(4): 831–847.

Kant, I. (1970a). 'Idea for a Universal History with a Cosmopolitan Purpose', in H. Reiss (ed.) *Kant's Political Writings*, Cambridge: Cambridge University Press.

—— (1970b). 'Perpetual Peace: A Philosophical Sketch', in H. Reiss (ed.) *Kant's Political Writings*, Cambridge: Cambridge University Press.

Kapstein, E. B. (1996). 'Shockproof: The End of Financial Crisis', *Foreign Affairs*, 74(1): 2–8.

Kates, J., Morrison, J. and Lief, E. (2006). 'Global health funding: a glass half full?' *Lancet*, 368(9531): 187–8.

Kaufmann, D. and Penciakova, V. (2011). 'Transparency, Conflict Minerals and Natural Resources: Debating Sections 1502 and 1504 of the Dodd–Frank Act'. Available at: http://www.brookings.edu/events/2011/12/13-transparency-resources#ref-id=20111214_mcdermott.

Kaufman, N. and Lindquist, S. (1995). 'Critiquing Gender-Neutral Treaty Language: The Convention on the Elimination of All Forms of Discrimination Against Women,' in J. Peters and A. Wolper (eds), *Women's Rights, Human Rights: International Feminist Perspectives*, New York: Routledge, pp. 121–222.

Keen, D. (2008). *Complex Emergencies*, Cambridge: Polity Press.

Keohane, R., Haas, P. and Levy, M. (1993). 'The Effectiveness of International Environmental Institutions', in P. Haas, R. Keohane and M. Levy (eds), *Institutions for the Earth: Sources*

of *Effective International Environmental Protection*, Cambridge, MA: MIT Press, pp. 3–26.
Keohane, R. and Victor, D. (2011). 'The Regime Complex for Climate Change', *Perspectives on Politics*, 9(1): 7–23.
Kern, A., Dhumale, R. and Eatwell, J. (2006). *Global Governance of Financial Systems: The International Regulation of Systemic Risk*, New York: Oxford University Press.
Kettler, H. and White, K. (2003). 'Valuing Industry Contributions to Public–Private Partnerships for Health Product Development', Switzerland, Initiative on Public–Private Partnerships for Health, www.iprsonline.org/resources/docs/ValuingIndustryContributions_KettlerWhite.pdf (accessed 26 January2012).
Keynes, J. (1933). 'National Self-Sufficiency', *The Yale Review*, 22(4): 755–69.
—— (1980) 'Shaping the Post-War World, the Clearing Union', in D. Moggridge (ed.) *The Collected Writings of J. M. Keynes: Vol. 25, Activities 1940–44*, Cambridge: Cambridge University Press.
Kickbusch, I., Hein, W. and Silberschmidt, G. (2010). 'Addressing Global Health Governance Challenges through a New Mechanism: The Proposal for a Committee of the World Health Assembly', *Journal of Law, Medicine & Ethics*, 38(3): 550–63.
Kierkegaard, S. (2008). 'International Cybercrime Convention', in L. Janczewski and A. Colarik (eds), *Cyber Warfare and Cyber Terrorism*, Hershey, PA: Information Science Reference, pp. 469–75.
Kirchner, E. (2007). 'Regional and global security: changing threats and institutional responses', in E. Kirchner and J. Sperling (eds), *Global Security Governance*, London: Routledge, pp. 3–22.
Kirton, J. and Guebert, J. (2009). 'Canada's G8 Health Diplomacy: Lessons for 2010', *Canadian Foreign Policy Journal*, 15(3): 85–105.
Korzeniewicz, R. (2012). 'Trends in World Income Inequality and the "Emerging Middle"', *European Journal of Development Research*, 24(2): 205–222.
Knake, R. (2010). *Internet Governance in an Age of Cyber Insecurity*, New York: Council on Foreign Relations.
Kneebone, S. (2006). 'The Pacific Plan: The Provision of "Effective Protection"?' *International Journal of Refugee Law*, 18(3–4): 696–721.
Krasner, S. (1982). 'Structural Causes and Regime Consequences: Regimes as Intervening Variables', *International Organization*, 36(2): 185–205.
—— (2001) 'Rethinking the sovereign state model', *Review of International Studies*, 27(5): 17–42.
Krause, K. (2004). 'Is Human Security "More Than Just a Good Idea"?' in M. Brzoska, and P. Croll (eds), *Promoting Security: But How and For Whom?* Bonn: BICC, 43–6.
Kregel, J. (2010). 'No Going Back: Why We Cannot Restore Glass-Steagall's Segregation of Banking and Finance', *Public Policy Brief no.107, Levy Economics Institute of Bard College*.
Kshetri, N. (2010). *The Global Cybercrime Industry: Economic, Institutional and Strategic Perspectives*, Heidelberg: Springer.
Kummer, M. (2011). 'The First Five Years: The Internet Governance Forum, or Towards New Models of Participatory Global Governance', in B. Gutterman (ed.), *IGF 2010 – Developing the Future Together: The Fifth Meeting of the Internet Governance Forum, Vilnius, Lithuania, 14–17 September 2010*, Nairobi: United Nations, pp. vi–xiii.
Kurtzman, J. (1993). *The Death of Money*, New York: Little, Brown and Co.
Lacina, B. and Gleditsch, N. (2005). 'Monitoring Trends in Global Combat: A New Dataset of Battle Deaths', *European Journal of Population*, 21(2–3): 145–166.

Lampedusa, G. di (1963). *The Leopard*, London: Fontana.
Lancaster, C. (2007). *Foreign Aid: Diplomacy, Development, Domestic Politics*, Chicago and London: University of Chicago Press.
Langan, M. (2012). 'Normative Power Europe and the Moral Economy of Africa–EU Ties: A Conceptual Reorientation of Normative Power', *New Political Economy*, 17(3): 243–70.
Langan. M. and Scott, J. (forthcoming). 'The Aid for Trade Charade', *Cooperation and Conflict*.
Langley, P. (2008). *The Everyday Life of Global Finance: Saving and Borrowing in America*, Oxford: Oxford University Press.
Larson, J. (1996). 'The World Health Organization's Definition of Health: Social versus Spiritual Health', *Social Indicators Research*, 38(2): 181–92.
Le Billon, P. (2008). 'Corrupting Peace? Peacebuilding and Post-conflict Corruption', *International Peacekeeping*, 15(3): 344–361.
Lee, D. (2012). 'Poverty and cotton in the DDA', in R. Wilkinson and J. Scott (eds), *Trade, Poverty, Inequality: Getting beyond the WTO's Doha Deadlock*, London: Routledge, pp. 72–90.
Lee, E. (1997). 'Globalisation and Labour Standards: A Review of the Issues', *International Labour Review*, 136(2): 173–89.
Lee, K. (2003). *Globalization and Health: An Introduction*, Hampshire: Palgrave Macmillan.
—— (2010). 'Civil Society Organizations and the Functions of Global Health Governance: What Role within Intergovernmental Organizations?' *Global Health Governance*, 3(2): 1–20.
Levy, M., Young, O. and Zurn, M. (1995). 'The Study of International Regimes', *European Journal of International Relations*, 1(3): 267–330.
Litfin, K. (1994). *Ozone Discourses: Science and Politics in Global Environmental Cooperation*, New York: Columbia University Press.
Luke, T. (1999). 'Eco-managerialism: Environmental Studies as a Power/Knowledge Formation', in F. Fischer and M. Hajer (eds), *Living With Nature: Environmental Politics as Cultural Discourse*, Oxford: Oxford University Press, pp. 103–20.
Loescher, G. (2001). *The Unhcr and World Politics: A Perilous Path*, New York: Oxford University Press.
Loescher, G. and Milner, J. (2005). 'Protracted Refugee Situations: Domestic and International Security Implications', *Adelphi Papers*, Oxford: Oxford University Press.
Loescher, G., Betts, A. and Milner, J. (2008). *The United Nations High Commissioner for Refugees (Unhcr): The Politics and Practice of Refugee Protection into the Twenty-First Century*, London: Routledge.
Lohmann, L. (2006). *Carbon Trading: A Critical Conversation on Climate Change, Privatisation and Power*, Uppsala: Dag Hammarskjold Centre and Corner House.
Lövbrand, E., Stripple, J. and Wiman, B. (2009). 'Earth System Governmentality: Reflections on Science in the Anthropocene', *Global Environmental Change*, 19(1): 7–13.
Lowes, S. (2012). 'The Legality of Extraterritorial Processing of Asylum Claims: The Judgment of the High Court of Australia in the "Malaysian Solution" Case', *Human Rights Law Review*, 12(1): 168–82.
Lumsdaine, D. (1993). *Moral Vision in International Politics: The Foreign Aid Regime, 1949–1989*, Princeton, NJ: Princeton University Press.
Lyall, F. (2011). *International Communications: The International Telecommunication Union and the Universal Postal Union*, Farnham: Ashgate.
Mackelm, P. (2002). 'Labour Law Beyond Borders', *Journal of International Economic Law*, 5(3): 605–45.

Malcolm, J. (2012). 'Arresting the Decline of Multi-Stakeholderism in Internet Governance', in J. Malcolm (ed.), *Consumers in the Information Society: Access, Fairness and Representation*, Kuala Lumpur: Consumers International, pp. 159–80.

Mailafia, O. (1997). *Europe and Economic Reform in Africa: Structural Adjustment and Economic Diplomacy*, London: Routledge.

Marchal, B., Cavalli, A. and Kegels, G. (2009). 'Global Health Actors Claim to Support Health System Strengthening – is this Reality or Rhetoric?' *PLoS Med* 6(4): e1000059. doi:10.1371/journal.pmed.1000059.

Marrus, M. (2002). *The Unwanted: European Refugees from the First World War through the Cold War*, Philadelphia: Temple University Press.

Martin, S. F. (2010). 'Gender and the Evolving Refugee Regime', *Refugee Survey Quarterly*, 29(2): 104–21.

Martinez-Alier, J. (2002). *The Environmentalism of the Poor: A Study of Ecological Conflicts and Valuation*, Cheltenham: Edward Elgar.

Marty, D. (2006). 'Alleged Secret Detentions and Unlawful Inter-State Transfers Involving Council of Europe Member States', 7 June, Council of Europe. Available at: http://www.therenditionproject.org.uk/pdf/PDF%2068%20[EP-MEM-2006-06%20Alleged%20Secret%20Detentions].pdf.

—— (2007). 'Secret detentions and illegal transfers of detainees involving Council of Europe member states: second report', 11 June. Available at: http://www.therenditionproject.org.uk/pdf/PDF%2072%20[EP-REP-2007-06%20Secret%20Detentions%20and%20Illegal%20Transfe.pdf.

Matas, D. and Simon, I. (1989). *Closing the Doors: The Failure of Refugee Protection*. Toronto: Summerhill Press.

McCoy, D., Chand, S. and Sridhar, D. (2009). 'Global Health Funding: How Much, Where it Comes From and Where it Goes', *Health Policy and Planning*, 24(6): 407–17.

McCoy, D., Kembhavi, G., Patel, J. and Luintel, A. (2009). 'The Bill & Melinda Gates Foundation's grant-making programme for global health', *Lancet*, 373(9675): 1645–1653.

McDaniel, P. and Malone, R. (2012). 'British American Tobacco's partnership with Earthwatch Europe and its implications for public health', *Global Public Health*, 7(1): 14–28.

McDonald, B. L. (2010). *Food Security*, Cambridge: Polity Press.

McInnes, C. and Lee, K. (2006). 'Health, Security and Foreign Policy', *Review of International Studies*, 32(1): 5–23.

McKenzie, R. (2011) (2010 online). 'Casino Capitalism with Derivatives: Fragility and Instability in Contemporary Finance', *Review of Radical Political Economics*, 43: 198–215, first published on 21 December, 2010.

McNamara, D. (2009). 'The Politics of Protection', Keynote Paper. 'Protecting People in Conflict & Crisis' Conference, Oxford: Oxford University Refugee Studies Centre, September.

McRae, H. and Cairncross, F. (1973). *Capital City*, London: Eyre Methuen.

Meadows, D. H., Meadows, D. L., Randers, J. and Behrens III, W. W. (1972). *The Limits to Growth: A Report for the Club of Rome's Project on the Predicament of Mankind*, New York: New American Library.

Méon, P. and Weill, L. (2008). 'Is Corruption an Efficient Grease?' *Laboratoire de Recherche en Gestion et en Economie*, Papier 2008–06.

Miall, H., Ramsbotham, O. and Woodhouse, T. (2005). *Contemporary Conflict Resolution*, Cambridge: Polity Press.

Milanovic, B. (2005). *Worlds Apart: Measuring International and Global Inequality*, Princeton, NJ: Princeton University Press.

Minear, L. (2005). 'Lessons Learned: The Darfur Experience', in N. Berhman (ed.), *Alnap Review of Humanitarian Action in 2004: Capacity Building*, London: Overseas Development Institute, pp. 73–122.
Minear, L., Clark, J., Cohen, R., Gallagher, D., Guest, I. and Wiess, T. G. (1994). 'Humanitarian Action in the Former Yugoslavia: The Un's Role, 1991–1993', *Watson Institute Occassional Paper*, 13, Providence, RI: Thomas J. Watson Jr. Institute, Brown University.
MMV (Medicines for Malaria Venture) (2012). 'Global Safety Board'. Available at: http://www.mmv.org/about-us/organisation-and-governance/global-safety-board (accessed 26 January 2012).
Moon, S., Szlezák, N. A., Michaud, C. M., Jamison, D. T., Keusch, G. T., Clark, W. C. and Bloom, B. R. (2010). 'The Global Health System: Lessons for a Stronger Institutional Framework', *PLoS Medicine*, 7(1): e1000193, doi: 10.1371/journal.pmed.1000193.
Montgomerie, J. (2008). 'Bridging the Critical Divide: Global Finance, Financialisation and Contemporary Capitalism', *Contemporary Politics*, 14(3): 233–252.
—— (2009). 'The Pursuit of (Past) Happiness? Middle-class Indebtedness and American Financialisation', *New Political Economy*, 14(1): 1–24.
Mooney, E. (2005). 'The Concept of Internal Displacment and the Case for Internally Displaced Persons as a Category of Concern', *Refugee Survey Quarterly*, 24(3): 9–26.
Morrissey, O., Milner, C. and McKay, A. (2007). 'A Critical Assessment of Proposed EU–ACP Economic Partnership Agreements', in A. Mold (ed.), *EU Development Policy in a Changing World: Challenges for the 21st Century*, Amsterdam: Amsterdam University Press, pp. 199–220.
Moss, T. and Bannon, A. (2004). 'Africa and the Battle over Agricultural Protectionism', *World Policy Journal*, 21(2): 53–61.
Moyo, D. (2009). *Dead Aid: Why Aid is Not Working and How There is a Better Way for Africa*, London: Allen Lane.
Mueller, M. (2010). *Networks and States: The Global Politics of Internet Governance*, Cambridge, MA: MIT Press.
Mueller, M., Mathiason, J. and Klein, H. (2007). 'The Internet and Global Governance: Principles and Norms for a New Regime', *Global Governance*, 13(2): 237–54.
Murphy, H. (2010). *The Making of International Trade Policy: NGOs Agenda Setting and the WTO*, London: Edward Elgar.
Myconos, G. (2005). *The Globalizations of Organized Labour: 1945–2005*, Basingstoke: Palgrave Macmillan.
Narayan, R. (2006). 'The Role of the People's Health Movement in Putting the Social Determinants of Health on the Global Agenda', *Health Promotion Journal of Australia*, 17(3): 186–8.
Nesvetailova, A. (2010). *Financial Alchemy in Crisis: the Great Liquidity Illusion*, London: Pluto Press.
—— (2013). 'Money and Finance in a Globalised Economy', in R. Palan (ed.), *Global Political Economy: Contemporary Theories*, London: Routledge.
Neumayer, E. (2005). 'Unequal Access to Foreign Spaces: How States use Visa Restrictions to Regulate Mobility in a Globalized World', in Global Commission on International Migration, *Global Migration Perspectives*, Geneva: Global Commission on International Migration.
Nkrumah, K. (1965). *Neocolonialism: The Last Stage of Imperialism*, London: Nelson.
Norheim-Martinsen, P. M. (2010). 'Beyond Intergovernmentalism: European Security and Defence Policy and the Governance Approach', *Journal of Common Market Studies*, 48(5): 1351–1365.

Norton-Taylor, R. (2012). 'Government pays Libyan dissident's family £2.2m over MI6-aided rendition', 13 December, *The Guardian*. Available at: http://www.guardian.co.uk/uk/2012/dec/13/libyan-dissident-mi6-aided-rendition.
NTIA (National Telecommunications and Information Administration) (1998), 'Improvement of Technical Management of Internet Names and Addresses; Proposed Rule'. Available at: http://www.ntia.doc.gov/federal-register-notice/1998/improvement-technical-management-Internet-names-and-addresses-proposed- (accessed 31 July 2012).
Nunn, S. and Price, A. (2004). 'Managing Development: EU and African Relations Through the Evolution of the Lome and Cotonou Agreements', *Historical Materialism*, 12(4): 203–30.
Nye, J. (1970). 'Comparing Common Markets: A Revised Neo-Functionalist Model', *International Organization*, 24(4): 796–835.
OCHA (2012). 'United Nations Trust Fund for Human Security'. Available at: http://www.unocha.org/humansecurity.
OECD (1999). *Codes of Conduct: An Inventory*, Working Party of the Trade Committee, TD/TC/WP(99)56/FINAL, Paris: OECD.
—— (2001). 'Recommendation to Untie Official Development Assistance to the Least Developed Countries', document DCD/DAC(2001)12/FINAL, Paris: OECD.
—— (2005). 'Paris Declaration on Aid Effectiveness', Paris: OECD.
—— (2011). 'OECD Guidelines for Multinational Enterprises', Paris: OECD.
Oels, A. (2005). 'Rendering Climate Change Governable: From Biopower to Advanced Liberal Governmentality', *Journal of Environmental Policy and Planning*, 7(3): 185–207.
Office for the Coordination of Humanitarian Affairs (1999). 'Guiding Principles on Internal Displacement', New York: UNOCHA.
Okereke, C., Bulkeley, H. and Schroeder, H. (2009). 'Conceptualising Climate Governance beyond the International Regime', *Global Environmental Politics*, 9(1): 58–78.
Oneal, J. R. and Russett, B. (1999). 'Assessing the Liberal Peace with Alternative Specifications: Trade Still Reduces Conflicts', *Journal of Peace Studies*, 36(4): 423–42.
Ooms, G., Stuckler, D., Basu, S. and McKee, M. (2010). 'Financing the Millennium Development Goals for Health and Beyond: Sustaining the "Big Push"', *Globalization and Health*, 6:17. Available at: http://www.globalizationandhealth.com/content/6/1/17 (accessed 27 January 2012).
Orbie, J. (2007). 'The European Union and the Commodity Debate: From Aid to Trade', *Review of African Political Economy*, 34(112): 297–311.
Orbie, J. and Babarinde, O. (2008). 'The Social Dimension of Globalization and EU Development Policy: Promoting Core Labour Standards and Corporate Social Responsibility', *European Integration*, 30(3): 459–77.
Orchard, P. (2010a). 'The Perils of Humanitarianism: Refugee and Idp Protection in Situations of Regime-Induced Displacement', *Refugee Survey Quarterly*, 29(1): 38–60.
—— (2010b). 'Protection of Internally Displaced Persons: Soft Law as a Norm-Generating Mechanism', *Review of International Studies*, 36(2): 281–303.
—— (2010c). 'Regime-Induced Displacement and Decision-Making within the United Nations Security Council: The Cases of Northern Iraq, Kosovo, and Darfur', *Global Responsibility to Protect*, 2(1): 1–26.
Organization for African Unity (1969). *Convention Governing the Specific Aspects of Refugee Problems in Africa*. Article II.
Ostrom, E. (1999). 'Coping with Tragedies of the Commons', *Annual Review of Political Science*, 2: 493–535.

Owen, R. (1845). *Robert Owen's Address to the Ministers of All Religions*, Philadelphia, PA.
Oxfam (2004). *Dumping on the World: How EU Sugar Policies Hurt Poor Countries*, Oxford: Oxfam.
—— (2005). 'What Happened in Hong Kong? Initial analysis of the WTO Ministerial', *Oxfam Briefing Paper No. 85*, Oxford: Oxfam.
—— (2006). *A Recipe for Disaster: Will the Doha Round Fail to Deliver for Development?* Oxford: Oxfam.
—— (2012). 'Oxfam calls on EU not to shut down "pharmacy of the developing world"', Press Release, 9 February 2012. Available at: http://www.oxfam.org.uk/applications/blogs/pressoffice/2012/02/09/oxfam-calls-on-eu-not-to-shut-down-%25E2%2580%2598pharmacy-of-the-developing-world%25E2%2580%2599/ (accessed 21 March 2012).
Page, S. (2006). 'Bringing Aid and Trade Together', in S. Page (ed.), *Trade and Aid: Partners or Rivals in Development Policy?* London: Cameron May, pp.11–34.
Palan, R. (2003). *The Offshore World*, Ithaca, NY: Cornell University Press.
—— (2009). 'The Proof of the Pudding is in the Eating: IPE in light of the Current of the Crisis of 2007/8', *New Political Economy*, 14(3): 385–393.
Palan, R., Murphy, R. and Chavagneux, C. (2010). *Tax Havens: How Globalization Really Works*, Ithaca, NY: Cornell University Press.
Panetta, L. (2009). 'Message from the Director: Interrogation and Policy Contracts (Statement to Employees by the Director of the Central Intelligence Agency Leon E. Panetta on the CIA's Interrogation Policy and Contracts)', 9 April. Available at: https://www.cia.gov/news-information/press-releases-statements/directors-statement-interrogation-policy-contracts.html.
Partridge, M. (2011). 'How the Economic Policies of a Corrupt Elite caused the Arab Spring', *New Statesman*. Available at: http://www.newstatesman.com/blogs/the-staggers/2011/06/economic-arab-egypt-region.
Paterson, M. and Stripple, J. (2010). 'My Space: Governing Individuals' Carbon Emissions', *Environment and Planning D: Society and Space*, 28(2): 341–62.
Paust, J. (2009). 'The Absolute Prohibition of Torture and Necessary and Appropriate Sanctions', *Valparaiso University Law Review*, 43: 1535–1575.
—— (2009). 'The Second Bybee Memo: A Smoking Gun', *Jurist*. Available at: http://jurist.org/forum/2009/04/second-bybee-memo-smoking-gun.php.
Payne, A. (2006). 'Blair, Brown and the Gleneagles Agenda: Making Poverty History, or Confronting the Global Politics of Unequal Development?' *International Affairs*, 82(5): 917–35.
Pearson, R. and Seyfang, G. (2002). '"I'll Tell You What I Want…": Women Workers and Codes of Conduct', in R. Jenkins, R. Pearson, and G. Seyfang, G. (eds), *Corporate Responsibility and Labour Rights: Codes of Conduct in the Global Economy*, London: Earthscan, pp. 43–60.
Pender, J. (2001). 'From "Structural Adjustment" to "Comprehensive Development Framework": conditionality transformed?' *Third World Quarterly*, 22(3): 397–411.
Personal communication. 2007. Interview 29 June 2007 – Cotton sector stakeholder, Nairobi, Kenya.
Petersmann, E. -U. (2004). 'The "Human Rights Approach" advocated by the UN High Commissioner for Human Rights and the International Labour Organisation: Is it Relevant for WTO Law and Policy?' *Journal of International Economic Law*, 7(3): 605–27.
Phillips, N. and Weaver, C. (eds) (2010). *International Political Economy: Debating the Past, Present and Future*, London: Routledge.

Phillips, J. and Spinks, H. (2012). 'Boat Arrivals in Australia since 1976', Canberra: Parliament of Australia Department of Parliamentary Services.
Philpott, D. (1999). 'Westphalia, Authority, and International Society', *Political Studies*, XLVII: 566–89.
PHM (2012). 'About the People's Health Movement'. Available at: http://www.phmovement.org/en/about (accessed 27 January 2012).
Piva, P. and Dodd, R. (2009). 'Where Did All the Aid Go? An in-depth analysis of increased health aid flows over the past 10 years', *Bulletin of the World Health Organization*, 87(12): 885–964.
Prügl, E. (1999). *The Global Construction of Gender: Home-Based Work in the Political Economy of the 20th Century*, New York: Columbia University Press.
—— (2002). 'Global Governance, Women-Friendly: The Promise of the ILO', *Global Social Policy*, 2(1): 9–12.
—— (2011). 'An ILO Convention for Domestic Workers: Contextualising the Debate', *International Feminist Journal of Politics*, 13(3): 438–41.
Rajan, R. (2010). *Fault Lines: How Hidden Fractures Still Threaten the World Economy*, Princeton, NJ: Princeton University Press.
Raper, M. (2003). 'Changing Roles of Ngos in Refugee Assistance', in E. Newman and J. van Selm (eds), *Refugees and Forced Displacement: International Security, Human Vulnerability and the State*, Tokyo: United Nations University, pp. 350–66.
Ravenhill, J. (ed.) (2008). *Global Political Economy*, 2nd edn. New York: Oxford University Press.
Ravinshankar, N., Gubbins, P., Cooley, R., Leach-Kemon, K., Michaud, C. M., Jamison, D. T. and Murray, C. (2009). 'Financing of Global Health: Tracking Development Assistance for Health from 1990 to 2007', *Lancet*, 373(9681): 2113–24.
Razafindrakoto, M. and Roubaud, F. (2006). 'Are International Databases on Corruption Reliable? A Comparison of Expert Opinion Surveys and Household Surveys in Sub-Saharan Africa', *Développement Institutions & Analyses de Long Terme, Document de Travail*, DT/2006-17.
Reich, M. (2000). 'Public-private partnerships for public health', *Nature Medicine*, 6(6): 617–620.
Reinhart, C. and K. Rogoff (2009). *This Time is Different: Eight Centuries of Financial Folly*, Oxford: Princeton University Press.
Republic of Kenya (2001). *Position Paper on the Textile Industry*, Nairobi: Government of Kenya. Available at: http://www.tradeandindustry.go.ke/documents/di_report_textile.pdf (accessed 8 October 2009).
Reuters (2011). 'Firms brace for UK bribery act, lawyers circle', 30 June. Available at: http://www.reuters.com/article/2011/06/30/us-britain-bribery-idUSTRE75T2HY20110630.
Revenue Watch Institute (2011). 'Costs and Criticisms: The Facts about Disclosure Rules'. Available at: http://www.revenuewatch.org/publications/fact_sheets/costs-criticisms-facts-about-disclosure-rules
Rhodes, R. A. (1996). 'The New Governance: Governing without Government', *Political Studies*, 44(4): 652–67.
Riddell, R. (2007). *Does Foreign Aid Really Work?* Oxford: Oxford University Press.
Riisgard, L. (2007). 'What's in it for Labour? Private Social Standards in the Cut Flower Industries of Kenya and Tanzania', *DIIS Working Paper no 2007/16*, Copenhagen: DIIS.
Riles, A. (2011). *Collateral Knowledge: Legal Reasoning in the Global Financial Markets*, Chicago, IL: University of Chicago Press.

Roberts, A. (1998). 'More Refugees, Less Asylum: A Regime in Transformation', *Journal of Refugee Studies*, 11(4): 375.
Rodriguez-Pinero, L. (2005). *Indigenous Peoples, Postcolonialism and International Law*, Oxford: Oxford University Press.
Ronit, K. and Schneider, V. (2000). 'Private Organizations and their Contribution to Problem-Solving in the Global Arena', in K. Ronit and V. Schneider (eds), *Private Organizations in Global Politics*, London: Routledge, pp. 1–33.
Rose-Ackerman, S. (2008). 'Corruption and Government', *International Peacekeeping*, 15(3): 328–343.
—— (2011). 'Anti-Corruption Policy: Can International Actors Play a Constructive Role?' *John M. Olin Center for Studies in Law, Economics, and Public Policy Research Paper No. 440*.
Rosen, W. (2008). *Justinian's Flea: Plague, Empire and the Birth of Europe*, London: Jonathan Cape.
Rosenau, J. (1995). 'Governance in the Twenty-First Century', *Global Governance*, 1(1): 13–43.
—— (2005). 'Governance in the Twenty-first Century', in R. Wilkinson (ed.), *The Global Governance Reader*, London: Routledge, pp. 45–67.
Rosenau, J. and Czempiel, O. (1992). *Governance without Government: Order and Change in World Politics*, Cambridge: Cambridge University Press.
Ruger, J. and Ng, N. (2010). 'Emerging and Transitioning Countries' Role in Global Health', *Saint Louis University Journal of Health Law & Policy*, 3(2): 253–90.
Ruggie, J. (1982). International Regimes, Transactions, and Change: Embedded Liberalism in the Postwar Economic Order, *International Organization*, 36(2): 379–415.
—— (1998). *Constructing the World Polity: Essays on International Institutionalization*, London: Routledge.
Rushton, S. (2011). 'Global Health Security: Security from Whom? Security from What?' *Political Studies*, 59(4): 779–96.
Rutherford, P. (1999). 'The Entry of Life into History', in E. Darier (ed.), *Discourses of the Environment*, Oxford: Blackwell, pp. 37–62.
Sachs, J. (2005). *The End of Poverty: Economic Possibilities of our Time*, New York: Penguin Press.
—— (2011). 'The Global Economy's Corporate Crime Wave'. Available at: http://www.project-syndicate.org/commentary/the-global-economy-s-corporate-crime-wave.
Sachs, W. (1999). *Planet Dialectics: Explorations in Environment and Development*, London: Zed.
Sally, R. (2002). 'Globalisation, Governance and Trade Policy: The WTO in Perspective', Global Dimensions (London: London School of Economics). Available at: http://www.lse.ac.uk/collections/globalDimensions/research/globalisationGovernanceAndTrade%20Policy/Default.htm (accessed 30 October 2012).
Samuel, A. (2004). *Hacktivism and the Future of Political Participation*, PhD thesis, Cambridge, MA: Harvard University.
Schaeffer, P. and Loveridge, S. (2002). 'Toward an Understanding of Types of Public–Private Cooperation', *Public Performance & Management Review*, 26(2): 169–89.
Schäferhoff, M., Schrade, C. and Yamey, G. (2010). 'Financing Maternal and Child Health – What are the Limitations in Estimating Donor Flows and Resource Needs?' *PLoS Medicine*, 7(7): e1000305, doi: 10.1371/journal.pmed.1000305.
Schieber, G., Gottret, P., Fleisher, L. and Leive, A. (2007). 'Financing Global Health: Mission Unaccomplished', *Health Affairs*, 26(4): 921–34.

Schuster, L. (2003). *The Use and Abuse of Political Asylum in Britain and Germany*, London: Frank Cass.
Schuurman, F. (ed,) (1993). *Beyond the Impasse: New Directions in Development Theory*, London: Zed Books.
Schwartz, H. (2009). *Subprime Nation: American Power, Global Capital and the Housing Bubble*, Ithaca, NY: Cornell University Press.
Schwenken, H. and Pabon, R. (2011). 'Roundtable Conversation of Domestic Workers' Activists about the ILO Convention', *International Feminist Journal of Politics* 13(3): 444–50.
Scott, J. and Wilkinson, R. (2011). 'The Poverty of the Doha Round and the Least Developed Countries', *Third World Quarterly*, 32(4): 611–27.
Seabrooke, L. (2006). *The Social Sources of Financial Power. Domestic Legitimacy and International Financial Orders*, Ithaca, NY: Cornell University Press.
Seimas Committee (2009). 'Findings of the Parliamentary Investigation by the Seimas Committee on National Security and Defence Concerning the Alleged Transportation and Confinement of Persons Detained by the Central Intelligence Agency of the United States of America in the Territory of the Republic of Lithuania', European Parliament. Available at: http://www.europarl.europa.eu/document/activities/cont/201203/20120326ATT41867/20120326ATT41867EN.pdf.
Sen, A. (1999). *Development as Freedom*, New York: Knopf.
Sengupta, A. (2011). 'Global Governance of Health: A Minefield of Contradictions and Sectional Interests', *Indian Journal of Medical Ethics*, 8(2): 86–90.
Shacknove, A. (1993). 'From Asylum to Containment', *International Journal of Refugee Law*, 5(4): 516–33.
Shaw, L. and Hale, A. (2002). 'The Emperor's New Clothes: What Codes Mean for Workers in the Garment Industry', in R. Jenkins, R. Pearson and G. Seyfang (eds), *Corporate Responsibility and Labour Rights: Codes of Conduct in the Global Economy*, London: Earthscan, pp. 101–12.
Siddiqi, J. (1995). *World Health and World Politics: The World Health Organization and the UN System*, London: Hurst & Company.
Sinclair, T. (2008). *The New Maters of Capital: American Bond Ratings Agencies and the Politics of Creditworthiness*, London: Cornell University Press.
Siskin, A. (2004). 'Visa Waiver Program', Washington DC: Congressional Research Services.
Sismondi, J. C. L. de (1827). 'L'Amérique', *Revue Encyclopédique*, 33.
Skran, C. (1995). *Refugees in Inter-War Europe: The Emergence of a Regime*, Oxford: Clarendon Press.
Slaughter, A. (1993). 'International Law and International Relations theory: a dual agenda', *American Journal of International Law*, 87(2): 205–239.
—— (2004). *A New World Order*, Princeton, NJ: Princeton University Press.
Soederberg, S. (2004). *The Politics of the New International Financial Architecture. Reimposing Neoliberal Domination in the Global South*, London: Zed.
Solum, L. (2009). 'Models of Internet Governance', in L. Bygrave and J. Bing (eds), *Internet Governance: Infrastructure and Institutions*, Oxford: Oxford University Press, pp. 48–91.
Spalding, A. (2010). 'Unwitting Sanctions: Understanding Anti-Bribery Legislation as Economic Sanctions Against Emerging Markets', *Florida Law Review*, 62: 351–426.
Sridhar, D. and Batniji, R. (2008). 'Misfinancing global health: a case for transparency in disbursements and decision making', *Lancet*, 372(9644): 1185–1191.
Srinivasan, T. (1999). 'Developing Countries in the World Trading System: From GATT, 1947, to the Third Ministerial Meeting of WTO, 1999', *The World Economy*, 22(8): 1047–64.

Standing, G. (1999). 'Global Feminization through Flexible Labour: A Theme Revisited', *World Development*, 27(3): 583–602.

—— (2008). 'The ILO; An Agency for Globalisation?' *Development and Change*, 39(3): 355–84.

Sterling-Folker, J. (2005). 'Realist Global Governance: Revisiting Cave! Hic Dragones and Beyond', in A. Ba and M. Hoffman (eds), *Contending Perspectives on Global Governance: Coherence, Contestation and World Order*, London: Routledge, pp. 17–38.

Stewart, F. and Wang, M. (2003). 'Do PRSPs empower poor countries and disempower the World Bank, or is it the other way round?' *QEH Working Paper Series*, QEHWPS108, Oxford: Queen Elizabeth House.

Stiglitz, J. (1998). 'Towards a New Paradigm for Development', Ninth Paul Prebisch Lecture, Geneva, United Nations, 19 October 1998. Available at: http://unctad.org/en/docs/prebisch9th.en.PDF (accessed 21 October 2012).

Stiglitz, J. and Charlton, A. (2006). 'The Doha Round after Hong Kong', paper prepared for 'An Assessment of the Doha Round after Hong Kong' conference, Manchester: University of Manchester.

Strange, S. (1976). 'International Monetary Relations', in A. Shonfield (ed.), *International Economic Relations of the Western World, 1959–1971*, Oxford: Oxford University Press.

—— (1986). *Casino Capitalism*, Oxford/Manchester: Basil Blackwell/Manchester University Press.

—— (1988). *State and Markets*, London: Pinter.

Stuckler, D., Basu, S. and McKee, M. (2011). 'Global Health Philanthropy and Institutional Relationships: How Should Conflicts of Interest be Addressed?' *PLoS Medicine*, 8(4): e1001020, doi: 10.1371/journal.pmed.1001020.

Subrahmanian, R. (2004). 'Promoting gender equality', in R. Black and H. White (eds), *Targeting Development: Critical Perspectives on the Millennium Development Goals*, London: Routledge, pp. 184–208.

Szlezák, N., Bloom, B., Jamison, D., Keusch, G., Michaud, C., Moon, S. and Clark, W. (2010). 'The Global Health System: Actors, Norms, and Expectations in Transition', *PLoS Medicine*, 7(1): e1000183, doi: 10.1371/journal.pmed.1000183.

Takasu, Y. (2010). 'Statement by H.E. Mr. Yukio Takasu … Introduction of draft resolution on human security', 16 July, New York. Available at: http://www.un.emb-japan.go.jp/statements/takasu071610.html.

Tallontire, A., Dolan, C., Smith, S. and S. Barreintos (2005). 'Reaching the marginalised? Gender value chains and ethical trade in African horticulture,' *Development in Practice*, 15(3–4), pp. 559–571.

Taylor, M. (2011). 'Race you to the Bottom … and Back Again? The Uneven Development of Labour Codes of Conduct', *New Political Economy*, 16(4): 445–62.

Terry, F. (2002). *Condemned to Repeat? The Paradox of Humanitarian Action*, Ithaca, NY: Cornell University Press.

Tesco (2011). *News Release: Tesco and the Sustainable Consumption Institute Join the Sustainability Consortium*. Available at: http://www.sci.manchester.ac.uk/uploads/tesco-and-the-sustainable-consumption-institute-join-the-sustainability-consortium---final.pdf (accessed 11 February 2013).

Tett, G. (2009). *Fool's Gold*, New York: Free Press.

Thérien, J.-P. (1999). 'Beyond the North–South Divide: The Two Tales of World Poverty', *Third World Quarterly*, 20(4): 723–42.

Thomas, C. (2001). 'Global governance, development and human security: exploring the links', *Third World Quarterly*, 22(2): 159–75.

Toporowski, J. (2009). 'It's Not About Regulation…', *DIIS Working Paper*, 2009:08, Copenhagen: Danish Institute for International Studies.
Torpey, J. C. (2000) *The Invention of the Passport: Surveillance, Citizenship, and the State*, Cambridge: Cambridge University Press.
Touré, S. (1962). 'Africa's Future and the World', *Foreign Affairs*, 41: 141–51.
Toye, J. and Toye, R. (2005). 'From Multilateralism to Modernisation: US Strategy on Trade, Finance and Development in the United Nations, 1945–63', *Forum for Development Studies*, 1: 127–50.
Traidcraft (2005). *Why More Free Trade Won't Help Africa: Through the Lens of Kenya*. Available at: http://www.traidcraft.co.uk/temp/radF74F6.pdf (accessed 8 October 2009).
—— (2012). 'What's Wrong with the Doha Negotiations on Agriculture?' Available at: http://www.traidcraft.co.uk/get_involved/campaign/wto/wto_faqs/doha_agriculture (accessed 21 October 2012).
Transparency International (2011). *Progress Report 2011: Enforcement of the OECD Anti-Bribery Convention*, Berlin: Transparency International.
Transparency International UK (2010). *The 2010 UK Bribery Act Adequate Procedures*, London: Transparency International UK.
U4 Anti-Corruption Resource Centre. (2010). 'UNCAC in a Nutshell: A Quick Guide to the United Nations Convention Against Corruption for Embassy and Donor Agency Staff', U4 Brief.
UN (1991). 'RESOLUTION 687 (1991), Adopted by the Security Council at its 2981st meeting, on 3 April 1991'. Available at: http://www.fas.org/news/un/iraq/sres/sres0687.htm.
—— (1992). *Agenda 21*, Rio: UN.
—— (1994). *Human Development Report: New Dimensions of Human Security*. Available at: http://hdr.undp.org/en/reports/global/hdr1994/chapters.
—— (2001). *Road Map Towards the Implementation of the United Nations Millennium Declaration: Report of the Secretary-General*, New York: United Nations.
—— (2004a). *A More Secure World: Our Shared Responsibility. Report of the High-level Panel on Threats, Challenges and Change*, New York: UN Dept of Public Information.
—— (2004b). *United Nations Convention Against Corruption*, New York: United Nations.
—— (2004c). *United Nations Global Compact*, New York: United Nations.
—— (2005). *In Larger Freedom: Towards Development, Security and Human Rights for All. Report of the Secretary-General, Fifty-ninth session*, 21 March, A/59/2005. Available at: http://www.un.org/largerfreedom/contents.htm.
—— (2006). *Human Security for All*, New York: United Nations Human Security Unit.
—— (2010). 'Joint Study on Global Practices in Relation to Secret Detention in the Context of Countering Terrorism', A/HRC/13/42 (20 May). Available at: http://www.unhcr.org/refworld/pdfid/4d8720092.pdf.
—— (2010a). Ch 7– 'Continuation of the Internet Governance Forum: Note by the Secretary-General', A/65/78–E/2010/68.
—— (2010b). Ch 1– *Human Development Report: The Real Wealth of Nations*. Available at: http://hdr.undp.org/en/reports/global/hdr2010.
—— (2010c). 'Joint Study on Global Practices in Relation to Secret Detention in the Context of Countering Terrorism', A/HRC/13/42.
—— (2011). 'Security Council Approves 'No-Fly Zone over Libya'. Available at: http://www.un.org/News/Press/docs/2011/sc10200.doc.htm.
—— (2011). *The Millennium Development Goals Report 2011*, New York: United Nations.
—— (2012a). 'Charter of the United Nations'. Available at: http://www.un.org/en/documents/charter.

—— (2012b). 'Millennium Development Goals'. Available at: http://www.un.org/millenniumgoals/index.shtml (accessed 28 January 2012).

—— (2012c). 'Security Council Fails to Adopt Draft on Syria'. Available at: http://www.un.org/News/Press/docs/2012/sc10536.doc.htm.

UN General Assembly (1951). Convention Relating to the Status of Refugees. Available at: http://www.unhcr.org/refworld/docid/3be01b964.html (accessed 12 February 2013).

UN General Assembly (1967). Protocol Relating to the Status of Refugees. Available at: http://www.unhcr.org/refworld/docid/3ae6b3ae4.html (accessed 12 February 2013).

UNCTAD (1994). *World Investment Report*, New York: United Nations.

—— (2010). *Economic Development in Africa Report 2010: South–South Cooperation: Africa and the New Forms of Development Partnership*, Geneva and New York: UNCTAD.

UNESCO (2008). *Human Security: Approaches and Challenges*, Paris: UNESCO.

UNHCR (1971). *A Mandate to Protect and Assist Refugees*, Geneva: Office of the United Nations High Commissioner for Refugees.

—— (1997). *The State of the World's Refugees: A Humanitarian Agenda*, Oxford: Oxford University Press.

—— (2000). *The State of the World's Refugees: Fifty Years of Humanitarian Action*, Oxford: Oxford University Press.

—— (2006a). '2005 Unhcr Statistical Report', Geneva: UNHCR.

—— (2006b). *The State of the World's Refugees: Human Displacement in the New Millennium*, London: Oxford University Press.

—— (2006c). *Statistical Yearbook: 2005*, Geneva: UNHCR.

—— (2011). State Parties to 1951 Convention relating to the Status of Refugees and the 1967 Protocol. Available at: http: //www.unhcr.org/protect/PROTECTION/3b73b0d63.pdf (accessed 12 February 2013).

—— (2011a). *Global Trends 2010*, Geneva: UNHCR.

—— (2011b). *Statistical Yearbook, 2010*, Geneva: UNHCR.

United Kingdom (UK) (2010). *Bribery Act* 2010.

United States (US) (1977). *Foreign Corrupt Practices Act*.

—— (2010). *Dodd–Frank Wall Street and Consumer Protection Act*.

United States Holocaust Memorial Museum (2012). 'German Jews During the Holocaust, 1939–1945'. Available at: http://www.ushmm.org/wlc/en/article.php?ModuleId=10005469 (accessed 21 March 2012).

UNSIC and World Bank (2010). *Fifth Global Progress Report 2010: A Framework for Sustaining Momentum*, Thailand: World Bank.

Unterhalter, E. (2005). 'Global Inequality, Capabilities, Social Justice: The Millennium Development Goal for Gender Equality in Education', *International Journal of Educational Development*, 25(2), 111–22.

UPU (Universal Postal Union) (2010). *Constitution. General Regulations*, Bern: International Bureau of the Universal Postal Union.

Uriminsky, M. (2001). 'Self Regulation in the Workplace: Codes of Conduct, Social Labelling and Socially Responsible Investment', *Management and Corporate Citizenship Working Paper*, 1, Geneva.

Valticos, N. (1998). 'International Labour Standards and Human Rights: Approaching the Year 2000', *International Labour Review*, 137(2): 136–47.

Vayrynen, R. (2001). 'Funding Dilemmas in Refugee Assistance: Political Interests and Institutional Reforms in Unhcr', *International Migration Review*, 35(1): 143–67.

Vink, M, and Meijerink, F. (2003). 'Asylum Applications and Recognition Rates in EU Member States 1982–2001: A Quantitative Analysis', *Journal of Refugee Studies*, 16(3): 297–315.

Vosko, L. (2002). 'The Shifting Role of the ILO and the Struggle for Global Social Justice', *Global Social Policy*, 2(1): 19–46.
W3C (World Wide Web Consortium) (2005). 'World Wide Web Consortium Process Document'. Available at: http://www.w3.org/2005/10/Process-20051014/ (accessed 2 August 2012).
—— (2012), 'Current Members'. Available at: http://www.w3.org/Consortium/Member/List. (accessed 1 August 2012).
Wade, R. (2003). 'What Strategies are Viable for Developing Countries Today? The WTO and the Shrinking of Development Space', *Review of International Political Economy*, 10(4): 621–44.
—— (2004). 'Is Globalization Reducing Poverty and Inequality?' *World Development*, 32(4): 567–589.
Wade, R. and Vestergaard, J. (2011) *The New Global Economic Council: Governance Reform at the G20, the IMF and the World Bank*, Copenhagen: Danish Institute for International Studies.
Waltz, K. (1999). 'Globalization and Governance', *PS: Political Science and Politics*, 32(4): 693–700.
Wapner, P. (1995). 'Politics Beyond the State: Environmental Activism and World Civic Politics', *World Politics*, 47(3): 311–40.
—— (2002). 'Horizontal Politics: Transnational Environmental Activism and Global Cultural Change', *Global Environmental Politics*, 2(2): 37–62.
Waterman, P. (2001). *Globalization, Social Movements and the New Internationalisms*, London: Continuum.
Webb, P. (2005). 'The United Nations Convention Against Corruption: Global Achievement or Missed Opportunity?' *Journal of International Economic Law*, 8(1): 191–229.
Webber, M., Croft, S., Howorth, J., Terriff, T. and Krahmann, E. (2004). 'The governance of European security', *Review of International Studies*, 30(1): 3–26.
Weber, M. (2004) 'Politics as a Vocation', in D. Owen and T. Strong (eds), *The Vocation Lectures*, Cambridge: Hackett, pp. 32–94.
Weisband, E. (2000). 'Discursive multilateralism: Global Benchmarks, Shame and Learning in the ILO Labour Standards Monitoring Regime', *International Studies Quarterly*, 44(4): 643–66.
Weiss, T. (2000). 'Governance, Good Governance and Global Governance: Conceptual and Actual Challenges', *Third World Quarterly*, 21(3): 795–814.
Weiss, T. and Pasic, A. (1997). 'Reinventing Unhcr: Enterprising Humanitarians in the Former Yougoslavia, 1991–1995', *Global Governance*, 3(1): 41–57.
Weismann, M. (2009). 'The Foreign Corrupt Practices Act: The Failure of the Self-Regulatory Model of Corporate Governance in the Global Business Environment', *Journal of Business Ethics*, 88: 615–661.
Whitehead, M., Jones, R. and Jones, M. (2007). *The Nature of the State: Excavating the Political Ecologies of the Modern State*, Oxford: Oxford University Press.
Whitman, J. (2003). 'Global Dynamics and the Limits of Global Governance', *Global Society*, 17(3): 253–72.
Whitworth, S. (1994), *Feminism and International Relations*, New York: St Martins Press.
Wigan, D. (2009). 'Financialisation and Derivatives: Constructing an Artifice of Indifference', *Competition and Change*, 3(2): 157–176.
—— (2010). 'Credit Risk Transfer and Crunches: Global Finance Victorious or Vanquished?' *New Political Economy* 15: 1.

WikiLeaks (2011). 'Secret US Embassy Cables'. Available at: http://wikileaks.org/cablegate.html (accessed 19 August 2012).

Wilkinson, R. (2002). 'Global Monitor: The World Trade Organization', *New Political Economy*, 7(1): 129–41.

—— (2006). *The WTO: Crisis and the Governance of Global Trade*, London: Routledge.

—— (2007). 'Global governance and the World Trade Organization', in G. Hook and D. Dobson (eds), *Global Governance and Japan: The Institutional Architecture*, London: Routledge, pp. 164–78.

Wilkinson, R. and Hulme, D. (eds) (2012). *The Millennium Development Goals and Beyond: Global Development after 2015*, London and New York: Routledge.

Wilkinson, R. and Scott, J. (eds) (2012). *Trade, Poverty, Inequality: Getting beyond the WTO's Doha Deadlock*, London: Routledge.

Willetts, P. (2011). *Non-Governmental Organizations in World Politics: The Construction of Global Governance*, London: Routledge.

Williams, O. and Rushton, S. (2011). 'Are the "Good Times" Over? Looking to the Future of Global Health Governance', *Global Health Governance*, 5(1): 1–16.

WiredSafety (2012). 'Overview of WiredSafety'. Available at: https://www.wiredsafety.org/about/ (accessed 1 August 2012).

Wolfowitz, P. (2004). 'Memorandum for the Secretary of the Navy: Order Establishing Combatant Status Review Tribunals', *US Department of Defense*.

World Bank (2003). *Striking a Better Balance: The Final Report of the Extractive Industries Review*, Washington DC: World Bank.

—— (2008). 'World Bank Statement on Chad–Cameroon Pipeline', Press Release, 9 September.

—— (2012). 'Six Questions on the Cost of Corruption with World Bank Institute Global Governance Director Daniel Kaufmann'. Available at: http://go.worldbank.org/KQH743GKF1.

WHO (2005). *Basic Documents. Forty-fifth Edition*, Geneva: World Health Organization.

—— (2011). 'WHO Reforms for a Healthy Future: Report by the Director-General. Executive Board Special session on WHO reform.' EBSS/2/2, 15 October 2011. Available at: who.int/gb/ebwha/pdf_files/EBSS/EBSS2_2-en.pdf (accessed 27 July 2012).

WSIS (World Summit on the Information Society) (2005). 'Tunis Agenda for the Information Society', WSIS-05/TUNIS/DOC/6(Rev. 1)-E.

WTO (2001). 'Doha Ministerial Declaration', WT/MIN(01)/DEC/1, 20 November.

—— (2011). 'Lamy hails "encouraging" third global review of Aid for Trade'. Available at http://www.wto.org/english/news_e/sppl_e/sppl201_e.htm (accessed 21 October 2012).

—— (2012). 'Understanding the WTO: Settling Disputes – a Unique Contribution'. Available at: http://www.wto.org/english/thewto_e/whatis_e/tif_e/disp1_e.htm (accessed 29 October 2012).

Young, A. and Peterson, J. (2006). 'The EU and the New Trade Politics', *Journal of European Public Policy*, 13(6): 795–814.

Young, O. (1994). *International Governance: Protecting the Environment in a Stateless Society*, Ithaca, NY: Cornell University Press.

Young, Z. (2002). *A New Green Order: The World Bank and the Politics of the Global Environmental Facility*, London: Pluto Press.

Zolberg, A., Suhrke, A. and Aguayo, S. (1989). *Escape from Violence: Conflict and the Refugee Crisis in the Developing World*, Oxford: Oxford University Press.

Index

activism: environmental 143, 144, 148, 149–50; Internet use 119, 123; labour standards 106, 108–10, 112
Ador, Gustave 185
advance market commitments (AMC) 133
Advisory Board on Human Security (ABHS) 20
advocacy groups: anti-corruption 63, 64, 67, 68, 69–71, 74–5; labour standards 109
Afghanistan 17, 72, 168, 171
Africa: Aid for Trade 87, 88; aid from China 43–4; climate change 148; corruption 62, 64, 65–6, 71–2, 73, 76; cotton production 42, 44, 89–90; effects of trade liberalisation 41, 85; internally displaced persons 184; Millennium Development Goals 37; refugees 183
African Court of Justice and Human Rights 184
African Union 16, 67, 183, 184
Agenda 21 146, 150, 151
agricultural production, North–South trade 79
agricultural subsidies 42, 44, 86
aid 30, 31, 33, 37, 38–40, *39*; Chinese aid to Africa 43–4; and corruption 64; health-related 132–3, 134, 135, 138, 139
aid agencies 30, 31, 39, 41, 44
Aid for Trade 86–90
air transportation 122–3
Al Qaeda 168
Amnesty International 17, 26, 167, 176
Angola 65, 71–2
Annan, Kofi 19, 20, 26, 30–1, 189
Antarctic protection 154
anthrax letter attacks 128, 139
anti-corruption legislation 63, 66, 67–70, 71–4
anti-discriminatory employment practices 105, 107
anti-globalisation movements 17
Anti-Phishing Working Group (APWG) 120, 122
apartheid 167
Apollo 8 mission 143
Arab League 16, 26
Arab Spring 62, 65, 119, 123
arbitrary detention 171–2

ASEAN regional forum 16
Asian Tsunami (2004) 14
al-Assad, Bashar 26
asset recovery 68
asylum seekers 182, 183, 187, 190–1, 192–3
AU *see* African Union
austerity programmes 59
Australia 170, 192–3, 199
Austria 19

Bank for International Settlements (BIS) 46, 54
banking crises *see* financial crises
Bank of England 52, 54, 60
Basel Committee on Banking Supervision (BCBS) 54, 57, 58; Basel 2 58–9; Basel 3 60
Beijing Women's Conference 31
Bhopal, India 144
bilateral trade arrangements 87, 100
Bill and Melinda Gates Foundation 133, 134–5, 137
biodiversity 32, 146, 154
biological weapons 24
BIS *see* Bank for International Settlements
Blair, Tony 24, 199
boomerang aid 88
borrowing, government 53
Bosnia 189
Bouazizi, Mohamed 62
Boutros-Ghali, Boutros 189
Brazil 39, 42, 131, 139–40; *see also* emerging economies
Bretton Woods Conference 40, 50, 51, 54, 82
Bretton Woods institutions (BWIs) *see* International Monetary Fund; World Bank
Bretton Woods poverty reduction paradigm 34, 35, 41
Bribe Payers' Index (BPI) 70–1
bribery *see* corruption
Bribery Act 2010, UK 67, 69–70
BRICS countries *see* emerging economies
British Board of Trade 118
Brundtland, Gro Harlem 131, 132, 145
Brundtland Commission 145

Bush, George W. 147, 168, 199; *see also* War on Terror
Business Environment Strengthening Technical Assistance Project (BESTAP), Malawi 87

Cambodia 72
Cameroon 72
campaigns 203
Canada 19, 20, 170
Capability Approach 35
capital controls 50, 52, 53, 55, 56
Capturing the Gains 93
carbon emissions 14–15, 146, 154–5
carbon offsetting 151, 155
carbon trading 154–5
carrier sanctions 191
Carson, Rachel 143
Cascading Style Sheets (CSS) 119, 122
Central Commission for the Navigation of the Rhine (CCR) 114, 115, 118, 120–1
Chad 72
Chang, Ha-Joon 84–5
chemicals, environmental effects 143, 144
chemical weapons 24
Cheney, Dick 73
Chernobyl 144
Chicago Climate Exchange 154–5
child labour 91, 100, 101
child mortality 32, 36, 133, 135, 138
Children's Summit (1990) 29
China: corruption 65; development aid 39, 43–4; economic growth 37; financial deposits 51; health governance 131; Internet controls 124–5; opium wars 79; and Syria 26; trade agreements 42; *see also* emerging economies
Chipko movement 144
Chirac, Jacques 24
Christmas Island 192, 193
Church, Frank 66
CIA 168–70, 171–2, 175–6, 177–8
City of London 51–2
civilian casualties 14
civil society organizations (CSOs) 201; anti-corruption soft law 74–5, 77; criticism of Aid for Trade 88; criticism of trade liberalisation 79, 85; environmental issues 148, 149–50, 158; ethical trade 90–3; and health 134, 136–7; human security 20–1; and security 17, 22
civil uprisings 62
classical liberal theories 82
Clean Air Act (1956), United Kingdom 149
Clean Development Mechanism (CDM) 154
climate change 14–15, 142, 146, 147–8, 154
Clinton, Bill 124
clothing industry 106
Cold War 187
collective bargaining 100, 101

Combatant Status Review Tribunals (CSRTs) 174
Commission for Sustainable Development (CSD) 147
Commission on Global Governance 2, 4
communications governance 114–27; Internet 117, 118–20, 121–2, 123–6; mechanisms of 120–3
communism 98
community security 18
Conferences of the Parties (CoPs) 148
conflict minerals 73
conflicts *see* wars
conservation organisations 144, 149
contraception 37
Convention against Torture and Other Cruel, Inhuman or Degrading Treatment or Punishment 165, 172, 173
Convention for the Protection and Assistance of Internally Displaced Persons in Africa 184
Convention on Combating Bribery of Foreign Public Officials in International Business Transactions 66, 67–8
Convention Relating to the Status of Refugees *see* Refugee Convention
coordination, security governance 16
Copenhagen Accord 148
copyright 116
Core Labour Standards (CLS) 100–5
corporate codes of conduct 91, 100, 105–7
corporations: anti-corruption soft law 70, 74–5; boomerang aid 88; capital controls avoidance 52; corruption 66, 69, 73–4; ethical trade 93; Internet governance 120, 122; mining 73–4, 75, 88; multinational 52, 97, 106; oil 73–4, 75, 76; pharmaceutical 33, 131, 132–3; *see also* private sector
corruption 62–78; costs of 64–6; defining 63–4; extractive industries 71–5; legislation 63, 66, 67–70, 71–4; soft law 70, 74–5
Corruption Perception Index (CPI) 64, 70–1
Côte d'Ivoire 72
cotton production 42, 44, 89–90
Council of Europe 67, 120, 121, 125–6, 164, 176
CounterBalance 88
credit crunch *see* financial crises
credit derivatives 49, 56–7, 58, 60
credit-rating agencies 46, 48, 56, 59, 60
critical theories, of trade 84–6, 87–8
CSOs *see* civil society organizations
currencies: deterritorialisation 55; exchange rate controls 50, 55
cybercrime 117, 120, 121, 122, 125–6
Cybercrime Convention 120, 125–6

DAC *see* Development Assistance Committee
Darfur, Sudan 194–5
debt crises 40, 57, 59, 60

debt relief 33, 40
Decent Work agenda 102–3, 110
Declaration of Fundamental Principles and Rights at Work 100, 101
Declaration on Human Rights *see* Universal Declaration of Human Rights
Democratic Republic of Congo (DRC) 64, 65–6, 72, 73
democratisation 65
demonstrations 62
Deng, Francis 193–4
Depression 49
deregulation, financial 53, 56, 57, 83, 84
derivatives 49, 56–7, 58, 60
Detainee Treatment Act (2005), USA 175
detention, secret 168, 170–3, 176–7
deterritorialisation of currencies 55
development 28–45; history of poverty governance 28–31, 33–4; and human security 19; Millennium Development Goals 28, 31–4, 35–7, 41–2, 133, 138–9; poverty reduction paradigms 34–5; poverty reduction strategies 40–2; and trade 42; *see also* aid
Development Assistance Committee (DAC) 30, 31; aid from member countries 38–9, *39*
Development Decade 28
diaspora communities 17
disasters: environmental 144; natural 14
diseases *see* infectious diseases
Dodd–Frank Wall Street and Consumer Protection Act, USA 73–4
Does Foreign Aid Really Work? (Riddell) 38
Doha Development Round 42, 79, 83–4, 85
dollar-a-day labour 84
dollar-a-day poverty 32, 35, 36–7
domain names 118, 125
Domestic Worker Convention 109, 110, 112
domestic workers 104–5, 109–13
DRC *see* Democratic Republic of Congo
drinking water 32
drug donation programs 133
duty-free quota-free market access 32, 42

Earth Day 144
Earth Summit 145–6
Earthtrends 153
ECHR *see* European Convention on Human Rights
Eco-Equity 150
eco-governmentality 157–8
Economic and Social Council 35
Economic Consequences of the Peace, The (Keynes) 50
economic growth 34, 35, 55–6, 82–3, 146
economic security 18
ecosystems 143, 152
education 32; environmental 147, 151
Egypt 62, 65, 124, 170
Elf oil corporation 76

elite initiatives 37
Elizabeth II, Queen 48
emancipation, security as 13
embedded liberalism 81, 82, 83
embezzlement *see* corruption
emerging economies 76–7, 131, 148
emissions trading 154–5
empowerment, of women 31, 32, 36
English language 116
enhanced interrogation techniques 168–9, 178
environmental disasters 144
environmental issues 142–59; activism 143, 144, 148, 149–50; carbon trading 154–5; climate change 14–15, 142, 146, 147–8, 154; legal agreements 153–4; sustainable development 32, 146, 147, 150
environmental legislation 149
environmental security 18
equality: employment 92, 100, 101, 103–5, 107; gender 31, 32, 36, 92, 103–5, 107
Esperanto 116
ethical trade 90–3
Ethical Trading Initiative (ETI) 90–1
ethnic cleansing 181
EU *see* European Union
Euromarket 51–3, 56
Europe: 2007-09 financial crisis 15, 47, 59; Council of 67, 120, 121, 125–6, 164, 176
European Commission 58, 60, 87, 89
European Convention on Human Rights (ECHR) 164, 167
European Court of Human Rights 167
European Investment Bank (EIB) 88
European Parliament 175
European Union 16, 82; agricultural subsidies 42, 86; Aid for Trade 87, 88; anti-corruption legislation 67; development aid 40; Emissions Trading Scheme 154; health governance 131; human rights monitoring 166; Kenyan textiles industry 79, 89–90; refugee policies 191; sovereign debt crisis 47, 59, 60
exchange rates, control of 50, 55
existential threats 13
experts 201
export processing zones (EPZs) 84, 90
extractive industries, and corruption 71–5
Extractive Industries Review (EIR) 71
Extractive Industries Transparency Initiative (EITI) 74–5
extreme weather events 15

fair wages 102
Fava, Giovanni Claudio 176
FCPA *see* Foreign Corrupt Practices Act
FDI *see* foreign direct investment
female employment 92, 103–5, 106–7; domestic workers 104–5, 109–13; homeworkers 107, 109; migrant workers 104–5

feminisation: of employment 103; of migration 104
Financial Action Task Force (FATF) 66
financial crises 40, 57, 58, 59, 60; 2007-09 global 15, 46–9, 58–60, 73, 139; Depression 49
financial innovations 50–1, 56–7
financialisation 49, 54, 56
financial regulation 46–60; and 2007-09 financial crisis 46–9, 58–60; and Bretton Woods 50, 51, 54; deregulation 53, 56, 57, 83, 84; Euromarket 51–3, 56; and neoliberalism 55–6; private 54, 56–9, 60
First World War 185
fiscal discipline 34, 42
five-year plans, national 41, 42
Food and Agriculture Organisation (FAO) 147
food security 18, 147, 153
force, use of 21–6
forced labour 100, 101, 105
forced migration 180–95; asylum seekers 182, 183, 187, 190–1, 192–3; internally displaced persons 66, 180, 183–5, *188*, 189, 193–5; refugees 66, 180, 181–3, 185–93, *188*
Ford, Gerald 66
Foreign Corrupt Practices Act (FCPA), USA 66, 67, 68–9, 71, 73
foreign direct investment (FDI) 64, 67, 69, 102
forests 144, 146, 152
Foucault, Michel 157, 158
Framework Convention on Global Health 137, 138
France 24, 76, 115, 185
fraud *see* corruption
freedom: of association 100, 101, 106; from fear and want 18; and security 13
free trade *see* trade liberalisation
French Revolution 115, 185
Friends of the Earth 143, 144, 149

G7 58, 66
G8 11, 16, 120, 130, 139
G20 11, 14, 16, 58, 130
G77 16
Gandhi, Indira 145
Gates, Bill 37
Gates Foundation 133, 134–5, 137
GATT *see* General Agreement on Tariffs and Trade
GAVI *see* Global Alliance for Vaccines and Immunization
Gawandia, Vijay 85–6
GEF *see* Global Environmental Facility
gender-based violence 36, 183
gender equality 31, 32, 36, 92, 103–5, 107
gender issues, refugee status 183
gender-neutral treaty language 104
General Agreement on Tariffs and Trade (GATT) 50, 81–2

Geneva Conventions 162, 164, 165, 168, 172, 175
genocide 22–3, 181
Germany 24, 170, 186; *see also* Nazi Germany
GHG (global health governance) 129; *see also* health governance
GHPs *see* public private partnerships
Global Alliance for Vaccines and Immunization (GAVI) 37, 132, 133–4, 136
Global Compact 67, 70, 100, 150
Global Corruption Barometer (GCB) 70–1
Global Environmental Facility (GEF) 146, 149
Global Environmental Outlook reports 153
Global Fund to Fight HIV/AIDS, Tuberculosis and Malaria (GFATBM) 130, 134, 139
global governance, definitions 3–5
global health governance (GHG) 129; *see also* health governance
Global Influenza Surveillance Network 132
globalisation: and inequality 35; and poverty reduction 34; of production 96, 99–100, 108
Global Programme to Eliminate Filariasis (GPEF) 133
global supply chains, and ethical trade 91–3
Global Witness 74
governance, definitions 4–5
Green Belt Movement 144, 150
Green Climate Fund 149, 154
green economy 150
greenhouse gas emissions 14–15, 146, 154–5
Greenpeace 143, 144, 149
Greenwich Meridian 116
growth *see* economic growth
Guantánamo Bay, Cuba 168, 171, 174
Guiding Principles on Internal Displacement 180, 183–5, 193
Gulf Cooperation Council (GCC) 16

H1N1 (Swine flu) 15, 131
H5N1 (Avian flu) 15, 128, 131, 132, 135, 139
habeas corpus rights 174–5, 178
Halliburton 73
Hardin, Garrett 155–6
Hazare, Anna 62, 78
Health for All target 138
health governance 128–41; and environmental degradation 147; health security 15, 18, 128, 139–40; philanthropic foundations 133, 134–5, 136–7; public private partnerships 132–4, 136–7, 140; World Health Organisation 11, 129, 130, 133, 136, 137, 147; *see also* infectious diseases
HIV/AIDS 15, 128, 133; funding 139; Millennium Development Goal 32, 36, 37, 138; UNAIDS 11, 130–1
Holocaust 186
homeworkers 107, 109
Hong Kong 105
horticulture 107

HTML (HyperText Markup Language) 119, 122
Huguenots 185
Human Development Index (HDI) 66
Human Development Reports 18–19
humanitarian organisations 184, 194
human rights 160–78; core rights 162, 163;
    Declaration on 29; and human security 21;
    international laws 160–4, 165–6, 171–4;
    War on Terror abuses 168–78
Human Rights Watch 17, 167, 176, 177
human rights workers 123
human security 13, 18–21
Human Security Network 19
Human Security Unit (HSU) 20
Hungary 187
Hurricane Katrina 17
Hussein, Saddam 24, 72, 193
HyperText Markup Language (HTML) 119, 122

IAEA *see* International Atomic Energy Agency
IATA *see* International Air Transport
    Association
IBRD *see* International Bank for Reconstruction
    and Development
ICANN *see* Internet Corporation for Assigned
    Names and Numbers
ICAO *see* International Civil Aviation
    Organisation
ICFTU *see* International Confederation of Free
    Trade Unions
ICRC *see* International Committee of the Red
    Cross/Crescent
ideas, security of 12–13
identity, security of 12–13
IDGs *see* International Development Goals
IDPs *see* internally displaced persons
IETF *see* Internet Engineering Task Force
IFIs *see* International Financial Institutions
IHL *see* International Humanitarian Law
IHRL *see* International Human Rights Law
ILO *see* International Labour Organisation
IMF *see* International Monetary Fund
income poverty 32, 35, 36–7
India: Bhopal disaster 144; corruption 64–5;
    demonstrations 62, 78; development aid 39;
    economic growth 37; environmental move-
    ments 144; health security 140; Narmada
    Dam project 148; opposition to social
    clauses 100; pharmaceutical industries 131;
    refugees 186; trade agreements 42; *see also*
    emerging economies
indigenous peoples 109
individual action, environmental 150–1, 155
Indonesia 14, 64, 105, 111–13, 132, 140
industrialisation 80, 84–5
inequality, rising global 35
infectious diseases 15, 28, 137; influenza 15,
    128, 131, 132, 135, 139; malaria 32, 36,
    133, 138, 139; Millennium Development
    Goals 32, 36, 37, 138; SARS 15, 128, 131,
    139; tuberculosis 133; vaccines 132, 133–4;
    virus sharing 132, 137; *see also* HIV/AIDS
influenza 15, 128, 131, 132, 135, 139
informal labour sector 103, 104–5
infrastructure 35, 38, 44, 86, 87
insecurity, acceptable levels of 13
Institute of International Finance (IIF) 58
intellectual property rights 81, 131
interest rates, control of 50
Intergovernmental Panel on Climate Change
    (IPCC) 14–15, 146, 154
internally displaced persons (IDPs) 66, 180,
    183–5, *188*, 189, 193–5
International Air Transport Association (IATA)
    122–3
International Atomic Energy Agency (IAEA)
    11, 24
International Bank for Reconstruction and
    Development (IBRD) 29, 50, 72
International Bill of Rights 162, 163
International Civil Aviation Organisation
    (ICAO) 116, 118, 122–3
International Commission on Intervention and
    State Sovereignty (ICISS) 21
International Committee of the Red Cross/
    Crescent (ICRC) 17, 164, 171, 173–4
International Confederation of Free Trade
    Unions (ICFTU) 100, 108
International Court of Justice 167
International Covenant on Civil and Political
    Rights (ICCPR) 162, 172
International Covenant on Economic, Social and
    Cultural Rights (ICESCR) 162
International Criminal Court 167
International Development Association (IDA)
    72
International Development Goals (IDGs) 30,
    31, 33
International Financial Institutions (IFIs) 102–3,
    200; *see also* International Monetary Fund;
    World Bank
International Health Regulations (IHR) 137
International Humanitarian Law (IHL) 162, 164,
    165–6, 171–4
International Human Rights Law (IHRL) 162,
    163, 165, 171–4
International Institute for Environment and
    Development (IIED) 149
International Institute for Sustainable
    Development (IISD) 149
International Labour Organisation (ILO) 28, 34,
    97–105, 109–10
international laws 5, 201–2; anti-corruption 63,
    67–8, 71–2; health-related 137–8; human
    rights 160–4, 165–6, 171–4; refugees 180,
    181–3; and security 17; and sovereignty
    23, 25
International Literary and Artistic Association
    116

International Monetary Fund (IMF) 11; anti-corruption mechanisms 64, 71–2, 75; financial regulation 46, 50, 58, 59; health 130; lending role 53, 55; neoliberal policies 83, 84; poverty reduction 31, 33, 40–2; purposes 40
International Organisation for Standardisation (ISO) 151, 202
International Organisation on Migration (IOM) 187
international peace 22
International Relations theory 6–7
International Telecommunication Union (ITU) 116, 117, 118, 121, 124
International Trade Organisation (ITO) 50, 82
International Trade Union Congress (ITUC) 108, 110
Internet Architecture Board (IAB) 118
Internet Assigned Numbers Authority (IANA) 124
Internet Corporation for Assigned Names and Numbers (ICANN) 118, 119, 124, 125
Internet Engineering Task Force (IETF) 118–19, 122, 125
Internet governance 117, 118–20, 121–2, 123–6
Internet Governance Forum (IGF) 119, 125
Internet Protocol Suite 117, 119, 122, 125
Internet Research Task Force (IRTF) 118
Internet Society 117, 118
IP addresses 118
IPCC *see* Intergovernmental Panel on Climate Change
Iran 193
Iraq 17, 23–5, 40, 72, 171
Iron Curtain 186
Israel 180, 186
issue framing 203
Italy 170
ITU *see* International Telecommunication Union

Japan 20, 87, 120, 128
Jewish refugees 186
Johannesburg Summit 147, 150
Joint Implementation 154
Jordan 170

Kampala Convention 184
Kant, Immanuel 5
Kapstein, Ethan 46, 47
Kaufmann, Daniel 64
Kellogg Brown & Root 73
Kennedy, John F. 29
Kenya 79, 89–90, 144
Keynes, John Maynard 50, 82
Keynesian economics 50, 55–6
kicking-away-the-ladder thesis 84–5
kleptocratic leaders 65, 66
knowledge 202–3

Korean War 186
Kurds 193
Kuwait 23–4
Kyoto Protocol 14, 146, 147–8, 154

labour certification schemes 106
labour internationalism 108
labour market flexibility 34
labour standards 96–113; activism 106, 108–10; Core Labour Standards (CLS) 100–5; corporate codes of conduct 91, 100, 105–7; and ethical trade 90, 91, 92; and International Labour Organisation 97–105, 109–10; and trade 99–100
landmines 19
languages, international auxiliary 116
Latin American debt crisis 57
League of Nations 98, 185
League of Nations High Commissioner for Refugees (LNHCR) 185–6
least developed countries, free market access 33
legislation: anti-corruption 63, 66, 67–70, 71–4; environmental 149; *see also* international laws; soft law
liberal institutionalists 82
liberalisation, trade *see* trade liberalisation
liberal peacebuilding 65
liberal theories: classical 82; of trade 80–4; *see also* neoliberalism
Liberia 72
liberty, right to 161, 163
Libya 25, 62, 65, 72, 170, 177
Limits to Growth, The 144
liquidity 46–7, 53, 56–7
Lithuania 170, 176
Lockerbie bombing 72
London School of Economics 48
Lotus Development Corporation 123

malaria 32, 36, 133, 138, 139
Malawi 87
Malaysia 104, 105, 111–13, 193
Malthus, Thomas 144
management, security governance 16
market-opening, criticism of 79–80, 84–5
Marshall Plan 51
Marty, Dick 176
maternal mortality 32, 37, 133, 135, 138
MDGs *see* Millennium Development Goals
measurement, standardisation of 116
medicines, access to 33, 131, 133
Medicines for Malaria Venture (MMV) 133
Memorandum of Understanding (MoU) 111–13
Mexico 20, 104
MI6 177
Microsoft 122
migrant workers 104–5, 109, 111–13
migration *see* forced migration
Military Commission Act (2006), USA 175, 178

Millennium Declaration 31, 33
Millennium Development Goals (MDGs) 28, 31–4, 35–7, 41–2, 133, 138–9
Millennium Summit 20, 28, 30–1
minimum wages 90, 91
mining corporations 73–4, 75, 88
Mobutu Sese Seko 64, 65
modernisation approach to development 29
money laundering 63, 64, 66, 68
Montreal Protocol 154
Morocco 170
mortgages 46, 56
Movement for the Survival of the Ogoni People (MOSOP) 144
multilateral environmental treaties (MEAs) 153
multinational corporations (MNCs) 52, 97, 106
Myanmar 188

Nakajima, Hiroshi 131
naming and shaming 99, 167, 203
Nansen, Fridthof 185–6
Narmada Dam project, India 148
national five-year plans 41, 42
National Sustainable Development Strategies 149
NATO 11, 16
natural disasters 14
natural resources 65–6, 71–5
navigation 114, 115, 118
Nazi Germany 54, 186
neo-colonialism 79, 85–6
neoliberalism 83–4; effects of economic policies 17; financial regulation 55–6; and labour standards 102; and poverty reduction 34, 35, 40–1
New Orleans 17
New Zealand 40
NGOs (non-governmental organisations) 201; anti-corruption advocacy 63, 64, 67, 68, 69–71, 74–5; and communications 115; criticism of Aid for Trade 88; and development 31, 37; environmental issues 143, 144, 146, 149–50, 158; ethical trade 90–3; human rights 167, 168; human security 20–1; internally displaced persons 194; Internet governance 117, 119; and Iraq 24–5; and labour standards 100, 102; and Millennium Development Goals 37; refugees 188; and security 16–17, 22
Nigeria 62, 64, 73, 144
Nixon Administration 66
Nkrumah, Kwame 85
non-intervention 23
Non-Proliferation of Nuclear Weapons treaty 24
non-refoulement 171, 173, 182
non-tariff barriers 81
norms 17, 23, 60, 157, 202
North–South divide 199, 200
North–South trade 79, 83–6

Norway 19, 54
nuclear disasters 144

Obama, Barack 73, 177
obligation overload 76
Occupy movement 17, 62, 78
ODA *see* official development assistance
Office for the Coordination of Humanitarian Affairs (OCHA) 20
official development assistance (ODA) 30, 31, 33, 37, 38–40, *39*; health-related 132–3, 134, 135, 138, 139
Ogata, Sadako 189
Ogoni People 144
oil corporations 73–4, 75, 76
oil crises 56, 58, 144
Oil-for-Food programme 72
oil spills 144
ontological security 12–13
Open Society Institute (OSI) 74
opium wars 79
Organisation for Economic Cooperation and Development (OECD) 29–30, 33, 41, 66, 67–8, 70
Organisation for Security and Cooperation in Europe (OSCE) 16
Organisation of African Unity 164, 183
Organisation of American States 164
organized crime 66
Ostrom, Elinor 156
Our Common Future 145, 151, 152
Our Global Neighbourhood 2
Oxfam 86
ozone depletion 144, 152, 154

Pacific Solution 192–3
Palestinian refugees 180, 186
Pandemic Influenza Preparedness Framework (PIPF) 132
pandemic preparedness 132, 139
Paris Declaration on Aid Effectiveness 39
participatory social auditing 92
patent protection laws 131
peace, international 22
peacekeepers 17, 189, 195
People's Health Movement (PHM) 136
personal security 18
pesticides 143, 144
pharmaceutical industries 33, 131, 132–3
philanthropic foundations 133, 134–5, 136–7
Philippines 64
Poland 170, 176
political security 18
population growth 144, 156
postal services 116
Post Washington Consensus (PWC) 102–3
poverty reduction 28–45; and environmental degradation 147; ethical trade 90–3; history 28–31, 33–4; and oil extraction

72; paradigms 34–5; Post Washington Consensus 102–3; strategies 40–2; and trade liberalisation 42, 83, 87; *see also* aid; development
Poverty Reduction Strategy Papers (PRSs) 31, 40, 41–2, 43, 84, 103
Powell, Colin 147
PPPs *see* public private partnerships
President's Emergency Plan for AIDS Relief (PEPFAR), USA 139
Primary Health Care (PHC) 138
primary schooling 32, 36
prisoners of war 162, 164, 168, 171
private sector: ethical trade 90–3; financial regulation 54, 56–9, 60; security companies 17; sustainable development 150; *see also* corporations; public private partnerships
privatisation 34, 42, 83, 84
protectionist trade policies 80, 84, 86, 99
protest movements 17; anti-corruption 62, 78; environmental 144, 148, 149–50; Internet use 119, 123; and Iraq 25
PRSs *see* Poverty Reduction Strategy Papers
public goods 197–8
public private partnerships (PPPs) 200; development 37; health 132–4, 136–7, 140; sustainable development 150
Publish What You Pay (PWYP) 74–5
Putin, Vladimir 124

Reagan, Ronald 41, 59
rebel groups 72
Recipe for Disaster: Will the Doha Round Fail to Deliver for Development? (Oxfam) 86
Red Cross/Crescent 17, 164, 171, 173–4
Reducing Emissions from Degradation and Deforestation (REDD) 154
Refugee Convention 181–3, 186
refugees 66, 180, 181–3, 185–93, *188*
regulation, security governance 16
religious communities 17
rendition 168, 171, 172
renewable resources 152
reproductive health 31, 32
return migration 111
Revenue Watch Institute (RWI) 74
Rhine, River 114, 115, 120–1
right to liberty 161, 163
right to life 161, 163
Rio+10 Summit 147, 150
Rio+20 Summit 147, 150
Rio Earth Summit 145–6
river transportation 114, 115
Road Map Towards the Implementation of the United Nations Millennium Declaration (UN) 31
Rohingya refugees 188
Romania 176
Roosevelt, Eleanor 186
Rostow, Kenneth 29
Royal Society for the Protection of Birds (RSPB) 144
Ruggie, John 80–1
Russia 24, 26; *see also* emerging economies
Russian Revolution 98, 185
Rwandan genocide 30

al-Saadi, Sami 177
Safe Third Country (STC) Agreements 191
sanctions: breach of WTO rules 99; human rights abuses 167; Iraq 24; and labour standards 99, 100; natural resources 72
Sanitary Conventions 137
sanitation 32
SAPs *see* Structural Adjustment Programmes
sarin gas attack, Tokyo 128
SARS 15, 128, 131, 139
satellite communications 117
Saudi Arabia 112
scientific monitoring, global 152–3
Second World War 161
securitisation 56–7
Security and Exchange Commission (SEC) 73–4
security governance 11–18; health security 15, 18, 128, 139–40; human security 18–21; online 117, 120, 121, 122; use of force 21–6
Sekou Touré, Ahmed 85
self-defence, justification for war 22
Sen, Amartya 35
sexual violence 183
sex workers 109
Shanghai Cooperation Organisation (SCO) 16
Shaping the 21st Century (DAC) 30, 31
Siemens AG 69
Sierra Club 144, 149
Sierra Leone 17, 65, 72
Silent Spring (Carson) 143
Singapore 105
slavery 161, 163
slum dwellers 32, 37
Small Island Developing States (SIDS) 148
smallpox 138
Smith, Adam 82
social clauses 99, 100
social floor 99
social justice 98
social media 17, 123
social movement unionism 108–9
social silence 49
social upgrading 93
soft law 202; anti-corruption 70–1, 74–5; internally displaced persons 180, 183–4
Somalia 30
South Africa 19, 107, 167; *see also* emerging economies
sovereignty 23, 25, 43, 76, 84
sovereignty as responsibility 193, 195
Spaceship Earth 143

Index 241

Srebrenica 189
Sri Lanka 14
standardisation 116, 202
Stanley, Albert 'Jack' 73
State of the World reports 152
Straw, Jack 177
Structural Adjustment Programmes (SAPs) 40–1, 43, 83
subprime mortgages 46
subsidies, agricultural 42, 44, 86
Sudan 194–5
Sustainable Consumption Institute (SCI) 93
sustainable development 32, 146, 147, 150
Sweden 170
Syria 26, 170

Taliban 168
tariff barriers 80, 83, 84
telegraph systems 114, 115–16
telephone systems 117
terrorism 66; War on Terror 168–78
Tesco 93
Tett, Gillian 49
Thailand 104, 140
Thatcher, Margaret 41
Thérien, Jean-Philippe 34–5
Third World Network 150
Thomas, Albert 98
Three Mile Island nuclear facility 144
Tokyo 128
Torrey Canyon 144
torture 161, 163, 168–70, 171, 172–3
trade 79–94; Aid for Trade 86–90; critical theories of 84–6, 87–8; dispute settlement 81; ethical 90–3; and labour standards 99–100; liberal theories of 80–4, 87; Millennium Development Goal 33; *see also* World Trade Organisation
Trade Justice campaigners 85, 88
trade liberalisation 34, 41, 42, 79–86; and corruption 65; criticism of 79–80, 84–6; deep 83–4; and inequality 35; non-tariff barriers 81; protectionist trade policies 80
Trade-Related Intellectual Property Rights (TRIPs) 131
trade union freedoms 100, 101, 102, 105
trade unions: criticism of Aid for Trade 88; criticism of trade liberalisation 79, 85; ethical trade 91, 92; and labour standards 98, 100, 102, 105, 108–10; social movement unionism 108–9
trafficking 105
tragedy of the commons 155–6
Transparency International (TI) 63, 64, 67, 68, 69, 70–1
tsunami 14
tuberculosis 133
Tunisia 62, 65
Turkey 193
Twitter 123

UDHR *see* Universal Declaration of Human Rights
Uganda 155
UNAIDS 11, 131
UNCAC *see* United Nations Convention Against Corruption
undocumented workers 111
UNDP *see* United Nations Development Programme
UNEP *see* United Nations Environment Programme
UNESCO 147
UNFCCC *see* United Nations Framework Convention on Climate Change
UNHCR *see* United Nations High Commissioner for Refugees
UNICEF 34, 133, 136
United Kingdom: 2007-09 financial crisis 47, 59; Aid for Trade 87; anti-corruption legislation 67, 69–70; British Board of Trade 118; City of London 51–2; development aid 40; environmental legislation 149; financial regulation 50, 51–3, 56, 60; and health governance 131; involvement in secret detention 170, 177; and Iraq 24; opium wars 79; protectionist trade policies 80, 84; refugee policies 183
United Nations 8, 199–200; anti-corruption legislation 63, 67, 68; Bretton Woods Conference 40, 50; Charter 22, 24, 161; Children's Summit (1990) 29; communications agencies 116, 117–18; Conference on the Human Environment 145; Convention on the Rights of Migrant Workers and their Families 113; Development Decade 28; Earthwatch 153; Emergency Relief Coordinator 194; environmental issues 145–8; Global Compact 67, 70, 100, 150; Human Development Index 66; Human Development Reports 18–19; human rights 29, 161–3, 165, 166, 167–8, 172, 173; human security 18–21; migrant workers 113; Millennium Development Goals 28, 31–4, 35–7, 41–2, 133, 138–9; Millennium Summit 20, 28, 30–1; Oil-for-Food programme 72; poverty reduction paradigm 34–5; secret detention investigations 176–7; summits on development 28, 29, 30–1; Working Group on Arbitrary Detention 172; World Summit (2005) 20; World Summit on the Information Society 118, 119; *see also individual bodies and agencies*
United Nations Convention Against Corruption (UNCAC) 63, 67, 68
United Nations Convention Against Transnational Organized Crime (UNCTOC) 67
United Nations Development Fund for Women (UNIFEM) 103

United Nations Development Programme (UNDP) 34, 130, 147
United Nations Educational, Scientific and Cultural Organisation (UNESCO) 147
United Nations Environment Programme (UNEP) 145, 147, 153
United Nations Framework Convention on Climate Change (UNFCCC) 146, 147, 148, 154
United Nations High Commissioner for Refugees (UNHCR) 180, 181, 182, 186–90, 191, 193, 194
United Nations Monitoring, Verification, and Inspection Commission (UNMOVIC) 24
United Nations Population Fund (UNFPA) 130
United Nations Secretary General 22, 189; *see also* Annan, Kofi
United Nations Security Council 11, 21–6, 30, 72, 189, 200
United States: 2007-09 financial crisis 47; agricultural subsidies 42, 44; Aid for Trade 87; anthrax letter attacks 128, 139; anti-corruption legislation 66, 67, 68–9, 71, 73–4; corporate corruption 66, 69, 73–4, 77; demonstrations 62, 78; environmental issues 147, 148; financial regulation 50, 52, 56, 60; and health governance 131; human rights monitoring 166; Internet governance 118, 119, 124; and Iraq 25; Kyoto Protocol 146; opposition to ITO 82; protectionist trade policies 80; refugee policies 186, 191; Supreme Court 174–5; War on Terror 168–78
Universal Declaration of Human Rights (UDHR) 29, 162, 182
Universal Postal Union (UPU) 116, 117, 120, 121
USSR 51

vaccines 132, 133–4
VeriSign 124
Via Campesina 150
violence, gender-based 36, 183
virus sharing 132, 137
visa controls 191
Vital Signs reports 152
Volapük 116
Volcker, Paul 72

W3C *see* World Wide Web Consortium
wages: fair 102; gender equality 105; minimum 90, 91
Wall Street 54, 62
War on Terror 168–78
wars: and corruption 65, 72; decline in 14; and human rights 161, 162, 164; justifications for 22–3; resource-related 65–6

Washington Consensus 34, 41, 83, 98; *see also* Post Washington Consensus
Watergate scandal 66
We the Peoples: The Role of the United Nations in the 21st Century (Annan) 30–1
White, Harry Dexter 54
WHO *see* World Health Organisation
WikiLeaks 123
Wildlife Conservation Society 144, 149
WiredSafety 120, 122
Wolfensohn, James 66–7
women's groups 31, 102
women's rights 31, 32, 36
women workers *see* female employment
working conditions *see* labour standards
World Bank 11; anti-corruption mechanisms 64, 66–7, 71–2, 75; creation of 29, 40; financial regulation 46, 50, 58; health 130, 133; labour standards 103; lending role 53, 55; neoliberal policies 83, 84; poverty reduction 31, 33, 38, 40–1; relationship with Wall Street 54; sustainable development 148–9
World Commission on Environment and Development 145
World Food Programme 29
World Health Assembly (WHA) 136
World Health Organisation (WHO) 11, 129, 130, 133, 136, 137, 147
World Intellectual Property Organisation (WIPO) 116, 118
World Resources Institute 149, 152–3
World Social Forum 150
World Summit (2005) 20
World Summit on Sustainable Development (WSSD) 147
World Summit on the Information Society 118, 119
World Trade Organisation (WTO) 34, 42, 79, 99; Aid for Trade 86; Doha Development Round 42, 79, 83–4, 85; and health 130; powers 81–2
WorldWatch Institute 149, 152
Worldwide Governance Indicators (WGI) 64, 70–1
World Wide Web Consortium (W3C) 119, 121–2, 125
World Wildlife Fund (WWF) 143
WTO *see* World Trade Organisation

YouTube 123

Zaire 64, 65–6
Zambia 88